Bertrand Russell's Philosophy

Bertrand Russell's Philosophy

edited by

George Nakhnikian

BOOKS

10 East 53d St., New York 10022
(a division of Harper & Row Publishers, Inc.)

B
1649
.R94
B37
1974

Published in the U.S.A. 1974 by
HARPER & ROW, PUBLISHERS, INC.
BARNES & NOBLE IMPORT DIVISION

ISBN 06 4950 77 8

Printed in Great Britain
by Ebenezer Baylis and Son Limited
The Trinity Press, Worcester, and London

CONTENTS

PREFACE

I remember the morning when the news of Russell's death reached me and my colleagues in the Department of Philosophy at Indiana University. What I felt was, I think, not unrepresentative. I felt grief and I felt subdued. But what I felt most of all was gratitude that such a magnificent man had walked among us and had, to the very end, remained magnificently himself. There was something full and well-rounded about Russell's life. The feeling of gratitude it inspired called for a tribute. And so the Department of Philosophy, together with the Department of Mathematics and the Department of the History and Philosophy of Science, organized a meeting at which we paid our tribute to Russell's memory. The meeting took place at Indiana University on March 12, 1970. The programme consisted of a paper by W. C. Salmon on Russell's philosophical accomplishment, a paper on Russell as a social reformer by Byrum Carter, the Chancellor of the Bloomington campus, and a rendition by Janos Starker of the Sarabande from Bach's Suite in D Minor. The Department of Philosophy also decided to arrange a symposium to meet in 1972 to commemorate Russell's centenary. The fourteen essays in this volume were written for that symposium held at Indiana University, March 9–11, 1972.

The essays range over Russell's logic and its philosophical implications, his ontology, his theory of knowledge, his theory of scientific method, and his political philosophy, including an eye-witness account of Russell's involvement in the politics of the Cold War. Most of the essays are arranged in pairs: Myhill and Cocchiarella, Sellars and Clark, Pears and Salmon (on memory), Wollheim and Nakhnikian, Schoenman and Sherman. Except for Salmon's paper, the second member of each pair is written in response to the first. The respondent on Professor Fitch's paper was Professor Michael Dunn. His remarks are not included separately because their substance was later incorporated by Professor Fitch in the present version of his paper.

I wish to thank my colleague, Milton Fisk, for taking charge of the arrangements for the symposium out of which this volume emerged, Mrs. Betty Neal for her invaluable assistance, and the rest of my departmental colleagues for their help.

Bloomington, Indiana   G. N.

LIST OF CONTRIBUTORS

Roderick M. Chisholm   Professor of Philosophy, Brown University, Providence, Rhode Island, USA

Romane Clark   Professor of Philosophy, Indiana University, Bloomington, Indiana, USA

Nino B. Cocchiarella   Associate Professor of Philosophy, Indiana University, Bloomington, Indiana, USA

Frederic B. Fitch   Professor of Philosophy, Yale University, New Haven, Connecticut, USA

Grover Maxwell   Professor of Philosophy, University of Minnesota, Minneapolis, Minn., USA

John Myhill   Professor of Philosophy, University of Birmingham, England

George Nakhnikian   Professor of Philosophy, Indiana University, Bloomington, Indiana, USA

David Pears   Student of Christ Church and Lecturer in Philosophy, University of Oxford, England

W. C. Salmon   Professor of History and Philosophy of Science, Indiana University, Bloomington, Indiana, USA

Ralph Schoenman   Formerly private secretary to Russell; Director, Studies in the Third World, 1776 Elm Ridge Rd., Pennington, New Jersey, USA

Wilfrid Sellars   Professor of Philosophy, University of Pittsburgh, Pittsburgh, Pennsylvania, USA

Edward Sherman   Associate Professor of Law, Law School, Indiana University, Bloomington, Indiana, USA

Richard Wollheim   Professor of Philosophy, University College, London, England

Frederic B. Fitch

Towards Proving the Consistency of Principia Mathematica

Bertrand Russell considered *Principia Mathematica*[1] to be one of his greatest achievements, if not his greatest. It is true that he was only one of the two co-authors, Alfred North Whitehead being the other, but many of the fundamental ideas involved in it, such as the theory of types, were primarily his, and probably also due to him was the main motive of the book, namely to show that all of mathematics can be viewed as merely a branch of logic.

No completely satisfactory proof of the consistency of *Principia Mathematica* (including the axioms of infinity and extensionality) has yet been presented, and perhaps none ever will. Results due to Gödel[2] and Rosser[3] show that such a consistency proof, if it exists at all, would have to be formulated in a metalogic that is stronger than, or at least different from, the system of logic of *Principia* itself. In the present paper, nevertheless, some steps are taken towards trying to carry out such a proof, partly in order to see more specifically what obstacles are encountered, and partly in the hope that Gödel's and Rosser's results are in some way not as final as they appear. The outcome of this investigation is that if the system N, defined below, satisfies the rule of modus ponens, then *Principia Mathematica* (including the axioms of infinity and extensionality) is indeed consistent. In other words, the *negative* problem of showing that an inconsistency does not arise in *Principia* is transformed into the *positive* problem of showing that the system N satisfies modus ponens. The latter problem is left unsolved in the present paper.[4]

An earlier form of the present paper was presented at the Russell Symposium

[1] Russell and A. N. Whitehead, *Principia Mathematica*, 2nd ed., Cambridge, 1925. I have elsewhere (*Journal of Symbolic Logic* 3 (1938) and 4 (1939)) proved the consistency of a ramified version of *Principia Mathematica* that lacks axioms of reducibility but includes axioms of infinity, extensionality, and choice.

[2] K. Gödel, "Über formal unentscheidbare Sätze der *Principia Mathematica* und verwandter Systeme I", *Monatshefte für Mathematik und Physik* 38 (1931).

[3] Barkley Rosser, "Extensions of Some Theorems of Gödel and Church", *Journal of Symbolic Logic* 1 (1936). Also "Gödel Theorems for Non-Constructive Logics", *Journal of Symbolic Logic* 2 (1937).

[4] This problem seems to be closely related to G. Takeuti's conjecture that the cut rule is redundant in Gentzen formulations of higher-order calculi (*Japanese Journal of Mathematics* 23). Takahashi is said to have proved Takeuti's conjecture to be correct ("A Proof of Cut-Elimination Theorem in Simple Type-Theory", *Journal of the Mathematical Society of Japan* 19, 4).

and was defective in the respect that the system N, as defined in it, was not actually as strong as was intended. This defect was discovered by Professor Michael Dunn, the commentator on the paper. A change has now been made in the definition of the system N, and the defect appears to be rectified. The nature of the change will be described in detail subsequently. The writer is greatly indebted to Professor Dunn for his ingenuity in uncovering the defect.

Three systems T, M, and N will be presented. System T is consistent and complete, but lacks an axiom of infinity. System M is slightly weaker than system T, and so it is also consistent and also lacks an axiom of infinity. Indeed, M is essentially the system of *Principia*, but without axioms of infinity and extensionality. System N is formulated differently from M, but it is equivalent to M provided that it, N, satisfies modus ponens. By comparing N with T and with systems like T, N can be shown not to have the denial of the axiom of infinity as one of its theorems. Hence if N satisfies modus ponens, the system M, being equivalent to N, would also fail to have the denial of the axiom of infinity as a theorem, and the axiom of infinity itself could then be added to M without destroying the consistency of M. A method due to Gandy[1] can be used to show that the axiom of extensionality can be further added to M without causing any inconsistency that was not previously present. The resulting extension of M is then a formulation of *Principia Mathematica* that includes the axioms of infinity and extensionality, and this formulation is consistent if N satisfies modus ponens. Details now follow.

A decidable system T is first constructed. Let ι be the type of individuals. If α and β are types, let (α) be the type of classes having members of type α, and let $(\alpha\beta)$ be the type of relations relating things of type α to things of type β. The symbols 'X_1', 'X_2', 'X_3', and so on, will serve as variables, with type indicated by a superscript. In particular, 'X_1^ι' 'X_2^ι' and so on, are variables of type ι. The symbols 'ι_1', 'ι_2', and so on, will serve as constants of type ι.[2]

The class of (well-formed) sentences for the system T is defined inductively as follows: Expressions of the form '$[a = b]$', where 'a' and 'b' are constants of type ι, are sentences of level 1. If 'p' and 'q' are sentences of respective levels n and m, then '$\sim p$' is a sentence of level $n + 1$, and '$[p \lor q]$' is a sentence of level $n + m$. If 'a' and 'x' are respectively a constant and a variable, each of type α, and if '$(\ldots a \ldots)$' is a sentence of level n that results from replacing all free

---

[1] R. O. Gandy, "On the Axiom of Extensionality: Part I", *Journal of Symbolic Logic* 21 (1956).

[2] The usage with regard to single quotation marks in this paper may be roughly described as follows: When single quotation marks are used to enclose an expression, the total expression (including the quotation marks) is assumed to act as a name of the enclosed expression, except that if the enclosed expression involves metalinguistic variables, these variables must, if the general context so suggests, be replaced by their values in suitable ways, and the reference will then be to expressions that result from such replacements rather than to the original enclosed expression itself.

occurrences of 'x' in '(...x...)' by 'a', then '[a ∈ x̂ (...x...)]' is a sentence of level $n + 1$, and 'x̂(...x...)' is a constant of type (α). If 'a' and 'x' are respectively a constant and a variable, each of type α, if 'b' and 'y' are respectively a constant and a variable, each of type β, and if '(...a...b...)' is a sentence of level n that results from replacing all free occurrences of 'x' and 'y' in '(...x ...y...)' respectively by 'a' and 'b', then '[a x̂ŷ(...x...y...) b]' is a sentence of level $n + 1$, and 'x̂ŷ(...x...y...)' is a constant of type (αβ). (The variables 'x' and 'y' are assumed to be distinct.)

The following rules define inductively the class of sentences which are theorems of T. The system T is identified with the class of its own theorems, so that the theorems of T are the same as the members of T. These rules provide that there are exactly three distinct individuals, but the rules could easily be modified to provide that there is any other finite number of individuals.

T-rule [=] for type ι. '[$u_i = u_j$]' is in T iff (if and only if) $i = j$ or $i, j > 2$.

T-rule [∼=] for type ι. '∼[$u_i = u_j$]' is in T iff '[$u_i = u_j$]' is not in T (or, equivalently, iff $i \neq j$ and $i, j \not> 2$).

T-rule [∨]. '[$p \lor q$]' is in T iff 'p' or 'q' is in T.

T-rule [∼∨]. '∼[$p \lor q$]' is in T iff '∼p' and '∼q' are in T.

T-rule [∼∼]. '∼∼p' is in T iff 'p' is in T.

T-rule of class abstraction. '[a ∈ x̂(...x...)]' is in T iff '(...a...)' is in T, where '(...a...)' results from replacing all free occurrences of 'x' in '(...x...)' by occurrences of 'a'.

T-rule of negative class abstraction. '∼[a ∈ x̂(...x...)]' is in T iff '∼(...a...)' is in T, where [etc.].

T-rule of relational abstraction. '[a x̂ŷ(...x...y...) b]' is in T iff '(...a...b...)' is in T, where [etc.].

T-rule of negative relational abstraction. '∼[a x̂ŷ(...x...y...) b]' is in T iff '∼(...a...b...)' is in T, where [etc.].

The above rules define T in such a way that the membership or non-membership of a sentence in T is always determined by the membership or non-membership in T of sentences of lower level, or else determined merely by the form of the sentence. Hence there exists a decision procedure for membership in T. Some derived rules will now be stated.

T-rule [∼]. '∼p' is in T iff 'p' is not in T (where 'p' is a sentence).

Proof. Induction will be used with respect to the level of 'p'. The basis of the induction is the case where 'p' is of level 1, and therefore is of the form '[$u_i = u_j$]', $i, j = 1, 2, 3, 4, \ldots$. The rule is true for this case by T-rules [=] and [∼=] for type ι. Next, consider the case where 'p' is of the form '[$q \lor r$]'. Since 'q' and 'r' are of lower level than 'p', the rule to be proved can be assumed to hold for 'p' chosen as 'q' and also for 'p' chosen as 'r'. But if '[$q \lor r$]' and '∼[$q \lor r$]' were both in T, then by T-rules [∨] and [∼∨] either 'q' and '∼q' would both be in T or 'r' and '∼r' would both be in T, contrary to the hypothesis of the induction. Furthermore, if neither '[$q \lor r$]' nor '∼[$q \lor r$]'

3

were in T, then T-rules [∨] and [∼∨] give the result that neither 'q' nor '∼q' would be in T or neither 'r' nor '∼r' would be in T, contrary to the hypothesis of the induction. The other cases, where 'p' is of one of the forms '∼[$u = u$]', '∼[$q \vee r$]', '∼∼q', '[$a \in \hat{x}(\ldots x \ldots)$]', and so on, are similar to the cases just considered.

'[p & q]', '[$p \supset q$]', and '[$p \equiv q$]' are defined respectively as abbreviations for '∼[∼$p \vee ∼q$]', '[∼$p \vee q$]', and '[[$p \supset q$] & [$q \supset p$]]'. The following three T-rules are easily derivable by use of the primitive T-rules [∨], [∼∨] and [∼∼] and the derived T-rule [∼]:

T-rule [&]. '[p & q]' is in T iff 'p' and 'q' are in T.

T-rule [⊃]. '[$p \supset q$]' is in T iff 'p' is not in T or 'q' is in T.

T-rule [≡]. '[$p \equiv q$]' is in T iff either 'p' and 'q' are both in T or neither of them is in T.

Some further T-rules are now derived:

T-rule of replacement of sentences. If 'p' and 'q' are sentences both of which or neither of which is in T, and if '$(\ldots p \ldots)$' is in T, where '$(\ldots p \ldots)$' is any sentence in which 'p' occurs zero or more times, then '$(\ldots q \ldots)$'. is in T, where '$(\ldots q \ldots)$' is the result of replacing 'p' by 'q' in zero or more places in '$(\ldots p \ldots)$'.

Proof. If no replacement is made, the rule is of course trivially true. Otherwise the procedure is to use induction with respect to the level of '$(\ldots p \ldots)$'. The basis of the induction is the case where '$(\ldots p \ldots)$' is 'p' itself, and '$(\ldots q \ldots)$' is 'q' itself. In this case 'q', and hence '$(\ldots q \ldots)$', must be in T, since 'p' and 'q' must both be in T. Next consider the case where '$(\ldots p \ldots)$' is different from 'p' but is of the form '[$r \vee s$]'. Since 'r' and 's' are of lower level than '[$r \vee s$]', the rule to be proved can be assumed to hold for '$(\ldots p \ldots)$' chosen as 'r' and also for '$(\ldots p \ldots)$' chosen as 's' .But then it clearly also must hold, by T-rule [∨], for '$(\ldots p \ldots)$' chosen as '[$r \vee s$]', since any replacements of 'p' by 'q' in '[$r \vee s$]' will correspond to replacements of 'p' by 'q' in 'r' or in 's'. More specifically if 'r_1' and 's_1' are the results of such replacements respectively in 'r' and 's', then '[$r_1 \vee s_1$]' is the result of the corresponding replacements in '[$r \vee s$]', and if '[$r \vee s$]' is in T then 'r' or 's' must be in T by T-rule [∨], and 'r_1' or 's_1' must be in T because the rule to be proved can be assumed to hold for '$(\ldots p \ldots)$' chosen as 'r' or as 's'; and finally '[$r_1 \vee s_1$]', which is '$(\ldots q \ldots)$', is in T by T-rule [∨]. The other cases, where '$(\ldots p \ldots)$' is not 'p' but is of some form other than '[$r \vee s$]', are similar to the case just considered.

T-rule of identity elimination for type ι. If '[$a = b$]' and '$(\ldots a \ldots)$' are in T, where 'a' and 'b' are constants of type ι and where '$(\ldots a \ldots)$' is any sentence in which 'a' occurs zero or more times, then '$(\ldots b \ldots)$' is in T, where '$(\ldots b \ldots)$' results from replacing 'a' by 'b' in zero or more places in '$(\ldots a \ldots)$'.

Proof. If no replacement is made, the rule is of course trivially true. Otherwise the procedure is to use induction with respect to the level of

'(…*a*…)'. The basis of the induction is the case where '(…*a*…)' is of the form '[*a* = *c*]' or of the form '[*c* = *a*]' (or of both forms), or of the form '∼[*a* = *c*]' or of the form '∼[*c* = *a*]' (or of both these two forms), where '*c*' is a constant of type ι. The T-rules [=] and [∼=] for type ι can be shown to give the required result for this case. Next consider the case where '(…*a*…)' is of the form '[*r* ∨ *s*]' and the rule to be proved is assumed to hold for '(…*a*…)' chosen as '*r*' and also for '(…*a*…)' chosen as '*s*'. This case is similar to the corresponding case in the proof of the T-rule of replacement of sentences, and the cases where '(…*a*…)' is of other forms, such as '∼[*r* ∨ *s*]', are similar to the present case.

T-rule of replacement of constants of type (α). If '*a*' and '*b*' are constants of type (α) such that for every constant '*c*' of type α, either '[*c* ∈ *a*]' and '[*c* ∈ *b*]' are both in T or else neither of them is in T, and if '(…*a*…)' is in T, where '(…*a*…)' is any sentence in which '*a*' occurs zero or more times, then '(…*b*…)' is in T, where '(…*b*…)' is the result of replacing '*a*' by '*b*' in zero or more places in '(…*a*…)'.

Proof. If no replacement is made, the rule is of course trivially true. Otherwise the procedure is to use induction with respect to the level of '(…*a*…)'. The basis of the induction is the case where '(…*a*…)' is of the form '[*d* ∈ *a*]', and the rightmost occurrence of '*a*' in '[*d* ∈ *a*]' is the only occurrence of '*a*' that is replaced. In this case '*d*' must be of type α, and '[*d* ∈ *b*]', which is '(…*b*…)', must be in T, because '[*d* ∈ *a*]' and '[*d* ∈ *b*]' must both be in T, since '[*d* ∈ *a*]' is in T. Consider next the case where '(…*a*…)' is of the form '[*r* ∨ *s*]'. This case is handled in the same way as the analogous case in the proofs of each of the preceding T-rules. Furthermore, the cases where '(…*a*…)' is of any of the forms '∼[*r* ∨ *s*]', '∼∼*r*', or '[*e* *x̂ŷ*(---*x*----*y*---)*f*]' can also be handled in essentially the same way, and so can the case where '(…*a*…)' is of the form '[*e* ∈ *x̂*(---*x*---)]' provided that '*a*' is different from '*x̂*(---*x*---)' or provided that even if they are the same, still the rightmost occurrence of '*x̂*(---*x*---)' in '[*e* ∈ *x̂*(---*x*---)]' is not one of the occurrences of '*a*' that is to be replaced by '*b*'. Finally consider the case where '(…*a*…)' is of the form '[*e* ∈ *x̂*(---*x*---)]' and '*a*' is the same constant as '*x̂*(---*x*---)', and furthermore the rightmost occurrence of '*x*(---*x*---)' in '[*e* ∈ *x̂*(---*x*---)]' is one of the occurrences of '*a*' that is to be replaced by '*b*'. First let all the occurrences of '*a*' (that is, of '*x̂*(---*x*---)') in '[*e* ∈ *a*]' that are to be replaced by '*b*', except for the rightmost occurrence of '*a*', be replaced by '*b*', and let the resulting sentence be '[*f* ∈ *a*]'. This sentence is in T by the previous case considered, assuming of course that the rule to be proved holds for all sentences of lower level than that of '[*e* ∈ *a*]'. But if '[*f* ∈ *a*]' is in T, then so is '[*f* ∈ *b*]' by the same reasoning that was used in the case that was the basis of the induction, and '[*f* ∈ *b*]' is '(…*b*…).' Hence '(…*b*…)' is in T as was to be shown.

T-rule of replacement of constants of type (αβ). If '*a*' and '*b*' are constants of type (αβ) such that for all constants '*c*' and '*d*' of respective types α and β, either

'$[c\ a\ d]$' and '$[c\ b\ d]$' are both in T or else neither of them is in T, and if '$(\ldots a\ldots)$' is any sentence in which 'a' occurs zero or more times, then '$(\ldots b\ldots)$' is in T, where '$(\ldots b\ldots)$' is the result of replacing 'a' by 'b' in zero or more places in '$(\ldots a\ldots)$'.

Proof. Similar to the proof of the previous T-rule.

A method will now be given for defining quantifiers over entities of type ι, that is, over individuals. If 'a' is a constant of type (ι), the expression 'Ea' will serve as an abbreviation for '$[[\iota_1 \in a] \vee [\iota_2 \in a] \vee [\iota_3 \in a]]$', where, in general, '$p \vee q \vee r$' is an abbreviation for '$[p \vee q] \vee r$'. If 'x' is a variable of type ι so that '$\hat{x}(\ldots x\ldots)$' is a constant of type (ι), the expression '$E\hat{x}(\ldots x\ldots)$' acts like an existentially quantified expression in the system T. More specifically, the following rule holds:

T-rule [E] for type ι. If 'x' is a variable of type ι, then '$E\hat{x}(\ldots x\ldots)$' is in T iff, for some constant 'a' of type ι, '$(\ldots a\ldots)$' is in T, where '$(\ldots a\ldots)$' results from replacing all free occurrences of 'x' in '$(\ldots x\ldots)$' by occurrences of 'a'.

Proof. Suppose that '$E\hat{x}(\ldots x\ldots)$' is in T, that is, suppose that '$[[\iota_1 \in b] \vee [\iota_2 \in b] \vee [\iota_3 \in b]]$' is in T, where '$b$' is '$\hat{x}(\ldots x\ldots)$'. Then by T-rule [V] and the T-rule of class abstraction, at least one of the sentences '$(\ldots \iota_1\ldots)$', '$(\ldots \iota_2\ldots)$' and '$(\ldots \iota_3\ldots)$' is in T, so there is a constant 'a' of type ι such that '$(\ldots a\ldots)$' is in T. Suppose, conversely, that there is some constant 'a' of type ι such that '$(\ldots a\ldots)$' is in T. Then by T-rule [=] for type ι, at least one of the sentences '$[a = \iota_1]$', '$[a = \iota_2]$' and '$[a = \iota_3]$' is in T, and so by the T-rule of identity elimination for type ι, at least one of the sentences '$(\ldots \iota_1\ldots)$', '$(\ldots \iota_2\ldots)$' and '$(\ldots \iota_3\ldots)$' is in T. Hence, by the T-rule of class abstraction and the T-rule [V], the sentence '$[[\iota_1 \in b] \vee [\iota_2 \in b] \vee [\iota_3 \in b]]$' is in T; that is, '$E\hat{x}(\ldots x\ldots)$' is in T.

Let 'Aa' serve as an abbreviation for '$[[\iota_1 \in a] \mathbin{\&} [\iota_2 \in a] \mathbin{\&} [\iota_3 \in a]]$', where '$a$' is a constant of type (ι) and where, in general, '$p \mathbin{\&} q \mathbin{\&} r$' is an abbreviation for '$[p \mathbin{\&} q] \mathbin{\&} r$'. If '$x$' is a variable of type ι, then '$A\hat{x}(\ldots x\ldots)$' acts like a universally quantified expression in the system T, and the following rule holds:

T-rule [A] for type ι. If 'x' is a variable of type ι, then '$A\hat{x}(\ldots x\ldots)$' is in T iff, for every constant 'a' of type ι, '$(\ldots a\ldots)$' is in T, where '$(\ldots a\ldots)$' results from replacing all free occurrences of 'x' in '$(\ldots x\ldots)$' by occurrences of 'a'.

Proof. Similar to the proof of the T-rule [E] for type ι.

If 'a' and 'b' are constants of type (ι), the expression '$[a = b]$' is an abbreviation for '$A\hat{x}[[x \in a] \equiv [x \in b]]$', where '$x$' is a variable type ι. The following rule is then derivable:

T-rule of identity elimination for type (ι). If '$[a = b]$' and '$(\ldots a\ldots)$' are in T, where 'a' and 'b' are constants of type (ι) and where '$(\ldots a\ldots)$' is any sentence in which 'a' occurs zero or more times, then '$(\ldots b\ldots)$' is in T, where '$(\ldots b\ldots)$' results from replacing 'a' by 'b' in zero or more places in '$(\ldots a\ldots)$'.

Proof. By T-rule [A] for type ι, T-rule [$\equiv$], and the T-rule of replacement of constants of type (α), choosing (α) as (ι).

Corresponding to each of the eight subclasses of the three-membered class $\{`\iota_1`, `\iota_2`, `\iota_3`\}$ it is easy to define a constant 'c' of type (ι) such that, for every constant 'a' of type ι, '$[a \in c]$' is in T iff 'a' is in the subclass in question. Call these eight constants 'γ_1', 'γ_2', ..., 'γ_8'. For example, if the subclass in question is $\{`\iota_2`, `\iota_3`\}$, then the corresponding constant, say it is 'γ_7', could be defined to be '$\hat{x}[[x = \iota_2] \lor [x = \iota_3]]$'. Let us assume that these eight constants have been defined. Reference to them is made in the following rule:

T-rule [$=$] for type (ι). If 'a' is of type (ι), then exactly one of the sentences '$[a = \gamma_1]$', '$[a = \gamma_2]$',..., '$[a = \gamma_8]$' is in T.

Proof. Let 'γ_i' be chosen in such a way that '$[\iota_j \in \gamma_i]$' is in T iff '$[\iota_j \in a]$', for $j < 4$. Then by T-rule [$=$] for type ι and the T-rule of identity elimination for type ι, the result is obtained that for all 'b' of type ι, '$[b \in a]$' is in T iff '$[b \in \gamma_i]$' is in T. By the definition of '$[a = \gamma_i]$', the T-rule [A] for type ι, and the T-rule [$\equiv$], it follows that '$[a = \gamma_i]$' is in T. It is easy to show that for $k \neq i$, '$[a = \gamma_k]$' is not in T.

If 'a' is a constant of type ((ι)), the expression 'Ea' will serve as an abbreviation for '$[[\gamma_1 \in a] \lor [\gamma_2 \in a] \lor \cdots \lor [\gamma_8 \in a]]$', while '$Aa$' will serve as an abbreviation for '$[[\gamma_1 \in a] \& [\gamma_2 \in a] \& \cdots \& [\gamma_8 \in a]]$'. The following two rules are in effect rules of quantification over classes of individuals.

T-rule [E] for type (ι). If 'x' is a variable of type (ι), then '$E\hat{x}(...x...)$' is in T iff, for some constant 'a' of type (ι), '$(...a...)$' is in T, where '$(...a...)$' results from replacing all free occurrences of 'x' in '$(...x...)$' by occurrences of 'a'.

Proof. Like the proof of T-rule [E] for type ι, except that T-rule [$=$] for type (ι) is used in place of T-rule [$=$] for type ι, while the T-rule of identity elimination for type (ι) is used in place of the T-rule of identity elimination for type ι.

A T-rule [A] for type (ι) can be similarly stated and can be proved like the corresponding rule for type ι. This method of defining quantifiers for the system T obviously can be extended step by step to quantifiers involving variables of successively higher and higher types (including relational types) provided that suitable identity relations for higher types are defined at the same time according to the following principles: for 'a' and 'b' of type (α), '$[a = b]$' is defined as '$A\hat{x}[[x \in a] \equiv [x \in b]]$', where '$x$' is a variable of type α. Also, for 'c' and 'd' of type ($\alpha\beta$), '$[c = d]$' is defined as '$A\hat{x}A\hat{y}[[x\,c\,y] \equiv [x\,d\,y]]$', where '$x$' and '$y$' are variables of respective types α and β. For the various identity relations thus obtained, as well as for the identity relations previously available, the following rule is easily provable:

T-rule of reflexivity of identity. (For 'a' of any type) '$[a = a]$' is in T.

Proceeding step by step to higher types, but using methods already used for lower types, the following three rules are clearly provable:

T-rule of substitution (or identity elimination). If '$[a = b]$' and '$(\ldots a \ldots)$' are in T, where 'a' and 'b' are constants of the same type and where '$(\ldots a \ldots)$' is any sentence in which 'a' occurs zero or more times, then '$(\ldots b \ldots)$' is in T, where '$(\ldots b \ldots)$' results from replacing 'a' by 'b' in zero or more places in 'a'.

T-rule [E]. If 'x' is a variable of any type α, then '$E\hat{x}(\ldots x \ldots)$' is in T iff, for some constant 'a' of type α, '$(\ldots a \ldots)$' is in T, where '$(\ldots a \ldots)$' results from replacing all free occurrences of 'x' in '$(\ldots x \ldots)$' by occurrences of 'a'.

T-rule [A]. If 'x' is a variable of any type α, then '$A\hat{x}(\ldots x \ldots)$' is in T iff, for every constant 'a' of type α, '$(\ldots a \ldots)$' is in T, where '$(\ldots a \ldots)$' results from replacing all free occurrences of 'x' in '$(\ldots x \ldots)$' by occurrences of 'a'.

A constant 'a' will be said to *belong to* a constant 'b' if '$[a \in b]$' is in T, and a constant 'a' will be said to be *related to* a constant 'b' by a constant 'f' if '$[a f b]$' is in T. Furthermore, a constant 'c' will be said to be 'f'-*hereditary* if the following is the case for all constants 'a' and 'b': if 'a' belongs to 'c' and if 'a' is related to 'b' by 'f', then 'b' belongs to 'c'. Define 'fH' as '$\hat{x}A\hat{u}A\hat{v}[[[u \in x]\ \&\ [u f v]] \supset [v \in x]]$'. Then the following rule is easily derivable:

T-rule [H]. '$[c \in fH]$' is in T iff 'c' is 'f'-hereditary.

The expression 'f_*' is called the *ancestral* of 'f' and is defined as '$\hat{x}\hat{y}A\hat{z}[[[x \in z]\ \&\ [z \in fH]] \supset [y \in z]]$' The following rules are then derivable:

T-rule $[*]_1$. '$[a f_* b]$' is in T iff 'b' belongs to every 'f'-hereditary constant that 'a' belongs to.

Proof. By the definition of 'f_*' and the T-rules of relational abstraction, [A], [&], [⊃], and [H].

T-rule $[*]_2$. '$[a f_* a]$' is in T, for 'a' of (any) type α, and 'f' of type $(\alpha\alpha)$.

Proof. By T-rule $[*]_1$.

T-rule $[*]_3$. If '$[a f b]$' is in T, so is '$[a f_* b]$'.

Proof. By T-rule $[*]_1$, since if '$[a f b]$' is in T, then 'b' clearly belongs to every 'f'-hereditary constant that 'a' belongs to.

T-rule $[*]_4$. If '$[a f_* b]$' and '$[b f_* c]$' are in T, so is '$[a f_* c]$'.

Proof. By T-rule $[*]_1$, since if 'c' belongs to every 'f'-hereditary constant that 'b' belongs to, and if 'b' belongs to every 'f'-hereditary constant that 'a' belongs to, then clearly 'c' belongs to every 'f'-hereditary constant that 'a' belongs to.

T-rule $[*]_5$. If '$[a f_* b]$' and '$[b f c]$' are in T, so is '$[a f_* c]$'.

Proof. By T-rules $[*]_3$ and $[*]_4$.

It will be said that 'b' is 'f'-*reachable* from 'a' if '$[a = b]$' or '$[a f b]$' is in T or if there is a finite sequence of constants 'c_1', 'c_2', ..., 'c_n', such that '$[a f c_1]$', '$[c_2 f c_3]$', ..., '$[c_{n-1} f c_n]$', '$[c_n f b]$' are in T.

T-rule $[*]_6$. If 'b' is 'f'-reachable from 'a', then '$[a f_* b]$' is in T.

Proof. By T-rule $[*]_1$, since if 'b' is 'f'-reachable from 'a', then clearly 'b' belongs to every 'f'-hereditary constant that 'a' belongs to. In the case that '$[a = b]$' is in T, use the T-rule of substitution.

Constants 'a' and 'b' will be said to be *equal* if '[a = b]' is in T, otherwise they will be said to be *unequal*.

T-rule $[*]_7$. If 'b' is not 'f'-reachable from 'a', '[a f_* b]' is not in T.

Proof. Consider the class C of constants that are 'f'-reachable from 'a'. This class can be shown to have a finite subclass D such that each member of C is equal to some member of D, since each type has at most some finite number of mutually unequal constants. Hence it is easy to find a constant 'd' such that the necessary and sufficient condition for being a member of C is belonging to 'd'. In fact if the members of D are 'd_1', 'd_2',..., 'd_n', then the constant 'd' can be chosen as '$\hat{x}[[x = d_1] \lor [x = d_2] \lor \cdots \lor [x = d_n]]$'. Now 'a' belongs to 'd', and 'd' is clearly 'f'-hereditary, but 'b' does not belong to 'd', Hence there is an 'f'-hereditary constant to which 'a' belongs but to which 'b' does not belong, and so, by T-rule $[*]_1$, '[a f_* b]' is not in T.

T-rule $[*]_8$. '[a f_* b]' is in T iff 'b' is 'f'-reachable from 'a'.

Proof. By T-rules $[*]_6$ and $[*]_7$.

T-rule $[*]$. '[a f_* b]' is in T iff '[a = b]' or '[a f b]' is in T or there is a finite sequence 'c_1', 'c_2',..., 'c_n' such that '$[a f c_1]$', '$[c_1 f c_2]$',..., '$[c_n f b]$' are in T.

Proof. By T-rule $[*]_8$.

The system T will now be modified in a trivial way in order to facilitate comparison with the systems M and N, soon to be defined. The modification consists in adding primitive (that is, undefined) quantifiers which are equivalent to the defined quantifiers of T, and in adding a primitive ancestral which is equivalent to the defined ancestral of T. This is done because there is need to have primitive quantifiers and a primitive ancestral in the systems M and N, and by having the same primitive concepts in the system T it becomes possible to show that all the theorems of M and N are theorems of T, although not all theorems of T are theorems of M and N. The class of sentences is therefore widened by adding the following further rules that are concerned directly or indirectly with sentence formation: (1) If '$E\hat{x}(\ldots x \ldots)$' is a sentence of level n, then '$\exists x(\ldots x \ldots)$' is a sentence of level $n + 1$. (2) If 'a_*' is a constant of type $(\alpha\alpha)$, then '$a_{(*)}$' is a constant of type $(\alpha\alpha)$. (3) If '[a f_* b]' is a sentence of level n, then '$[a f_{(*)} b]$' is a sentence of level $n + 1$. Thus the new primitive concepts are existential quantifiers formed by use of the symbol '∃', and ancestrals of a special sort formed by use of the symbol '(*)'. In the system T, however, these new concepts are equivalent to the old ones to which they correspond, and this is guaranteed by adding the following further primitive rules for membership in T:

T-rule $[\exists]_0$. '$\exists x(\ldots x \ldots)$' is in T iff '$E\hat{x}(\ldots x \ldots)$' is in T.

T-rule $[\sim\exists]_0$. '$\sim\exists x(\ldots x \ldots)$' is in T iff '$\sim E\hat{x}(\ldots x \ldots)$' is in T.

T-rule $[(*)]_0$. '$[a b_{(*)} c]$' is in T iff '$[a b_* c]$' is in T.

T-rule $[\sim(*)]_0$. '$\sim[a b_{(*)} c]$' is in T iff '$\sim[a b_* c]$' is in T.

Notice that when the above rules are used, it still remains true that membership or non-membership of a sentence in T can always be decided by reference

9

to sentences of lower level. Also, all previously stated rules concerning T are still derivable, such as the T-rule [$\sim$]. The following further rules are now easily derivable. '$\forall x(\ldots x \ldots)$' abbreviates '$\sim \exists x \sim(\ldots x \ldots)$'.

T-rule [$\exists$]. If 'x' is a variable of type α, then '$\exists x(\ldots x \ldots)$' is in T iff, for some constant 'a' of type α, '$(\ldots a \ldots)$' is in T, where [etc.].

T-rule [$\sim\exists$]. If 'x' is a variable of type α, then '$\sim\exists x(\ldots x \ldots)$' is in T iff, for every constant 'a' of type α, '$\sim(\ldots a \ldots)$' is in T, where [etc.].

T-rule ($\forall$). If 'x' is a variable of type α, then '$\forall x(\ldots x \ldots)$' is in T iff, for every constant 'a' of type α, '$(\ldots a \ldots)$' is in T, where [etc.].

T-rule [$\sim\forall$]. If 'x' is a variable of type α, then '$\sim\forall x(\ldots x \ldots)$' is in T iff, for some constant 'a' of type α, '$\sim(\ldots a \ldots)$' is in T, where [etc.].

T-rule [(*)]. '$[a f_{(*)} b]$' is in T iff '$[a = b]$' or '$[a f b]$' is in T or there is a finite sequence 'c_1', 'c_2', \ldots, 'c_n' such that '$[a f c_1]$', '$[c_1 f c_2]$', \ldots, '$[c_n f b]$' are in T.

T-rule [$\sim$(*)]. '$\sim[a f_{(*)} b]$' is in T iff '$\sim[a = b]$' and '$\sim[a f b]$' are in T and, for every finite sequence 'c_1', 'c_2', \ldots, 'c_n' (of constants of the same type as 'a' and 'b'), at least one of '$\sim[a f c_1]$', '$\sim[c_1 f c_2]$', \ldots, '$\sim[c_n f b]$' is in T.

The definition of '$[a = b]$' for the case where 'a' and 'b' are not of type ι, the definition of 'fH' and the definition of 'f_*' are now to be understood as modified by using quantifiers of the form '$\forall x$' in place of quantifiers of the form 'Ax'. This change will not invalidate any results so far obtained because of the fact that '$\forall x(\ldots x \ldots)$' is in T iff '$A\hat{x}(\ldots x \ldots)$' is in T. In particular the T-rule of substitution (that if '$[a = b]$' and '$(\ldots a \ldots)$' are in T, so is '$(\ldots b \ldots)$') will continue to hold and to play the role of axioms of extensionality for T. The reason for making this change in quantifiers in the definitions of '$[a = b]$', 'fH' and 'f_*' is that the latter expressions have to be used not only in the system T, where both '$\forall x$' and '$A\hat{x}$' have the requisite properties of universal quantifiers, but also in the systems M and N, where '$\forall x$' has these properties but '$A\hat{x}$' does not.

A system M will now be defined by rules M1–M13 below. The class of all sentences is defined in the same way for M as for T. The system M is a non-constructive form of the system of *Principia Mathematica*, without axioms of infinity, choice or extensionality. It is easy to show that the rules M1–M13 are all satisfied by the system T, so that every theorem of M is a theorem of T, and M is therefore clearly consistent. Later it will be shown that the denial of the axiom of infinity is not a theorem of M and that the axiom of infinity can be added to M without destroying consistency if the system N, to be defined below, satisfies the rule of modus ponens.

Outermost square brackets will generally be omitted from now on. The rules defining M are as follows:

M1. If 'p' and '$p \supset q$' are in M, so is 'q'.

M2. If '$(\ldots a \ldots)$' is in M for every constant 'a' of type α, then '$\forall x(\ldots x \ldots)$' is in M, where '$x$' is a variable of type α, and '$(\ldots a \ldots)$' is the result of replacing all free occurrences of 'x' in '$(\ldots x \ldots)$' by occurrences of 'a'.

M3. Every sentence which is a truth-table tautology is in M.

M4. '$\forall x(\ldots x \ldots) \supset (\ldots a \ldots)$' is in M, where [etc.].

M5. '$\forall x[(\ldots x \ldots) \supset (---x---)] \supset [\forall x(\ldots x \ldots) \supset \forall x(---x---)]$' is in M.

M6. '$p \supset \forall x p$' is in M (where 'p', being a sentence, contains no free occurrences of 'x').

M7. '$[a \in \hat{x}(\ldots x \ldots)] \equiv (\ldots a \ldots)$' is in M, where [etc.].

M8. '$[a \, \hat{x}\hat{y}(\ldots x \ldots y \ldots) \, b] \equiv (\ldots a \ldots b \ldots)$' is in M, where [etc.].

M9. '$a \, f_{(*)} \, a$' is in M.

M10. '$[a f b] \supset [a f_{(*)} b]$' is in M.

M11. '$[a f_{(*)} b] \supset [[b f_{(*)} c] \supset [a f_{(*)} c]]$' is in M.

M12. If 'a' is of type ι, then '$a = a$' is in M.

M13. If 'a' and 'b' are of type ι, then '$[a = b] \supset [(\ldots a \ldots) \supset (\ldots b \ldots)]$' is in M, where '$(\ldots b \ldots)$'. is the result of replacing 'a' by 'b' in one or more places in '$(\ldots a \ldots)$'.

We may think of M1 and M2 as providing rules of direct consequence for the system M, and M3–M13 as providing the axioms. Then by an M-proof could be meant a well-ordered (possibly infinite) class of sentences such that each sentence of the class either is an axiom or is a direct consequence by M1 or M2 of sentences that are in the class and that precede it in the well-ordering. It is possible to define a weaker subsystem of M, to be called M_0, by replacing the phrase, "is in M", by the phrase, "is an axiom of M_0", everywhere in M2–M13, and revising M1 to read, " 'q' is a direct consequence (for M_0) of 'p' and '$p \supset q$' ". The system M_0 is constructive in the sense that the class of its theorems (members) is recursively enumerable and its proofs are finite in length. M_0 is essentially equivalent to usual formulations of *Principia Mathematica* if the axioms of infinity, choice and extensionality are omitted.

Preparatory to defining the system N, the following abbreviations are introduced:

'$[f \mid g]$' for '$\hat{x}\hat{y} \exists z[[x f z] \, \& \, [z \, g \, y]]$',

'f^0' for '$\hat{x}\hat{y}[[x = y] \, \& \, [f = f]]$',

'f^1' for 'f',

'f^2' for '$[f \mid f]$',

'f^3' for '$[[f \mid f] \mid f]$', and so on.

The expression '$[f \mid g]$' may be called the *relative product* of 'f' with 'g', and the expressions 'f^0', 'f^1', and so on, may be called the *relative powers* of 'f'. These notions will be useful in relating the system N to the system T. The following two T-rules are easily derivable:

T-rule for relative powers. The necessary and sufficient condition for '$a \, f^m \, b$' to be in T is: for $m = 0$, that '$a = b$' is in T; for $m = 1$, that '$a f b$' is in T; for $m = n + 1 > 1$, that there is a sequence 'c_1', 'c_2', ..., 'c_n' such that '$a f c_1$', '$c_1 f c_2$', ..., '$c_n f b$' are in T.

T-rule $[(*)]_1$. '$a \, f_{(*)} \, b$' is in T iff, for some non-negative integer n, '$a f^n b$' is in T.

Given a disjunction '$p \lor q$' of sentences 'p' and 'q', the leftmost occurrence of 'p' in '$p \lor q$' will be said to occupy position L in '$p \lor q$', and the rightmost occurrence of 'q' in '$p \lor q$' will be said to occupy position R in '$p \lor q$'. It will also be said that any sentence 'p' occupies position I (the identity position) in 'p' itself. If 'p' occupies position L in 'q' and if 'q' occupies position R in 'r', then it will be said that 'p' occupies position LR in 'r', and similarly for other cases. Thus, for example, 'q' occupies position RRL in '$[r \lor [p \lor q]] \lor s$', while '$p$' occupies position LRL in the same expression. Of course an expression may occupy several different positions in another expression. Positions of the kind described here may be said to be *disjunctive positions*, that is, positions of disjuncts in a disjunction, though the identity position is a disjunctive position only in a vacuous sense. References to positions are to be understood as references to disjunctive positions. Hereafter the notation 'Φp' (possibly with a numerical subscript attached to 'Φ') will be used to stand for 'p' itself or for any disjunction in which 'p' has a disjunctive position. When 'Φp' is used in this way to stand for a disjunction, and when 'Φq' is used shortly afterwards to stand for another disjunction, then 'Φq' is to be understood as standing for the result of replacing 'p' by 'q' in exactly one position in the disjunction for which 'Φp' stands. When 'Φp' stands for 'p' itself, then of course 'Φq' stands for 'q' itself.

The systems T, M, and N are subclasses of the class of all sentences. As in the case of system M, all the rules used to define N are rules that also hold for system T. Consequently, N, like M, is a subclass of T and is therefore clearly free from contradiction.

The system N is now defined by way of the following set of thirteen rules, N1–N13.[1] This definition will later be revised in the direction of further strengthening N so as to overcome a deficiency discovered by Professor Michael Dunn.

N1 (N-rule [$\lor$]). If the sentences 'p' and '$\sim p$' occupy disjunctive positions in the same disjunctive sentence, then that disjunctive sentence is in N.

N2 (N-rule [$\sim\lor$]). If '$\Phi\sim p$' and '$\Phi\sim q$' are in N, so is '$\Phi\sim[p \lor q]$'.

N3 (N-rule [$\sim\sim$]). If 'Φp' is in N, so is '$\Phi\sim\sim p$'.

N4 (N-rule [$\exists$]). If 'x' is a variable of type α, and if '$\Phi(\ldots a \ldots)$' is in N, where 'a' is a constant of type α, then '$\Phi\exists x(\ldots x \ldots)$' is in N, where '$(\ldots a \ldots)$' is the result of replacing all free occurrences of 'x' in '$(\ldots x \ldots)$' by 'a'.

N5 (N-rule [$\sim\exists$]). If 'x' is a variable of type α, and if '$\Phi\sim(\ldots a_1 \ldots)$', '$\Phi\sim(\ldots a_2 \ldots)$', '$\Phi\sim(\ldots a_3 \ldots)$', $\ldots$ are in N, where 'a_1', 'a_2', 'a_3', $\ldots$ are all the constants of type α, then '$\Phi\sim\exists x(\ldots x \ldots)$' is in N, where, for $i = 1, 2, 3, \ldots$, '$(\ldots a_i \ldots)$' is the result of replacing all free occurrences of 'x' in '$(\ldots x \ldots)$' by 'a_i'.

---

[1] The method used here for defining N has affinities with the Anderson-Belnap tree-proof method (A. Anderson and N. Belnap, "A Simple Proof of Gödel's Completeness Theorem", *Journal of Symbolic Logic* 24, 4 (1959)).

N6 (N-rule [cls]). If '$\Phi(\ldots a \ldots)$' is in N, so is '$\Phi[a \in \hat{x}(\ldots x \ldots)]$', where [etc.].

N7 (N-rule [$\sim$cls]). If '$\Phi\sim(\ldots a \ldots)$' is in N, so is '$\Phi\sim[a \in \hat{x}(\ldots x \ldots)]$', where [etc.].

N8 (N-rule [rel]). If '$\Phi(\ldots a \ldots b \ldots)$' is in N, so is '$\Phi[a \, \hat{x}\hat{y}(\ldots x \ldots y \ldots) b]$', where [etc.].

N9 (N-rule [$\sim$rel]). If '$\Phi\sim(\ldots a \ldots b \ldots)$' is in N, so is '$\Phi\sim[a \, \hat{x}\hat{y}(\ldots x \ldots y \ldots) b]$', where [etc.].

N10 (N-rule [(∗)]). If '$\Phi[a \, f^n \, b]$' is in N, where n is a non-negative integer, then '$\Phi[a \, f_{(∗)} \, b]$' is in N.

N11 (N-rule [$\sim$(∗)]). If '$\Phi\sim[a \, f^n \, b]$' is in N for each non-negative integer n, then '$\Phi\sim[a \, f_{(∗)} \, b]$' is in N.

N12 (N-rule [=]). If 'a' and 'b' are constants of type ι and if '$\Phi\forall x[\sim[a \in x] \lor [b \in x]]$' is in N, so is '$\Phi[a = b]$'.

N13 (N-rule [$\sim$=]). If 'a' and 'b' are constants of type ι and if '$\Phi\sim\forall x[\sim[a \in x] \lor [b \in x]]$', is in N, so is '$\Phi\sim[a = b]$'.

The rules N12 and N13 are not really required since identity between individuals need not be taken as undefined in systems M and N, but we treat identity between individuals as undefined in M and N in order to facilitate comparison with system T, where it *does* seem desirable to treat such identity as undefined. The rules N10 and N11 could also be omitted were it not for the fact that there is need for the undefined concept of the ancestral in order to show as easily as possible that the denial of the axiom of infinity is not a theorem of system N and therefore, if N satisfies modus ponens, also not a theorem of system M.

The rule N1 may be regarded as stating, in effect, that certain sentences are axioms for N, and each of the other rules N2–N13 may be regarded as stating, in effect, that corresponding to a specified sentence there is a class of sentences (in some cases consisting of a single sentence) which jointly have the specified sentence as a d.c. (direct consequence for system N). It is then to be understood that every sentence 'p' which is an axiom for N is in N (that is, is a theorem of N), and that if 'q_1', 'q_2',... are in N and jointly have 'p' as a d.c., then 'p' is in N. Furthermore, if some sentence 'p' is in N, the reason for its being in N must be either that it is an axiom for N or that it is a d.c. of sentences that are in N. Consequently, one way to show that all sentences of N have some property is to show that every axiom for N has the property and that every sentence which is a d.c. of sentences which have the property has the property.

Two easily derived N-rules are now stated:

N-rule [$\forall$]. If 'x' is a variable of type α, and if '$\Phi(\ldots a_1 \ldots)$', '$\Phi(\ldots a_2 \ldots)$',... are in N, where 'a_1', 'a_2',... are all the constants of type α, then '$\Phi\forall x(\ldots x \ldots)$' is in N, where [etc.].

N-rule [$\sim\forall$]. If 'x' is a variable of type α, and if '$\Phi\sim(\ldots a \ldots)$' is in N, where '$a$' is a constant of type α, then '$\Phi\sim\forall x(\ldots x \ldots)$' is in N, where [etc.].

The definition of the system N as given above is the same as that used in an earlier version of this paper, but this definition gives a weaker version of N than was intended. Specifically, Professor Michael Dunn has shown the writer that the following two theorems are not derivable in this previous version:

$$\exists x[(\ldots x \ldots) \vee \sim \exists y(\ldots y \ldots)]$$
$$[a \; \hat{x}\hat{y}[[x f y] \vee \sim [a f_{(*)} b]]_{(*)} b]$$

One way to overcome this weakness and to cause the above sentences to be theorems of N is to extend the concept of 'disjunctive' position in such a way that '$\sim \exists y(\ldots y \ldots)$' would have a position in the first of these two sentences and '$\sim [a f_{(*)} b]$' would have a position in the second. In order to do this in a sufficiently general way, some further concepts must first be introduced.

A *quasi-sentence* is defined as any expression obtained by replacing in a sentence zero or more constants by variables of the same types as those constants. Similarly, a *quasi-constant* is defined as any expression obtained by replacing in a constant zero or more other constants by variables of the same types as those constants. In particular, therefore, every sentence is a quasi-sentence, and every constant and every variable is a quasi-constant.

Let the boldface symbols '**a**', '**b**', and '**c**' hereafter stand for arbitrary quasi-constants, and let the boldface symbols '**p**', '**q**', and '**r**' hereafter stand for arbitrary quasi-sentences. Consider a sentence '*s*' containing an occurrence of a quasi-sentence of the form '$[\mathbf{a} \in x(\ldots x \ldots)]$', where '$(\ldots x \ldots)$' is a quasi-sentence in which the variable '*x*' occurs zero or more times. We say that '*q*' is a *contraction* of '*s*' if '*q*' is a sentence obtained from '*s*' by replacing an occurrence of '$[\mathbf{a} \in x(\ldots x \ldots)]$' by an occurrence of '$(\ldots \mathbf{a} \ldots)$' (at the same time, if necessary, making a change of bound variables in '$(\ldots x \ldots)$' so that variables in '**a**' that are free in '$[\mathbf{a} \in x(\ldots x \ldots)]$' remain free in '$(\ldots \mathbf{a} \ldots)$'). It is of course to be understood that '$(\ldots \mathbf{a} \ldots)$' is the result of replacing all occurrences of '*x*' that are free in '$(\ldots x \ldots)$' by occurrences of '**a**'. The notion of contraction also includes a similar case where a quasi-sentence of the form '$[\mathbf{a} \; \hat{x}\hat{y}(\ldots x \ldots y \ldots) \mathbf{b}]$' is replaced by '$(\ldots \mathbf{a} \ldots \mathbf{b} \ldots)$' (with similar requirements for change of bound variables).

A contraction of a contraction of a sentence '*s*' is also said to be a contraction of '*s*'. A contraction of '*s*' which has no further contraction is said to be a *final contraction* of '*s*'. It is clear that any sentence which has a contraction has a final contraction.

The N-rules [cls], [$\sim$cls], [rel], and [$\sim$rel] are now to be replaced by following stronger N-rule:

Contractional N-rule. If a sentence '*p*' has a contraction, and if a final contraction of '*p*' is in N, then '*p*' is in N.

The concept of (disjunctive) position will next be defined in a more general way than before. The new definition will not always assign (disjunctive) positions within sentences that have contractions, but there is no need for such an assignment because the contractional N-rule applies to such sentences without regard to (disjunctive) positions.

The concept of *location* (for quasi-sentences) is first defined: (1) Each quasi-sentence is trivially located in itself and is said to have location I in itself. (2) If a quasi-sentence '**p**' has some location P in a quasi-sentence '**q**', then '**p**' has location PL in '[**q** $\vee$ **r**]', and location PR in '[**r** $\vee$ **q**]'. (3) If '**p**' has some location P in '**q**', then '**p**' has location $P\sim$ in '$\sim$**q**' and location PE in '$\exists x$**q**' (where 'x' is a variable), and it has location PA in '$x\hat{y}$**q**$_{(*)}$' (where 'x' and 'y' are variables).

If '$\sim$' occurs an odd number of times in the name of a location, the location is said to be *negative*, otherwise *positive*. A (*disjunctive*) *position* is now redefined in a more general way as *any positive location*. For example, '$\sim\exists y(\ldots y \ldots)$' has location I in itself and so has location IR in '[$(\ldots x \ldots) \vee \sim\exists y(\ldots y \ldots)$]' and location IRE in '$\exists x[(\ldots x \ldots) \vee \sim\exists y(\ldots y \ldots)]$'. The latter location is clearly a positive location and so is a (disjunctive) position. On the other hand, '$\exists y(\ldots y \ldots)$' has location $I\sim RE$ in '$\exists x[(\ldots x \ldots) \vee \sim\exists y(\ldots y \ldots)]$'. This location is negative and so is not a disjunctive position. As another example, '$\sim\exists y(\ldots y \ldots)$' has location $IL\sim\sim E$ in '$\exists x\sim\sim[\sim\exists y(\ldots y \ldots) \vee (\ldots x \ldots)]$'. This is a positive location and so is a (disjunctive) position. Indeed, for this reason, the latter sentence can be shown to be in N, and so can the sentence '$\exists x(\ldots x \ldots) \vee \sim\exists y(\ldots y \ldots)]$'. For similar reasons the sentence '[a $\hat{x}\hat{y}[[x f y] \vee \sim[a f_{(*)} b]]_{(*)} b$' can also be shown to be in N. Thus the deficiencies pointed out by Dunn appear to be overcome.

Notice that one sentence may occur in another without having a location (in our technical sense) in that other. For example, 'p' occurs in '$\exists y[\hat{x}[(\ldots x \ldots) \vee p] \in y]$' but has no location in it. (The latter sentence, furthermore, has no contraction, and no sentence other than it itself has a location in it).

A (disjunctive) position in the *old* sense will now be called a *primary* (disjunctive) position. Such a position may now be defined as a location whose name does not contain the symbols '$\sim$', 'E', or 'A'. The rule N1 (N-rule [$\vee$]) must be restricted by replacing the phrase "disjunctive positions" by the phrase "primary disjunctive positions", since otherwise the new definition of disjunctive position would make N1 too strong and would cause N no longer to be a subclass of T (since T would not satisfy such a strong version of N1), and N would no longer even be consistent.

When these changes have been made in the definition of the system N, it remains true that N is a subclass of T and therefore consistent. It is not known, however, whether N satisfies the rule of modus ponens (expressed as M1 for system M).

Some metatheorems about systems M and N are now presented:

Theorem 1. Every axiom for M is in N; that is, all sentences that are in M by M3–M13 are also in N.

Proof. It is known that rules N1–N3 give rise to all tautologies of two-valued logic (expressed in terms of 'V' and '$\sim$'),[1] so that N satisfies M3. It is easy to show that N also satisfies each of M4–M13.

Theorem 2. If N satisfies modus ponens, then every theorem of M is a theorem of N.

Proof. N satisfies M1 by hypothesis and satisfies M2 by N-rule [∀] above. Hence, under the given hypothesis, N satisfies M1–M13 by Theorem 1.

Theorem 3. Every theorem of N is a theorem of M.

Proof. Each of N1–N13 can be shown to be satisfied by M.

Some further abbreviations are now introduced. The symbol 'Λ' (denoting the empty class of individuals) is defined as '$\hat{x}\sim[x = x]$', where 'x' is a variable of type ι. Similarly, 'V' (denoting the universal class of individuals) is defined as '$\hat{x}[x = x]$'. Next, 'F' is defined as '$\hat{x}\hat{y}\exists u \forall w[[w \in y] \equiv [[w = u] \vee [w \in x]]]$', where '$x$' and '$y$' are variables of type (ι), and 'u' and 'w' are variables of type ι. The constant 'F' denotes the relation between two classes when the second results from adding a member to the first. Thus '$\Lambda\ F^n\ V$' would mean that the universal class could be reached from the empty class by n successive additions of one member each, and '$\Lambda\ F_*\ V$' would mean that the universal class is finite, that is, that the axiom of infinity is false. Thus '$\sim[\Lambda\ F_*\ V]$' may be regarded as a formulation of the axiom of infinity (cp. *125·16 of *Principia Mathematica*). Its contradictory, '$\Lambda\ F_*\ V$', will be shown not to be in N or M if N satisfies modus ponens.

It is clear that '$\Lambda\ F^0\ V$', '$\Lambda\ F^1\ V$', and '$\Lambda\ F^2\ V$' are not theorems of T, but that '$\Lambda\ F^3\ V$' is a theorem of T. On the other hand, T could easily be modified so that '$\Lambda\ F^3\ V$' would fail to be a theorem of T but '$\Lambda\ F^4\ V$' would be a theorem of T. In fact, for each $n > 0$, it is not hard to construct a modified version T_n of T such that '$\Lambda\ F^m\ V$' is in T_n for $m \geqslant n$ but not for $m < n$. Now for each such T_n it is clear that N is a subclass of T_n just as N is a subclass of T. Hence the following theorem:

Theorem 4. '$\Lambda\ F^n\ V$' is not in N for any non-negative integer n.

Theorem 5. '$\Lambda\ F_{(*)}\ V$' is not in N.

Proof. The only rule according to which '$\Lambda\ F_{(*)}\ V$' could be in N is the N-rule [(∗)], that is N10. But this rule requires the premise that '$\Lambda\ F^n\ V$' is in N, where n is some non-negative integer; and because of Theorem 4 no such premise can be established.

Theorem 6. If N satisfies modus ponens, '$\Lambda\ F_{(*)}\ V$' is not in M.

Proof. By Theorems 2 and 5.

Theorem 7. If N satisfies modus ponens, '$\Lambda\ F_*\ V$' is not in M.

Proof. It is easy to see that '$\hat{x}[\Lambda\ F_{(*)}\ x]$' is an '$F$'-hereditary constant to which the constant 'Λ' belongs (using terminology in connection with the system M that was originally designed to be used in connection with the system T). Hence, if '$\Lambda\ F_*\ V$' were in M, then 'V' would belong to every 'F'-hereditary

---

[1] For example, the Anderson-Belnap tree-proof rules (ibid.) clearly give rise to all tautologies of two-valued logic.

constant to which 'Λ' belongs, and so 'V' would belong to '$\hat{x}[\Lambda \; F_{(*)} \; x]$', that is, '$V \in \hat{x}[\Lambda \; F_{(*)} \; x]$' would be in M. But then '$\Lambda \; F_{(*)} \; V$' would be in M, contrary to Theorem 6.

Theorem 8. M is consistent and, if N satisfies modus ponens, remains so when '$\sim[\Lambda \; F_* \; V]$' (the axiom of infinity) is added as a further axiom.

Proof. M is consistent since it is a subclass of the consistent system T. If the addition of '$\sim[\Lambda \; F_* \; V]$' to M were to produce a contradiction, then in a parallel way the implication '$\sim[\Lambda \; F_* \; V] \supset [p \; \& \sim p]$' would be provable in M, and hence, by well-known methods, '$\Lambda \; F_* \; V$' would be provable in M, contrary to Theorem 7.

If M* and M$_0^*$ are the systems obtained by adding the axiom of infinity respectively to systems M and M$_0$, and if N satisfies modus ponens, then the constructive system M$_0^*$ must be consistent since it is a subsystem of the consistent system M*. If the axiom of extensionality is added to M$_0^*$, and if M$_0^*$ is consistent, the result is a consistent system, as can be seen by applying a method due to Gandy.[1] This method is applicable to M* as well as to M$_0^*$, so it is also true that the axiom of extensionality can be added to M* without destroying consistency. The result of adding the axiom of extensionality to M$_0^*$ gives a system that may be called M$_0^E$, while the result of adding it to M* may be called M^E. The system M$_0^E$ is essentially the system of *Principia Mathematica* when formulated as a constructive system that includes axioms of infinity and extensionality, and M^E is a slightly stronger non–constructive system. Both these systems must be consistent if N satisfies modus ponens.

[1] ibid.

John Myhill

The Undefinability of the Set of Natural Numbers in the Ramified Principia

Russell, as is well known, saw no philosophical justification for the *simple* theory of types, and consequently the *ramified* theory is his "official" logic. Nonetheless, in the second edition of *Principia Mathematica* the "axiom of reducibility" is included as a primitive proposition (**12·1**) and not adjoined as an explicit hypothesis to theorems requiring it for their proof (as are the axiom of infinity and the multiplicative axiom). As was early pointed out, the addition of the axiom of reducibility makes the simple and ramified theories indistinguishable. His reasons for accepting this axiom are, he states, "largely inductive, namely that many propositions which are nearly indubitable can be deduced from it, and that no equally plausible way is known by which these propositions could be true if the axiom were false, and nothing which is probably false can be deduced from it".[1] Again, he defends its introduction on the ground that "*if mathematics is to be possible* [my italics] it is absolutely necessary that we should have a method of making statements which will usually be equivalent to what we have in mind when we (inaccurately) speak of 'all properties of *x*' ".[2] The necessity of the axiom from this (pragmatic) point of view results from three circumstances in particular: (1) the impossibility of stating, without its help, the Leibnizian principle that two things are identical if and only if they have the same properties; (2) the inadequacy of the usual definition of '*x* is a natural number' if stated in terms of the ramified hierarchy; and (3) the fact that if real numbers are introduced into this hierarchy they are divided into "levels" so that the least upper bound of a bounded set of reals of one level will in general be a real of a higher level, and there is no level which is *closed* under the operation of taking least upper bounds of its bounded subsets, i.e. no level which behaves like the classical continuum. There have been mathematicians, notably Hermann Weyl, who have refused to admit impredicative definitions in mathematics, and have accepted this splitting of the classical continuum into levels or orders as an inevitable consequence of their position. Such mathematicians have usually taken the natural numbers as fundamental, and however prepared they are to weaken the results of classical analysis, or to complicate the proofs of those results which remain, it is unlikely that they would accept the

[1] *Principia Mathematica*, 2nd ed., 1925, vol. I, p. 50.
[2] ibid., vol. I, p. 166.

ramified *Principia* as a codification of their underlying logic, because of the difficulty we numbered (2).

Let us state this difficulty more precisely. Suppose that we have given acceptable definitions of 'zero' and 'successor', say for definiteness Russell's own. Then classically we say that x is a *natural number* if x belongs to every set that contains o and is such that wherever it contains y, it contains the successor of y. In symbols

$$x \in N \equiv (\forall \alpha)(o \in \alpha \wedge (\forall y)(y \in \alpha \rightarrow y + \mathbf{I} \in \alpha) \rightarrow x \in \alpha).$$

If we like we can write this definition in terms of properties instead of sets, but in either case the difficulty is the same: we cannot quantify over *all* α of the required type (actually it is type 3) but only over all α of a certain *order*. For in the ramified *Principia* sets (or properties) are divided into orders as well as types, and the totality of all sets (or properties) of a given type is as illegitimate as the totality of all sets whatsoever. In order therefore to make the above definition even well-formed there must be a subscript, say k, on α to indicate the level or order of sets or properties which we have in mind. Thus x is a natural number if and only if it has all the kth-level hereditary properties of o. Now suppose we wish to establish some property of all natural numbers by induction, i.e. suppose we have proved $\varphi(o)$ and $\varphi(a) \rightarrow \varphi(a + \mathbf{I})$ and wish to infer $(\forall x \in N)\varphi(x)$. If φ is a kth-level property this inference is immediately justified by the definition, and if φ is of some level less than k there is again no difficulty since every property of any level $<k$ is automatically of level k, or at least coextensive with a property of level k. But in general φ will be of level $>k$; this will always be the case if φ contains clauses of the form $y \in N$, since this in primitive notation contains the quantification $(\forall \alpha_k)$. Now every $x \in N$ has by definition all k^{th}-level hereditary properties of o, but we see no way to infer that it has the higher-level hereditary property φ. Thus however large we pick k, there will be instances of mathematical induction (in particular any induction on properties containing clauses $y \in N$, which most interesting properties of natural numbers do contain), which cannot be carried out in our formalism.

Russell's way out of this difficulty, as we have seen, was to adopt the axiom of reducibility. According to this axiom, every property is coextensive with a predicative property; thus if x has all hereditary predicative properties of o, it has *all* hereditary properties of o, and we can use induction on *all* properties, of however high a level, even with $k = 3$ in the definition of N. (A property is *predicative* if it is of the next level above that of its argument.) However it is quite evident that Russell was not at all happy with this solution, and in Appendix B of *Principia*, vol. 1, he produces another. This claims to show that *mathematical induction can be saved without using the axiom of reducibility.*

Specifically, let us define

$$N_{k+1} = \{x | (\forall \alpha_k)(o \in \alpha \wedge (\forall y)(y \in \alpha \rightarrow y + \mathbf{I} \in \alpha) \rightarrow x \in \alpha)\}.$$

Then in Appendix B, Russell claims to prove, *without using the axiom of reducibility*, a general proposition (**89·29**), having as a special case the result[1] that

$$N_k = N_6 \quad (k > 6).$$

Suppose he had in fact done this, then we would define N as simply N_6 and then we could prove

$$\varphi(0) \land (\forall y)(\varphi(y) \to \varphi(y + 1)) \to (\forall x \in N)\varphi(x)$$

for all φ of no matter how high an order.

In his paper in the Schilpp Russell volume,[2] Gödel observed that Russell's proof of ***89·29** is defective, and enquired whether a correct proof could be given. The main purpose of this paper is to answer this question in the negative. More precisely, we show that if we define N_k as above (no matter how great k is) we can *not* prove that $N_k = N_m$ for any $m > k$. That is, if we define the set of natural numbers as consisting of all those things which have all k^{th}-order hereditary properties of 0, then we cannot prove that these things have all m^{th}-order properties of 0, where $m > k$; i.e. we cannot prove the principle of mathematical induction in the form

$$\varphi(0) \land (\forall x)(\varphi(x) \to \varphi(x + 1)) \to (\forall x \in N_{k+1})\varphi(x)$$

where φ has order greater than k.

To show this impossibility, we need to formalize the ramified *Principia* more completely than was done by Russell (in Section **12**). We shall use the formalization given by Schütte in his book *Beweistheorie*,[3] except that we shall simplify his treatment by considering only sets and not relations. If anyone objects that *Principia* itself dealt not with sets but with properties in intension (propositional functions), he has only to omit the axiom of extensionality from what follows, and make whatever further adjustments then become necessary; if the principle of mathematical induction is not derivable in the stronger system (with extensionality), it is *a fortiori* not derivable in the weaker one without.

A *signature* (used as a subscript indicating type) is a finite sequence $m_1, \ldots, m_k$ of natural numbers such that $k \geqslant 1$ and

$$m_1 > m_2 > \cdots > m_k = 0.$$

[1] The reader may wonder how I arrived at the curious number 6, since ***89·29** mentions the number 3. The reason is notational; ***89·29** says that the third-order ancestral R_{*3} of any one-many or many-one relation (e.g. successor) is the same as its kth-order ancestral for any $k > 3$. In particular something which has all the third-order hereditary properties of 0, has *all* hereditary properties of 0 (cf. ***89·01**). But Russell counts the orders of properties relative to the order of the things that have the properties, not absolutely as we do (*Principia*, p. 58), so that his third-order properties are our fifth-order properties. The set of all things that have all fifth-order hereditary properties of 0 is a sixth-order set denoted, by us, as N_6.

[2] P. A. Schilpp (ed.), *The Philosophy of Bertrand Russell*, Evanston, Ill., 1944.

[3] K. Schütte, *Beweistheorie*, Berlin, 1960.

These "types" combine what we previously called types (in the sense of the simple theory) and orders or levels. 'Type' will always be used in this sense henceforth. The intuitive picture is as follows. Type o consists of individuals, which are also said to have level o. Type m,σ, where σ is a type, is the collection of all those sets of objects of type σ which can be defined using quantification only over objects of level $<m$. An object of type m,σ will be said to have level m. Thus type 10 consists of all sets of individuals which can be defined using only quantifiers ranging over individuals, type 210 consists of all sets of objects of type 10 which can be defined using only quantifiers ranging over individuals and objects of level 1 (i.e. of type 10), and so on. Atomic *formulas* are of the forms $x_\sigma \in y_{m\sigma}$ and $x_\sigma = y_\sigma$, where identity is taken as primitive in order to avoid difficulty (1) mentioned above. As axioms we take the axioms of the many-sorted predicate calculus, the usual properties of identity (reflexivity, transitivity, symmetry and substitutivity) and the following two:

A.
$$(\exists x_{m\sigma})(\forall y_\sigma)(y \in x \leftrightarrow \cdots y-)$$

where in $\cdots y-$ all bound variables have level $<m$ and all free ones have level $\leq m$; and

B.
$$(\forall y_\sigma)(y_\sigma \in a_{m\sigma} \leftrightarrow y_\sigma \in b_{m\sigma}) \to a = b.$$

We can also add if we like some form of the axiom of infinity, but this is not necessary for our purposes (see footnote 2, p. 26).

The x of axiom *A* is unique by axiom *B*, and we denote it by

$$\{y_\sigma| \cdots y-\}_{m\sigma}.$$

The following convention will be useful: we write 1 for 10, 2 for 210, 3 for 3210, etc. and likewise *mn* for $m, n, n-1, \ldots,$ o. With these conventions we take natural numbers as type 2 objects, viz.

$$\Lambda_1 \equiv \{x_0|x \neq x\}_1$$
$$(x_0)_1 \equiv \{y_0|y = x\}_1$$
$$(x_1)_2 \equiv \{y_1|y_1 = x\}_2$$
$$a_1 \cup b_1 \equiv \{x_0|x_0 \in a \vee x_0 \in b\}_1$$
$$0_2 \equiv \{\Lambda_1\}_2$$
$$s(x_2) \equiv \{y_1|(\exists z_1 w_0)(w_0 \notin z_1 \wedge z_1 \in x_2 \wedge y_1 = z_1 \cup (w_0)\}_2.$$

Thus the natural numbers are 0_2, $1_2 \equiv s(0_2)$, $2_2 \equiv s(1_2)$, etc. It is around the formalization of this 'etc.' that our problem centres.

Suppose that a certain integer $k \geq 3$ is chosen and we define

$$N_{k+1} \equiv \{x_2|(\forall y_{k,2})(0_2 \in y \wedge (\forall u_2)(u \in y \to s(u) \in y) \to x \in y)\}_{k+1,2}$$

then N_{k+1} is the set of all those things which possess all k^{th}-level hereditary properties of o. We have to show that N_{k+1} does not provably satisfy induction with respect to properties of level $>k$, i.e. that we cannot prove

$$o_2 \in b_{m,2} \wedge (\forall u_2)(u \in b \to s(u) \in b) \to N_{k+1} \subset b \qquad (*)$$

for $m > k$.

In fact we shall show something much stronger than this, namely that *no* definition of the set of natural numbers will suffice. Specifically: let $N_{k+1}(x_2)$ be *any* formula with the properties that

$$N(o) \qquad (1)$$

and

$$N(x_2) \to N(s(x_2)) \qquad (2)$$

are each provable in the ramified *Principia*, and let no subscript of level $>k$ occur in $N(x_2)$. Then $(*)$ is not provable for $m > k$.

We shall show this by exhibiting a *model* which makes A, B and the identity axioms true and yet makes the formula $(*)$ false (for a suitable b). It will follow that Russell's proof in Appendix B is fallacious, and that no correct proof of his stated result can be given. Further this cannot be remedied by defining e.g. *à la* Quine

$$N_{4,2}(x_2) \equiv (\forall y_3)(x \in y \wedge (\forall z_2)(s(z) \in y \to z \in y) \to o \in y)$$

nor (as will appear later) by adjoining any *finite* number of additional axioms (except for the trivial case where the resulting system is either inconsistent or possesses only models with a finite ground type).

Call the given system RP (for "Ramified *Principia*"). Form from it a system $RP(u)$ by adjoining a constant u_2 of type 2 with the axioms

C.	$u_2 \in N_{k+1}$
Do.	$u \neq o_2$
D1.	$u \neq 1_2$
D2.	$u \neq 2_2$

and so on. By a familiar argument $RP(u)$ is consistent; for if a contradiction could be deduced from axioms A,B,C and the Ds, it would involve only finitely many of these last, say the first 10,000; but then a contradiction could be deduced from axioms A,B and

C'.	$10,001 \in N_{k+1}$
D'o.	$10,001 \neq o$
D'1.	$10,001 \neq 1$
D'2.	$10,001 \neq 2$

etc. Now C' is provable in RP (by (1)–(2)); and while not all of the formulas $D'n$ are provable in RP, they are all provable in an extension of RP formed by adjoining an axiom to the effect that there are more than 10,000 individuals. Since this latter system is evidently consistent, so is $RP(u)$.

But being consistent, $RP(u)$ possesses a *model*, i.e. an interpretation which makes all its axioms, and consequently all its theorems, true. Such a model has the form

$$M \equiv (\mathbf{D}_0, \mathbf{D}_{10}, \mathbf{D}_{20}, \mathbf{D}_{210}, \ldots, \theta, \mathbf{E})$$

where for each type σ, $\mathbf{D}_\sigma$ is the set of objects assigned as values to variables of type σ, $\theta \in \mathbf{D}_2$ is the interpretation of u, and $\mathbf{E}$ is the interpretation of $\in$. To say this is a model of RP(u) means that the axioms A–D hold in it, i.e. in the first place that

$$(\forall x_1 \in \mathbf{D}_{\sigma 1}) \ldots (\forall x_n \in \mathbf{D}_{\sigma n})(\exists y \in \mathbf{D}_{m\tau})(\forall z \in \mathbf{D}_\tau)(\mathbf{E}(z,y) \leftrightarrow \ldots z\text{---})$$

where each σ_ι has level $\leqslant m$, and where each bound variable occurring in $\ldots z$— is restricted to some $\mathbf{D}_\mu$ where μ has level $<m$. And here we define the *level* of a signature as the first number occurring in it.

In the second place we have

$$a,b \in \mathbf{D}_{m\sigma} \wedge (\forall x \in \mathbf{D}_\sigma)(\mathbf{E}(x,a) \leftrightarrow \mathbf{E}(x,b)) \to a = b$$

corresponding to axiom B; thirdly we have the translation of $u_2 \in N_{k+1}$, which we abbreviate as $N_\mathbf{E}(\theta)$. Finally, for any defined object

$$t_\sigma \equiv (\imath x)\psi(x)$$

of RP we now define $t_\mathbf{E} \equiv (\imath x \in \mathbf{D}_\sigma)\psi_\mathbf{E}(x)$, where $\psi_\mathbf{E}$ is obtained from ψ by writing everywhere $\mathbf{E}$ for $\in$ and $(\forall y \in \mathbf{D}_\tau)$ for $(\forall y_\tau)$; corresponding to the axioms D, θ is distinct from all the objects $(o_2)_\mathbf{E}$, $s_\mathbf{E}(o_2)_\mathbf{E}$, $s_\mathbf{E}s_\mathbf{E}(o_2)_\mathbf{E}, \ldots$ with this notation.

From this model M we now construct another one, M', in which axioms A–B hold but (∗) is false. We have

$$M' \equiv (\mathbf{D}'_0, \mathbf{D}'_{10}, \mathbf{D}'_{20}, \mathbf{D}'_{210}, \ldots, \mathbf{E}')$$

and we must define all these things. If σ has level $\leqslant k$, we let $\mathbf{D}'_\sigma \equiv \mathbf{D}_\sigma$. If σ has level $>k$, then $\sigma = m\tau$ for some $m > k$ and we take $\mathbf{D}'_\sigma$ to be the collection of *all* subsets of $\mathbf{D}'_\tau$. $\mathbf{E}'$ is defined by two cases as follows: if $y \in \mathbf{D}_\sigma$ where the level of σ is $\leqslant k$, then '$\mathbf{E}'(x,y)$' means $\mathbf{E}(x,y)$; if the level of σ is $>k$, then '$\mathbf{E}'(x,y)$' means $x \in y$.[1]

We claim that A–B hold in M' but (∗) does not. Thus (∗) is not deducible from A–B; i.e. induction for N_{k+1} is not provable in the ramified *Principia*.

To say that A holds in M' is to say that

$$(\forall x_1 \in \mathbf{D}'_{\sigma_1}) \ldots (\forall x_n \in \mathbf{D}'_{\sigma n})(\exists y \in \mathbf{D}'_{m\tau})(\forall z \in \mathbf{D}'_\tau)(\mathbf{E}'(z,y) \leftrightarrow \ldots z\text{---})$$

[1] There is a minor technical difficulty here; in order for this definition to make sense the various domains $\mathbf{D}_\sigma$ of M must be disjoint. To ensure this, suppose they are *not* disjoint; then we form a new model

$$M^* \equiv (\mathbf{D}^*_0, \mathbf{D}^*_{10}, \ldots)$$

by setting $\mathbf{D}^*_\sigma \equiv \mathbf{D}_\sigma \times \{\sigma\}$, $\theta^* \equiv (\theta, 210)$ and $\mathbf{E}^* ((x,\sigma), (y,\tau)) \equiv \mathbf{E}(x,y) \wedge (\exists m) (\tau = m\sigma)$. This has disjoint $\mathbf{D}^*_\sigma$'s and satisfies A–D; then we form M' using M^* instead of M.

where each σ_i has level $\leqslant m$ and where each bound variable in $\ldots z-$ is restricted to $\mathbf{D'_\mu}$, where μ has level $< m$. There are two cases according as $m \leqslant k$ or $m > k$. In the former case all the $\mathbf{D'_\sigma}$ and $\mathbf{D'_\mu}$ in the given formula can be replaced by $\mathbf{D_{\sigma_i}}$ and $\mathbf{D_\mu}$; likewise $\mathbf{E'}$ can be replaced by $\mathbf{E}$, and the given formula simply says that A holds in M, which was so by construction. If $m > k$, '$\mathbf{E'}(z,y)$' means $z \in y$ and the formula simply says that there is a subset y of $\mathbf{D'_\tau}$ consisting of all z satisfying $\ldots z-$, which is trivially true.

To say that B holds in M' is to say that

$$a,b \in \mathbf{D'_{m\sigma}} \wedge (\forall y \in \mathbf{D'_\sigma})(\mathbf{E'}(y,a) \leftrightarrow \mathbf{E'}(y,b)) \to a = b.$$

Here again, if $m \leqslant k$ the primes can be omitted without changing the meaning and B holds in M' because it holds in M. If $m > k$, '$\mathbf{E'}$' means $\in$ and B simply says that two coextensive subsets of $\mathbf{D'_\sigma}$ are identical.

We proceed to show that (∗), namely

$$0_2 \in b_{m,2} \wedge (\forall u_2)(u \in b \to s(u) \in b)) \to (\forall y_2)(N(y) \to y \in b),$$

fails in M' for $m > k$. This means that

$$(\exists b \in \mathbf{D'_{m,2}})(\mathbf{E'}((0_2)_{\mathbf{E'}}, b) \wedge (\forall u \in \mathbf{D'_2})(\mathbf{E'}(u.b) \to \mathbf{E'}(s_\mathbf{E}(u), b)) \wedge$$
$$(\exists y \in \mathbf{D'_2})(N_\mathbf{E'}(y) \wedge \daleth\mathbf{E'}(y,b))). \qquad (3)$$

Here $t_{\mathbf{E'}}$ is formed from t as $t_\mathbf{E}$ was, except that we write $\mathbf{E'}$ instead of $\mathbf{E}$ and $\mathbf{D'_\sigma}$ instead of $\mathbf{D_\sigma}$.

Since $m > k$, all the explicitly written $\mathbf{E}$'s in (3) are interpreted as $\in$, so what we need is a $b \in \mathbf{D'_{m,2}}$ and a $y \in \mathbf{D_2}$ such that

$$(0_2)_{\mathbf{E'}} \in b \qquad (4)$$
$$u \in \mathbf{D'_2} \wedge u \in b \to s_{\mathbf{E'}}(u) \in b \qquad (5)$$
$$N_{\mathbf{E'}}(y) \qquad (6)$$

and

$$y \notin b \qquad (7),$$

We set $b \equiv \{0_{\mathbf{E'}}, s_{\mathbf{E'}}0_{\mathbf{E'}}, s_{\mathbf{E'}}s_{\mathbf{E'}}0_{\mathbf{E'}}, \ldots\}$ which is the same as $\{0_\mathbf{E}, s_\mathbf{E}0_\mathbf{E} s_\mathbf{E}s_\mathbf{E}0_\mathbf{E}, \ldots\}$ the set of "standard" non-negative integers of M (or M'); and we set $y \equiv \theta$. Then (4)–(5) and (7) are trivial; but so is (6) because $N_{\mathbf{E'}}(\theta)$ contains no subscript of level $> k$ and so is equivalent to $N_\mathbf{E}(\theta)$ which is simply axiom C holding in M.[1,2]

---

[1] The reader may be curious as to what Russell's actual mistake was, in Appendix B. The Appendix is a thorny text indeed, full of slipshod notations which it taxed the patience of this reader to correct, and I am not at all sure I got to the heart of his error since there are so many superficial ones which can be corrected in various ways (and one does not know which is the right correction, i.e. which one represents just what Russell had in mind). To give the reader some idea of what we are up against, at the very beginning he defines

$$\text{Cls induct}_m \equiv \{\rho \mid (\forall \mu_m)(\Lambda \varepsilon \mu \wedge (\forall \eta \gamma)(\eta \varepsilon \mu \to (\eta \cup (y)\varepsilon \mu \to \rho \varepsilon \mu)\}$$

and proves (∗89·12) $\rho \varepsilon \text{Cls induct}_3 \to (\exists \mu_2)(\rho = \mu_2)$. The definition of Cls induct$_m$ is, however,

Let us return briefly to the difficulty numbered (1) at the beginning of the paper (Leibniz's law). Can we prove that if two (say) individuals have all their k^{th}-order properties in common for sufficiently large k then they have *all* their properties in common? Again the answer is *no*. We give the proof in outline only. Let RP_0 be like RP except that the identity-sign and its axioms are dropped and axiom B replaced by

B'. $\qquad\qquad (\forall x_\sigma)(x \in a_{m\sigma} \leftrightarrow x \in b_{m\sigma}) \land \ldots a \longrightarrow \ldots b—$

Define identity of order k between individuals by

$$x_0 \overline{\overline{k}} y_0 \equiv (\forall z_{k,0})(x \in z \leftrightarrow y \in z).$$

Then the problem is: can we prove (for sufficiently large k) that

$$x_0 \overline{\overline{k}} y_0 \land x \in a_{k+1,0} \rightarrow y \in a \quad ? \qquad\qquad (**)$$

As before we construct a model in which the axioms A and B' are true and $(**)$ is false. The trick is (again as before) to give the types of level $\leqslant k$ a non-standard interpretation and the types of level $> k$ the interpretation they receive in simple type-theory. More precisely, let the domain $\mathbf{D}_0$ of individuals be any set (with at least 2 elements); let $\mathbf{D}_{m\sigma}$ consist of all subsets of $\mathbf{D}_\sigma$ if $m > k$, and all subsets of $\mathbf{D}_\sigma$ that can be defined without referring to any particular individual[1] if $m \leqslant k$; let variables x_σ be interpreted as ranging over $\mathbf{D}_\sigma$ and let $\in$ be interpreted as $\in$; then the axioms A and B' come out true while evidently $(**)$ is false if $a \equiv \{x\}$. So Leibniz's law is not provable in full generality for any $\overline{\overline{k}}$. This result is a good deal less interesting than the previous one about induction, since no reasonable person would imagine that it was provable. (In

---

defective; the order of ρ ought to be signified, and it is not. If this order is signified as $m - 1$, then if ρ has order 2 *89·12 reduces to the tautology $(\exists \mu_2) (\rho_2 = \mu_2)$; and if ρ has any other order, *89·12 is not even well formed. One can correct this mistake by always writing $Cls_m(\rho)$ instead of $\rho\epsilon\ Cls\ induct_m$ (I think!); but a more serious error occurs in line 3 of the proof of *89·12, which reads (without hypotheses)

$$\exists! \alpha - \beta \cdot \alpha \subset \beta \cup \iota y \cdot \supset \cdot \alpha = \beta \cup \iota y$$

which is false on the face of it. Whether it can be replaced by something which is not false so as to give a correct proof of 89·16 I don't know. At any rate the main result of the present paper shows that not *all* of his errors can be corrected.

[2] The proof goes over in the presence of the axiom of infinity or indeed of any *finite* number of consistent additional axioms $Q_1, \ldots, Q_n$. The only modification is that we use, in constructing the model M', not the number k but a number $k^* \geqslant k$ which is also $\geqslant$ all type levels occurring in $Q_1, \ldots, Q_n$. M' is a model of $A, B, Q_1, \ldots, Q_n$ but not a model of $(*)$ for $m > k^*$, so $(*)$ is not provable from $A, B, Q_1, \ldots, Q_n$. Of course, $Q_1, \ldots, Q_n$ must satisfy the trivial conditions mentioned at the beginning of the proof.

[1] In detail. For any permutation p of $\mathbf{D}_0$, and any set α belonging to the simple type-hierarchy over $\mathbf{D}_0$, define $p[\alpha]$ inductively by $p[x] \equiv p(x)(x\epsilon\mathbf{D}_0)$, $p[\alpha] \equiv \{p[y]/y\epsilon\alpha\}$, and call α *invariant* if $p[\alpha] = \alpha$. Now let $\mathbf{D}_{m\sigma}$ consist of all invariant subsets of $\mathbf{D}_\sigma$ if $m \leqslant k$, and of *all* subsets of $\mathbf{D}_\sigma$ if $m > k$.

fact Russell, *Principia Mathematica*, vol. 1, p. 169, says that "in this case [i.e. in the absence of the axiom of reducibility] strict identity would *have to be* [my italics] taken as a primitive idea"—thereby implying that he thought Leibniz's law was *obviously* unprovable.) Still it is nice that we can prove it to be unprovable.

We conclude with some remarks as to the philosophical interpretation of our main result (the one about induction). It shows that the property of being a natural number (in Russell's sense) is not predicatively definable from $\in$, or even from $\in$ and $=$ taken as primitive. There are two possible philosophical reactions according as one's mathematical philosophy has a classical or a constructive tendency. In the former case, one would reason that the result shows that impredicativity is present in mathematics from the very beginning, i.e. the natural numbers, and that consequently any philosophy of mathematics which repudiates impredicative definitions *ipso facto* repudiates mathematics itself. This would lead to the acceptance of simple type-theory or one of its extensions—e.g. Zermelo-Frankel set theory—as a reasonable codification of mathematical practice. If on the other hand one's mind has a constructive bent, one would find it unthinkable that the notion of "finite cardinal" (say of type 2, or equivalently the notion of "finite set of individuals") required the understanding of an *arbitrary* (impredicative) *set of sets of sets of individuals*! Our result shows that the notion of "finite" can only be defined impredicatively from $\in$ and $=$, but since that notion is clear to the constructivist and impredicative definitions are not, the constructivist must infer that $\in$ (and $=$) are not sufficient primitives for the development of mathematics, and that either "finite" or some equivalent idea ("natural number" or the "ancestral") is needed as another basic notion.[1] This would lead one in the direction of either intuitionism or formalism, depending on one's attitude towards higher types. The ramified *Principia* itself falls uncomfortably between these two positions, and apparently does not correspond to any coherent philosophy of mathematics; certainly not to any philosophy that makes mathematics possible.

---

[1] Note that the objection is not directed towards Russell's definition of the individual natural numbers 0,1,2,... (though most constructivists object to that too, on quite other grounds) nor even to his definition of 'cardinal number'. It is directed towards his definition of *the set of* natural numbers; to his definition of *finiteness*, which separates the natural numbers from the infinite cardinals.

Nino B. Cocchiarella

Formal Ontology and the Foundations of Mathematics[1]

In his paper, "The Undefinability of the Set of Natural Numbers in the Ramified *Principia*", Myhill has shown that the general concept of a natural number or finite cardinal—*general* enough, that is, to yield the induction schema—is not definable in terms of ramified type theory in essentially its original form and without the axiom of reducibility. In my commentary I shall examine Myhill's concluding philosophical remarks within the context of general metaphysics or what below I call *formal ontology*. I shall especially be concerned with the sense in which ramified type theory (without the axiom of reducibility) purports to represent a constructive philosophy of mathematics. In addition, I shall sketch several forms of realism according to which the claim that "impredicativity is present in mathematics from the beginning" is true in an especially apt and interesting sense that goes beyond that intended by Myhill.

1. *Mathematical Logic as Formal Ontology*

Gödel has remarked that mathematical logic "has two quite different aspects. On the one hand, it is a section of Mathematics treating of classes, relations, combinations of symbols, etc., instead of numbers, functions, geometric figures, etc. On the other hand, it is a science prior to all others, which contains the ideas and principles underlying all sciences."[2] In the former case, mathematical logic is principally, though not only, a *calculus ratiocinator*. Under that aspect, beyond consistency, no special heed need be paid a formal system regarding the philosophical significance of its grammatical forms and the viability of the primitive concepts and assumptions expressed by means of these forms. In the latter case, however, it is quite otherwise. As a science prior to all others, Gödel's description of mathematical logic is comparable to Aristotle's description of metaphysics. Only, as a science which is prior to all others, metaphysics, according to Aristotle, is therefore the science of the "modes" or "categories of being". Where the particular, specialized sciences, including mathematics, are concerned with but their own special "modes of being", metaphysics and now mathematical logic under its second aspect—or what we might instead call *formal ontology*—

[1] The author was supported in part by NSF grant GS-28605.
[2] K. Gödel, "Russell's Mathematical Logic", in P. A. Schilpp (ed.), *The Philosophy of Bertrand Russell*, Evanston, Ill., 1944.

is concerned with the study and development of alternative formalizations regarding the systematic co-ordination of all the "modes" or "categories of being" under the most general laws. Usually, and perhaps most appropriately since this is where ontological commitment comes in, each "mode of being" within a particular formal ontology is represented by a type of bindable variable whose syntactical role is intended to reflect in some philosophically coherent way the ontological role of that "mode of being". Under this second aspect, mathematical logic, or formal ontology, is concerned with the adequacy of formal systems as alternative formulations of the deepest structural maps of reality.[1]

Viewed in this way, each feature of a proposed formal system is to be evaluated in terms of its purported philosophical significance, how well, for example, it functions as a proposed metaphysical map of reality. Different metaphysical schools, of course, will be interested in different ways of understanding a formal system as a map of reality. Conceptualists, for example, would view the grammar of a formal system together with its logistic behaviour as a proposed formal map of the structuring powers of human cognition, a proposed map, that is, of the structure of constructive cognitive processes of the human mind. Operations of the system must then be devised with limitations built into them that reflect in an appropriate manner the limitations of these same constructive powers of the mind. It is much in this sort of way that the constructivist attitude in the philosophy of mathematics must be understood. Realists, on the other hand, would construe the operations and elements of the formal map as having ontological significance independently of the constructive power of the human mind. Limitations built into the system, whether they apply to the notion of grammatical well-formedness or to the logistic behaviour of the ontological grammar, are evaluated then on grounds other than the nature of thought and its inherent limitations. Some of the most obvious of such grounds for limitation pertain to the way the implicit metaphysical scheme underlying the system proposes to resolve the known antinomies.

Leibniz, as Gödel has pointed out, was one of the first expositors of this view of mathematical logic. Leibniz himself referred to such a formal system as a *characteristica universalis*. But it was not until Frege and Peano that any significant attempt at the construction of a formal ontology was made. Frege called his system a *Begriffsschrift*, indicating, as Gödel remarks, that "Frege was chiefly interested in the analysis of thought".[2] Frege himself in a response to Schröder's criticisms of his *Begriffsschrift* stated "that, unlike Boole's, his logic is

---

[1] cf. G. Bergmann, "Ontological Alternatives", in E. D. Klemke (ed.), *Essays on Frege*, Urbana, Ill., 1968, p. 148: "Logic without ontology is merely a calculus. A calculus acquires philosophical import only if its author claims that it is an ideal language (*Begriffsschrift*), i.e. that it perspicuously reflects an adequate ontology."

[2] Gödel, op. cit.

not a *calculus ratiocinator*, or not merely a *calculus ratiocinator*, but a *lingua characteristica*".[1]

Now this Fregean emphasis on concepts (*Begriffe*) and the nature of thought is significant. For although it would seem, because of this emphasis, that Frege is a conceptualist and that therefore his logic would reflect certain limitations in the nature of human concept formation, it turns out that Fregean concepts are real, objective entities of a "mode of being" which is independent of minds and the subjective ideas by means of which minds think. To be sure, Fregean concepts are not self-subsistent entities, but their ontological dependence is upon the individual objects "falling under" them and not, apparently, upon the nature of thought. Their ontological dependence consists only in their being "unsaturated". They are nevertheless "real" entities in so far as Frege takes quantification over them as having ontological significance.[2] In this regard, Frege's ontology is realistic, though somehow it is also an analysis of thought.[3]

I shall not try to account here for this apparent ambiguity in the Fregean enterprise. I mention it in part because it is an ambiguity which Russell apparently shared (or perhaps even inherited from Frege) in the construction of his own formal ontology, the ramified theory of types, and which he never himself adequately resolved. As a formal embodiment of the Russell-Poincaré "vicious circle principle", the ramified theory of types purports to represent a limitation in the powers of human concept formation, specifically a limitation regarding impredicative concept formation. Adjoining the axiom of reducibility to this formal ontology, however, can be justified only by taking a realistic attitude, an attitude which Russell clearly accepted in at least some of his writings.[4] The two attitudes taken together: the attitude, on the one hand, that the limitations imposed on both the ontological grammar and the logical constructions based upon that grammar are dictated by one's conceptualist views regarding at least the "higher-order" portion of one's ontology; and the attitude, on the other hand, that the reality represented by one's ontological grammar and the operations on that grammar is independent of mind and the nature of thought;

---

[1] J. van Heijenoort, "Logic as Calculus and Logic as Language", *Synthese* 17, 3 (1967), p. 324.

[2] Bergmann, op. cit., p. 135, construes Frege's concepts as syncategorematic entities, but his only reason for this seems to be their ontological dependence on objects. We shall here understand a primitive symbol of a formal ontology to be a syncategorematic sign—and the entity, if any, it represents to be a syncategorematic entity—if it is not a substituend for (and the entity is not "indicated" by) any type of variable in the grammar of the system.

[3] cf. R. Grossman, "Frege's Ontology", in Klemke (ed.), *Essays on Frege*, for a discussion of this issue in regard to Frege's ontology.

[4] For example, in his *Introduction to Mathematical Philosophy*, he says that "logic is concerned with the real world just as truly as zoology, though with its more abstract and general features" (p. 169). We might note that the realism implicit in the reducibility axiom is one in regard to classes and not properties (or, in Russell's terminology, propositional functions). Indeed, Russell first referred to the axiom as "the axiom of classes". What is peculiar about this is that Russell took his formal ontology to be a "no class" ontology.

these two attitudes though apparently not formally inconsistent, seem not to result in a philosophically coherent formal ontology. It is within this sort of context that I understand Myhill's concluding remark that "the ramified *Principia* itself falls uncomfortably between these two positions, and apparently does not correspond to any coherent philosophy of mathematics . . ." (p. 27).

Let us note that where Myhill speaks to the question of a coherent philosophy of mathematics, I have referred instead to the problem of a philosophically coherent formal ontology. The distinction is minor or not depending on how broad one's criteria are for the coherence of a philosophy of mathematics. Certainly, since the problem of the nature of mathematical existence is an ontological problem *par excellence*, every philosophically coherent formal ontology must contain a coherent philosophy of mathematics.[1] Tolerance forbids, I would suppose, maintaining the converse.

2. *Ontological Grammar as the Theory of (Onto)Logical Form*

Now a particular formal ontology has two principal parts to which we should turn in evaluating its philosophical coherency. There is first of all that part which I have called its ontological grammar. This essentially is a theory of logical form. Secondly, there is the logistic behaviour that is ascribed to that grammar. Different metaphysical systems when formalized may have the same or very similar ontological grammar while differing quite radically in the logistic behaviour of that grammar.[2] More difficult to assess, some metaphysical systems when formalized may differ significantly in their grammar while having in some appropriate sense a "similar" underlying logic. What makes the latter situation difficult to assess is how the difference in grammar can be given genuine ontological significance as opposed to signifying merely variant notational schemes for the same implicit metaphysical framework. For example, Quine's "branched quantifiers" can be used so as to apply only to individual variables and would appear in this regard to commit us only to individuals. Nevertheless, the underlying logic for these branched quantifiers is "similar" to a weak but still

---

[1] Most proposals regarding the construction of a philosophically coherent formal ontology are programmatic and fragmentary and do not purport to constitute a completed metaphysical system. The importance of formally constructing such partial or fragmentary ontologies is not at issue here. Nor is it being suggested that a fragmentary ontology which defers the question of mathematical existence is for that reason incoherent. Of course, if such a fragmentary ontology cannot be extended so as to contain a coherent account of the nature of mathematical existence, especially *vis-à-vis* that of concrete or physical existence, then it does indeed represent a philosophically incoherent ontology, even if only fragmentarily. For this reason, metaphysical programmes should not long defer the question of containing a coherent philosophy of mathematics.

[2] See N. Cocchiarella, "Properties as Individuals in Formal Ontology", *Nous* 6 (1972), for a description of two realistic formal ontologies, one with, one without, complex properties and relations.

essentially incomplete second-order logic in which the variables of second order range over functions (many-one relations).[1] Shall we say that the formal ontology which utilizes branched quantifiers is committed to functions or not? No doubt a relevant and nontrivial answer can be given in terms of a deeper investigation of the notion of "similarity in underlying logic" than we have time for here.

One species of the notion of a "similarity in underlying logic" which we should be cautious of here is that whereby a "many-sorted" logic is "reduced" to a "similar" one-sorted logic by the introduction of primitive predicate constants designating the different "modes of being" indicated in the original logic by the different types or "sorts" of variables. If in the original formal ontology "being" is not a genus, i.e. if the different "modes of being" are intended to be ontologically incomparable, then such a "reduction" to a one-sorted logic will distort the original intent by rendering the different "modes of being" as merely different *kinds* of being and, in effect, thereby render "being" a genus. This is not to discount the value of such a "reduction" in regard to investigating some of the formal properties of the original system. Montague, for example, was able to characterize, by means of such "reductions", a rather general method for proving when a "many-sorted" theory is not finitely axiomatizable.[2] Similarly, the underlying logic of systems with modal operators can be "reduced" to a "similar" first-order logic by adding a "possible-world" parameter to each of the original predicate expressions in essentially the same way that tensed language can be so "reduced" by adding a time-parameter 'at t' to each of the original predicate expressions. Of course, the intent of the original ontology is quite distorted by such a "reduction" if the whole point was not to have ontological commitment to "possible worlds" or "moments of time"—at least certainly not as a *kind of individual*. In addition, because modal operators, unlike a possible-world or time-parameter, may be iterated and have occurrences within the scopes of other occurrences, certain aspects of "internality", aspects which are fundamental to some metaphysical schools, disappear or become "external" relationships after such "reductions", thereby further distorting the intent in constructing formal ontologies for these metaphysical schools. Again, however, let us be clear that there is much value in turning to such "reductions". On the other hand, we should be cautious in drawing any metaphysical conclusions from the fact that there are such "reductions", especially if the notion of a quantifiable variable (of a given type) is to serve as any sort of criterion for ontological commitment.

Now if ontological grammar really is a significant factor in the evaluation of the philosophical coherency of a formal ontology, then it is appropriate to require some statement of the criteria by means of which we might so evaluate

[1] cf. W. van O. Quine, *Philosophy of Logic*, Englewood Cliffs, N.J., 1970, pp. 89–91.

[2] See R. Montague, "Semantic Closure and Non-Finite Axiomatizability", in his *Infinitistic Methods*, New York 1959.

such a grammar. In this regard I should like to suggest that the principle function or most important feature of an ontological grammar—and hence the principle criterion by which it is to be evaluated—is the special way it purports to represent or provide an account of the nature of predication. In other words, the purpose, or at least one of the most important purposes, of a formal ontology is to provide a philosophically coherent theory of predication, a theory, that is, of the nature of the "linkage" between distinct categories or "modes of being" through which it purports to explain the unity and coherence of reality. It is primarily in its account of the nature of predication that a formal ontology indicates the manner in which it is to be taken as a map of reality. But then, how such an ontology views predication can be discerned only by turning to its ontological grammar. For only through that grammar can we view reality in the way its advocates intend their description of reality.

Even a metaphysical school which insists that there is but one category or "mode of being" (categorial monism) must give some account of predication. Nominalism, for example, has only one sort of quantifiable variable in its ontological grammar. One variant of this metaphysical school interprets the role of predication as being absorbed by that of predicates which are now construed as syncategorematic signs.[1] How this amounts to a philosophically coherent theory of predication is by no means obvious. Logical atomism attempts a fuller account through its interpretation of predication as a "picturing" of atomic configurations of objects. Lesniewski's *mereology* and Leonard's and Goodman's *calculus of individuals* are more detailed attempts at a nominalistic theory which appears to interpret predication as some sort of part-whole relation. Lesniewski's fuller system, which he himself called "ontology", is a rather ingenious development of the scholastic medieval theory of supposition.

3. *Type Theory, A Non-Realist, Constructivist Formal Ontology*

What now of Russell's theory of predication? How in a more specific way might we understand the philosophical incoherency of his ramified theory of types (with the axiom of reducibility)? Obviously, Russell was led to his theory as a result of his famous paradox. As an aside, we might note that his paradox has two forms, one in regard to the class of all classes that are not members of themselves, the other in regard to "the predicate: to be a predicate that cannot be predicated of itself".[2] In this regard, we might note that Russell's proposed solution, viz., the ramified theory of types, is primarily a theory of predication and secondarily, through his notation of class abstracts as incomplete symbols,

---

[1] See W. van O. Quine and N. Goodman, "Steps towards a Constructive Nominalism", *Journal of Symbolic Logic* 12, 4 (1947), pp. 105–22.

[2] Russell, "Letter to Frege", in J. van Heijenoort (ed.), *From Frege to Gödel*, Cambridge, Mass., 1967, p. 125.

a theory of the membership relation. Here, it is Russell in the role of metaphysician or philosopher who is constructing primarily a formal ontology and attempting thereby a coherent philosophy of mathematics.

Now, apparently, for Russell all paradoxes ultimately devolve upon what he construes as the ontological error of self-predication. But self-predication, as is well-known, is easily ruled out by a simple stratification of ontological types. That would seem to be the appropriate response of a *realist* who took self-predication as the source of paradox. Moreover, I see no reason why such a realist cannot take self-predication and all unstratified or cyclical predication-chains as simply false on ontological grounds, that is on pain of contradiction otherwise, rather than as meaningless. The development of such a realist ontology would appear to be very much along the lines of Quine's "New Foundations", though it may differ from "New Foundations" in retaining a distinction between individual and predicate variables.[1] Type theory, of course, whether simple or ramified, rules out all unstratified predication-chains as meaningless. In this regard, I should like to suggest that type theory, whether simple or ramified, does not represent a theory of predication corresponding to any realist ontology.

The ontological grammar of ramified type theory does seem, however, an appropriate representation of a conceptualist ontology. For adherents of this metaphysical school understand each "higher-order" entity as being the product of a possible mental construction and therefore as having no ontological content independently of the elements involved or presupposed in such a construction. In this respect, predication represents a relationship between the elements of some presupposed totality and a constructible rule or form of classification which classifies the elements of this totality according to the manner of its construction. The constructible totality of such rules of classification becomes in turn a presupposed totality subject to constructible classificatory rules, only now of course of a "higher" type. Quite appropriately then, according to this informal and intuitive sketch, self-predication as well as all unstratified predication-chains must be viewed as meaningless. That is, the ontological grammar for this sort of metaphysical system should contain at least the distinctions of the simple theory of types. Russell's additional ramification of the types, however, introduces a grammatical framework within which the intuitive concept

---

[1] By allowing predicate variables to occupy subject positions of themselves as well as of other predicate variables, we are construing predicate variables as substituends of individual variables; and, accordingly, we should thereby understand the values of predicate variables to constitute a *kind* of individual. (See Cocchiarella, op. cit., for an alternative development of a similar sort.) The distinction between concrete and abstract individuals might be expressible within the system—especially if only monadic predicate variables are used—without resorting to the introduction of *descriptive* or *categorematic constants*. Such a system, with or without an extensionality axiom, would seem to be rather similar to Jensen' system NFU, "NF with Urelements", in Jensen, "On the Consistency of a Slight (?) Modification of Quine's 'New Foundations'", *Synthese* 19 (1968), pp. 250–63.

of *constructibility* involved in this theory of predication may be given a more appropriate logistic description than that available with just simple types. To be sure, a prohibition against impredicative concept formation can be formulated within the ontological grammar of the theory of simple types. For example, consider the predicative theory of simple types that is a fragment or proper sub-theory of the ramified theory of types (without the axiom of reducibility).[1] The point is, however, that this predicative theory of simple types really is only a fragmentary representation of the intended theory of constructive predication. It excludes, for example, rules or methods of classifying, say, individuals, that are constructible not only by quantifying over the totality of individuals but by also quantifying over the totality of rules constructible by quantifying only over individuals, etc. I can think of no philosophically coherent theory of predication that actually disallows such rules or methods of classification while insisting on all those allowed for in a predicative theory of simple types. In this regard, we should perhaps not think of the ramified types as somehow doubly typed, or as distinguished into a type and an "order", as though there were two and not one theory of predication being represented. Indeed, ramified types seem to make far better sense than simple types alone as the grammatical basis of a formal ontology. And of course it is precisely this "better sense" which the axiom of reducibility nullifies. For the axiom stipulates that any rule or method of classifying that involves the ramification of types in its construction is at least extensionally equivalent to a rule or method of classifying which involves only simple types in its construction. It is in this sense that the addition of an axiom of reducibility to the ramified theory of types renders the latter a philosophically incoherent formal ontology.

But how can ramified type theory without the reducibility axiom be the basis of a coherent constructivist philosophy of mathematics? Quite clearly it needs to be supplemented, but the supplementation must be in accordance with the basic metaphysical framework. In this regard we might note that the hierarchy of types which the ontological grammar of type theory "shows forth" or expresses in a global way reflects a process of *iteration* which is a necessary feature of limited or finitistic constructive thought. Both Frege and Russell, of course, took the general concept of iteration or of *etcetera*, or equivalently the concept of the "ancestral", to be definable in "purely logical" terms, which, in our present terminology, is to say that they took it to be expressible within the primitive framework of their respective formal ontologies. Frege however was a realist and though Russell wrote at times as though he too was a realist, we nevertheless find the ramified theory of types to be philosophically coherent as a representative of a conceptualist ontology. Accordingly, Myhill's result comes to the fore of our consideration in pointing out that the general concept of

---

[1] In terms of Myhill's formulation, this is the set of theorems of RP in which only variables of a simple type occur. (A type signature $m_1, \ldots, m_k$ is a simple type if, for $1 < i \leqslant k$, $m_{(i+1)} = m_i - 1$.)

iteration, or of *etcetera*, or equivalently of the "ancestral"—i.e. *general* enough so as to define a notion of *finite cardinal* which would yield the induction schema— cannot be defined in terms of ramified type theory in its original form and with- out the axiom of reducibility. I, for one, however, do not see why a conceptual- ist ontology cannot, within the bounds of its restrictive constructive conditions, allow for the existence of such a sufficiently general concept of iteration *within* as well as *without* its formal representation. In this regard I am in agreement with Myhill's concluding remarks regarding the options open to a constructive position in the philosophy of mathematics. I might add, however, that I do not see any reason why we need to supplement and thereby alter the ontological grammar of ramified type theory. An acceptable form of the supplementation needed can be made strictly in terms of the sanctioned logistic behaviour of that grammar.

4. Set-Theory in a Predicative Second Order Logic

I also agree with Myhill's concluding remark against the realist's diagnosis of his result, namely that "impredicativity is present in mathematics from the beginning, and that consequently any philosophy of mathematics which re- pudiates impredicative definitions *ipso facto* repudiates mathematics itself" (p. 27). Myhill, however, apparently has in mind only that form of realism in which the predicative/impredicative distinction is without ontological content in categorematic terms. Impredicativity is present for this form of realism only through the strength of its axioms; its allowance, for example, in the com- prehension clause of bound variables of the same type as that initially being existentially quantified over in its form of the comprehension principle. Other than making this sort of allowance, the predicative/impredicative distinction comes to naught in this form of realism.

But there are forms of realism in which this distinction has ontological content in categorematic terms, i.e. in terms according to which it is a distinction between categories or "modes of being", which in our present terminology is to say that it is represented through a distinction between bind- able variables. And for this kind of realism the observation that "impredicativity is present in mathematics from the beginning" is true in a way not intended by Myhill.

In order briefly to describe several variants of this form of realism consider standard second order logic with set-abstraction as an individual term-making operation. Existentially positing membership as a relation satisfying extensionality and the unrestricted form of *the conversion principle* for sets, i.e. the principle

(1) $$(\forall F)(\forall y)[y \in \{x|F(x)\} \leftrightarrow F(y)]$$

amounts essentially to (a variant of) Frege's formal ontology, which by Russell's paradox is easily shown to be inconsistent. Let us note, however, that the comprehension principle

(CP) $$(\exists F)(\forall x_1)\ldots(\forall x_n)[F(x_1,\ldots,x_n)\leftrightarrow \varphi]$$

where φ is a formula of the present grammar in which the *n*-place predicate variable 'F' has no (free) occurrences and 'x_1',..., 'x_n' are among the distinct individual variables occurring free in φ, is utilized in the derivation of this contradiction. The instance in question asserts that non-self-membership is a complex property:

(2) $$(\exists F)(\forall y)[F(y)\leftrightarrow y\notin y]$$

The complexity of non-self-membership is at least two-fold: first, it is the *complement* of a property, viz. the property of self-membership; and secondly, it is the complement of a *relational property*, and therefore is itself a relational property. That membership is a relation is another instance of (CP):[1]

(3) $$(\exists R)(\forall x)(\forall y)[R(xy)\leftrightarrow x\in y]$$

Now instead of *standard second order logic*, let us consider a version of *predicative second order logic* with set-abstraction as an individual term-making operation. As a formal ontology, only predicative properties and relations are acknowledged here as being quantified over by the bound predicate variables. To signalize this, let us use $\forall!$ and $\exists!$ rather than $\forall$ and $\exists$ when affixed to predicate variables. (We shall continue to apply $\forall$ and $\exists$ to individual variables, however.) The comprehension principle now takes the form:

(CP!) $$(\forall!G_1)\ldots(\forall!G_k)(\exists!F)(\forall x_1)\ldots(\forall x_n)[F(x_1,\ldots,x_n)\leftrightarrow \varphi]$$

where φ, according to the present grammar, is a formula in which no predicate constants occur and in which no predicate variable has a bound occurrence, 'G_1',..., 'G_k' are all the predicate variables occurring (free) in φ, 'x_1',..., 'x_n' are among the distinct individual variables occurring free in φ, and 'F' is an *n*-place predicate variable which does not occur in φ. Other than this replacement of (CP) by (CP!) and using $\forall!$ and $\exists!$ in place of $\forall$ and $\exists$ when affixed to predicate variables, the remaining axioms of second order logic are retained.

We should note, however, that the present system differs from Church's formulation of the predicative functional calculus of second order (without propositional variables) in his *Introduction to Mathematical Logic*, Section 58, by

---

[1] Instead of (CP) we could focus on the principle of universal instantiation of a formula for a predicate variable:

$$(\forall F)\Psi \rightarrow \check{S}^{\,F}_{\varphi}(x_1,\ldots,x_n)\ \Psi\ |$$

But it is known that given the remaining axioms of second order logic these two principles are equivalent. We shall assume here that the version of second order logic being discussed has (CP) and not the instantiation law as one of its axioms.

having the following qualified form of the universal instantiation principle for predicate variables:[1]

(UI!) $(\exists !F)(\forall x_1)\ldots(\forall x_n)[F(x_1,\ldots,x_n)\leftrightarrow\varphi]\rightarrow[(\forall !F)\Psi\rightarrow \check{S}^F_\varphi(x_1,\ldots,x_n)\Psi|]$

Of course, by (UI!) and (CP!) we also have:

(4) $\qquad\qquad (\forall !G_1)\ldots(\forall !G_k)[(\forall !F)\Psi\rightarrow \check{S}^F_\varphi(x_1,\ldots x_n)\,\Psi|]$

where φ, 'F', 'G_1',..., 'G_k', 'x_1',..., 'x_n' are as described in (CP!) above.[2] In Church's formulation this last principle (4), *without the quantifier prefix on the predicate variables occurring (free) in φ*, is an axiom schema, and (CP!), without the same initial quantifier prefix, is therefore a theorem schema of that system. In the present system, however, the quantifier prefix cannot be discharged without assuming

$$(\exists !F_j)(\forall y_1)\ldots(\forall y_i)[F_j(y_1,\ldots,y_i)\leftrightarrow G_j(y_1,\ldots,y_i)]$$

for each $j\leqslant k$ and where 'G_j' and 'F_j' are *i*-place predicate variables. The point to this last restriction is to indicate that though predicate variables bound by $\forall$! and $\exists$! have only predicative properties and relations as values, *free occurrences* of predicate variables, and therefore *predicate constants* as well, may refer to impredicative properties and relations.[3]

In this last regard, consider adding '$\in$' to the system as a 2-place predicate constant satisfying extensionality and the conversion principle for sets that are the extensions of predicative properties:

(Conv!) $\qquad\qquad (\forall !F)(\forall y)[y \in \{x|F(x)\}\leftrightarrow F(y)]$

---

[1] (UI!) follows directly from:

$$(\forall x_1)\ldots(\forall x_n)[F(x_1,\ldots,x_n)\leftrightarrow\varphi]\rightarrow[\Psi\leftrightarrow \check{S}^F_\varphi(x_1,\ldots,x_n)\,\Psi|]$$

which in turn is easily proved by an inductive argument on the structure of Ψ. Note that the proof of (UI!) does not depend on (CP!).

[2] Relative to the remaining axioms, (CP!) and (4) are equivalent to one another.

[3] An analogous situation holds in quantified first order modal logics where *bound occurrences* of individual variables are allowed to refer only to objects existing in the world in question, whereas *free occurrences* of individual variables, and *individual constants* as well, may refer to possible individuals existing in other related worlds but not actually existing in the world in question. In these contexts, it is false to claim, as some have claimed, that assertion of formulas containing free variables is at best a convenience which can always be replaced by assertion of the universal closure of these formulas.

Incidentally, the fact that *predicate constants* may refer to impredicative properties or relations is the reason why such constants are not allowed to occur in instances of (CP!) in its role as an axiom schema. (CP!) might entail such an instance by (UI!), but then the antecedent of (UI!) must be satisfied regarding such a predicate constant. And normally, such satisfaction will have to be stipulated in the form of a *meaning postulate*.

Also, because formulas containing no bound predicate variables may contain free predicate variables or constants that refer to impredicative properties or relations, we should be fore-warned not to confuse the *ontological* predicative/impredicative distinction with a *syntactical* distinction between formulas containing, as opposed to those not containing, bound predicate variables.

Significantly, Russell's argument no longer yields a contradiction. What follows instead, by (UI!), is that non-self-membership is not a predicative property:

(5) $$\sim(\exists!F)(\forall\gamma)[F(\gamma)\leftrightarrow\gamma\notin\gamma]$$

And of course from this it follows that membership is not a predicative relation:[1]

(6) $$\sim(\exists!R)(\forall x)(\forall\gamma)[R(x,\gamma)\leftrightarrow x\in\gamma]$$

But then that membership is an impredicative relation would seem hardly a point to dispute here since its present implicit characterization essentially involves quantification over properties. Accordingly, stipulating a particular instance of the conversion principle

(7) $$(\forall\gamma)[\gamma\in\{x|\ldots x\ldots\}\leftrightarrow\ldots\gamma\ldots]$$

where '$\ldots x\ldots$' is a formula in which '$\in$' occurs amounts to extending the membership axioms so as to include the conversion principle for at least some of the sets that are extensions of impredicative properties.[2] And of course, *some such stipulations must be made if we are to have a sufficient set-theoretical basis for mathematics in the present ontology.* This is our first form of realism according to which "impredicativity is present in mathematics from the beginning".

5. A Categorematic Predicative/Impredicative Dichotomy in a Realist Ontology

Our second form of such a realism is obtained by meshing the present version of predicative second order logic with standard second order logic. Only, we shall use $\forall$ and $\exists$ when affixed to predicate variables to refer to impredicative properties and relations as well. We retain, in other words, $\forall!$ and $\exists!$ for signalizing quantification over predicative properties and relations, but, in addition, we utilize $\forall$ and $\exists$ to refer to *all* properties, whether predicative or not. The usual axioms for standard second order logic are retained, including (CP), but we need to add:

(8) $$(\forall F)\varphi\rightarrow(\forall!F)\varphi$$

which stipulates that whatever holds regarding all properties (relations) holds therefore also for all predicative properties (relations).[3]

---

[1] If membership were a predicative relation, then, by (UI!) and (CP!), so too is non-membership, from which it follows that non-self-membership is a predicative property. But Russell's argument shows that the latter is false.

[2] Because of the impredicativity of membership, all open formulas in which '$\in$' occurs non-vacuously are construed here as representing impredicative properties and relations.

[3] The axiomatic basis, so far, then is: a complete axiom set for first order logic; distribution laws for $\forall$ and $\forall!$ when affixed to predicate variables; a law regarding vacuous quantification of predicate variables; and (CP), (CP!) and (8). We assume modus penens and that universal generalizations of theorems are also theorems.

The point of this form of realism is to make explicit the ontological commitments that are suppressed in the above from allowing quantification only over predicative properties and relations. In the weaker system, because '∈' is there not a substituend for any bound variable, it is plausible that membership be construed as a syncategorematic notion. In that regard, no ontological commitment is made—at least not via the bound predicate variables—to a *membership relation*.[1]

In the present stronger ontology, however, membership is definitely to be construed as being a relation, though of course not a predicative relation. In making this explicit, rather than introduce '∈' as a predicate constant, let us instead take it to be a 2-place predicate variable and then, in the manner of a Ramsey-sentence, existentially posit membership as a relation satisfying extensionality and the conversion principle (Conv!), for predicative properties.[2] Of course (5), and therefore (6), follow by (UI!) from the membership axiom (as an open formula with '∈' free). That is, it is provable, as in the weaker system, that membership is not a predicative relation—only here it is also provable that the entity in question is a relation and therefore an impredicative relation. But again, as in the weaker system, this fact is hardly surprising since the implicit characterization of membership essentially involves quantification over properties.[3] Of course, more in the manner of (7) above needs to be added to the membership axiom so that conversion holds for at least some general types of impredicative properties;[4] for example, the property of being indiscernible

---

[1] It is perhaps appropriate then, relative to the weaker ontology, to place all mention there of impredicative properties and relations in scare-quotes, thereby indicating that though informally convenient the terminology, if construed literally, is ontologically misleading.

[2] In describing the pure form of a formal ontology it is preferable not to include any descriptive or categorematic constants among the primitives of its ontological grammar. This procedure is especially appropriate in the present ontology because with general quantifiable predicate variables additional axioms regarding '∈' can all be summed up in the form of a finite conjunction. The final axiom for membership is then a Ramsey-sentence with no descriptive constants and which existentially binds '∈' as a 2-place predicate variable. Its lack of descriptive constants distinguishes this axiom as a pure ontological posit as opposed to other Ramsey-sentences for empirical theories and in which occur descriptive constants belonging to the observation vocabulary of an applied form of the formal ontology.

[3] A similar observation would seem to apply to any concept whose axiomatic or implicit characterization within first order logic requires infinitely many axioms. As a rule, concepts that can be recursively but not finitely characterized within first order logic can be finitely characterized within the present ontology through quantification over properties. Such concepts are impredicative according to the present realist ontology.

[4] Along Fregean lines, we could stipulate that set descriptions which do not satisfy conversion all denote the empty set:

$$(\forall F)(\sim (\forall y)[y \in \{x \mid F(x)\} \leftrightarrow F(y)] \to \{x \mid F(x)\} = \{x \mid x \neq x\})$$

where identity is understood as indiscernibility. Note that this gambit is not so readily available in the weaker system with quantification only over predicative properties and relations, since indiscernibility with respect to predicative properties does not justify substitutivity in all contexts. Perhaps, then, that system should be supplemented with a primitive syncategorematic (or impredicative?) identity notion satisfying full substitutivity.

from either of several specified individuals (doubleton axiom),[1] or the property of being a member of a member of a given set (union axiom), or the property of being a subset of a given set (power set axiom).[2] And of course, as in the weaker system, even here some such stipulations must be made if we are to have a sufficient set-theoretical basis for mathematics in the present stronger ontology. This is our second form of a realism according to which "impredicativity is present in mathematics from the beginning".

6. Simples and the Abstract Being of Sets in a Realist Ontology

Finally, let us briefly consider the "mode of being" of sets in this Fregean type of ontology. They are, of course, individuals, i.e. objects, but nevertheless they are quite different in their "mode of being" from concrete or empirical objects. Is there some way of expressing this difference categorematically by means of the present type of ontological grammar? Simply positing their existence as one kind of individual without attempting to indicate how their abstract nature differs from that of concrete or empirical objects seems to leave the ontology philosophically incomplete at one of its basic junctures. And pointing out that they are the *extensions* of properties can hardly be said to be an account of this difference.[3]

---

[1] This property as well as all those that comprehend a set through a finite enumeration is impredicative because indiscernibility (identity) involves quantification over properties.

[2] These latter complex properties are impredicative because membership is an essential component of each. The power set axiom is also impredicative in the sense intended by Myhill since the given set in question is a member of its power set.

Incidentally, because the conversion principle is basic to the Fregean view of sets as the extensions of properties, we should consider ways of maximizing it. One such way is von Neumann's *maximization principle* which stipulates that a "class" is (represented by) a set if and only if it cannot be mapped on to the universal class. Reformulated in terms of the present ontological grammar, this amounts to the following *maximization principle for conversion*: conversion holds between a set and its comprehending property if and only if the individuals possessing that property cannot be mapped on to the totality of individuals. In symbols:

(MPC) $(\forall F)((\forall y)[y \in \{x \mid F(x)\} \leftrightarrow F(y)] \leftrightarrow$
$\sim (\exists R)[(\forall x)(\forall y)(\forall z)(R(x,y) \,\&\, R(x,z) \rightarrow y = z) \,\&$
$(\forall x)((\exists y)R(x,y) \rightarrow F(x)) \,\&\, (\forall y)(\exists x)(F(x) \,\&\, R(x,y))])$

Note that this maximization principle, like von Neumann's original version, entails Zermelo's *separation axiom* and Fraenkel's *replacement axiom*. Moreover, assuming an appropriate characterization of ordinal numbers and the fact that conversion fails for the set of all ordinal numbers (Burali-Forti's paradox), (MPC) entails that the ordinal numbers can be mapped on to the totality of individuals, i.e., each individual can be associated with an ordinal number, from which the well-ordering theorem—and therefore also the axiom of choice (for sets)—follows.

[3] In the Fregean type of ontology, sets are identified with the extensions of properties:

$$\text{Set}(y) =_{df} (\exists F) y = \{x \mid F(x)\}$$

where identity is understood as indiscernibility.

In regard to this question, let us note that the theory of predication represented by the present ontological grammar, which really is only an extended form of (our earlier variant of) Frege's grammar,[1] is essentially a form of the Aristotelian inherence theory. Being, in this ontology, is not a genus, and predication or the unity of the categories is explained through the notion of primary being and the inherence of secondary "modes of being" in the primary. Properties and relations, according to this theory, have only a secondary or dependent "mode of being". This is their status as unsaturated or non-self-subsistent entities. Individual objects, or at least concrete or empirical individual objects, have primary being on the other hand. They are saturated, self-subsistent entities.[2]

But what of the individual being of sets? (We shall assume that sets are the only abstract individuals in this ontology.) As saturated entities are they therefore also self-subsistent primary beings? Certainly, as abstract individuals they are not concrete or empirical objects. But is not their abstractness itself a form of dependent or purely relational being? We shall assume that it is, though, since they are saturated entities, their mode of dependence is not that of properties and relations. I should like to propose here, relative to this Fregean type of ontology, that the difference in the "mode of being" of sets from that of concrete or empirical objects derives from the fact that sets have a purely relational mode of being via an impredicative relation.

In explanation of this proposal, let us note that according to the original Fregean approach to this type of ontology, sets or extensions are saturated surrogates for properties and relations. Where for logico-mathematical reasons we want to speak of (structural) properties of properties, e.g. the cardinality of a property, we must instead, according to this view, speak of properties of sets, where the sets, by conversion, have as members exactly the objects possessing the properties for which they are surrogates. Of course, because of Russell's paradox the original conversion principle exchanging sets for properties in a

---

[1] In the Fregean type of framework, the quantifiers $\forall$ and $\exists$ when affixed to individual variables represent *second-level functions* (whose "arguments", roughly, are *first-level functions*: properties and relations whose "arguments" are individual objects). When affixed to predicate variables, they represent *third-level functions* (whose "arguments" are second- and first-level functions). There are no fourth-level functions in this type of ontology. And although these "quantifiers" and those definable in terms of them (e.g., quantifiers for 'at most one', 'at most two', etc., 'exactly one', 'exactly two', etc.), as well as the set-abstraction operator, are the only second- and third-level functions actually considered by Frege, the framework does not exclude there being other second- and third-level functions not definable in terms of these. (We ignore here Frege's use of the definite description operator.)

[2] My own preferred ontological framework superficially resembles the Fregean but supplements the latter with temporal and causal modalities (indicated by quantifiable formula operator variables) and events or processes (indicated by quantifiable propositional variables). However, in my ontology individuals are also unsaturated entities as well as properties and relations (and, of course, modalities too). Here, only events or processes viewed propositionally have saturated being. The theory of predication involved, of course, is not a form of the Aristotelian theory of inherence.

one-to-one manner requires modification. That is, membership as a relation between saturated entities cannot be a perfect mirror-image of predication as a "linkage" or "nexus" between saturated and unsaturated entities, especially in the case of saturated entities that are themselves surrogates for properties. Naturally, the form which the modification is to take should have some ontological motivation, and in the present Fregean type of ontology both the modification and its motivation are in terms of the predicative/impredicative dichotomy among properties and relations. But this dichotomy presupposes a distinction between *complex* and *simple* properties and relations. Impredicative properties and relations are of course complex because they essentially involve or presuppose quantification over properties or relations. Conjunctive, disjunctive and negative predicative properties are, of course, also complex, but their complexity does not involve or presuppose quantification over properties or relations. However, ultimately—at least relative to a given level of ontological analysis which fixes the framework for the conceptual purposes at hand—the predicative status of complex predicative properties and relations must devolve upon the simple (predicative) properties and relations from which they are generated. If there were no such presumed simples, then the predicative/impredicative distinction would be without ontological content.[1]

For purposes of distinguishing simple from complex properties and relations, let us introduce into our present Fregean type of ontological grammar the quantifiers $\forall^c$ and $\exists^c$. When affixed to predicate variables these quantifiers range over simple properties and relations. However, we shall also affix them to individual variables and (definitionally) understand them when so affixed to range over individuals that possess simple properties:[2]

---

[1] This need not mean that such simple properties and relations are *absolute* and not *relative* in character. Perhaps every level of ontological analysis must presuppose simples among its individuals as well as among its properties and relations. But relative to a deeper level of analysis these same simples may turn out to be complex (cp. an analysis of macro-physical objects and their basic properties and relations in terms of micro-physical objects and their basic micro-states). We need not assume that this descent into ever deeper levels of ontological analysis must reach a final deepest level with absolutely simple objects and properties and relations. Whether an Aristotelian inherence theory of predication must assume such an absolute level will be left open here.

[2] We could affix $\forall$! and $\exists$! to individual variables and (definitionally) understand them in a similar manner:

$$(\forall !x)\varphi = d_f (\forall x)[(\exists !F)F(x) \rightarrow \varphi]$$

But note that by (CP!) the complement of a predicative property is also a predicative property. Thus, since bivalence holds in this ontology and we are assuming the existence of predicative properties, every individual possesses a predicative property here. However, since the complement of a simple property is not itself simple, not every individual need possess a simple (predicative) property—and we shall shortly argue that sets themselves do not. In an earlier version of this paper, I confused (partly because of my aversion to absolute simples) the role which simple properties have in this ontology with that of predicative properties. A query from Bas van Fraassen led me to the present version.

$$(\forall^c_x)\varphi = df (\forall x)[(\exists^c F)F(x) \to \varphi]$$

The only form which the comprehension principle takes in regard to simples is:[1]

(CPᶜ) $(\forall^c G)(\exists^c F)(\forall x_1)\ldots(\forall x_n)[F(x_1,\ldots, x_n) \leftrightarrow G(x_1,\ldots, x_n)]$

A qualified version analogous to (UI!) of universal instantiation of formulas representing simple properties and relations is easily proved. (We shall need to assume the distribution of $\forall^c$ over conditionals, however.) And that simple properties (relations), are predicative will follow from

(9) $(\forall! F)\varphi \to (\forall^c F)\varphi$

which stipulates that whatever holds of all predicative properties (relations) holds also for all simple properties (relations).

What we now propose in this development of the ontology is that simple properties and relations can be possessed only by concrete or empirical objects, i.e. simple properties and relations are the basic features characterizing the concrete physical universe. Of course, many complex properties and relations, impredicative as well as predicative, also characterize the physical world and are in that sense physical properties and relations. Indeed, the concrete objects of the universe obtain their individuation or self-identity precisely through such impredicative and therefore complex physical properties. Nevertheless, on this proposal, the concretion of such objects is accounted for through their possession of simple (predicative) properties.

On this proposal, the proposition that sets are the only abstract individuals would be expressed by:

(10) $(\forall y)[\sim(\exists^c G)\ G(y) \to (\exists F)\ y = \{x | F(x)\}]$

where identity is understood as indiscernibility. Similarly, the proposition that no concrete object is a set would be expressed by:

(11) $(\forall^c y)(\forall F)\ y \neq \{x | F(x)\}$

which is provably equivalent to the principle that no set possesses a simple property:

(12) $(\forall F)\sim(\exists^c G) G(\{x | F(x)\})$

Here in this last principle we find an ontological basis for distinguishing the abstract nature of sets from the physical nature of concrete or empirical objects. As saturated surrogates for properties and relations, sets have a purely relational

---

[1] Predicate constants introduced to represent simple properties or relations must be stipulated to do so by *meaning postulates*. This should obviate the need for meaning postulates for predicate constants intended to represent complex predicative properties or relations, since their predicative nature will be determined by their decomposition into simple properties and relations.

mode of being. That is, the abstract being of sets, though saturated, cannot be separated from the being of their members. And the relation in question is of course *the impredicative membership relation*, a quasi-mirror-image of the predication "nexus" through which properties and relations have their form of dependent being, viz. unsaturated being. And, finally, *it is precisely because sets have a purely relational mode of being via the impredicative membership relation that they fail to possess any simple properties*. That is, if structural logico-mathematical properties of properties are reconstrued in this ontology as properties of sets, then implicit in the content of these "higher-order" properties is their ontological side-stepping of the totality of properties, which implicitly renders them impredicative. These are the "primary" properties of sets, i.e. the properties which sets have primarily because they are saturated surrogates of properties or relations. They are the properties, in other words, which sets have primarily through the impredicative membership relation which is the basis for the purely relational mode of being of sets and which, because of its impredicativity, renders these "primary" properties of sets as themselves impredicative. Of course, because of bivalence, each set, in regard to each predicative property, must have either that property or its complement. But because satisfaction of bivalence is the only reason for a set to possess a predicative property, it will possess such a property only by default. Possession of a simple (predicative) property, however, can never be by default for that would amount to rendering the property complex. Accordingly, sets do not possess simple properties. And of course from this it follows that they do not stand in simple relations. Therefore, assuming that sets are the only abstract individuals acknowledged in this Fregean type of ontology, concretion or the physical nature of concrete or empirical objects is to be accounted for by their possession of simple properties. This, of course, is exactly what we proposed above. And this, finally, is our third form of a realism according to which "impredicativity is present in mathematics from the beginning".

Roderick M. Chisholm

On the Nature of Acquaintance:
A Discussion of Russell's Theory of Knowledge

Russell's contributions to the theory of knowledge fall within three broad areas. First, there are his attempts to deal with what, in *The Problems of Philosophy* of 1912, he called the problem of appearance and reality. There are, he seemed there to hold, three very different sorts of individual thing in the world—"minds", material things, and "sense data"—and the problem was that of determining the relation of the third to the first and the second. Later, he attempted to reduce the first and the second of these things to the third; that is to say, he attempted to reduce "minds" and material things to sense-data. Later still, he attempted to reduce all three to events. And, after that, he attempted to reduce events to entities of still another sort ("bundles of qualities"). I think it must now be conceded that these various attempts were unsuccessful, but, as we know, they had extraordinary influence upon the work of other philosophers.

Secondly, there was what some have called Russell's quest for certainty—his doctrine of knowledge by acquaintance, his various attempts to answer the question "What are the objects of acquaintance?", and his views about those matters of fact which he took to constitute the basis of empirical knowledge. There are some who now believe that the problems with which Russell was here concerned were not genuine ones. My own view, however, is that they are genuine problems and that Russell has thrown as much light upon them as has any other philosopher of the present century.

And, thirdly, there is Russell's concern with what we might call epistemic justification. He assumes that our claims to know are justified only in virtue of certain relations obtaining between those propositions constituting the objects of those claims and those propositions constituting what he calls the basis or foundation of our knowledge, and he takes it to be the task of the epistemologist to bring these relations to light. The task of articulating these principles is, in all essential respects, like what is involved in articulating the principles of logic and the principles of ethics. Russell's contributions to this area are, I think, very important indeed and not yet sufficiently appreciated.

I have been invited to discuss "some matter related to Russell's views on the foundations of knowledge in experience". I have chosen the nature of acquaintance as my topic because it does thus relate to Russell's views on the foundations of knowledge in experience and because what Russell has to say about it is central to the first two of the three areas I have distinguished. I am sorry that his theory of "non-demonstrative inference" must remain undiscussed.

Russell defined his technical use of the term "acquaintance" by reference to direct awareness. In "Knowledge by Acquaintance and Knowledge by Description" (1911), his first published discussion of the topic, he wrote: "I say that I am *acquainted* with an object when I have a direct cognitive relation to that object, i.e. when I am directly aware of the object itself. When I speak of a cognitive relation here, I do not mean the sort of relation which constitutes judgment, but the sort which constitutes presentation."[1] He adds, in *The Problems of Philosophy* (1912), that acquaintance involves, not "knowledge of *truths*", but "knowledge of *things*".[2] But if acquaintance does not involve knowledge of truths, nevertheless, Russell thinks, it provides us with the basis of our knowledge of truths.

What are the objects of acquaintance? Russell makes this summary statement in *The Problems of Philosophy*:

We have acquaintance in sensation with the data of the outer senses, and in introspection with the data of what may be called the inner sense—thoughts, feelings, desires, etc.; we have acquaintance in memory with things which have been data either of the outer senses or of the inner sense. Further, it is probable, though not certain, that we have acquaintance with Self, as that which is aware of things or has desires toward things.

In addition to our acquaintance with particular existing things, we also have acquaintance with what we shall call *universals*, that is to say, general ideas, such as *whiteness, diversity, brotherhood*, and so on.[3]

In this passage, Russell is inclined to say that we are acquainted with *ourselves*, but in his later writings he is inclined to deny that we are acquainted with ourselves. To understand the nature of acquaintance, as Russell conceived it, we should consider the reasons for his vacillation with respect to this point.

What is the relation between acquaintance with sense data and acquaintance with ourselves? The following passage occurs in Russell's first essay on acquaintance:

In introspection, we seem to be immediately aware of varying complexes, consisting of objects in various cognitive and conative relations to ourselves. When I see the sun, it often happens that I am aware of my seeing the sun, in addition to being aware of the sun; and when I desire food, it often happens that I am aware of my desire for food. But it is hard to discover any state of mind in which I am aware of myself alone, as opposed to a complex of which I am a constituent. The question of the nature of self-consciousness

[1] This paper first appeared in the *Proceedings of the Aristotelian Society*, n.s., 9 (1910–11); references to it here are to *Mysticism and Logic*, New York 1929.

[2] References are to *The Problems of Philosophy*, London 1950. For the above quotations see pp. 44 and 48.

[3] ibid., pp. 51–2.

is too large, and too slightly connected with our subject, to be argued at length here. It is difficult, but probably not impossible, to account for plain facts if we assume that we do not have acquaintance with ourselves. It is plain that we are not only *acquainted* with the complex "Self-acquainted-with-*A*", but we also *know* the proposition "I am acquainted with *A*".[1]

Supposing that the *A*, to which Russell here refers, is a sense datum, should we say that when a man thus knows that he is acquainted with a certain sense-datum *A*, then there are *three* different things which are objects of his acquaintance—first, the man himself; secondly, the sense datum *A*; and, thirdly, what Russell calls "the complex 'Self-acquainted-with-*A*'"? To answer this question, let us look further at those things he calls "sense data".

In *The Problems of Philosophy*, as I have said, Russell seemed to hold that the individual things of the world comprise at least three different types of entity: "minds", material things, and "sense data". (It is difficult for us now, I think, to see why Russell introduced the word 'mind' into his discussion. A mind, he said, is whatever is acquainted with anything. But he also said that he, Russell, is acquainted with sense data. Why, then, did he seem to posit still another entity and say, not that *he* is acquainted with a certain sense datum, but that *his mind* is acquainted with it?) Why does Russell say that there are sense data?

The facts that led Russell to say that there are sense data are the same as those that have led other philosophers to say that, in addition to the things that appear to us in various ways, there are the various appearances which those things present to us when they appear to us in those ways. We know that by changing the conditions under which we perceive the material things around us, we can produce changes in the way those things appear to us. Using Russell's example, we may note that, just by altering our spatial position with respect to a table, we can alter the spatial appearance that the table presents. (We now know that the facts in question must be put with some caution. We should not say "By walking around the table we can make the table *appear to have a different shape*". But we could say "By walking around the table we can make the table *appear differently shapewise*". In sketching the table as it appears from the various places, we could produce a different shape for each of the different places.)[2] We do not perceive any physical thing unless that physical thing appears to us in some way, and the way in which it does appear to us depends in part upon our own psychological and physiological condition.

Russell was surely right in saying that there is a sense in which a rectangular table-top may look rhomboidal if viewed from the corner of the table. But I think he was mistaken in inferring from this fact, as he seemed to do, that a

---

[1] *Mysticism and Logic*, p. 211.

[2] cf. *Human Knowledge: Its Scope and Limits*, New York 1948, p. 208: "Until we learn to draw, we think that a rectangular object always looks rectangular; and we are right, in the sense that an animal inference causes us to judge it to be rectangular."

rectangular table-top, *if* thus viewed, will present to us an appearance that really *is* rhomboidal. (If "*x* appears rhomboidal" implies "*x* presents an appearance which is rhomboidal", does "*x* appears more than 80 years old" imply "*x* presents an appearance which is more than 80 years old"? Or does "*x* appears dissatisfied" imply "*x* presents an appearance which really is dissatisfied"?) The facts about sense data with which Russell began could be expressed in the locution "*x* appears in such-and-such a way to *y*" where the '*x*' would designate a material thing and the '*y*' the person that perceives that thing. We could also use the passive voice and say "*y* is appeared to in such-and-such a way by *x*". (Or, if we don't like the sound of the expression 'to be appeared to', we could introduce the technical synonym 'to sense' and say "*y* senses in such-and-such a way with respect to *x*".) This would have the advantage of enabling us to detach the 'by *x*' (or 'with respect to *x*') on those occasions, hallucinatory or otherwise, when the person referred to by '*y*' could be said, in Russell's terminology, to be aware of a sense datum or appearance which is not an appearance *of* any material thing. On those occasions, the person would be appeared to but he wouldn't be appeared to by anything. (He would sense but he would not sense with respect to anything.)

If we look at the matter this way, our procedure, and the resulting account of acquaintance, will be somewhat different from Russell's. For we will conclude that Russell was mistaken in assuming that appearances, like "minds" (i.e. persons) and material things, are to be treated as individual things in the world. If I am right, "he is aware of a red sense datum" does not describe a relation between two individual things—a man and a sense datum. It describes a state of one thing. It says that the man is appeared to in a certain way, i.e. that he is sensing in a certain way (possibly the way in which all of us sense when we perceive a red thing in the appropriate conditions).[1]

How many things, then, are involved when a man is acquainted with a sense datum? Let us call the man '*S*' and assume that he is appeared to in the way one is ordinarily appeared to when one observes a red thing under certain standard observation conditions. We have rejected Russell's locution "*S* is directly aware of a red sense datum". Let us now consider two alternative locutions:

(1) There exists an *x* such that *S* is identical with *x* and *x* is directly aware that *x* is appeared to redly.

(2) There exists an *x* such that *S* is identical with *x* and *x* is directly aware of *x* being appeared to redly.

If we adopt locution (1), we will be tempted to say that the object of the man's awareness is the thing designated by '*x*'—that is to say, *the man* himself. If we

[1] My own views on this topic are developed in further detail in *Perceiving: A Philosophical Study*, Ithaca 1957, pp. 115–25, and in "On the Observability of the Self", *Philosophy and Phenomenological Research* 30 (1969), pp. 7–21. The latter paper also appears in P. Kurtz (ed.), *Language and Human Nature: A French-American Philosophers' Dialogue*, St. Louis 1971.

adopt locution (2), we will be tempted to say that the object of the man's awareness is the thing designated by '*x* being appeared to redly'; this thing, presumably, is a *state*, or *event* (and would seem to be an instance of what Russell called a "complex"). But in neither case will we say the man is directly aware of a red *sense datum*, where this is assumed to be an entity other than the man and other than any state of the man.

In suggesting that there *is* something designated by '*x* being appeared to redly', we are assuming that locution (2) above implies:

(3) There exists an *x* and a *y* such that (i) *S* is identical with *x*, (ii) *y* is identical with *x* being appeared to redly, and (iii) *x* is directly aware of *y*.

It seems to me that this assumption is correct: (2) does imply (3), and (1) implies (2). And (1) is certainly a fairly perspicuous way to describe the fact in question.

If we recognize these facts, we are not likely to quarrel about whether it is the man himself, or whether it is a certain state of the man, that is the object of his acquaintance. The important thing would seem to me to be this: one cannot be directly aware of *an individual thing* without thereby being directly aware of that thing being in some *state* or other; and one cannot be directly aware of any *state* without thereby being directly aware of some *individual thing*.

Russell spoke, however, of "the elusiveness of the subject in introspection".[1] In the passage cited above, from "Knowledge by Acquaintance and Knowledge by Description", he said that it is "hard to discover any state of mind in which I am aware of myself alone, as opposed to a complex of which I am a constituent". But how are we to take "I am directly aware of myself alone"? There are at least two possibilities. We could take it to mean the same as "I am directly aware of myself and not directly aware of any other individual thing". Or we could take it to mean the same as "I am directly aware of myself and yet not directly aware of my being in any state". If we take it in the second sense, then we must conclude that no one is ever directly aware of himself alone. But if we take it in the first sense, then we may conclude that there are many occasions on which a man is directly aware of himself alone.

Russell wondered whether his theory of acquaintance "in any way implies a direct consciousness of a bare subject".[2] On any interpretation, surely, the answer

---

[1] *Logic and Knowledge*, ed. R. C. Marsh, London 1956, p. 163. The passage appears in the third of the three papers entitled "On the Nature of Acquaintance", which first appeared in the *Monist* in 1914.

[2] "We are thus forced to ... ask ourselves whether our theory of acquaintance in any way implies a direct consciousness of the bare subject. If it does, it would seem that it must be false; but I think we can show that it does not. Our theory maintains that the datum when we are aware of experiencing an object O is the fact 'something is acquainted with O'. The subject appears here, not in its individual capacity, but as an 'apparent variable'; thus such a fact may be a datum in spite of incapacity for acquaintance with the subject." *Logic and Knowledge*, p. 164; this quotation is also from the third of the three papers. "On the Nature of Acquaintance".

is negative. If by "a direct consciousness of a bare subject", he means being aware of oneself without being aware of oneself being in any state, then we have no such consciousness. And if by "a bare subject", he means a subject that isn't in any state, then there isn't any such subject; for everything—or at least every individual thing except God, if he exists—is at every moment at which it exists in *some* state or other. But from the fact that there is no "direct consciousness of a bare subject" we must not draw the erroneous conclusion that no one is ever directly acquainted with himself.

Consider in this context what Russell called, in *The Problems of Philosophy*, the data of "the inner sense" ("We have acquaintance in sensation with the data of the outer senses, and in introspection with the data of what may be called the inner sense—thoughts, feelings, desires, etc. . . ."). In *An Inquiry into Meaning and Truth* (1940), Russell said that we are directly aware of our own propositional attitudes. "It is clear," he wrote, "that we can be aware of believing or desiring something in just as immediate a way as we can be aware of a red patch that we see."[1] And this is certainly true. If a man is directly aware, as he may be, of his desire to eat, then we can say, very much as before, either (1) "There exists an x such that x is directly aware that x desires to eat" or (2) "There exists an x such that x is directly aware of x desiring to eat". As before, we can say either that the man is directly aware of himself or that he is directly aware of his being in a certain state. And in the latter case, we will be saying, not simply that the man is aware of a certain state—we will be saying that he is aware of *his* being in that state: "there exists an x such that x is directly aware of x desiring to eat".

This is not to say that, in thus being aware of oneself as being in a certain state, one is aware of oneself as *being* a self. If we characterize a self, as Russell had characterized what he called a "mind", by saying it is the sort of thing that can be directly aware of things, then it is quite possible for a man to be aware of himself as being in a certain state without thereby being aware of himself as being the kind of thing that can be thus directly aware. What we have said is quite consistent with Russell's later observation that, if a man always lived alone, "he would never be led to distinguish between 'there is a table' and 'I see a table'; in fact, he would always use the former phrase, if one could suppose him using phrases at all. The word 'I' is a word of limitation, meaning 'I, not you'; it is by no means part of any primitive datum."[2]

Russell also said many times, of course, that the self is a "logical construction" and he seems to have thought that propositions ostensibly about the self could be reduced to propositions about other things in much the way in which, according to his view, propositions about cardinal numbers can be reduced to

---

[1] *An Inquiry into Meaning and Truth*, New York 1940, p. 205.
[2] ibid., p. 182.

propositions about classes.[1] But I think it is fair to say that he never even suggested how what he had called the data of "inner sense" can be reduced to propositions that do not refer to the self. Following the principles of *Principia Mathematica*, we could, if we had the time and patience, take a simple proposition of arithmetic, such as "two and two are four" and re-express it in terms solely of the logic of classes. But consider the datum expressed by "I am directly aware of my having been earlier directly aware that I wanted to eat". Russell has given us no principles enabling us to re-express that in terms that do not refer to the self.

As we have seen, Russell also said, in 1912, that "in addition to our acquaintance with particular existing things, we also have acquaintance with what we call *universals*, that is to say, general ideas, such as *whiteness, diversity, brotherhood*, and so on. . . . Awareness of universals is called *conceiving*, and a universal of which we are aware is called a *concept*."[2] Note that Russell speaks here of conceiving, not of having a concept. A man who *has* a concept, say, of whiteness, as distinguished from a man who is *directly aware* of whiteness, is a man who knows what it is for a thing to be white, or what it would be for a thing to be white. Having a concept is thus dispositional rather than being a matter of direct awareness. I suggest that, when Russell says we may become directly aware of universals, he has in mind something of this sort: in being directly aware of something as being white, one is able to abstract the property whiteness and then to become directly aware of it—the property whiteness—as being had, i.e. instantiated or exemplified. In other words, a man may be such that, if there exists an x such that he is directly aware of x being white, then there exists a y such that he is directly aware of x as exemplifying y—or of y as being exemplified by x. Or, to take Russell's example of diversity, the man may be such that, if there exists an x and a y such that he is directly aware of x as being other than y, then there exists a z such that he is directly aware of x as being related to y by z.

And why not? How else could the man begin to acquire his concepts?

Russell obviously wanted to base his theory of conception upon his theory of

---

[1] cf. *My Philosophical Development*, London 1957, pp. 135–6: "The subject, however, appears to be a logical fiction like mathematical points and instants. It is introduced, not because observation reveals it, but because it is linguistically convenient and apparently demanded by grammar. Nominal entities of this sort may or may not exist, but there is no good ground for assuming that they do. The functions that they appear to perform can always be performed by classes or series or other logical constructions, consisting of less dubious entities. If we are to avoid a perfectly gratuitous assumption, we must dispense with the subject as one of the actual ingredients of the world."

[2] *The Problems of Philosophy*, p. 52. cf. "Knowledge by Acquaintance and Knowledge by Description", in *Mysticism and Logic*, pp. 212–13.

acquaintance.[1] But is his theory of acquaintance broad enough to accomplish this purpose? Given the concepts that we do have, and given the things that Russell lists as possible objects of acquaintance, is it plausible to say that we have, somehow, acquired all our concepts from our direct awareness of such objects? When Russell talks about our concepts, he usually gives examples that apply to physical things. This leads us to ask: might it not be that sometimes we are directly aware of physical things?

Russell was quite definite about the answer to this question: we are never directly aware of physical things.[2] But not everything that he says about direct awareness, or acquaintance, supports this contention, and some of the things he says about it seem to suggest the opposite. Among the objects of acquaintance, he often says, are those things that one can designate by the use of purely demonstrative expressions—those things that we can "name" (in Russell's rather special sense of 'name'). "What distinguishes the objects to which I can give names from other things is the fact that these objects are within my experience, that I am acquainted with them. . . ."[3] The demonstrative 'this', he said, is a proper name *par excellence*. Anything I can refer to, using such a word purely demonstratively, is an object of acquaintance, something of which I am directly aware. Now, surely, I can use the word 'that' purely demonstratively to refer to any of those things I now directly *perceive*—e.g. *that* house, across the river. Why *not* say that I am directly aware of the house that I see and hence that it is an object of my acquaintance? We could then say, not only that there is something (namely, myself) which I am directly aware of as being appeared to in a certain way, but also that there is a second thing (namely, the house) which I am directly aware of as appearing in that way. We could say, in other words: "There exist an x and a y such that x is directly aware of y appearing red to x" (or "x is directly aware of x as being appeared red to by y"). Perhaps we could even add that there are certain occasions on which a man may be directly aware of a certain thing, say, a house, not only as *appearing red*, but also as *being red*. This would be the epistemological view that some people have called "direct realism". This view, as I have said, is considerably broader than Russell's, but it would enable him to carry out the theory of conception which he had proposed. Thus if there are things and we can be directly aware of those things as being red, then there are things and we can be directly aware of them as having or

---

[1] This, of course, is the point of Russell's "acquaintance principle": "Whenever a relation of supposing or judging occurs, the terms to which the supposing or judging mind is related by the relation of supposing or judging must be terms with which the mind in question is acquainted"; *Mysticism and Logic*, pp. 220–1. If the person or self is a "logical fiction", then, presumably, this principle could be reformulated without any reference to "the supposing or judging mind". But it is difficult to imagine what the reformulation would be.

[2] See his discussion of this question in "The Nature of Sense-Data: A Reply to Dr. Dawes Hicks", *Mind*, n.s., 22 (1913).

[3] See "On the Nature of Acquaintance", in *Logic and Knowledge*, p. 167.

exemplifying the colour red. And similarly for the other properties which, as we ordinarily say, we can perceive the physical things around us to have.

Why didn't Russell accept this view, then? He assumed this: one cannot be directly aware of an object as being so-and-so unless one's belief, with respect to that object, that it *is* so-and-so is capable of withstanding "methodological doubt". Is there something that I am directly aware of as being, say, a cube? Russell would have reasoned as follows: (1) if there is an x such that I am directly aware of x as being a cube, then it would be impossible for me now to doubt that there is such an x; but (2) it is possible for me now to doubt that I am directly aware of anything as being a cube ("Perhaps I am hallucinated or dreaming, or possibly someone is doing something to my eyes and brain"); and therefore (3) there is no x such that I am directly aware of x as being a cube. Given that I am now looking at a cube, the second premise, as many philosophers will be eager to point out, is problematic at best. "*Can* you really doubt that the thing before you is a cube—that there is a cube that you are now perceiving?" But suppose we give Russell the second premise. The difficult question is: why should we accept the first?

There is a way of conceiving direct awareness, and if we do conceive it in that way, then, although we can say of a man that he is directly aware of many states of himself, we can never say of anyone that he is directly aware of the states of any external physical thing—any physical thing that is other than himself. This sense of direct awareness may be suggested by the following schema:

S is directly aware of the fact that $p = Df\ p$ and necessarily if p then S knows that p.

But this use of 'necessarily' would not have been acceptable to Russell. And the definition would not allow him to say that anything we can refer to by means of a purely demonstrative expression is an object of our acquaintance.

One final question about acquaintance: Russell said that acquaintance involves knowledge of *things* but not knowledge of *truths*. Why not knowledge of truths? If I am acquainted with myself as sensing in a certain way, don't I thereby *know* that I'm sensing in that way? ("It is plain that we are not only *acquainted* with the complex 'Self-acquainted-with-A', but we also *know* the proposition 'I am acquainted with A'."[1]) Russell said that acquaintance involves not "the sort of relation which constitutes judgment, but the sort which constitutes presentation"[2]. I cannot be sure of what Russell had in mind here, but I suggest he may have reasoned somewhat like this:

[1] *Mysticism and Logic*, p. 211.

[2] ibid., p. 209. It should be noted that at the time Russell wrote this passage (in "Knowledge by Acquaintance and Knowledge by Description") he accepted the so-called "multiple relation theory of judgment" which he thought enabled him to dispense with propositions. See "On the Nature of Truth", in *Philosophical Essays*, London 1910, esp. pp. 172ff, and *Principia Mathematica*, 2nd ed., Cambridge 1925, vol. I, pp. 42–7.

(1) A man's awareness cannot be said to be knowledge of a *truth* unless it involves belief in a proposition that is true. But (2) direct awareness is *de re*, or nonpropositional, rather than *de dicto*, or propositional. The proper expression of the content of direct awareness may be put as "There is an *x* such that he is directly aware that *x* is so-and-so"; but the expression following the 'aware that'—namely, '*x* is so-and-so'—is not the expression of a proposition. Therefore (3) a man's direct awareness cannot be said to be knowledge of a truth.

What of the first premise? Can't a man have a belief that is true without his thereby believing a proposition that is true? I would say that he could. Suppose we said—what is suggested by Russell's theory of conception—that whenever there is a thing of which a man is directly aware, then there is some property which is such that he is aware of that thing as having that property. For example, if there is some thing such that the man is aware of that thing as being red, then the property redness is, so to speak, such that the man is aware of it as being had. What, then, would be a true belief *de re*? We could say that a man has a true belief *de re* if there is some thing *x* and some property *y* such that (1) *x* has *y* and (2) *x* is believed by the man to have *y*. So it was a mistake, I think, to suggest that acquaintance, being knowledge of *things*, is not also knowledge of *truths*.

Wilfrid Sellars

Ontology and the Philosophy of Mind in Russell

In *My Philosophical Development* Russell writes: "I have maintained a principle which still seems to me completely valid, to the effect that if we can understand what a sentence means, it must be composed entirely of words denoting things with which we are acquainted or definable in terms of such words."[1] He excludes logical words; in the first place the connectives, which, though they are not, of course, meaningless, do not denote. He also, interestingly enough, excludes without comment the quantifiers 'all' and 'some'. He then adds: "we can eliminate the need of this limitation by confining our principle to sentences containing no variables and containing no parts that are sentences."

Russell first formulated a "principle of acquaintance" in his classic little book *The Problems of Philosophy*. And it is indeed true that in a sense Russell can be said to "have maintained" a principle of acquaintance throughout the intervening years. But much water went over the dam between 1912 and 1959, and a study of the history of this principle will throw light on the development of Russell's philosophy of mind. In *The Problems of Philosophy* the principle reads:

Every proposition which we can understand must be composed fully of constituents with which we are acquainted.[2]

A number of questions naturally arise when considering this principle. In the first place, what is "acquaintance"? I shall give this question a more detailed discussion shortly. Initially, however, it is sufficient to note that Russell conceives of acquaintance as a basic cognitive *relation*. He also refers to it as an *act*. Here it suffices to note that relation words, except, of course, when he extends the term 'relation' to include "monadic" relations, are, for Russell, essentially many-place predicates.[3] What are the terms of this relation? Russell tells us that acquaintance is a relation between a "subject" and an "object", and represents it by the schema

$$S—A—O$$

which has the logical form '$x R y$'.[4]

---

[1] *My Philosophical Development*, New York 1959, p. 169.

[2] *The Problems of Philosophy*, London 1912, p. 91.

[3] Not all relations, of course, are, in any ordinary sense, "acts". Nor are all "acts" two- (or more)-place relations. Indeed, a striking feature of many contemporary philosophies of mind is the attempt to construe ostensibly transitive verbs standing for mental acts as intransitive, or one-place, acts.

[4] Some philosophers who have used the above schema have been tempted to take 'A' to stand for an act construed as a mental particular.

I lay aside for the moment ontological questions concerning acquaintance as act or relation, and pick up its character as cognitive. Acquaintance is a form of "knowledge". Russell distinguishes between "knowledge of *truths*" and "knowledge of *things*". The former expression is "applicable to the sort of knowledge which is opposed to error, the sense in which what we know is *true*, the sense which applies to our beliefs and convictions, i.e. to what are called *judgments*. In this sense of the word we know *that* something is the case. This sort of knowledge may be described as knowledge of *truths*. Acquaintance, on the other hand, belongs to the category of knowledge of *things*." This, he tells us, "is the sense in which we know sense data".[1]

But though acquaintance is distinguished from knowledge of truths, the two modes of knowledge are intimately related to one another. Thus:

If I am acquainted with a thing which exists, my acquaintance gives me the knowledge that it exists.

How are we to construe the "it" of the clause "that it exists"? The answer is found in the sentence which follows:

But it is not true that, conversely, whenever I can know that a thing of a certain sort exists, I or someone else must be acquainted with the thing.

This surely entitles us to construe the previous sentence as telling us that if I am acquainted with a thing which exists, my acquaintance gives me that knowledge that it—a thing *of a certain sort*—exists. Of course, by "of a certain sort" Russell *may* simply mean "answering to a certain description", in which case the specific overtones of the word 'sort' are to be neglected. But then, again, he may not. The importance of this point will emerge shortly.

The object terms to which a subject stands in the relation of acquaintance includes both particulars and non-particulars. The paradigm of the former is sense data. The latter include both universals and facts. Among the facts with which we are acquainted are facts which themselves involve acquaintance, e.g. the fact that we are acquainted with a certain sense datum. Whether the subject of acquaintance is itself ever an object of acquaintance is a question to which Russell devotes considerable attention and which he finds difficult to answer.

But before we take a closer look at some of these questions, let us return to the Principle of Acquaintance. Notice that as formulated in *The Problems of Philosophy* the principle has a preamble, so to speak, which reads as follows:

The fundamental principle in the analysis of *propositions containing descriptions* is this. [my italics]

What sort of items does he have in mind as constituents for such propositions?

---

[1] *The Problems of Philosophy*, pp. 69–70.

Clearly they will include particulars, e.g. sense data, themselves objects of acquaintance, which serve as a frame of reference in terms of which "described" objects are picked out, thus: the chair which is responsible for *these* (sense data) is a Hepplewhite. Also among the constituents of these propositions are attributes and relations which are either, in a pre-analytic sense, involved in "the meaning" of the descriptive phrase, or "predicated" of the object described. Are there any other constituents? According to the theory of descriptions, the material object which is responsible for *these* (sense data) is not a constituent of the above proposition, for perspicuously formulated, it turns out to be, not a subject-predicate proposition about the chair, but rather a general statement which is about *everything*. As reformulated, it contains a variable of quantification which takes all particulars or, at least, all material objects as its values. Is not Russell therefore committed by his principle to the claim that to understand the original statement, we must *somehow* be acquainted with everything? Since it would entail that in some global sense we are acquainted with items which far transcend in number the items with which, on any occasion, we are severally acquainted, it would raise serious problems for the whole idea of acquaintance. If, as Quine argues, bound variables are the bearers of reference or, to use Russell's term, denotation, it would be difficult for Russell to avoid this consequence. Russell never seems to have seen this problem—at least in these terms.[1]

I now return to the topic of the epistemic or cognitive character of acquaintance, and to the question whether the subject is an object of acquaintance to itself. The epistemic character of acquaintance stands out very clearly in the passage in *The Problems of Philosophy* in which the concept is introduced:

We shall say that we have *acquaintance* with anything of which we are directly aware, without the intermediary of any process of inference or any knowledge of truths. Thus in the presence of my table I am acquainted with the sense-data that make up the appearance of my table—its colour, shape, hardness, smoothness, etc.; all these are things of which I am immediately conscious when I am seeing and touching my table. The particular shade of colour that I am seeing may have many things said about it—I may say that it is brown, that it is rather dark, and so on. But such statements, though they make me know truths *about* the colour, do not make me *know the colour itself* any better

---

[1] The alternative of tying all reference to demonstratives, and construing quantification (at least over particulars) as having purely syntactical meaning, amounts to a semantical solipsism of this present moment. It is interesting to note that Russell always took radical solipsism seriously. In later years, particularly when wrestling with positivist accounts of meaning and verification, his robust sense of reality expressed itself in attempts to refute it. His early (1914) essay on "The Relation of Sense-Data to Physics", reprinted in *Mysticism and Logic*, London 1917, was, however, as is well known, one of the primary sources of logical positivism. There, in a mood inspired by Ockham, he wrote "It would give me the greatest satisfaction to . . . establish physics on a solipsistic basis" (*Mysticism and Logic*, p. 152).

than I did before: so as concerns *knowledge of the colour itself*, as opposed to *knowledge of truths about it*, I know the colour perfectly and completely when I see it, and no further *knowledge of it itself* is even theoretically possible. Thus the sense data which make up the appearance of my table are things with which I have acquaintance, things immediately known to me *just as they are*.[1]

With this passage in mind let us follow Russell's soul-searchings about self-acquaintance. In *The Problems of Philosophy*, Russell argues that we not only know *that there is* a subject particular, we also are, or can be, acquainted with it. He makes the latter claim, however, not without a certain amount of hesitation. The source of this uneasiness is not difficult to trace. It lies in what he finds it possible to say about objects of acquaintance in the cases which he takes as his paradigm. Thus, consider the dark brown sense datum of which he is immediately conscious when looking at his table. He writes: "I know the colour perfectly and completely ... no further knowledge of it itself is even theoretically possible." To be sure he is speaking here of a "particular shade of colour" and shades of colour are, of course, universals and not particulars. But the context makes it clear that Russell, although his language is loose, is thinking not of a "particular" shade of colour in the sense of one certain shade of colour as contrasted with others, but of a *particular* which is an instance of that shade. Thus it is sense data as particulars which he has in mind when he concludes the above passage by writing that "the sense data which make up the appearance of my table are things ... immediately known to me just as they are".

In other words, although acquaintance with a dark brown sense datum is not knowledge *that*, i.e. knowledge of a fact or truth, nevertheless acquaintance brings it about that it is "known to me" just *as it is*, i.e. *as being a rather dark brown*. In a subsequent chapter on intuitive knowledge (Chapter 11), Russell speaks of a "kind of self-evident truths" which are "immediately derived from sensation". He carefully distinguishes between sense data and the self-evident truths which we know about them. Sense data themselves are neither true nor false. "A particular patch of colour which I see, for example, simply exists: it is not the sort of thing that is true or false."[2] He attempts to distinguish two kinds of self-evident truths of perception, though he suggests that "perhaps in the last analysis the two kinds may coalesce".

First, there is the kind which simply asserts the *existence* of the sense datum without in any way analysing it. We see a patch of red, and we judge "there is such-and-such a patch of red", or more strictly "there is that"; this is one kind of intuitive judgment of perception. The other kind arises when the object of sense is complex, and we subject it to some degree of analysis. If, for instance, we see a *round* patch of red we may judge "that patch of red is round".... Our judgement analyses the datum into colour and shape, and then recombines them by stating that the red colour is round in shape.

[1] *The Problems of Philosophy*, pp. 73–4; my italics.
[2] ibid., pp. 177, 178.

One point stands out clearly from these passages, namely that although the acquaintance with the sense datum is not *as such* a knowledge of a truth or fact, it is so intimately connected with knowledge of certain facts about the sense datum that the latter can be said to be "immediately derived from" the former. There is, so to speak, no gap between them, no possible slip between knowing the datum and knowing that it is red.

Now, if this is what acquaintance with sense data amounts to, we would expect that if we were acquainted with the subject, then here also something would be immediately known to me just as it is; we would expect that so far as concerns knowledge of the subject itself, as contrasted with knowledge of truths about it, one knows the subject *perfectly* and *completely* when one is acquainted with it, and *no further knowledge of it itself is even theoretically possible.* We would seem forced to conclude that if we cannot say *this,* then we are simply *not* acquainted with the subject. But Russell neither boldly tells us that we have perfect knowledge of the subject, nor that we are not acquainted with the subject. Instead, he tells us that "complicated arguments can be adduced on either side" of the question and after some weighing of the pros and cons concludes rather lamely that "acquaintance with ourselves seems probably to occur". He makes a feeble effort to reconcile this conclusion with what would seem to be the obvious implications of the paradigm case of sense data, by saying that in the case of the subject, "the acquaintance is hard to disentangle from other things".

Two years later in the essay "On the Nature of Acquaintance"[1] Russell takes a radically different stance. Although he still claims that we have intuitive knowledge of the existence of a subject particular, as when we are acquainted with the fact that *something* is acquainted with *this* (sense datum), we are not acquainted with the subject particular itself. We grasp it as *the particular which* is acquainted with a certain sense datum.

Now the primary thrust of Russell's discussion in "On the Nature of Acquaintance" is the appeal to introspection. He simply agrees with Hume[2]

---

[1] Reprinted in *Logic and Knowledge*, London 1956, edited by Robert Charles Marsh. Page references are to *Logic and Knowledge*.

[2] Russell draws on a well-known passage from Hume, but uses it to make a somewhat different point from that intended by its original author. Hume fails—or thinks he fails—to find an item which has perceptions. He sees no need to posit such a term, believing, paradoxically, that it makes sense to speak of perceptions without a perceiving subject. I say "paradoxically" because the verbal noun 'perception' makes sense only by virtue of its relation to the subject-predicate statement form '*x* perceives'. Just what is to be made of this depth-grammatical point is, of course, a matter of controversy. But it would seem clear that one who regards grammar as misleading should come up with a way of describing the data of introspection which doesn't use verbal nouns which imply a subject. Russell, who came to warn against the dangers of taking ordinary grammar at its face value, subsequently attempted to do this as Hume did not. But Russell at the time we are considering heeded the call of grammar and, believing that a subject term *is* necessary, found it. To be sure, he finds it only as *the item which* is acquainted with e.g. this circular red patch. Nevertheless he *finds* it in that he knows intuitively that there is such an item.

that no subject is "found". "Hume's inability to perceive himself was not peculiar, and I think most unprejudiced observers would agree with him." Russell proceeds to argue that even if on occasion some rare adept were to find himself, we should have to interpret 'I' as others use it, and the adept on other occasions, as a description rather than "a true proper noun in the logical sense". But though *this* argument takes it to be a simple matter of fact that we don't find the subject, it is followed by a passage which begins:

If it is true, as it seems to be, that subjects are not given in acquaintance, it follows that nothing can be known as to *their intrinsic nature*. We cannot know, for example, that they differ from one another, nor yet that they do not differ.

This, of course, does not entail that if subjects were given in acquaintance, their intrinsic nature would be known. Yet it strongly suggests it. A moment later he restates his point.

The definition of what is "mental" as what involves subjects is inadmissible, in view of the fact that we do not know *what subjects are*.[1]

It seems to me legitimate to infer that Russell has been struck by the idea that if we were acquainted with the subject, we would know what the subject is, its "intrinsic nature", as we know what a red sense datum is when we are acquainted with it. Notice that in "On the Nature of Acquaintance" Russell isn't claiming that the subject is a bare particular, only that *our awareness* of it is bare, lacking as it does the power to give us an intuitive knowledge of what the subject is.

Although the above reconstruction of Russell's thought seems reasonable enough, it is open to a telling objection. One who offers this objection agrees that according to Russell, when one is acquainted with an object, "one knows the object perfectly and completely", but argues that, as the very term suggests, what is thus known is the *identity* of the object. When one is, in the ordinary sense, acquainted with somebody, one knows *who* that person is.[2] When one knows, i.e. is acquainted with, Bismarck, one knows who Bismarck is. This does not mean that at least in the ordinary sense, the converse is true, i.e. that to know who Bismarck is, one must be acquainted with him. But it does seem clear that one who can be said to know or to be acquainted with Bismarck has a special claim to know who he is. Again, when one knows or is acquainted with Bismarck, one knows *that* Bismarck exists. As before, this does not mean that the converse is true, i.e. that to know that Bismarck exists, one must be acquainted with him. Yet one who is acquainted with Bismarck has a special

[1] "On the Nature of Acquaintance", pp. 164, 165; my italics.
[2] Compare Russell's introductory remarks on knowledge by acquaintance and knowledge by description, pp. 83ff. of *The Problems of Philosophy*.

claim to know that he exists. Is it not in these features of our ordinary use of "acquaintance" that we are to find the clues for a correct interpretation of the cognitive character of Russell's "knowledge by acquaintance"?

To this question, the answer is, of course, yes—but not an unqualified yes. To warrant an unqualified yes, we must replace "the clues" by "clues". But what the objector wants is to replace the claim that when one is acquainted with an object, one knows what the object is in the sense of knowing the *intrinsic nature* of the object, by the claim that when one is acquainted with an object, one simply knows *what* object it is, where knowing *what* something is is the neuter parallel of knowing *who* somebody is. (I shall use the term 'which' for this sense of 'what'.) He also wants to replace the claim that by virtue of being acquainted with an object one knows *that* the object is of a certain sort, by the claim that by virtue of being acquainted with an object, one simply knows that the object exists. And, indeed, if the implications of knowledge by acquaintance are construed along the objector's lines, then the fact that we don't know the "intrinsic nature" of the subject would scarcely count against the idea that we are acquainted with it. The fact that Russell simply appeals to Hume's experiment and its negative outcome would be accounted for.

To all this, the proper reply is that *both* themes are present in Russell's account. Furthermore, they are both present in the implications of the common sense use of 'acquaintance'. One who knows, i.e. is acquainted with Bismarck, is in a privileged position with respect to knowing not only *who* he is, and *that* he exists, but also *what sort* of person he is, *what* he is like. Special weight would be given to his testimony as to Bismarck's character.

I pointed out above that in that ordinary sense of 'knows' in which it means "is acquainted with",

　　x knows *y*

entails but is not entailed by

　　x knows who *y* is

and

　　x knows that *y* exists.

Russell, working within the tradition which draws, or attempts to draw, a sharp distinction between knowledge and probable opinion, requires of

　　x knows which *y* is

and

　　x knows that *y* exists

a standard of certainty which leads him to think that the knowledge *of y* which ensures these pieces of knowledge is itself "perfect" and "complete". And he is tempted to think that "*x* is acquainted with *y*" is not only a sufficient, but also a necessary, condition of "*x* knows who *y* is" and "*x* knows that *y* exists". It is only when he came to the conclusion in "On the Nature of Acquaintance" that we are not acquainted with the subject, that we find him stressing that we can be acquainted with the fact that the subject exists (i.e. that *something* is acquainted with O) "in spite of incapacity for acquaintance with the subject".[1]

I agree, then, that *part* of the epistemic character of acquaintance is a matter of the relation between "x knows (i.e. is acquainted with) y" on the one hand and "x knows *what* (in the sense of *which*) y is" and "x knows that y exists" on the other. I simply add that another part of the epistemic character of acquaintance is a matter of the relation between "x knows (i.e. is acquainted with) y" and "x knows *what* (i.e. of what sort) y is".

But unless I am very much mistaken, this concession is likely to be met with an impatient response on the following lines.

You have failed to take into account the central theme of Russell's distinction between "knowledge by acquaintance" and "knowledge by description". Knowledge by description is expressed in language by statements involving the use of descriptive phrases of the form 'the so and so'. Knowledge by acquaintance is expressed by logically proper names.

To see what the objector is driving at let us look once again at non-technical uses. We note that people not only *have* names, they are *called* by names—not only in absence, but, as the term itself suggests, in presence. Thus, one who knows Bismarck can seek him out and address him by name. One who knows him by name *need* not be acquainted with him. But, then, one who knows him by name need not be able to seek him out and address him by name. He may know him only as the German Chancellor who is called Bismarck, and lack the information necessary to construct a recipe for confronting him. Indeed, since he is not in a position to address Bismarck as Bismarck, 'Bismarck' in his vocabulary does not have the full force of a *name*. One who not only knows Bismarck by name, but is acquainted with him, is in a privileged position with respect to seeking him out and addressing him by name. Furthermore, the people with whom one is acquainted and can address by name provide a fixed system of pegs from which to hang definite descriptions. Acquaintances, then, are like familiar cities on a map. Knowing them, one knows how to get to the others. If I know Bismarck, I can find his Uncle Franz and his teacher Joseph.

Transposed into a Russellian Key, this becomes the idea that only things which are objects of acquaintance can be named. The theme that names are what persons are addressed by takes over. 'This' and other demonstratives are claimed to have a primary use in which they are the names of particulars with which one is in the technical sense acquainted. And it is these names which are the firm (if fleeting) pegs of reference to which descriptions are tied.

Now all this is an old story. What is its relevance to the topic at hand? The answer lies in the fact that for Russell, the meaning of a proper name which is *really* a proper name is simply the object named. Russell sees that 'this' is not a mere label, that associated with it is a characteristic pattern of use. Thus, he tells

[1] "On the Nature of Acquaintance", p. 164.

us that the object described as "the object of attention of a given subject at a given moment" is the object "which this subject . . . will call 'this'". This pattern, however, is not what 'this' means, at least in the sense of *denotes*, and Russell is particularly concerned to warn us that "it would be an error to suppose that 'this' *means* 'the object to which I am now attending' ".[1]

With the above qualification, Russell's account of 'this' agrees in spirit with the label theory of names, the theory that names have reference but lack sense. He assumes that for a token of 'this' to have a sense, is for it to be shorthand for one or more descriptions. The idea that a demonstrative, or a name, for that matter, could be conceptually tied to a cluster of descriptive phrases without being shorthand for it, though implicit in his account of the use of "emphatic particulars" ('this', 'here', 'now', 'I'), does not occur to him.

We are now in a position to see what the objector had in mind in his second assault. If the linguistic correlate of knowledge by acquaintance is (1) a *term*, not a *proposition*, (2) a term which is a *true proper name*, rather than a *descriptive phrase*, then, surely, the knowledge by acquaintance of an object O can be neither (1) the knowledge *that* O is of a certain character nor (2) the knowledge *of* O as *the item which* is of a certain character. The content of knowledge by acquaintance must be pure *this* without a *such*. The theme the objector is stressing is well expressed by the following passage from "On the Nature of Acquaintance":

At any given moment, there are certain things of which a man is "aware", certain things which are "before his mind" . . . if I speak to myself, and denote [these things] by what may be called "proper names", rather than by descriptive words, I cannot be in error. So long as the names which I use really are names at the moment, i.e., are naming things to me, so long the words must be objects of which I am aware, since otherwise the words would be meaningless sounds not names of things. There is thus at any given moment a certain assemblage of objects to which I could, if I chose, give proper names; these are the objects of my "awareness", the objects "before my mind", or the objects that are within my present "experience".[2]

Now all this is very true and telling. Whether he is clear about it or not, Russell should deny that acquaintance as such is acquaintance with an object *as being of a certain character*. And he *does* introduce acquaintance to provide *named* items to serve as reference pegs for descriptions. Nevertheless, it would be a mistake to infer that Russell doesn't recognize a conceptual tie between knowing an object by acquaintance and knowing certain intimate facts about it, thus that it is of a certain kind or that it has a certain intrinsic nature. Although knowledge of objects by acquaintance is not identical with knowledge of such facts, it makes this knowledge available by being what it is, i.e. acquaintance.

[1] ibid., p. 168.
[2] ibid., p. 130.

This connection between acquaintance and knowledge of facts was, after all, present in the ordinary language paradigms which guided Russell's thought.

Although I must confess to a certain feeling of puzzlement as to why Russell didn't offer an explicit argument of the form

If I were acquainted with the subject, I would know its intrinsic nature
I do not know its intrinsic nature
Therefore I am not acquainted with the subject,

I do think that I have made a case for the idea that this argument is almost on the tip of his pen. In any event, I propose to push this interpretation a bit further and to show that it provides additional insight into the development of Russell's thought.

In an attempt to get a better idea of knowing what a particular is in the sense of knowing its "intrinsic nature", let us take a closer look at the example he discusses in Chapter 11 of *The Problems of Philosophy*. The example, it will be remembered, is "a circular patch of red". In knowing what this object is, we know it to be a circular patch of red.

There are three points to stress. In the first place, 'red' is functioning here as a word for a kind of matter or stuff. In contemporary terminology it is a "mass term". In the second place, 'patch of red' is a sortal expression formed from this mass term which applies to portions of red as 'puddle of water' applies to portions of water. In the third place, although we know both that the object is a patch of red we are knowing *what* it is as we are not by virtue of knowing that it is circular. For although both these facts about the datum are intuitively known and are non-relational, the fact that it is made of a certain stuff pertains to its nature or what it is, in a way in which the fact that it is circular does not. But although I stress these points, I do not mean to imply that Russell does. I do, however, wish to suggest that these features of his example were not unnoticed by Russell and that they are part of the "tacit knowledge" which guides his thought.

To put the point bluntly, in Russell's paradigm case of knowledge by acquaintance, we know what O is by knowing of what stuff it is. If we combine this with our earlier analysis we will construe Russell as thinking, though not in so many words, that if we were acquainted with the subject, we would know "what I am" not just in the sense of being acquainted with an *adjectival* fact about myself, let alone a *relational* fact about myself; rather we would know of what stuff I consist. No sortal fact about myself which did not convey *this* information would count as knowledge of my "intrinsic nature". This construction of Russell's thought would account for the impact on Russell of James's classic paper "Does 'Consciousness' Exist?". James (quoted by Russell) writes,

To deny plumply that 'consciousness' exists seems so absurd on the face of it—for undeniably 'thoughts' do exist—that I fear that some readers will follow me no further. Let me then immediately explain that I mean only to deny that the word stands for an entity, but to insist most emphatically that it does stand for a function. There is, I mean, no aboriginal stuff or quality of being contrasted with that of which material objects are made, out of which our thoughts of them are made; but there is a function of experience which thoughts perform, and for the performance of which this quality of being is involved. That function is *knowing*.

My thesis is that if we start with the supposition that there is only one primal stuff or material in the world, a stuff of which everything is composed, and if we call that stuff 'pure experience', then knowing can easily be explained as a particular sort of relation towards one another into which portions of pure experience may enter. The relation itself is a part of pure experience; one of its 'terms' becomes the subject or bearer of the knowledge, the knower, the other becomes the object known.[1]

It is clear that James's "primal stuff", the material of which everything is composed, and which he calls "pure experience" is a collective reference to such stuffs as colour, sound, etc. Russell's "patch of red" would be a portion of this primal stuff.

At this stage Russell, then, is looking for a particular to be the subject term of a relation of acquaintance. He is intrigued by James's suggestion, but is highly sceptical about the idea that $S—A—O$ can be dissolved into a complex relation between clusters of portions of neutral stuff, especially where the objects of knowledge are *facts* or *truths* rather than perceptual *things*. Thus he notes that James "considers knowledge of things rather than knowledge of truths".[2]

Holding to the irreducibility of acquaintance and to its relational character, Russell insists that such stuffs as colour fall on the object side of the relation.

I cannot think that the difference between my seeing the patch of red, and the patch of red being there unseen, consists in the presence or absence of relations between the patch of red and other objects of the same kind. It seems to me possible to imagine a mind existing for only a fraction of a second, and ceasing to exist before having any other experience.[3]

If, then, Russell, like James, thinks of particulars as made of qualitative stuff (as this red patch consists of red), and therefore thinks of the subject for which he is looking as made of some qualitative stuff or other, the crucial fact is that, like James, he finds no unique mind stuff on the subject side, and finds most implausible the suggestion that the subject could be one portion of "pure experience" serving as the subject or bearer of the relation knowing to another portion serving as object. As before, we note that given the power of acquaintance to yield perfect and complete knowledge of the intrinsic nature of

[1] *Logic and Knowledge*, pp. 141–2.
[2] ibid., p. 159.
[3] ibid., p. 148.

particulars which we found in the case of sense data, we can argue that *since* we do not know the qualitative stuff of which the subject is made, we cannot be acquainted with it.

The philosophy of mind which Russell develops in "On the Nature of Acquaintance" and *The Problems of Philosophy* is, as he subsequently put it, a highly relational view. This is already clear from his account of acquaintance. The aptness of the characterization is reinforced by his analysis of belief. This analysis is so familiar, having played the role of dialectical foil for several generations of philosophers, that I shall make no independent attempt to assess its strengths and weaknesses. Rather I shall look at it through Russell's eyes in an attempt to understand why he came to reject it, and why he came to hold the radically different positions developed in *The Analysis of Mind* and, much later, in *An Inquiry into Meaning and Truth*.

We have seen that, according to Russell, we are acquainted with objects (both particulars and universals), and with facts. In the latter case we have intuitive knowledge, in a strong sense, of the fact. Thus in *The Problems of Philosophy* he writes, "in all cases where we know by acquaintance a complex fact consisting of certain terms in a certain relation, we say that the truth that these terms are so related has the first and absolute kind of self-evidence, and in these cases the judgment that the terms are so related *must* be true. Thus this sort of self-evidence is an absolute guarantee of truth." We must, however, be careful to distinguish between the *acquaintance* with the fact, and the *judgment* which accompanies it and is made true by the fact. According to Russell, the acquaintance with the fact has the form

S— acquainted with — fact.

The object of acquaintance, the fact, occurs as a single term, a "single complex whole".[1] Thus if the fact with which one is acquainted involves two juxtaposed colour patches, one is acquainted with the fact *this-being-next-to-that*

S—A— (this being next to that)

or

S—A— (that this is next to that).

The judgment, on the other hand, "analyses" the complex whole or fact, and does so by having the form

S—J— (this, (being) next to, that).

To put the contrast more perspicuously, in PMese form, acquaintance with the fact has the relational form

Acquainted with(S, (this being next to that))

whereas the judgment has the form

Judges (S; this, being next to, that).

Thus, using a common sense example, Russell writes:

Suppose we first perceive the sun shining, which is a complex fact, and thence proceed

---

[1] *The Problems of Philosophy*, pp. 213–14, 215.

to make the judgment "the sun is shining". In passing from the perception to the judgment, it is necessary to analyse the given complex fact: we have to separate out "the sun" and "shining" as constituents of the fact.[1]

I shall not pause to press the question as to how acquaintance with the fact that aRb can be epistemic, in the sense of *constituting* knowledge of a being R to b (as contrasted with making such knowledge possible), without the acquaintance taking account of the constituents and structure of the fact. To do so would take me into the problem of the role of the given or self-evident in knowledge—the idea that certain facts as non-conceptual entities are "self-evident" or "self-presenting" and constitute an epistemic base which justifies beliefs. What I wish to stress is not why Russell thinks it proper to construe acquaintance with fact as a dyadic relation, but why he doesn't construe judgment or, which is the same thing,[2] belief as a dyadic relation.

The answer, as is well known, is that belief can't have the form

    Believes (*S*, fact)

because false beliefs are beliefs, yet what they believe is not a fact. He considers, only to reject, the possibility that false belief might have the form

    Believes (*S*, falsehood)

on the ground that the idea that there are objective falsehoods "though not logically refutable, is a theory to be avoided if possible". Thus he rejects the analysis according to which the objects of beliefs are propositions (as objective entities), some of which have the property of being true or obtaining, and as such are facts, while the rest are false.[3]

We can avoid the need for objective falsehoods by construing belief as a many termed relation "in which the mind and the various objects concerned all occur severally". Thus, in spite of appearances to the contrary, Othello's belief that Desdemona loves Cassio does not have the dyadic form

    (1) Believes (Othello, that Desdemona loves Cassio)

but rather the four-termed form

    (2) Believes (Othello; Desdemona, loving, Cassio)

for "Desdemona and loving and Cassio must all be terms in the relation which exists when Othello believes that Desdemona loves Cassio".[4]

Russell tells us that in the fact expressed by (2) the relation of believing is the "cement" which holds together the "bricks": Othello, Desdemona, loving and

---

[1] ibid., p. 214.

[2] Russell, who is sensitive to the contrastive use of 'belief' and 'knowledge', uses 'judgment' as a generic term which covers both mere belief and, to use a contemporary turn of phrase, 'justified true belief', which is that form of knowledge which isn't *acquaintance* with fact.

[3] It is important to bear in mind that, throughout his career, Russell (1) insisted that extra-mental reality includes *facts* as well as *things*, and (2) refused to construe facts as a sub-category of propositions.

[4] *The Problems of Philosophy*, p. 196.

Cassio in that order. This is reflected by the fact that in (2) 'believes' is functioning as a *predicate*, whereas the other expressions, including 'loving' are functioning as *names*. Thus, although 'loves' is a relation word, and although in the fact that Desdemona loves Cassio, if there is such a fact, the relation loving would serve as "cement" and Desdemona and Cassio as "bricks", nevertheless *in the belief-fact*, loving is just one of the "bricks" and "not cement".

Before exploring the distinction between relations as bricks and relations as cement, which Russell subsequently believed to be the Achilles heel of the theory, let us note that Russell offers a simple account of true belief, according to which the fact expressed by

(3) Believes (*S*; *a*, *R*, *b*)

in which *believing* is the cement and *R* one of the bricks, is a true belief-fact just in case

(4) *R*(*a*, *b*)

expresses a fact in which *R* is the cement and *a* and *b* the bricks. Notice, again, that in (3) 'believes' is the predicate and '*R*' a name, whereas in (4) '*R*' is the predicate.

Just a few years after advancing the theory, Russell abandoned it. Looking back at the situation some forty years later, in *My Philosophical Development*, Russell tells us why:

I abandoned this theory, both because I ceased to believe in the "subject" and because I no longer thought that a relation can occur significantly as a term, except when a paraphrase is possible in which it does not so occur.[1]

This brief statement does, indeed, contain the heart of the matter. Two lines of thought combined to lead him away from his 1912–14 position. In the first place he came to abandon the idea that either acquaintance or belief is to be construed as a relation between an entity called the "subject" and the objects of acquaintance or belief. We have seen that by 1914 he had concluded that we are not acquainted with such an entity, though we are acquainted with the fact that there is one. By 1917 he had moved closer to neutral monism. He tells us in *Lectures on the Philosophy of Logical Atomism* that although "I do so far find very great difficulty in believing it . . . I think some of the arguments I used against neutral monism [in "On the Nature of Acquaintance"] are not valid."[2] He is clearly itching to use Ockham's razor, and, in the year following the publication of the lectures, wields it. He had now persuaded himself that not only is he not acquainted with the subject, he does not have intuitive knowledge that it exists. It has become one of those suppositious entities which "may exist, but we have

[1] *My Philosophical Development*, p. 182.
[2] p. 222. Originally published in the *Monist*. The lectures were reprinted in *Logic and Knowledge*; page references are to the latter.

no reason to suppose that they do".[1] It is an inferred entity which is to be replaced by a logical construction.

Along with the subject go mental acts. "I am at a loss to discover any actual phenomenon which could be called an 'act' and could be regarded as a constituent of a presentation. . . . It seems to me imperative, therefore, to construct a theory of presentation and belief which makes no use of the 'subject' or 'act' as a constituent of a presentation." Such a theory will necessarily be, he tells us, a "less relational theory of mental occurrences".[2] Notice, however, that since, when *x* is a logical construction, predications of *x* are to be exhibited as predications of the constituents of *x*, and since many of the latter predications will be relational, the effect of abandoning the subject is to make the resulting philosophy of mind "less relational" only in a Pickwickian sense. It means only that fewer mental phenomena have as form

$$xRy$$

where '*x*' denotes an entity akin to a subject and '*R*' stands for an unanalysable mental relation.

In "On Propositions"[3] and in *The Analysis of Mind*[4] to which it is a prelude, Russell lays great stress on images. "We have thus, so far, two sorts of mental 'stuff', namely (*a*) sensations, which are also physical, and (*b*) images, which are purely mental. Sensations do not 'mean', but images often do, through the medium of belief." He shortly asks "Are sensations and images, suitably related, a sufficient stuff out of which to compose beliefs?"[5] and answers in the affirmative both with respect to the "content" or "what is believed", and the believing of it.

This brings me to the point that although in "On Propositions" and *The Analysis of Mind* Russell rejects the

(Subject or act)-content-object

type of analysis, which he attributes to Meinong, according to which (1) all acts of belief are alike, (2) the content is a feature of the belief state by virtue of which it is correlated with its object, (3) the object is either a fact or a falsehood, he offers an analysis which has, superficially, a similar structure. He writes:

In Lecture I we criticized the analysis of a presentation into act, content and object. But our analysis of belief has three very similar elements, namely the believing, what is believed and the objective.[6]

He tells us that whereas in the case of presentations (e.g. sensation) no act is to

---

[1] ibid., p. 306.

[2] ibid., pp. 305, 306.

[3] An essay first published in 1919, and reprinted in *Logic and Knowledge*. Page references are to the latter.

[4] London 1921.

[5] "On Propositions", pp. 306, 307.

[6] *The Analysis of Mind*, p. 233.

be found, "the believing is an actual experienced feeling, not something postulated, like the act". As for the content of a belief, it may "consist of words only, or of images only, or of a mixture of the two, or of either or both together with one or more sensations". As for the objective, although he borrows Meinong's term, it has a quite un-Meinongian meaning. The objective of a belief is the fact that makes it true, if it is true, or that makes it false, if it is false.

Before following up this theme, a preliminary look is necessary at the second reason which contributed, according to Russell, to his abandonment of his original theory of belief, namely that "I no longer thought that a relation can occur significantly as a term, except when a paraphrase is possible in which it does not so occur". This seems to mean that all significant sentences in which a relation word ostensibly stands for a term can be paraphrased by a sentence in which it does not. Thus in

> Love is rarely reciprocated

'love' ostensibly stands for an entity which is asserted to have the property of being rarely reciprocated. The sentence in question can, however, be paraphrased as

> If one person loves another, rarely does the latter love the former

in which 'loves' functions as it does as in

> Plato loves Socrates

i.e. to characterize Plato and Socrates rather than to refer to something which is itself being characterized.

Consider, also,

> *precedes* is a transitive relation.

Can this not be "paraphrased" as

> $(x)\,(y)\,(z)\,(x \text{ precedes } y \cdot y \text{ precedes } z \rightarrow x \text{ precedes } z?)$

It is not clear that when such a paraphrase is available, it is identical in sense with the sentence paraphrased. And what exactly is to be said about such an apparent counter example to his thesis as

> Love is a relation?

Russell has two options: (1) he can rather implausibly deny that the sentence is significant; (2) he can deny that the grammatical subject of the sentence is the relation-word 'love'. What he actually does is to hesitate between the two. In effect he tells us that *if* the grammatical subject of the sentence is the relation-word 'love', then the sentence is meaningless as violating the theory of types. If, on the other hand, the sentence is significant, it is because it is a surrogate for

> 'Loves' is a relation-word.

Thus in "Logical Atomism",[1] he writes:

---

[1] First published in *Contemporary British Philosophy* (2 vols.), edited by J. H. Muirhead, London, 1924–5. It was reprinted in *Logic and Knowledge*, to which page references will be made.

The following words ... by their very nature, sin against the [doctrine of types]: attribute, relation, complex, fact, truth, falsehood ... to give a meaning to these words, we have to make a detour by way of words or symbols and the different ways in which they may mean. ... We can significantly say "attribute-words and relation-words have different uses" but we cannot significantly say "attributes are not relations". By our definition of types, since relations are relations, the form of words, 'attributes are relations' must be not false but meaningless ... nevertheless the statement "attribute-words are not relation-words" is significant and true.[1]

Much later, in *My Philosophical Development,* he tells us that when a sentence involving a non-relating use of a relation-word cannot be translated into a sentence in which it relates, then the sentence in question is nonsense.[2]

Russell must be thinking that

Attributes are not relations

that is,

(x) (x is an attribute $\rightarrow$ x is not a relation)

lacks significance, because he thinks that a substitution instance would be, for example,

Precedes is an attribute $\rightarrow$ precedes is not a relation

both the antecedent and consequent of which lack significance, if 'precedes' is a relation-word. On the other hand

'precedes' is an attribute-word $\rightarrow$ 'precedes' is not a relation-word

is both significant and true. Since Russell does not spell this out, however, it is not clear that this is a fair representation of his reasoning. Notice that the above could *not* be his reasoning if, when he says, as he does, that "relations are relations", he would allow that this is significant in a way in which 'attributes are not relations' is not. There is no reason, however, to believe that he would. It can have exactly the same status, for he needs it only as the surrogate for 'relation-words are relation-words', a forceful reminder that relation-words are many-placed, so that if, in either

precedes is an attribute

or

precedes is a relation

'precedes' is a relation-word, the context is nonsense as an attempt to fit together in a sentence

(—) precedes (—)

with

(—) is an attribute

or

(—) is a relation.

Now if our interpretation of Russell is correct, he is claiming that a significant

[1] ibid., p. 334.
[2] *My Philosophical Development*, p. 160.

sentence doesn't contain a dyadic relation-word '*R*', unless the word is functioning in that sentence as does the '*R*' in

$R(a, b)$.

This means that in the sentence

Believes (S; a, R, b)

the relation-word '*R*' either does not occur, or the sentence is not significant. This poses a dilemma for Russell's early theory of belief. For if the relation-word '*R*' does not occur, then S's belief would seem to have nothing to do with the relation R, whereas if the relation-word '*R*' does occur, then the belief sentence itself is nonsense.

One might attempt to escape through the horns by arguing that, strictly speaking, the belief has the form

Believes (S; a, R-hood, b)

and that the belief attributed to S has to do with the relation R, because the belief sentence contains the word '*R*-hood'. But Russell now insists that the only way in which a sentence can have to do with the relation R, is by containing the relation word '*R*' *functioning as a relation-word*, and *this* '*R*-hood' cannot do *unless the sentence containing it can be paraphrased in terms of* '*R*' *functioning as a relation-word*. This stops the escape through the horns.

The first sign of Russell's dissatisfaction with his 1912–14 theory is found in *Lectures on the Philosophy of Logical Atomism*. He argues, as before, that belief is not to be construed as a 2-term relation between a subject and an entity which, in the case of a true belief, is a fact, and, in the case of false belief, an objective falsehood. And he concludes, as before, that "the belief does not really contain a proposition as a constituent, but only contains the constituents of the proposition as constituents". But after this sketch of his 1912–14 theory, he continues:

> I want to try to get an account of the way that a belief is made up. That is not an easy question at all. You cannot make what I should like to call a map-in-space of a belief. . . . The point is in connection with there being two verbs in the judgment; and with the fact that both verbs have to occur as verbs, *because if a thing is a verb it cannot occur otherwise than as a verb.*[1]

Using his earlier example of Othello's false belief that Desdemona loves Cassio, he remarks that

you have this odd state of affairs that the verb 'loves' occurs in that proposition and seems

[1] pp. 221–5; my italics. It should be noted that Russell has previously announced his intention to use the word 'verb' both for linguistic items (e.g. 'love') and for the extra-linguistic item (e.g. love) for which they stand: " . . . it is not only the proposition that has the two verbs, but also the fact which is expressed by the proposition has two constituents corresponding to verbs. I shall call these constituents verbs for the sake of shortness, as it is very difficult to find any word to describe all those objects which are denoted by verbs" (p. 217).

to occur as relating Desdemona to Cassio, whereas, in fact, it does not do so, but yet it does occur as a verb, it does occur in the sort of way that a verb should do.

In other words (1) the verb 'loves' occurs; (2) it occurs in the way in which it occurs when the sentence in which it occurs makes a commitment to somebody loving somebody. Yet in spite of the fact that Desdemona doesn't love Cassio, the belief sentence is true. He continues:

I mean that when *A* believes that *B* loves *C*, you have to put a verb in the place where 'loves' occurs. You cannot put a substantive in its place. Therefore it is clear that the subordinate verb . . . is functioning as a verb, and seems to be relating to terms, but as a matter of fact does not, when the judgement happens to be false. This is what constitutes the puzzle about the nature of belief.

Russell reminds us of the temptation to construe false belief as a relation between a subject and an objective falsehood, an objective state of affairs which does not exist. But, like Odysseus, he does not heed the siren's song:

Every theory of error sooner or later wrecks itself by assuming the existence of the nonexistent. As when I say "Desdemona loves Cassio", it seems as if you have a nonexistent love between Desdemona and Cassio. But that is just as wrong as a nonexistent unicorn.

After crediting Wittgenstein for the discovery that beliefs have a radically different form from the sort of facts he had previously been discussing, Russell stresses once again "the impossibility of treating the proposition believed as an independent entity, entering as a unit into the occurrence of the belief", and "the impossibility of putting the subordinate verb on a level with its terms as an object term in the belief".[1]

Russell does not come up with an answer to his "puzzle" in *Lectures on the Philosophy of Logical Atomism*. He does not yet accept neutral monism, although he has abandoned the "pin-point ego" or "metaphysical subject" in favour of a logical construction out of experiences. Indeed, he argues that if there are irreducible facts of the two verb kind, "that . . . may make neutral monism rather difficult". He points out, on the other hand, that "there is the theory that one calls behaviourism", which "would altogether dispense with these facts containing two verbs, and would therefore dispose of that argument against neutral monism". According to Russell neutral monism "does not distinguish between a particular and experiencing that particular", and since he is still strongly inclined to think that such a distinction is necessary to account for "emphatic particulars", he remains unconvinced. He does, however, permit himself to express the hope

---

[1] It is worth pausing to note that Russell expresses the conviction that "perception, as opposed to belief, does go straight to the fact and not through the proposition" (p. 228). See above, p. 69.

that "in the course of time" he will find out whether "neutral monism is true, or is not".[1]

At this stage, then, Russell has abandoned his old theory on the ground that it requires the "loves" of the subordinate clause to be a singular term and not a verb. Yet he still insists that belief must be a relation between a mind, which he now construes as a logical construction out of experiences, and *not* a proposition, but rather the constituents of the proposition. He is clearly still thinking of the constituents of the proposition not as symbols, but as things symbolized. But how can the relation *love* be a term of the belief relation without occurring as a substantive rather than a verb? And even if it occurs as a verb, how can it do so without binding Desdemona and Cassio into a non-existent complex?

Russell sees the need for further thought about the nature of relations. Looking back from the vantage point of 1924, by which time he had constructed a new theory, he writes: "My own views on the subject of relations in the past were less clear than I thought them to be, . . . the subject of relations is difficult, and I am far from claiming now to be clear about it." To this he adds, however, "I think that certain points are clear to me." I have already touched on those features of his views which he relates to his theory of types, and which culminate in the thesis that "attributes and relations differ from substances by the fact that they suggest a structure, and that there can be no significant symbol which symbolizes them in isolation. All propositions", he continues, "in which an attribute or a relation *seems* to be the subject are only significant if they can be brought into a form in which the attribute is attributed or the relation relates . . . the proper symbol for 'yellow' is not the single word 'yellow', but . . . '*x* is yellow' . . . similarly the relation *precedes* must not be represented by this one word, but by the symbol '*x* precedes *y*'."[2]

I have already pointed out that in his new theory Russell accepts, but reinterprets, Meinong's distinction between act, content and object. For our present purposes, it is the latter two which are more important.[3] Roughly, the content of a belief is a propositional occurrence, an event which *means* that Desdemona loves Cassio, and is true in case she does and false in case she doesn't. This propositional token is a complex of symbols: a symbol for Desdemona, a symbol for Cassio and a symbol for the relation loves.

How does this help? In the first place, the constituents of the propositional event are symbols. Thus, the belief statement asserts of Othello that he is related to a token of the proposition "Desdemona loves Cassio" and that he is so by being related to tokens of the symbols 'Desdemona' 'loves' and 'Cassio'. We

---

[1] ibid., p. 280.

[2] ibid., pp. 333, 337–8.

[3] The distinction between the "act" and the "content" is motivated by the widely shared idea that the same content can be believed, entertained, questioned etc., and, perhaps, desired, etc. Russell, however, notes that a case can be made (with Spinoza) for the idea that the supposed differences in act simply reflect differences in content.

ascribe to Othello a propositional state in which a certain symbol is functioning as a verb-symbol. Thus we do justice to the idea that a verb-symbol must always function as a verb-symbol. *We*, of course, who do the ascribing, do not *use* the verb-symbol 'loves', but rather use its name. Our ascription of belief has the form

  Believes (Othello, 'Desdemona loves Cassio')

or, in finer grain, something *like*

  Believes (Othello, 'Desdemona', 'loves', 'Cassio').

We shall see in a moment that the latter won't do as it stands, and that the problem of what to replace it by is no easy one. But before following through with the propositional event, what about the relation of the propositional event to the something in the world which makes it true or false? Here also we must preserve the principle that relations occur only as relating. This time, however, we are concerned with the relations themselves and not with relation words. One way of preserving the principle is to claim that what makes the propositional event false is the objective falsehood that Desdemona loves Cassio. We would do so, however, only at the expense of having love relate Desdemona to Cassio in a non-existent love of Desdemona for Cassio.

A more attractive alternative is to say that what makes the propositional event false is the fact, albeit a negative one, that Desdemona does not love Cassio. This, too, preserves the principle, for, although in this formulation, the word 'not' has intruded between 'Desdemona' and 'Cassio', put more perspicuously, the fact has the form

  The fact that not-(Desdemona loves Cassio).

Yet many philosophers find negative facts as objectionable as objective falsehoods. And, after all, if love occurs as relating, why does it not, here also, find Desdemona and Cassio in a non-existent love? The answer would seem to be that the idea of a relation occurring *as relating* includes the case of its occurring *as not relating* as when love does not relate Desdemona to Cassio. The proper contrast to "occurring as relating" is not the latter, but rather "occurring as a term".

But although the situation seems to be promising with respect to *each part* of the principle that relations occur only as relating, a serious difficulty comes to light when we attempt to put the two parts, i.e.

  1. Relation-words occur only as relating (i.e. as "verbs")
  2. Relations occur only as relating

together. The difficulty stands out most clearly if we try the following account of the truth of Othello's belief:

The belief ascribed to Othello by

  (B) Believes (Othello; 'Desdemona', 'love', 'Cassio')

is true just in case there exists the fact

  (F) Loves (Desdemona, Cassio).

For surely we have to say

'Desdemona' is the symbol for Desdemona

'Cassio' is the symbol for Cassio

and, which is the rub,

(M) 'Love' is the symbol for love.

In (F) *love* occurs as relating, it relates Desdemona to Cassio. But surely in (M) *love* occurs as the objective term of a symbolizing relationship. Since the *love* of (F) must be identical with the *love* of (M), the principle that relations occur only as relating is violated. What to do?

Russell at this time took a new look at Bradley's puzzle about relations. Bradley had, in effect, argued that in order for

(1) *Rab*

to be true, where '*a*' stands for *a*, '*b*' for *b* and '*R*' for *R*, the items the symbols stand for, namely *a*, *b*, and *R*, must be related. The mere collection *a*, *b*, *R* is not a fact, and if '*Rab*' stood for the collection, it would be a collection of expressions and not a statement. But if *a*, *b*, and *R* are related, there is a fact-making relation R' which relates them. And if (1) is to be true, and not a mere list of symbols, it must affirm that this relation obtains. To do so it must refer to this relation. Since it does not do so explicitly, it must do so implicitly. When made explicit, therefore, (1) becomes

(2) R' *Rab*

where 'R'' stands for R', the other symbols having meaning as before. Once again the items the symbols stand for must be related. The mere collection *a*, *b*, *R*, R' is not a fact, and if '$R'Rab$' stood for the collection, it would be a collection of expressions and not a statement. But if *a*, *b*, *R*, R' are related, there is a fact-making relation R'' which relates them, and if (2) is to be true, and not a mere list of symbols, it must affirm that this relation obtains. To do so it must refer to this relation. Since it does not do so explicitly it must do so implicitly. When made explicit, therefore, (2) becomes

(3) $R''R'ab$

. . .

In *Philosophy*, Russell replies to Bradley's argument, which he seems to have construed along the above lines, although he does not spell it out in detail,[1] as follows:

Bradley has been misled, unconsciously, by . . . the fact that the *word* for a relation is as substantial as the *words* for its terms. Suppose *A* and *B* are two events and *A* precedes *B*. In the proposition "*A* precedes *B*" the word 'precedes' is just as substantial as the word '*A*' and '*B*'. The relation of the *two* events *A* and *B* is represented in language by the time or space order of the *three* words '*A*' 'precedes' and '*B*'. But this order . . . *is an actual relation, not a word for a relation*. The first step in Bradley's regress does have to be taken in giving verbal expression to a relation, for the word for a relation does have to be related to the

---

[1] Bradley, of course, does not highlight the semantical aspect of the regress which is essential to Russell's reply.

words for its terms. But this is a linguistic, not a metaphysical, fact and the regress does not have to go any further.[1]

In other words, Russell grants, in this passage, that '*AB*' would be a mere collection of names without the word 'precedes', but points out that '*A* precedes *B*' is not a mere collection, but rather a relational structure, and that it means what it does, not simply because it contains these three words, but because it contains them *in a certain order*. Thus, the fact that an '*A*', a 'precedes' and a '*B*' occur in that order says that *A* and *B* stand in the relation *preceding*.

Russell does, indeed, stop the regress—but, unfortunately at a stage in which it causes him almost as much trouble as if he had let it continue. For Russell is telling us that the proposition

(P) *A* precedes *B*

which has *three* words, says that

(F) *A, B* exemplify *preceding*

—a fact in the expression of which *four* words occur, and in which *the relation-word occurring as a relation-word* is 'exemplify' and *not* 'precedes'. Three words standing *in a triadic relation* say what is also said by the use of four words in a four-term relation. It is obvious that the regress will continue unless we take the following drastic step. We argue that the *only way* in which the fact that *A, B* exemplify *preceding* can be expressed, is by placing the words for *A, B* and precedence in a *triadic* relation. This would entail that '*A, B* exemplify *preceding*' is a *triadic* fact in which the terms are an '*A*' and a '*B*' on the one hand and a 'precedence' on the other. The relation would clearly have to be something like *having an 'exemplify' between them*. It would follow that the job of the word 'exemplify' is a peculiar one. It would have the auxiliary job of making it possible for certain substantives to have an 'exemplify' related to them in a certain way. Above all, the verb 'exemplify' is otiose, since what can be done with it in our example can also be done without it by placing the substantives in a certain triadic relationship to each other without the use of an auxiliary expression. When the auxiliary expression is used, the sentence '*A, B* exemplify *preceding*' expresses a three-termed fact by means of a symbolic fact which only ostensibly has four terms. When the auxiliary expression is not used, as in '*preceding (A, B)*', we have a sentence which is a symbolic fact containing three terms and which expresses the structure of a three-termed fact. Notice that the fact of which the structure is expressed is an *exemplification* fact in the sense that it is a fact appropriately expressed by a sentence containing the predicate 'exemplify', though it contains no term corresponding to this word.

Notice also that although we can say that 'exemplify' stands for exemplification, the moment we start taking it to stand for a *constituent* of the fact that *A, B* exemplify *preceding*, we abandon our gain and are back in Bradley's clutches.

[1] *Philosophy*, New York 1927, p. 253; my italics. Published in England under the title *Outline of Philosophy*. Page references are to the American edition.

Now to make Russell's move *when he makes it*, in the above passage, amounts to treating ordinary relation words as substantives, and 'exemplify' or 'stand in' as the only *verb* which really functions as a verb. Thus, surface grammar aside,

> *A* precedes *B*

has been reparsed as

> Preceding (*A, B*)

and the verb 'stand in' of

> *A* and *B* stand in preceding

as an "otiose" auxiliary symbol which makes the proposition in which it occurs a three-termed propositional fact, which, if true, expresses a three-term exemplification or *standing in* fact.

That I am not misinterpreting the position to which Russell, to some extent unwittingly, commits himself, is confirmed by the following passage from *The Analysis of Matter*. He writes:

Words which symbolize relations are themselves just as substantial as other words. If we say "Caesar loves Brutus" the word 'love', considered as a physical event, is of exactly the same kind as the words 'Caesar' and 'Brutus', but is supposed to mean something of a totally different kind. . . . *There is in the above sentence a relation which is symbolized by a relation, not by a word; this is the three-term relation of love to Caesar and Brutus. This is symbolized by the order of the words—i.e. by a three-term relation.*[1]

Notice that the three-term relation of love to Caesar and Brutus is the relation of *standing in* or *exemplification* of the above analysis.

Now, even if we were to grant that there is such a thing as a relation (or "tie") which relates love to Caesar and Brutus, and which can only be expressed by placing 'Caesar', 'Brutus' and 'love' in a triadic relation, with or without the use of an auxiliary symbol, this would not help Russell explain the manner in which *ordinary* relation words like 'love' and 'precedes' have meaning. For, as Russell himself notes, "in order to mention this relation [i.e. the relation of *standing in*] it is necessary to treat 'love' grammatically as a substantive, which tends to confuse the distinction between a substantive and a relation." Since Russell has other fish to fry in *The Analysis of Matter*, he does not pursue the topic other than to claim, rather optimistically, that "it is not very difficult to avoid the false suggestions due to this peculiarity of language, when once the danger of them has been pointed out".

It is possible, however, to interpret Russell as holding *both* that there is a *tie* in the world between love, Caesar and Brutus, which is expressed by a *triadic* relation between the corresponding words, *and* that there is a *relation* in the world between Caesar and Brutus which is expressed by placing the words 'Caesar' and 'Brutus' in a *dyadic* relation. In other words Russell might be

---

[1] *The Analysis of Matter*, London 1927, p. 243. Final italics mine.

holding that the moves which were made above with 'exemplify' can *also* be made with respect to 'precedes'. He does, indeed, consider the possibility of making this move with respect to ordinary relation-words. The puzzle comes in with the "also". For the spirit of the move, *at the level at which Russell makes it in his reply to Bradley*, is that the "meaning" of 'stand in' or 'exemplify' consists in its being an auxiliary symbol which enables a relation of three names to express a tie between three objects (two particulars, and the abstract object *love*). Yet to make the same move *at the level of ordinary relation-words* is to argue that the latter, e.g. 'precedes', do not denote objects, e.g. the object *preceding*, but *themselves* have only the kind of "meaning" which consists in being auxiliary symbols which enable a relation of names to express a relation between objects. To make the move at the 'exemplify' level, and in the way in which Russell makes it, implies that 'precedes' denotes an object in the world. To make the move at the 'precedes' level is to imply that it does not. Thus to make the move at *both* levels is to imply that 'precedes' does and does not denote an object in the world, and, hence, to be trapped in a paradox. It is only because Russell was not clearer about his options and their implications that it would be inaccurate to say that he remained trapped in this paradox throughout his subsequent career.

One way of grasping Russell's predicament is by contrasting his analysis with one which, though structurally quite similar, avoids the above inconsistency. Thus, if one thinks of abstract singular terms as metalinguistic distributive singular terms thus

Preceding = the 'precedes'

where the latter singular term functions much as 'the lion' as in 'the lion is tawny', or 'a prophet' as in 'a prophet is not without honour',[1] and if one interprets 'exemplify' as the converse of 'is true of', and the thesis that relating relation-words (i.e. predicative relation words) are auxiliary symbols would apply to exemplification statements as the claim that

One says that $\left\{\begin{array}{l} a, b \text{ exemplify precedence} \\ \text{the 'precedes' is true of } a, b \end{array}\right\}$ by placing
$\left\{\begin{array}{l} \text{an '}a\text{' and a '}b\text{' and a 'precedence'} \\ \text{an '}a\text{' and a '}b\text{' and a 'the 'precedes' '} \end{array}\right\}$ in a triadic structure,
with or without the use of the auxiliary symbol
$\left\{\begin{array}{l} \text{'exemplify'} \\ \text{'is true of'} \end{array}\right\}$.

With: $\left\{\begin{array}{l} a, b \text{ exemplify precedence} \\ \text{the 'precedes' is true of } a, b \end{array}\right.$ Without: $\left\{\begin{array}{l} \text{precedence } (a, b) \\ [\text{the 'precedes'}] \, (a, b) \end{array}\right.$

[1] The point of the examples is to make more intuitive the idea that there might be singular terms, sentences involving which are equivalent to universally quantified sentences, and hence the idea that statements about preceding might be statements about all 'precedes' s.

Since

The 'precedes' is true of *a, b*,

and hence

Preceding is exemplified by *a, b*

is logically equivalent to

Precedes (*a, b*)

[**NB**; *not* 'preceding (*a, b*)'], one can now apply the same thesis about relating relation-words to this level, thus:

> One says that precedes (*a, b*) by placing an '*a*' and a '*b*' in a conventionally selected dyadic structure, with or without the use of the auxiliary symbol 'precedes'.

> With: Precedes (*a, b*)   Without: a_b

This structuring of the situation would explicate the manner in which the nominalized relation-word 'preceding' is connected with the relating (predicative) relation word 'precedes', and would explain why some sentences involving nominalized relation-words can be significant even though they are not logically equivalent to sentences involving a corresponding predicative relation-word. An example would be 'preceding is a relation' which becomes

The 'precedes' is a relation word.

It would also make clear that the relation between 'preceding (*a, b*)' and 'precedes (*a, b*)' is logical equivalence and not synonymy.

That Russell considered the possibility of treating not only such words as 'exemplify' and 'stand in', which have traditionally been said to stand for ontological ties, but also ordinary predicative relation-words (e.g. 'precedes'), as auxiliary symbols is clear from his new theory of the truth of belief, first formulated in the essay "On Propositions" and elaborated in *The Analysis of Mind*. The most explicit statement is to be found in *Philosophy*, almost immediately after he has resolved Bradley's paradox by making the above move at the level of ontological ties. Thus in the chapter which follows his discussion of Bradley, he writes

When we say "lightning precedes thunder", the word 'precedes' has quite a different relation to what it means to that which the word 'lightning' and 'thunder' have to what they respectively mean. Wittgenstein[1] says that what really happens is that one establishes a relation between the word 'lightning' and the word 'thunder', namely the relation of having the word 'precedes' between them.[2]

Russell continues by saying that this view "may be quite correct"—a surprisingly lukewarm endorsement of the view which is exactly what he

---

[1] Russell refers to the *Tractatus* and presumably has in mind 3.1432.
[2] *Philosophy*, p. 265.

needs—and by pointing out that "it is sufficiently odd to make it not surprising that people have thought the word 'precedes' means a relation in the same sense in which 'lightning' means a kind of event". It is clear that Russell hasn't fully grasped the significance of Wittgenstein's insight. Thus, it is not surprising that he both draws upon it, and makes statements which are incompatible with it, saying in one breath that relation-words are auxiliary symbols, and in the next that relation-words denote relations.

Wittgenstein's point, of course, was that the *only* way in which a relational fact involving *n* terms can be expressed is by placing *n* substantives in a counterpart *n*-adic relation. Russell seems to think that it is enough to say that in some cases an *n*-adic fact can be expressed by an *n*-adic relation between substantives, whereas in other cases, *n*-adic facts are expressed by an $(n + 1)$-adic relation between *n* substantives and one verb. Thus he writes

In the phrase '*A* is to the left of *B*', even if we treat 'is-to-the-left-of' as one word, we have a fact consisting of *three* terms with a *triadic* relation, not two terms with a dyadic relation. The linguistic symbol for a relation is not itself a relation, but a term as solid as the other words of the sentence. Language might have been so constructed that this should not have been always the case: a few especially important relations might have been symbolized by relations between words. For instance '*AB*' might have meant '*A* is to the left of *B*'. ... But the practical possibilities of this method ... are obviously very limited. ... Hence the linguistic statement of the fact is a more complex fact than that which it asserts.[1]

But, of course, though Russell is right about the "practical possibilities" of a method of symbolizing relations which dispenses with auxiliary symbols, he misses Wittgenstein's point that *even when auxiliary symbols are used*, dyadic relations between things are expressed by *dyadic* relations between the expressions which designate them. It is because he has failed to see this, that he was led to make his reply to Bradley at the level of the tie between Caesar and Brutus on the one hand and *love* on the other, which involves construing ordinary relation words as denoting entities in the world.

With these distinctions and strategies under our belt, let us return to the problem of belief. We are asking how we can give the truth conditions for the belief ascribed to Othello by

(B) Believes (Othello, 'Desdemona', 'loves', 'Cassio').

The initial answer was that the belief is true just in case

(F) Desdemona loves Cassio.

The problem arose, however, that this is correct only if

(M) 'Loves' symbolizes *loves*,

which seems to require that the 'loves' on the right is a substantive expression which stands for a term in a symbolizing relationship. How can the relating relation of (F) be identical with a term of (M)?

---

[1] "On Propositions", p. 316.

What light has been thrown on this puzzle by the above discussion of the Bradley paradox? The answer is that even in the absence of a general theory of meaning, we are now in a position to by-pass the puzzles raised by (M), for we can now construe (B) as having the form

Believes (Othello: ['Desdemona' R 'loves' 'Cassio'])

where this says that the propositional event occurring in Othello consists of a symbol for Desdemona and a symbol for Cassio with a 'loves' between these two symbols. The word 'loves' no longer appears as a constituent of the propositional event, hence we no longer have to specify that 'loves' symbolizes *loves*, but only that

A propositional event consisting of a 'Desdemona' and a 'Cassio' with a 'loves' between them signifies that Desdemona loves Cassio.

And on the right hand side of *this*, 'loves' occurs as a *verb*. Our specific problem about relation words occurring only as relating has disappeared.[1]

But although this strategy is available for the analysis of (B), it should not surprise us to find that Russell fails to avail himself of it. Russell limits his use of this strategy to what he calls "image-beliefs". The concept is a confused one, but it is easy to understand why Russell is attracted by it. Russell asks us to consider a memory belief in which the propositional content involves an image of a certain window to the left of a certain fire. This is a complex image "which we may analyse, for our purposes, into (*a*) the image of the window, (*b*) the image of the fire, (*c*) the relation that (*a*) is to the left of (*b*)".[2] In other words, "for our purposes" the image of [the window to the left of the fire] consists of a constituent image of the window which is to the left of a constituent image of the fire. If we could pretend that the image *qua* image was a propositional event, and the constituent images his referring expressions, then the situation would be

Russell has an image of the window to the left of an image of the fire

which would ascribe to Russell a true propositional event just in case

The window was to the left of the fire.

The relation of the images would correctly represent the relation of the objects.

Now I take it as obvious that images as such are not propositions and therefore a symbol to refer to an object is not, even in the case of images, a matter of similarity. I also take it to be obvious that a dyadic relation between symbols which represents a dyadic relation between objects need not be the *same* relation as the relation it represents, and that even if it were the same, it would be a contingent fact, which is in some sense a matter of "convention", that it

---

[1] That the solution covertly challenges a parallel principle to the effect that propositions occur only as propositions, will be noticed by the student of the *Tractatus*. I shall return to this point later on.

[2] "On Propositions", p. 316.

was so. Russell, himself, distinguishes between the image as image, and the frame of mind by virtue of which the image serves as an instrument of belief.

Now it is clear that if this frame of mind is construed as a belief that the window and the fire were like *this*, we would have abandoned the idea that the image *itself* is functioning as the belief proposition. The belief would now be a propositional state which refers (*a*) to the window and to the fire, and (*b*) to the image of the window and to the image of the fire, and affirms the former to be related as, in a certain respect, are the latter. The simplicity of the analysis would have vanished, as would the idea that it is the images being related which says that the objects are related. Rather it would now be as items to which the belief refers, that the images would contribute to this assertion.

If, on the other hand, the image is the whole content of the proposition, then the fact that the image of the fire is to the left of the image of the window *need not* have meant that the window was to the left of the fire. The fact that it means "to the left of" is simply a special case of the general principle that a dyadic relation of objects is expressed by a dyadic relation of terms. The relation *may* be the same, there may be a *point* to its being the same, but even if it is not the same, the proposition means what it does as directly as if it were. Thus Russell's image proposition *could* mean that the window was *to the right of the fire*. This might involve a loss in convenience and learnability, but the proposition would mean what it meant as directly as if it meant "to the left of".

I stress this point, because, as we shall see, Russell held at this time that image-propositions which empirically resemble the states of affairs which would make them true are the primary bearers of reference and truth. Basic verbal propositions are only indirectly meaningful and true. Thus in "On Propositions" he writes: " '*A* is to the left of *B*' means the image-proposition, and is true when this is true, and false when it is false."[1]

Russell points out that no image as such can be negative. He concludes that image-propositions are always positive. Now, of course, if one means by 'image-proposition', a proposition consisting entirely of images, this would be, of course, a non sequitur. A proposition consisting of images could contain an image, e.g. a black dot, by virtue of which it functioned as the contradictory of the same image complex without the dot. What Russell has in mind, of course, is that notness is not a perceptible quality or relation. It would be nonsense to suppose that images which are negative could mean that certain objects were negative, as images which are juxtaposed can mean that certain objects are juxtaposed. It is clear, therefore, that Russell means by an image-proposition a proposition which not only consists entirely of images, but is such that every semantically relevant feature of the images is a feature by virtue of which they (*a*) represent objects, e.g. the window and the fire, (*b*) represent

---

[1] "On Propositions", p. 319.

these objects as of such and such a quality in standing in such and such empirical relations.[1]

If all image-propositions are positive, word-propositions, on the other hand, are, Russell tells us, "of two kinds, one verified by a positive objective, the other by a negative objective".[2] He ties the distinction between positive and negative word propositions to the distinction between positive and negative facts. He thus reaffirms his position that there are negative facts. Now, in one sense this is obviously true. Not only are there negative facts, but they are indispensable. The issue, however, as Wittgenstein saw, is not "are there negative facts?" but "are there negative *basic* facts about objects?" Wittgenstein argued that basic statements are true because they correctly picture objects; thus '*aRb*' pictures *a* and *b*, because '*a*' being in a certain dyadic relation to '*b*' (they have an '*R*' between them) represents correctly how *a* and *b* stand to each other. Now logical words "do not represent"[3] and do not enter into the picturing relationship. No proposition of the form 'not-(*aRb*)' is true by virtue of picturing *a* and *b*. By virtue of what, then, is 'not-(*aRb*)' true? Wittgenstein failed, in the *Tractatus*, to see that he is committed to the view that 'not-(*aRb*)' is true because some (positive) atomic proposition incompatible with '*aRb*', thus '*aR'b*', does correctly represent *a* and *b*. Thus, '*a* does not precede *b*' is true because '*a* succeeds *b*' is true.

A standard objection to this move is that the incompatibility of *preceding* and *succeeding* would itself be a negative fact, and an "objective" one at that. "If one is going to allow objective negative facts about relations, why not allow basic negative facts? Why not say that what makes 'not-(*aRb*)' true is the fact that not-(*aRb*)?" The answer involves taking seriously the idea that "basic proposition" is not only a *logical* idea, but an *epistemic* one. Basic propositions are what the world makes true or false. Thus we must not confuse the irreducibility of negative facts with the basic-ness of negative facts. And we must not confuse the idea that negative facts are as objective as positive facts, with the idea that they are as basically true of objects as are positive facts.

Now, if basic propositions are true because they correctly picture objects, no true basic proposition *can* be negative. And if 'not-(*aRb*)' cannot be true by virtue of picturing a and b, its truth, if it is true, *must* be grounded in the truth of an incompatible positive proposition. We must say not just that no true basic propositions are negative, but that no basic propositions *tout court* are

---

[1] It is interesting to note that instead of making this purely logical point about the absence of negation from image-propositions, Russell ties it to a psychological point which reveals the fundamental unclarity of his concept of an image proposition. "There is no 'not' in an image proposition; the not belongs to the feeling, not to the content of the proposition" (p. 317). The "belief feeling" would seem to be the feeling that *this* is *not* how things stood with the window and the fire.

[2] "On Propositions", p. 317.

[3] *Tractatus* 4.0312.

negative. Russell accepts this, for his basic propositions are image-propositions, and none of these is negative. What, then, does he think it could mean to say that the world contains negative facts?

Now, according to the above analysis, the negative fact by virtue of which the truth of 'not-(aRb)' is grounded in the truth of '$aR'b$' is the negative conceptual fact about the propositional forms '$---R---$' and '$---R'---$' that they cannot both be true when the blanks are filled by 'a' and 'b' in the same order. In the *Tractatus* Wittgenstein argues that no atomic proposition can be *logically* incompatible with another atomic proposition. If this means that no atomic proposition can have the form 'not-p' it is a direct consequence of the Tractarian theory of propositions. If, on the other hand, it means that every combination of atomic propositions can be true, it is incompatible with the Tractarian theory of the hook-up of propositions with objects.

Wittgenstein disguised the situation by arguing that "reality is the obtaining and non-obtaining of atomic states of affairs. (The obtaining of states of affairs we also call a positive, their non-obtaining a negative fact.)"[1] By recognizing that all atomic states of affairs are positive, this thesis implies that the reason why 'aRb' is false is because the state of affairs it expresses does not obtain. But if this is to be equivalent to the idea that 'aRb' *mispictures* a and b, it must entail the obtaining of a state of affairs which is mispictured by 'aRb'. As he came to see,[2] his argument requires that basic predicates come in families of competing determinates. The theme of non-contradictory incompatibility is one side of the coin; the theme that if one member of the family is not true of certain objects another member must be, is the other. Familyhood is a necessary feature of discourse about objects, and the fact that a certain conceptual framework contains the families it does is a fact about the framework. But although incompatibilities are *objective* facts, they are not facts about *objects*, which, for Wittgenstein, are always particulars.

Now suppose we grant that for it to be a fact that not-(aRb) is simply for the proposition 'not-(aRb)' to be true, thus dispensing with "objective" negative facts, i.e. negative facts as nonlinguistic entities. Suppose we say that, in general, what makes molecular propositions true or false is the truth or falsity of positive atomic propositions. What, then, of the latter? What makes them true? *Prima facie*, there are two alternatives:

(1) objects
(2) atomic facts.

If we opt for the former, and say, for example, that it is a and b which make 'aRb' true, the objection is invariably raised that while a and b can be responsible for the *referential* success of 'aRb', they cannot be responsible for its success in characterizing them as standing in the relation R. Why not? Well, the objector

---

[1] *Tractatus* 2.06.
[2] "Logical Form", *Proceedings of the Aristotelian Society* (1928).

continues, *a* and *b* *merely as a* and *b* are logically neutral with respect to any of the relations in which *a* and *b* might stand. Hence it must be something other than *a* and *b* *merely as a* and *b* which is responsible for the characterizing success of '*aRb*'. Now if he were to continue by arguing that this something other than *a* and *b* *merely as a* and *b* must be a third entity, he would have fallen into Bradley's trap and we could ignore him. But suppose he agrees that *a* and *b* (as contrasted with *a* and *b* *and some tertium quid*) are indeed responsible for this success, but insists that it is not *a* and *b* *merely as a* and *b*, but *a* and *b* *as configured* which is so responsible. Do not *a* and *b* *as configured* constitute a fact?

But must we choose between

> *a* and *b* *merely as a* and *b* make '*aRb*' true

and

> The fact that *aRb* makes '*aRb*' true?

Obviously we don't have to choose between

> Mrs. O'Leary's cow *merely as* Mrs. O'Leary's cow caused the Chicago fire

and

> Certain facts about Mrs. O'Leary's cow caused the Chicago fire.

Of course certain facts about Mrs. O'Leary's cow *explain* the fact that the fire took place. But it was the cow, by kicking over the bucket, that brought the fire about. But it will be said, aren't

> The cow, by kicking over the bucket . . .

and

> The fact that the cow kicked over the bucket . . .

only superficially different? Differences which for some purposes are superficial, can be crucial for others. For ontology, the difference is crucial.

As we press the question "What makes a certain kind of proposition true?" in the direction of basic propositions, we find ourselves saying that such and such a proposition is true if and only if such and such more basic propositions are true. And this can be paraphrased as 'such and such is a fact if and only if such and such are the more basic facts'. But when we reach the level of basic statements, an account of this kind is no longer available. Consider the parallel questions:

> What makes '(Tom and Dick) or (Jack and Harry) will be there' refer to something?
> The fact that the sentence is equivalent to 'Tom and Dick will be there or Jack and Harry will be there' and 'Tom and Dick' and 'Jack and Harry' refer to something.
> What makes 'Tom and Dick will be there' refer to something?
> The fact that the sentence is equivalent to 'Tom will be there and Dick will be there' and 'Tom' and 'Dick' refer to something.
> What makes 'Tom' refer to something?

Clearly a different kind of answer is required for the last question. What kind? Surely an account of the complex causal-historical-linguistic (C-H-L) relationships which exist between those who have this name (as the name of a particular person) in their vocabulary, and the person in question.

It would be out of the question to say

'Harry' refers (in L) to Harry *because*
x refers to y (in L) $=_{df} x =$ 'Tom' and $y =$ Tom or
$\qquad x =$ 'Dick' and $y =$ Dick or
$\qquad x =$ 'Harry' and $y =$ Harry or
. . . .

Surely the situation is parallel in the case of truth. The answer will be of the form

a, b make 'aRb' true because, aRb and in our linguistic community, 'a' stand in certain C-H-L relations to a, 'b' stands in such and such C-H-L relations to b, and expressions consisting of two referring expressions with an 'R' between them are involved in such and such inference patterns and in propensities to respond in perceptual situations to objects $(\hat{x}, \hat{y})$ such that xRy.

It is by virtue of this, that we can say not only

aRb

so, 'aRb' is true

but

'aRb' is true *because* aRb.

And the relevant C-H-L facts can be formulated without the use of fact expressions or propositional singular terms.

Thus, properly understood, the claim that it is not just a and b, but the fact that aRb, which makes 'aRb' true, is seen to be a mislocating of the idea that what *explains* the truth (i.e. the semantical correctness of asserting) 'aRb' is certain complex C-H-L facts about a and b which, together with the fact that aRb, entail the semantical correctness of asserting 'aRb'.

I have gone into this excursus on Wittgenstein not only because Russell at this period was under his influence, but because the above themes from the *Tractatus* provide a useful background against which to present Russell's views on truth. The first thing to note is that Russell accepts Wittgenstein's idea that the basic bearers of truth are positive propositions. He also accepts the idea that the basic bearers of truth are propositions in which n-adic relations of referring expressions express n-adic relations of objects. This is because for Russell the basic bearers of truth are image-propositions. "The simplest case" of "the formal correspondence which makes truth or falsehood" is, he tells us in "On Propositions",

the case of a dyadic relation which is the same in the fact and in the image-proposition. You have an image of A which is to the left of your image of B: this occurrence is the image-proposition. If *A* is to the left of *B*, the proposition is true; *if A is not to the left of B it is false.*[1]

I postpone, for a moment, comment on the italicized statement. For it must be stressed once again that Russell's basic propositions are without exception pictures in a literal sense which is reminiscent of Hume's account of belief. Since all basic matter-of-factual truths are of this kind, he is particularly concerned to argue[2] that basic temporal truths conform to the pattern. Thus an image of *A* followed by an image of *B* can be (if one "proceeds to believe the sequence") an image-proposition to the effect that *A* is followed by *B*. How central a role these image propositions play emerges when he continues:

The *phrase* '*A* is to the left of *B*' means the image-proposition, and is true, when that is true and false when that is false.

Russell has simply abandoned the idea that the sentence '*A* is to the left of *B*' might be a primary bearer of truth. Forgetting that this sentence might be construed as an '*A*' and a '*B*' *dyadically* related by having an 'is to the left of' between them, he writes:

In the phrase '*A* is to the left of *B*', even if we treat 'is to the left of' as one word, we have a fact consisting of *three* terms in a triadic relation, not two terms with a dyadic relation.[3]

Russell overlooks the obvious objection that '*A* is to the left of *B*' can scarcely "mean" the image-proposition in the sense of synonymy, if they differ so radically in structure. Russell must be thinking, to pick up an earlier theme, that the phrase '*A* is to the left of *B*' expresses a triadic tie between two particulars and a relation, whereas the image proposition expresses a dyadic relation between the two particulars. But there is no hope of illumination in this direction.

The second point to be noted is that for Russell, what makes a basic atomic proposition (an image-proposition) false is not the non-existence of a positive fact, but a negative fact, thus, in his example, the fact that *A* is *not* to the left of *B*. Russell's awareness of the indispensability of negative facts in explaining truth and falsity as they pertain to basic propositions, leads him to stress the wrong negative facts. If, with Wittgenstein, he had accepted the thesis that the world consists of what can be pictured, then, agreeing with Wittgenstein that all pictures are positive, he would have had to abandon, *not* 'negative facts', but the (weird) idea that negation belongs to the extra-conceptual order.

In the concluding section of this paper, I shall return to the topic of Russell's

---

[1] "On Propositions", p. 319; my italics.
[2] ibid., p. 318.
[3] ibid., p. 316.

theory of belief, and, completing this circle, his principle of acquaintance. But before I do so, I must touch on another dimension of Russell's later ontology, which also impinges on his philosophy of mind. He became convinced that not only are we not acquainted *with* a particular which is the subject term of mental relations; there *is* no such particular—for the simple reason that there are no particulars, *period*. The argument he offers is not easy to reconstruct, for although he presents it on a number of occasions, the formulation is invariably allusive, relying on intuitive transitions and cavalier references to historical controversies. But, although the argument is a tissue of confusions, the fact that it is so commonly endorsed, as well as the key role it has played in Russell's development, require that it be examined. This examination will lay the ground work for a subsequent discussion of other influences of Russell's views on ontology on his latter philosophy of mind.

The global form of the argument is

Particulars would be *bare* particulars.

The idea of bare particulars is absurd.

Therefore, there are no particulars.

How is the major premise established? Consider the proposition

a is *f*.

Suppose we take this at its face value as a subject-predicate proposition. *a* is, then, a particular, and 'is *f*' an adjectival predicate which ascribes the quality of being red to *a*. The question arises "What sort of thing is *a*?" We can answer "*a* is a particular". Here we use a *category* sortal. What about *empirical* sortals? Russell tells us in *My Philosophical Development* that "common names", which is his term for sortals, "are unnecessary. The statement that Socrates is a man has the same meaning as Socrates is human."[1] Thus suppose we did find an empirical sortal which applies to *a*, thus:

a is a *K*

this statement would, by the preceding, be identical in meaning with a statement involving only non-sortal predicates, thus

a is $f_1, f_2, \ldots f_n$

where 'f_1', ... 'f_n' are predicates which constitute the criteria for being a *K*. Thus any attempt to answer the question

What sort of item is *a*, which is *f* ?

leads to a statement which re-raises the original question, thus,

What sort of item is *a*, which is $f_1, \ldots f_n$?

We are left with the category sortal,

a is a particular.

Now this, by *itself*, would not constitute a commitment to the idea that *a* is a bare particular. For even if we grant that 'particular' is the only *sortal* which is true of *a*, and not reducible to adjectival predication, it could not be claimed,

---

[1] *My Philosophical Development*, p. 166.

under penalty of contradiction, that *a* is *characterless*, for it is, *ex hypothesi*, *f*.

Indeed we might counter attack, using Russell's own example of a circular patch of red, to argue that there is an empirical sortal which is true of *a* and which cannot be paraphrased away into adjectival predications, namely,

> *a* is *a patch of red*

where 'red' stands for a kind of stuff.

But there is another strand in the argument which, if valid, would undercut any such move. Russell reminds us that

> *a* is red

tells us that *a* has a certain quality. Now things *do* have qualities; and, in a sense, the above statement *does* tell us that *a* has a certain quality, i.e. redness. In *Human Knowledge: Its Scope and Limits*, Russell asks us to consider two alternatives:[1]

> (1) Things are constituted by qualities
>
> (2) Things are neither qualities nor bundles of qualities; but, rather, particulars which have qualities.

By asking us to consider these alternatives, Russell, in effect, substitutes for

> *a* is red

the proposition

> *a* has (the quality) redness.

Now, although these two propositions are intimately related, it would be a mistake to assume that they are synonymous. If they are not—and, indeed, they are not—to replace one by the other is to run the risk of confusion. And confusion is exactly what occurs. For the question

> What sort of thing is *a*, which *is f*?

now becomes

> What sort of thing is *a* which *has f-ness*?

As before, empirical sortals are reduced to adjectival predications. Previously, this reduction led us from '*a* is a K' to '*a* is $f_1 \ldots f_n$', which still tells us something that *a* is—even if only adjectivally. Now, however, we end up with

> *a* has (qualities) f_1-ness $\ldots f_n$-ness.

We asked what sort of thing *a* is, and the answer we are given tells us what *a has*. In other words the argument this time *does* lead to bare particulars, for whereas before we could say

> *a* isn't bare because it *is* red

this time we would have to say

> *a* isn't bare because it *has* redness.

We could never say what *a is*, except to categorize it as a particular, but only what it *has*. And to say what something *has* is not to say what it *is*. *a* becomes a haver of qualities or, in Russell's words, "an unknowable substratum, an

---

[1] *Human Knowledge: Its Scope and Limits*, New York 1948, pp. 292–3.

invisible peg from which properties would hang like hams from the beams of a farmhouse".[1]

Finding the notion of such a particular absurd, Russell reparses particulars as complexes of qualities. He introduces a relational predicate 'compresent with' with the form

compresent with $(Q_1, \ldots Q_n)$

such that the thing, *a*, previously construed as a particular of which non-relational predicates are true, becomes a complex of qualities to which individual qualities belong.[2] Russell answers one obvious objection by pointing out that since complexes of qualities can be referred to by description, and hence need not be referred to by enumerating their constituents,

a contains Q_1

need not be analytic if true. For '*a*' can be short for a descriptive phrase which picks out a complex in terms of some of its constituents or in terms of its relation to other complexes.[3]

I have been stressing the predicative character of 'red' in '*a* is red'—as con-trasted with the singular-term-ish-ness (ostensibly the name-hood) of 'redness'. I have asserted that it is a mistake to construe

a is red

as synonymous with

a has redness.

Those philosophers (and among them are *distinguished* philosophers) who take these statements to be synonymous, differing only in surface grammar, do, indeed, face the dilemma posed by Russell—either bare particulars or bundles of qualities. I am happy to be able, as I think, to slip between the horns of this dilemma. But I enjoy the scholastic niceties of the continuing debate between those who find themselves impaled on one or the other horn.

Russell reparses 'red' as 'redness', and, in general, adjectives as substantives. However, he does *not* reparse relation words. Indeed he lays great stress upon this fact. Thus, his argument about particulars does not rest on a general theory of predication which would require him to reconstrue

a is next to *b*

---

[1] *My Philosophical Development*, p. 161.

[2] Actually this contrived predicate is a concealed form of the predicate 'jointly exemplified by a particular'. But the dialectic necessary to show this would take me away from the topic of this paper.

[3] The answer to all this is not that there are no complexes of qualities. There are, just as there are qualities. It is, as I have argued on several occasions, that the move to complexes of qualities is (*a*) unnecessary, (*b*) conceals a reference to particulars. The believer in particulars who admits that *a* has redness, has not, *pace* Russell, been forced to reparse '*a* is red' as '*a* has redness'. Thus he too can insist that even though *a* is not identical with redness, or even with a bundle of qualities which includes redness, nevertheless *a* is **red**, and hence not bare.

as

    a and *b* stand in juxtaposition

where 'stand in' is the relational parallel of the 'has' of

    a has redness.

Nor does he reparse verbs as verbal nouns, thus

    Romeo loves Juliet

as

    Romeo and Juliet stand in (the relation) loving.

Indeed, as we have seen, he makes a stronger claim. He tells us that substantive relation words are dispensable, whereas predicate relation words are not, and, indeed, that the former are significant only when sentences containing them "can be translated into sentences in which the relation words perform their proper function of denoting a relation between terms".[1]

To sum up,

    a is red

is reparsed as

    redness is a constituent of (the bundle of qualities) *a*

not simply because of the idea that for a non-logical expression to have meaning is for it to name an object—although Russell is not untarred with this brush, for, at least in his later work, he refuses to reparse relational predicates as names of objects. Once one-place predicates have been turned into names of bundles of qualities, Russell has a way of stopping the dialectic which led to bare particulars in the case of one-place predicates. For consider

    a is next to *b*

—if we ask "What are *a* and *b*, which are next to each other?" we now have the answer

    a and *b* are complexes of qualities.

Indeed we have the more satisfying answer,

    a and *b* are colours.

For Russell accepts the genuinely subject predicate character of 'redness is a colour'.[2] Thus, as Russell sees it, we can accept the genuinely predicative character of relation words without being committed to the absurdity of bare particulars.

This claim throws light on the development of Russell's conception of the problem of universals. In *The Problems of Philosophy* Russell's argument was that we need words which do not refer to particulars in order to make statements. The words he finds necessary are predicates. We may, perhaps, dispense with one-place predicates such as 'white', but the only promising way of doing so requires the two-place predicate 'is similar to' (or some variant of this

---

[1] *My Philosophical Development*, p. 173.

[2] "There are still universals denoted by predicates such as colour, sound, taste, etc. . . . I should regard 'red is a colour' as a genuine subject-predicate proposition, assigning to the 'substance' *red* the quality colour" (ibid., p. 171).

expression). An attempt to dispense with this two-place predicate by the same strategy simply re-introduces it. The immediate conclusion to be drawn is that if we need two-place predicates, then the original attempt to dispense with one-place predicates simply because they aren't names of particulars was misguided. The reason for dispensing with one-place predicates has disappeared. To be sure, the possibility of dispensing with one-place predicates in favour of many-place predicates remains, but until this programme has been satisfactorily carried out, we may accept one-place predicates at their face value.

But although this is the thrust of Russell's argument in *The Problems of Philosophy*, he confuses the issue by assuming that to prove the need for *predicates* is *ipso facto* to prove the need for abstract singular terms; that to prove the need for 'is similar to' is to prove the need for 'similarity'; that to prove the need for 'white' is to prove the need for 'whiteness'. The mediating link is the name theory of meaning. Predicates have meaning, and what they stand for is abstract objects—whiteness, similarity.

When this theme is added, the above argument constitutes strong pressure for the view that, surface grammar aside, in

a is f

'f' is a name of an object—not, to be sure, a particular but an abstract object, a quality. It would also, however, support the view that in

a resembles b

'resembles' is the name of the relation. But if these conclusions are accepted, the original problem—what distinguishes a statement from a list of names—notoriously recurs, though at a level which includes a new category of names. Bradley takes his revenge. When he came to appreciate this, Russell abandoned the name theory of meaning for predicates. Whether he found a satisfactory substitute is a topic to which I will turn at the end of this paper.

My purpose in reminding you of these facts is not to rehash the problem of abstract entities, but to throw light on central themes in Russell's philosophy of mind. For Russell came to see the problem of universals, not as the problem "Are there objects which are not particulars?" This question he has no hesitation answering in the affirmative. Rather it becomes the problem as to what it is in reality which corresponds to predicative expressions, i.e. relation words used predicatively—since one-place predicates have been deprived of their predicative status.[1]

Russell considers and rejects two views but fails to come up with a positive view which satisfies him. He rejects the view that there are *objects* of which verbal nouns and other nominalizations of relation words are the names: juxtaposition, similarity, loving. He also rejects the view (essentially that of Frege) according to which predicative words correspond to, or to use

[1] As has already been noted above, this is not quite true. Russell regards

Red (ness) is a colour

as a true subject-predicate proposition, with 'is a colour' as a one-place predicate.

Russell's word, "denote" predicative entities (e.g. *is similar to, not* similarity).

Before concluding this paper by examining the implications of our discussion for the principle of acquaintance, let us consider briefly the later vicissitudes of Russell's theory of belief. Looking back on the twenties from the vantage point of 1956, Russell tells us that for a time he accepted Wittgenstein's suggestion that '*A* believes *p*' has the form

'*p*' says *p*

According to this suggestion, *A*'s believing *p*, where this is an episodic rather than dispositional belief, consists in the occurrence in the subject *A*, himself a logical construction out of events, of an event which is a token of a proposition which says *p*. Wittgenstein, of course, did not mean, as Russell took him to, that the "inner" proposition token belongs to a conventional language as, for example, an auditory image, let alone that it is in the language used by the person who makes the belief statement.[1] Wittgenstein simply requires that the "inner" proposition token be synonymous with the expression which follows 'says' as in

'Desdemona loves Cassio' says *Desdemona loves Cassio*.

It should be obvious that for Wittgenstein the 'Desdemona loves Cassio' to the right cannot be, in the basic Tractarian sense, an occurrence of the proposition "Desdemona loves Cassio", for propositions occur in the Tractarian sense only in truth functional contexts. Clearly, a special use is being made above of a token of the design 'Desdemona loves Cassio' in which it gives semantical information about the "inner" token. How it does this is an enigma wrapped in Tractarian metaphor. The information is, presumably, *shown* rather than *said*.[2]

Interestingly enough, Russell's new theory in *An Inquiry into Meaning and Truth* is not as different from Wittgenstein's as he believes. But whereas Wittgenstein fails to explain, save by metaphor, just *how* '*D* loves *C*' occurs in 'Othello believes Desdemona loves Cassio', i.e. in

'Desdemona loves Cassio' says Desdemona loves Cassio

Russell makes an attempt to do so and fails to pull it off.

The core of Russell's account is that

Othello believes Desdemona loves Cassio

doesn't assert a relation between Othello and *Desdemona loves Cassio*, but rather ascribes to Othello a certain state. This state is of the sort which would be

---

[1] In *An Inquiry into Meaning and Truth*, Russell interprets Wittgenstein's analysis as, in effect, construing '*A* believes *p*' as

A believes '*p*'

but this is surely a mistake.

[2] Wittgenstein's elaboration, "Here we have no coordination of a fact and an object, but a coordination of facts by means of a coordination of their objects", simply enriches the account by relating it to his thesis that one says that *aRb* by placing an '*a*' in a counterpart relation to a '*b*'.

expressed, if Othello were to use language, by an utterance which is similar in meaning, to a relevant degree, to 'Desdemona loves Cassio'.

But how is 'Desdemona loves Cassio' occurring, and how do we avoid the familiar paradox? Russell thinks it sufficient to say that we are not concerned with its truth value. But this is little help. He tells us that we *are* concerned with its significance, with what it expresses. This suggests that in the belief context 'Desdemona loves Cassio' stands for a kind of mental state, the kind of state which would find a linguistic expression in this sentence. This thesis amounts, in contemporary terms, to the "adverbial theory" of the objects of belief. We would thus have

   O believes *D*-loves-*C*-ly

or, using the nominalizing language of states

   O is in a *D loves C* state of belief.

Presumably a *D loves C* state is a complex state consisting of state components. How do we cut it up? Leaving aside the subtle issues raised by Wittgenstein, let us simply try

   O is in a state which consists of a *D* state of thought, a *loves* state of
   thought and a *C* state of thought

where the state components *somehow* fit together to make up a *D loves C* state.

But a *D loves C* state, for Russell, is not only a state of a certain kind. It is capable of being either true or false. If true, it "indicates" a fact. Again a *D* state is not only a state of a certain kind, it picks out Desdemona. And when Russell believes that Socrates loves Plato, the *Socrates* state picks out a person who lived in Athens more than two thousand years ago.

We are therefore confronted with the questions

   What is it for a *D* state to pick out Desdemona?
   A *C* state to pick out Cassio?
   A *loves* state to pick out loving?
   A *D loves C* state to "indicate" a fact?

With these questions, we return to our opening topic, for the Russell of 1912 and the immediately following years would have said that for a *D loves C* state to be about *D*, loving, and *C*, is for the subject to be acquainted with certain objects. Thus, if '*D*' and '*C*' were logically proper names, then the state would involve a relation of acquaintance between Othello on the one hand and Desdemona, loving, and Cassio on the other. Since they are not, the acquaintance would relate the *attributes* in terms of which Othello picks out Desdemona and Cassio.[1]

---

[1] I have argued above, p. 59, that the principle of acquaintance would also require an encompassing acquaintance with the range of values of the variable of quantification. Russell seems never to have taken this requirement into account and it is clear that taking it seriously would have interesting repercussions in both ontology and the philosophy of mind. But I refrain from following up this line of thought on the present occasion.

Russell continued to adhere to the principle of acquaintance. But he modified it. How? In the first place he abandoned the account of sensation according to which it is a relation between a subject term and a sense datum. He tells us that his "abandonment of the relational character of sensation led me to substitute 'noticing' for 'acquaintance' ". He came to think that sensation is, as such, non-cognitive. He put this by saying that the sensation of a colour patch is just the colour patch itself. One can see what he is trying to say by comparing it with the adverbial theory according to which the *esse* of a sensed red patch is its being sensed. What he says won't do as it stands, for it leaves out of account the relation, however non-cognitive, by virtue of which a sensation belongs to a person. The point is relatively unimportant, however, because he replaces sensation as an act of acquaintance with *noticing*. Noticing *is* epistemic, and it is *relational*, though not a relation between a "pin-point" or "metaphysical" subject and what the subject notices. He sketches a causal account of noticing in terms of bodily states, including beliefs. But in spite of these changes in its content, the form of the principle remains essentially the same. In the passage from *My Philosophical Development* which was quoted in my opening paragraph, he tells us that the principle, "which still seems to me completely valid", is to the effect that if we can understand what a sentence means, it must be composed of words denoting things with which we are acquainted, or definable in terms of such words. After qualifying the principle by confining it to sentences containing no variables and containing no parts which are sentences, Russell tells us that "in that case, we may say that if our sentence attributes a predicate to the subject, or asserts a relation between two or more terms, the words for the subject and for the terms of the relation must be proper names in the narrowest sense".[1]

Now in the new dispensation, proper names in the 'narrowest sense' are names *of* qualities. Thus, among the words we understand is 'red', which stands for the quality redness. Since the principle tells us that we are acquainted with what 'red' denotes, we naturally ask: What is it to be acquainted with redness? "Red and blue are words for certain kinds of experiences, and we get to know what these words mean by hearing them when we are noticing *red* things and *blue* things".[2] Presumably, understanding the word 'red' is a dispositional state which involves being able to use the word correctly as a name for the object, redness, when one is perceptually confronted by a quality complex which contains it as a constituent.

But what of relations? Here is the rub. There are *objects* which are qualities, but no objects which are relations. What is to take the place of the earlier notion that we are acquainted with temporal succession, with spatial juxtaposition, the relation *north of*? Qualities are entities to which the mind can respond, or,

[1] *My Philosophical Development*, p. 169.
[2] ibid.

at least are elements of quality complexes to which the mind can respond. They can be singled out and named. They become causally involved in mental activity, sometimes directly, sometimes indirectly by virtue of their symbolic representatives. In the case of relations, however, he allows no relational objects of which a parallel account might be given.

Russell tells us that he has failed to "descry some entity denoted by relation words and capable of some shadowy kind of subsistence outside the complex in which it is embedded".[2] Notice that this report is not unambiguous. It could mean that he has failed to descry *any* entity denoted by relation words, or it could mean that while he has descried entities denoted by relation words, these entities are not capable of "subsistence" outside the "complexes" in which they are "embedded". The distinction is important, for if the latter is the case, there would seem to be no reason why these entities could not be given linguistic labels. Russell would have descried Fregean concepts, those intrinsically unsaturated entities which feed on objects. But he would have encountered none whose appetite was unsaturated.

Russell is clearly uneasy. Yet his uneasiness does not tempt him to reparse

> *a* succeeds *b*

as

> *a* and *b* stand in a relation of succession

or the more parsimonious

> Succession (*a, b*)

and hence to admit into his ontology two or more place counterparts of qualities, and to construe them as objects which can be descried and named.

Russell falls back on the idea that there are relational *facts* which he identifies with "relational complexes". "It is as certain as anything can be that there are relational facts such as '*A* is earlier than *B*'."[2] Russell is here speaking in a philosophical tone of voice, and clearly means that such facts are "in the world", i.e. are as independent of mind as physical things. Perhaps, although relational facts cannot be named, but only affirmed or asserted, and although they contain no relational object or entity which can be labelled, we can nevertheless give an account of our ability to "think of relations" in terms of relational facts, which satisfies the principle of acquaintance.

Perhaps we should say that to understand 'succeeds' we must have descried not a fact which has the entity succession as a constituent, but rather a fact of the kind expressed by sentences of the form '*x* succeeds *y*'. But this requires that we use the form

> Mind descries that *a* succeeds *b*

and we would be confronted once again with a violation of the principle that propositions occur only as propoundings, i.e. not as substantives. This time,

---

[1] ibid., p. 173.
[2] ibid., p. 172.

however, we would be precluded from the nominalistic move of identifying this with

Mind descries '*a* succeeds *b*',

for to do this would be to assimilate descrying to belief, and hence to face the question "How do we come to be able to use 'succeeds' significantly?" all over again.

The answer must surely be that rather than accounting for our acquiring the ability to use 'succeeds' significantly, the descrying of facts of the form '*x* succeeds *y*' represents the fruits of the process of acquiring the ability to use 'succeeds' significantly. Russell is still looking for an *epistemic* act of acquaintance which makes the meaningful use of the corresponding symbols possible. He is trapped in the myth of the given. The alternative is to realize that epistemic abilities are patterns of non-epistemic connections. It is not by being epistemically related to *facts* of the form that *xRy* that we acquire the ability to "think of the relation *R*"; rather we acquire this ability by acquiring *inter alia* the propensity to respond to *objects* which are *R* to one another with sentences of the form '*xRy*', and to fit these sentences into certain inference patterns.

The "knowledge by acquaintance" with particulars, qualities and facts which Russell takes to be a substratum which supports the meaningful use of symbols, is simply the effective exercise of the very abilities it is supposed to support. Notice, therefore, that one could espouse a principle of acquaintance to the effect that all the basic descriptive predicates which one can fully[1] understand are expressions which have served to express perceptual knowledge, without turning this into a foundational theory of concept acquisition. Russell clearly began with the latter, and it shaped his thinking. It is equally clear, however, that there is much in his later work which points the way out of this labyrinth.

---

[1] I write "fully", because a blind man has a "partial" understanding of colour words though he is unable to use them in perceptual contexts.

Romane Clark

Ontology and the Philosophy of Mind in Sellars' Critique of Russell

Professor Sellars quotes Russell:

I want to try to get an account of the way that a belief is made up. That is not an easy question at all. You cannot make what I should like to call a map-in-space of a belief. . . . The point is in connection with there being two verbs in the judgment; and with the fact that both verbs have to occur as verbs, *because if a thing is a verb it cannot occur otherwise than as a verb.* (Sellars' italics)

Sellars footnotes Russell's remarks, pointing out that Russell deliberately uses 'verb' "both for linguistic items (e.g. 'love') and for the extra-linguistic item (e.g. love) for which they stand".[1]

    Russell's remark here is puzzling: what is it for a thing to occur as a verb, if that thing is not (as Russell's quasi-technical usage permits) a linguistic item? But in the context of Russell's earlier thought it is not difficult to see what bothers him. (It is a merit of Sellars' excellent essay that he has extracted, sharpened and related several issues like this from Russell's many writings.) What bothers Russell is the true ascription of false judgments to someone. What bothers him about the true ascription of false judgments to someone is that although there are, he believes, facts which make true our true beliefs there are not, he believes, entities which make false our false beliefs. Yet false beliefs are of course meaningful, and they are moreover false because of the way the world, in addition to thought, happens to be. What is there which makes the belief significant, although false? And what corresponds in reality to the verb in a false judgment? Russell early raised these questions in a rather special form: what is it to which a mind (say, Othello's) is related when it judges falsely (say, that Desdemona loves Cassio?)

    Russell, we know tried several ways of answering this question within the framework of his assumptions about facts and things and knowing minds. One early attempt[2] was to locate the significance of false beliefs at least in part in the existence of objects which Russell took to be the objects of reference of elements

---

[1] See Sellars, W., "Ontology and the Philosophy of Mind in Russell", p. 74, this volume. The reference is to Russell's *Lectures on the Philosophy of Logical Atomism*, pp. 224–5. Page references are to the reprinted version appearing in *Logic and Knowledge*, ed. R. C. Marsh, London 1956.

[2] *The Problems of Philosophy*, London 1912. See Chapter 12, "Truth and Falsehood".

of the belief. It is these, he then thought, to which the mind is related even in false judgments. It is these which account for the significance of the false belief. These objects are said by Russell to be known by acquaintance or else by description in terms of objects known by acquaintance. The falsity of a judgment was then to be explained in terms of the fact that the existing objects of reference are not actually so related among themselves as to form a complex, a fact, which suitably matches the belief. (The belief itself is a structure of referring elements the verbal expressions of which are taken by Russell to be names.) Thus, Othello believes falsely that Desdemona loved Cassio because, although (fiction aside) Desdemona and Cassio exist and although couples do stand in that special relation of affection which Othello ascribed to Desdemona and Cassio, still Desdemona and Cassio are not, actually, related as Othello believes them to be. The elements of the complex required to make the belief true exist but the complex does not. One of these elements of the required complex is the relation in which Desdemona and Cassio are wrongly believed to stand. For Russell at this time, it, quite as much as Desdemona and Cassio, is an object of reference of some element of the belief. But it, in Russell's later technical usage, is also a *verb*. Othello, on the earlier account, must stand in some relation to *that*, to the verb, in his erroneous judgment of Desdemona's inconstancy.

Russell, in this earlier account, trades heavily upon a distinction sharply drawn between two ways of characterizing the mind's relation to reality. There is acquaintance and there is judging. He contrasted the simplicity of the former with the complexity of the latter. The epistemological simplicity which Russell finds in the psychical act of acquaintance spills over into his ontology. It is matched (in the expression of thought) by the syntactical and semantical simplicity of (primitive) names. The epistemological complexity which Russell finds in the psychical act of judgment similarly spills over into his ontology and is similarly matched (in the expression of thought) by the syntactical and semantical complexity of sentences.

In a perspicuous language, a name is a syntactical unit with no further, syntactically significant, parts. (Obviously, by contrast, the material embodiments of names, tokens of them, contain discernible material parts.) A sentence, in a logically perspicuous language, is a complex structure of syntactically distinct elements. These are conventionally distinguished in some manner in their material occurrences. Semantically, the names of a perspicuous language are associated with single items, whatever (concrete or abstract, simple or complex) these may be. But sentences by contrast are two-valued and their truth-valuations presuppose the prior assignments of objects to their syntactically distinct, primitive non-logical elements. So, in these two dimensions, syntactically and semantically, the simplicity of names in the expression of our thought matches, and may be thought to reinforce, the characterization of the act of acquaintance as an epistemologically simple act.

In fact, however, the epistemological simplicity of acquaintance is characterized by Russell, at this time, negatively: it is a mental occurrence which involves no knowledge of truths and so involves no inference. It is an apparent consequence of this negative characterization of these acts that they cannot be acts of classification, identification, or characterization of the nature of the object of the act. For each of these last acts presumably involves some prior knowledge of truths. The expression of each such act, presumably, would be recorded in a full sentence. But acquaintance, Russell insists, is not like this.

Sellars, however, suspects that Russell was, at least tacitly, committed to characterizing knowledge by acquaintance as knowledge of the nature of the object known. Apparently, then, if Sellars is right in this and if I am right in my account of Russell's negative characterization of the act of acquaintance, Russell is (at least tacitly) inconsistent in his views on acquaintance. However, Russell so clearly and emphatically stresses in *The Problems of Philosophy* that acquaintance is direct knowledge of things, and he so specifically contrasts knowledge of things with knowledge of truths, that my preference is to save him from the charge of logical schizophrenia at the price of charging Sellars with misunderstanding.

This issue leads a bit away from our present concern with the role of verbs in judgment. But it is important in understanding Russell's view of the kind of knowledge we can have of verbs. Moreover, it is too central to Sellars' account of Russell's developing thought to ignore, and too complex to relegate to a footnote, so we had better take time out to let Sellars speak for himself on this. Sellars writes:

Although I must confess to a certain feeling of puzzlement as to why Russell didn't offer an explicit argument of the form

If I were acquainted with the subject, I would know its intrinsic nature
I do not know its intrinsic nature
Therefore I am not acquainted with the subject

I do think I have made a case for the idea that this argument is almost on the tip of his pen.

Sellars goes on to consider Russell's example of an object of acquaintance, "a circular patch of red", writing:

There are three points to stress. In the first place, 'red' is functioning here as a word for a kind of matter or stuff. . . . In the second place, 'patch of red' is a sortal expression formed from this mass term which applies to portions of red as 'puddle of water' applies to portions of water. In the third place, although we know both that the object is a patch of red and that it is circular, in knowing that it is a patch of red we are knowing *what* it is as we are not by virtue of knowing that it is circular. For although both these facts about the datum are intuitively known and are non-relational, the fact that it is made of a certain stuff pertains to its nature or what it is, in a way in which the fact that it is circular does not. But although I stress these points, I do not mean to imply that Russell does. . . .

To put the point bluntly, in Russell's paradigm case of knowledge by acquaintance, we know what object O is by knowing of what stuff it is.[1]

Sellars' push on Russell's views at this point is a nudge toward Kantian cognitive holism and away from classical empiricism. Evidently, these issues are larger than the dimensions of a parenthetical remark. But some smaller things can be said which are pertinent here. First, *we* at any rate have been sensitized to differences between adjectives and sortal expressions. (Stuff, after all, comes in amounts. It is things, by contrast, which vary in the intensity or degree to which they manifest certain sensible qualities. I have more water than you if my glass of water is bigger than yours. I do not have something redder than you if my patch of red is bigger than yours, and I do not have more red than you but more of a red patch.) It seems implausible to suppose that Russell consciously, but without remarking the fact, construed expressions for sensible qualities on the pattern of those for mass terms or the sortals formed from them. And it seems to me that there is a more plausible reading of his remarks from the *Problems* than that he did this unconsciously. Surely, it may be that in speaking of red patches he intended nothing more than to make reference to something red, to a red thing. We are, we may suppose him to be saying, directly and non-inferentially aware of something red in an act of sensible acquaintance. The contrast between Sellars' view of Russell and mine is reflected in the following inference patterns (think of 'X' as 'red'): forming a sortal expression from a mass term, X, we have:

This is an amount of X

X is a Y

Ergo, this is an amount of a Y,

but taking the adjectival role of expressions for the sense qualities as dominant:

This is X

X is a Y

Ergo, this is Y-ed.

Despite Russell's talk of "a patch of red", I find it implausible to suppose that Russell indeed thought of sense data as particular amounts of sensible qualities rather than simply as red particulars. He would, I believe, have rejected the first inference pattern for 'red' as an instance of 'X'. Splashes of colour on canvas or in the sky, I am forced to construe as literal (in the first instance,) or figurative, (in the second,) references to amounts of pigmented material.

Note in any case that Russell does *not* (in the *Problems*) take it to be either clear or obvious at the outset what the object of an act of sensible awareness is. The concept of the act is not, as he describes it, such that solely from the ascription of an occurrence of the act to an agent we can infer what sort of entity it is

[1] Sellars, this volume, p. 66.

with which the agent of the act is sensibly acquainted. That remains an open question for Russell, one to be determined by a separate inquiry. In fact, in the *Problems*, Russell offers in the initial chapter a *separate argument* to show that the objects of acts of sensible acquaintance cannot, reasonably, be supposed to be physical things. From this, he goes on to conclude that it is reasonable to suppose that what they really are, commonsense to one side, is sense data. The argument he offers is, I think, not very persuasive and certainly it is not a demonstration. But the relevant fact here is that is that he thinks it is a point that needs making separately on its own. It scarcely seems possible then that Russell thought that acquaintance was to be correctly conceived as a mental act which either is, or presupposes, knowledge of the intrinsic nature of the object known.

Even if Russell's sense data indeed were amounts of sensible stuff with which psychical agents are acquainted in immediate, sensuous experience, and even if sensible qualities should in fact constitute the intrinsic natures of the entities they qualify, even then it still does not follow that acquaintance is knowledge of the intrinsic natures of the objects known. For one may surely be aware of something (indeed one may even know the sensible character of the thing of which he is aware), without thereby knowing that the sensible character does constitute the intrinsic nature of the object of awareness. (Should the object of awareness be a physical object, a view which we know Russell thought to be unreasonable but which also is not one which he claims to have shown logically impossible, presumably then it would *not* constitute its intrinsic nature.) We might now paraphrase Sellars in this way: "To put the point bluntly, in Russell's paradigm case of knowledge by acquaintance, we know the object O without knowing what O is." This paraphrase at least has the merit of being consistent with Russell's insistence that knowledge by acquaintance "is essentially simpler than any knowledge of truths, and *logically independent* of knowledge of truths".[1]

If we are right in this lengthy parenthetical discussion, Russell took acquaintance to be a mental act of a particularly simple, one-dimensional sort. It was direct awareness of things. It was logically independent of any acts of judgment. Acts of judgment, by contrast, are complex occurrences. The propositions by which their content may be expressed must consist, Russell insisted, wholly of items with which we are (already?) acquainted, if these are propositions which we understand. Presumably he meant that the elements of the propositions refer to entities with which we are (already?) acquainted.

Acquaintance with sensible particulars is, in the standard case, an instance of a psychical agent causally interacting with his environment. But judgment is not in general like this. We think, often, in the absence of the object of thought or its causes, and often we judge truly in such cases. The correspondence of a judgment with the fact which makes it true is only occasionally concurrent with an interaction between a thinking agent and his sensuous stimulation by

---

[1] *The Problems of Philosophy*, Chapter 5, first paragraph; my italics.

the very objects of thought or their causes. Only in the special case of perceptual judgments is sensuous stimulation a necessary condition for the occurrence of the psychical act. On Russell's theory[1] the correspondence between true judgments and their matching facts, and the relation "making true", are not interactions between knowing minds and an agent's surroundings. This is so, on Russell's theory, even though the making of particular, singular, judgments presupposes prior acts of acquaintance and so prior causal stimulations.

So far, the two ways in which a mind is, for Russell, related to reality, acquaintance and judgment, have been contrasted in two basic respects. Acts of acquaintance with sensible particulars are causal interactions. Acts of judgment need not be. Acts of acquaintance are logically simple acts, presupposing no further distinct psychical acts. But acts of judgment are logically complex acts, presupposing acts of acquaintance (and presumably also an act of predicating one object of acquaintance, a universal, of another, a particular, in simple singular affirmative judgments).

Russell, I believe, confused the simplicity of the act of acquaintance, probably tacitly reinforced in his thinking by the syntactical simplicity of a suitable vehicle for its expression, with the simplicity of the object of the act. He transferred, I suspect, different senses in which the act and its expression may be thought to be simple, to the object of the act, ontologically characterized. For, unlike those singular judgments which presumably "involve" the logically distinct acts of reference and ascription, the performance of which actually constitutes the making of the judgment, the act of acquaintance is direct and self-contained. It is an occurrence the happening of which presupposes no other, constitutive psychical acts. And this is reinforced by "the logically proper name" as the syntactical vehicle for the linguistic expression of the act of primitive awareness. As the name is syntactically complete and primitive, without syntactically distinct parts, as the psychical act is complete and primitive, without pyschically distinct occurrences, so too the object of the act might thought to be ontologically primitive and without ontologically distinct parts. The sense datum is a paradigm of an entity which has no further entities constitutive of it. It is an element whose existence is relative to various interactions in the causal order but it is an element which has no ontologically distinct parts. In this special latter sense, it is complete, simple, and ontologically independent. The relevant simplicity and independence is, however, if I am correct in my understanding of Russell, not that which Sellars finds on the tip of Russell's pen, all but put down on paper. Red expanses have, for that matter, smaller patches as (spatial) parts. And so, too, physical objects have physical parts. The objects of acquaintance have, then, parts. What we can infer from the occurrence of an act of acquaintance alone is not which of these kinds of things is the object of the act. The relevant point is that the act is an act of awareness of *an object*

[1] ibid., Chapter 12.

rather than a complex. The object of acquaintance is the sort of thing which one can know directly, which one can name. It is a thing having no onto-logically diverse parts or constituents in the way in which complexes must. The objects of awareness are complete, simple, and independent by contrast with the dependence and complexity of that which makes true our true judg-ments. These last, unlike the objects of acquaintance, have ontologically diverse elements as constituents. These last, as complexes which can be asserted but not named, have their being only in their constituents.

Objects of acquaintance are the ontologically diverse constituents, not parts, occurring in the complex structures Russell calls facts.[1] The ontological con-trast is, for Russell, between facts and things. It is the simplicity and priority of the epistemological act and of its verbal expression which Russell transfers to the objects of acts of acquaintance. And it is the complexity and dependence of the epistemological act and its verbal expression which Russell transfers to the complexes which make true those acts of judgment which are true. Russell's order of dependence in Being is a consequence of the simplicity and priorities he finds in his epistemology at this early stage in his thought.

So far, our characterization of Russell has stressed his ontological responses to the sharp epistemological distinction he drew between the psychical acts of acquaintance and judgment. But none of this explains the initial questions arising from the quotation which initiates this paper. Why does he come, then, in his later writing, to stress "two-verb sentences"? And what does he mean by a verb "occurring as a verb"?

Russell's characterization of knowledge by acquaintance has been discussed here in terms of awareness of sensible particulars. But Russell is a Platonist in the *Problems*, and acquaintance is also the primitive mental act by which we gain awareness of abstract entities, the universals. And judgment, he claims, always involves reference to at least one universal. How then does the verb 'loves' occur in the two-verb ascription of Othello's false belief to Othello and how does it occur in the facts which make true our true judgments? Russell, in the *Problems*, says this:

We spoke of the relation called 'judging' or 'believing' as knitting together into one complex whole the subject and objects. In this respect, judging is like any other relation. Whenever a relation holds between two or more terms, it unites the terms into a complex whole. . . . When an act of believing occurs, there is a complex, in which 'believing' is the uniting relation, and subject and objects are arranged in a certain order by the 'sense'

---

[1] Russell speaks in *The Problems of Philosophy* of acquaintance with facts as well as things. (See, e.g., the discussion in Chapter 13, "Knowledge and Error", p. 211.) It seems clear from his discussion that he has in mind perception as a species of knowledge. It is unfortunate, then, that he uses the term 'acquaintance' here as well as for direct knowledge of things. For while perceptual knowledge, like knowledge of things by acquaintance, is direct, non-inferential and causally mediated, it is radically different in being knowledge of truths. He is more careful in Chapter 11, "On Intuitive Knowledge". See, e.g., pp. 117-18.

of the relation of believing. Among the objects, as we saw in considering 'Othello believes that Desdemona loves Cassio', one must be a relation—in this instance, the relation 'loving'. But this relation, as it occurs in the act of believing, is not the relation which creates the unity of the complex whole consisting of the subject and objects. The relation 'loving', as it occurs in the act of believing, is one of the objects—it is a brick in the structure, not the cement. The cement is the relation 'believing'.[1]

And so we have an answer to our two questions for Russell at the time of the *Problems*. The verb 'loves' occurs in complexes as relating ("cementing together") the subject terms of the complex. The verb occurs in "two-verb" judgments, i.e. in the context of the ascription of beliefs to persons, as an object, an item among other items to which the agent of the belief makes reference.

It is evident that, if "judging" is a relation like any other relation, this account will not do. For one thing, it will not do since expressions for the relation will be terms of varying degree, requiring varying numbers of argument expressions to complete them, in varying contexts. For if the objects of belief are entities joined by the relation of believing then that relation will sometimes hold among few things and sometimes among more. Othello's belief about Desdemona and Cassio is a belief about three things on Russell's account. It is about Desdemona, Cassio, and loving. Othello's belief that Cassio is treacherous is, presumably, a belief about two things on Russell's account. It is about Cassio and treachery. "Belief" is, then, in the first instance, a four-termed relation, and in the second instance, a three-termed one. But this is not possible.

This is not, however, the ground upon which Russell comes later, in the *Lectures on the Philosophy of Logical Atomism*, to reject his earlier account of belief. It is rather that he comes to think that, in "two-verb judgments", "both verbs have to occur as verbs", and, more generally, that "if a thing is a verb it cannot occur otherwise than as a verb".[2]

Apparently, in the *Problems*, verbs occur in complexes as abstract objects, attributes and relations, which qualify or relate particulars and in doing so create the particular structure or complex there then is. It is by abstracting what is common to their various exemplifications that a knowing mind can come to be aware of the universal itself, and this awareness is acquaintance with the abstract object. In judgment, the universal occurs as an object of reference. It is a nameable. It is 'loving' not 'loves' to which the mind makes reference. In its exemplifications, the universal occurs as that sort of object which determines or gives the structure to the complex in which it occurs.

It is, perhaps, possible to see how Russell might come to give up the more specific point about two-verb contexts in his later writing. For it is plausible to assume that Russell comes to see that an analysis of an agent's belief needs to

---

[1] ibid., pp. 199–200.
[2] *Lectures on the Philosophy of Logical Atomism*, reprinted in R. C. Marsh (ed.), *Logic and Knowledge*, London 1956.

preserve the content of the belief and not merely the correspondence of the elements of the belief with extra-linguistic items of reference. Othello, after all, had certain beliefs, elements of which corresponded not merely to Desdemona, Cassio, and loving, but to the belief that Desdemona loved Cassio. It is plausible to assume that Russell comes to see that it will not do to say that the verb, 'believes', is the "cement which gives order to the belief". 'Othello believes that Desdemona loves Cassio' becomes, on such an account, 'Othello believes that Desdemona stands in the relation loving to Cassio'. But of course Othello may believe that Desdemona loves Cassio without believing this latter thing at all. Russell may be viewed as coming to see that an account of how it is possible that beliefs be false, is not necessarily a theory of believing.

But, in fact, Russell's changing views seem to be more radically motivated than the suggestion above can account for. For he not only says that in two-verb judgments both verbs must occur as verbs, but he also goes on to say the much more general thing, that verbs cannot occur otherwise than as verbs. And this suggests not merely a repudiation of his earlier account of false belief, but a dramatic rejection of his earlier Platonism together with its associated epistemological baggage, acquaintance with abstract entities.

This is, to me at least, an exciting shift in Russell's developing, or at least changing, thought. It has always seemed puzzling that the radical doctrine, that there are diverse kinds of Being some of which cannot be named or referred to, was so selectively exploited. Frege, after all, had his unsaturated concepts which could not be the objects of singular reference, but statements, he argued, named one of the truth-values. Russell, in his earlier period, apparently held that complexes can be asserted but not named, but argued then that psychical agents could be acquainted with relations and qualities and properties. The objects of acquaintance are objects which can be named. We find now that in the *Lectures*, still impelled by epistemological considerations to his ontological conclusions, Russell enlarges the category of non-nameables. He now holds both that complexes, facts, are not the objects of singular reference, and cannot be, and also that "verbs" as well are not the objects of singular reference, and cannot be. ("A verb cannot occur other than as a verb.")

I assume that, in saying that a verb cannot occur save as a verb, Russell is saying in part that singular judgments are not the sort of entity whose linguistic expression makes reference to abstract objects through the occurrence of abstract singular terms. The verbs which occur in the expression of the thought are the constituents of a correct logical formalization of the expression, or formalizations of them are. But a correct formalization of a verb is not a noun. Accordingly, the complex which makes true a true judgment (and Russell still maintains in the *Lectures* that there are facts, as separate, non-nameable complexes) is a structure in which the objects of reference of the judgment are related in a given way. But the objects of reference do not include an object to which the verb refers. The complex is not a complex of objects, particular and abstract, standing in a pattern of exemplification. His rejection of the object-copula-object theory of predication is now explicit. (This rejection was of course already present, although more tentatively, in the *Problems*. For even there, although he held that we can be and indeed on occasion are acquainted with universals, the occurrences of relations in complexes were the binding materials (the "cement") which formed or united (concrete) objects into structures, not objects among objects. And this seems very close to holding that "verbs occur only as verbs".) Now, verbs no longer get associated with corresponding, abstract entities of the sort putatively referred to by abstract singulars, not even in the ascription of false beliefs to a psychical agent. Nor, presumably, do they get associated in oblique discourse with Fregean senses, those abstract entities which constitute the sense of the verbs in their standard occurrences in direct discourse. Russell, it seems, holds, at the time of the *Lectures*, a truly radical theory of non-nameables. Even in the context of Othello's false belief about Desdemona it is the unsaturated binding material, '_____ loves . . .', and not an abstract entity (to which Russell refers by 'loving'), which occurs.

This does not entail that there are, on the theory, no abstract entities and in particular no universals. Abstract singular expressions remain to be accounted for. But ordinary singular judgments are not now viewed as vehicles requiring singular reference to them. And ascriptions of judgments to psychical agents no longer wait upon determination of their truth-value for the determination that there exists an explicit reference to a universal as an object of belief. The Platonistic theme must be argued directly now in terms of the occurrences, not of verbs, but of abstract singulars. But however that further argument may go, and however Russell may characterize on the new theory his old problem of significantly ascribing false beliefs, an important fact emerges. It is this, that Russell in the *Lectures* comes down on the Fregean side of the two main theories of predication. This is an important fact, having as it does both immediate and remote formal consequences,[1] and suggesting as it does further metaphysical and ontological commitments.

We call Russell's (Fregean) theory of predication "the no-copula theory"; the other theory of predication we call "the copula theory". Syntactically, on the copula theory, singular affirmative judgments are, in a perspicuous language, formalized by sentences the syntactical elements of which are singular terms together with an operator which takes pairs of singular terms into sentences. Set theory is a paradigm of the copula-theory, with the membership symbol joining pairs of singular terms to yield a sentence. Conditions may of course be placed on the terms upon which the copula operates when one defines the

---

[1] Immediate formal consequences have been investigated and developed in considerable detail in Nino B. Cocchiarella's important recent papers, "Properties as Individuals in Formal Ontology", *Nous* 6 (1972); "Whither Russell's Paradox of Predication?" forthcoming in *Logic and Ontology*, ed. M. K. Munitz, New York; "Fregean Semantics for a Realist Ontology", forthcoming in *Notre Dame Journal of Formal Logic*.

sequences of expressions which are to count as sentences. We may, for example, segregate the singular terms in a familiar way into levels and require perhaps that terms of successive levels must flank the copula.

The Platonic theory of predication is also a copula-theory. The system of *Principia Mathematica* might be viewed as a rather natural expression of its logic. A more explicit representation of the theory would, however, introduce explicitly an operator, a copula, which, in a manner analogous to the symbol for membership in set theory, joins pairs of singular terms (perhaps of certain orders) to yield a sentence.

If the fundamental formal fact about copula theories consisted just in the accessibility of terms on either side of the copula to quantification, then the literal appearance of the copula might, perhaps, be considered merely a nota-tional device merely underscoring the syntactical completeness of the terms it joins. But the interest in the copula theory does not reside solely in the acces-sibility of the singular terms, particularly of those occurring in predicate posi-tion to the right of the copula, to quantification. There are further formal functions for the copula to fulfil as well, as we shall argue. If so, it is desirable that a perspicuous notation explicitly represents these further functions.

Syntactically, on the no-copula theory, singular, affirmative judgments are formalized by sentences in which all the open places occurring in one style of expression, the predicate, are filled by singular terms, yielding thus a sentence. Predicates, and singular terms as well, may be further distinguished into further distinct sorts (e.g. as sortals, mass terms, or qualities), and predicates of varying numbers of open places may of course occur. It is a feature of the no-copula theory that predicates cannot significantly occupy the open places in predicates, and that predicates are not accessible to the quantifiers.

Ontologically, there are distinct metaphysical motivations of Platonic, on the one hand, or anti-Platonic on the other, sorts pushing in the direction of the one theory or the other. If the formal theory is coupled with an analysis of the concept "makes true"[1] then there emerge, as we have seen with Russell, distinct characterizations of the nature of the complexes, the facts, which make true our true assertions. Complexes which make true the true atomic assertions of a no-copula theory are simply structures of particulars. They are, on the copula theory, particulars standing in the relation of exemplification to abstract individuals.

If, however, as is usual, we consider only classical valuations for the semantics of the two types of theory, and if we restrict our attention to first-order logical theories of these sorts, the same assignments of individuals to the individual constants, and of *n*-tuples of individuals to the predicate constants of either

---

[1] See, for instance, Bas C. van Fraassen's interesting paper, "Facts and Tautological Entailments", *Journal of Philosophy* 66 (1969), and my attempt to sketch a semantics for predicate-modifiers which appeals to facts, "Concerning the Logic of Predicate Modifiers", *Nous*, 4 (1970).

theory may be made, quite ignoring the copula, with the same consequent truth-valuations for matching sentences in either theory. The distinction between copula and no-copula theories may then seem otiose. That it is not is, I think, surely evident with the advent of higher-order logics and general quantification theory. But apart from this, there remain important differences between the two theories of predication even on the level of extended first-order logics which have implications for Russell's later account. It is to these further differences that I wish to turn now.

If the copula is an essential ingredient in the formalization of the logic of our thoughts, then it ought, we may suppose, to be meaningful to ask whether there are diverse copulas and various forms of predication. But, on the other side, if the no-copula theory is the right theory of the logic or predication, then there are, it would seem, not styles of predications but merely different sorts of predicates. For the most part, contemporary theorizing has, in this respect and apart from set theory, gone the way of the no-copula theory. It is difficult to find articulate accounts which explicitly embrace a copula theory in the sense in which that would involve different forms of the copula in a significant way. One exception to the general trend, one person who explicitly argued for styles of copula and so for varying forms of predication, was the late Everett W. Hall. Hall, in a book-length argument, developed a kind of objectivist's theory of value, but a most unique kind. There are values, he thought, in the (Russellian) sense in which there are facts. They are not properties of things. They are not nameables to which we can make reference with abstract singulars like 'goodness'. They are not abstract entities whose ascription to objects is reflected in the occurrence of value-predicates (like 'good') in simple, singular, affirmative judgments. Rather, Hall thought, 'ought' is the fundamental valuative concept in terms of which others are ultimately understood, and the function of 'ought' is not as a predicate nor as a modal operator on sentences. It is rather a form of the copula. 'John is here' has, in the realm of value, Hall thought, a matching assertion: John ought to be here. The indicative nominalizing form, 'John's being here is the case' has a matching nominalization: John's being here ought to be the case. Both nominalizations, with their abstract references to (possible) states of affairs, are in fact implied by the simpler sentences, in which no nominalizations occur, which were cited in the preceding sentence. Those simpler sentences each exploit a mood of speech not a modal inflection. Each, but in different styles of predication, predicates his presence of the individual, John. The one predicates his presence in an affirmative, declarative way, literally in the declarative mood. The other predicates it, not in a declarative way, requiring for its truth the matching fact of John's presence, but in an evaluative way. It is, of course, not the purpose here to defend or even develop the detail of Hall's special form of value objectivism. The point here is that it is a rare expression of a theory which, if correct, requires that the copula is an essential ingredient of any adequate theory of predication precisely because there are diverse forms of predication, and distinct copulas, to be accounted for.

Hall went on, in a little known paper, to argue that there were additional forms of predication and so other forms of the copula.[1] All this is fun, I think, and, at least, it affords an example of what could be involved in trying to take seriously a copula theory of predication. Unfortunately, however, it is at best an interesting, if exotic, alternative to standard procedure. For surely the standard response, tacit in actual writings, would become explicit if challenged in this way. That response is this: why suppose there are diverse forms of predication and styles of the copula? Everything you say can be accounted for by assuming instead merely that there is one form of predication but many styles and varieties of predicates. And, since we already recognize various styles and varieties of predicates anyway, surely it is intellectually cleaner to attempt to analyse valuations and the other cases in the standard way. This at least has the merit of not populating our ontologies with proliferating species of non-objects: facts, values, . . ., whatnot.

But there is a last point to be made for the copula theorist. It is appropriate to raise it here, and then end with it, for it leads back to Russell and once more to Sellars's discussion of Russell's developing thought. It takes us to Sellars' discussion of Russell's "negative facts".

If, by contrast with Russell's no-copula theory, we assume that the copula is an essential logical ingredient in the expression of the judgments we make, then, it seems, there are three points upon which we might drape modal (and other) modifiers when we come to qualify simple judgments. This is something of a novelty, for, while we are used to discussions of modality *de dicto* or *de re*, this suggests a further richness. The questions are, now, first: what are the three points of qualification on the copula theory? Second, do we in fact require all three?

The logical form of simple, singular, affirmative judgments is, on the copula theory, this: singular term-copula-(abstract) singular terms. (Ontologically, there is a push to suppose that judgments of these forms will be made true, or will be satisfied, by there obtaining various types of complexes: facts, values, . . ., whatnot, in which the objects associated with the singular terms are related in the distinct, specific, ways indicated by the values of the copula.) Evidently, by contrast with the no-copula theory, there is now available an extra position for placing modal-like qualifiers on the basic sentence frame. Consider for instance negation. On the no-copula theory we have two formal ingredients, a singular (subject) term, say 'a', and a predicate frame, say '$\_F$', from which the singular, affirmative sentence, 'Fa', is formed. To negate this we seem to have these options: we can treat negation as expressed by a (*de dicto*) unary sentence operator which takes sentences into sentences, thus: 'It is not the case that Fa',

---

[1] "The Forms of Sentences and the Dimensions of Reality", which appears in a collection of Hall's papers edited by E. M. Adams, *Categorical Analysis*, Chapel Hill, N.C., 1964, pp. 69–90.

or, symbolically, '-*Fa*'; or we can treat negation as an operator on predicates, creating predicates from predicates, thus: 'is non-*F*', or, symbolically, '__$\bar{F}$'; or, negation may take both forms and we can set down implicational laws expressing the relations among sentences of each kind.

On the copula theory, by contrast, there is a position for yet a third form of negation. Historically, when our native language was more inflected than it is today, this occurred in the natural expression of thought. For, historically, negation occurred not merely as a sentence operator or predicate operator, but as a modifier of the copula. 'Willy-nilly' is a vestigial appendage of our linguistic heritage. In general, there once occurred the negated copulas, 'nis', 'nam', 'nil', contracting together negation and the declarative, tensed, copula. Further generalizing over this phenomenon, we see that there are three distinct modal-like qualifiers possible on the copula theory; those which modify the sentence, those which modify the predicate, and, now, those as well which modify the coupla. Moreover, not only negation can be viewed as occurring at each point. We say as well such things as 'It is possible that *a* is *F*', '*a* is-possibly *F*', and '*a* is a possible-*F*-er'. We might also say, with minor awkwardness, such things as 'It will be the case that *a* is *F*', '*a* will *F*', and even '*a* is a future *F*-er'. So, there is a richness to the copula theory not enjoyed by the no-copula theory. Is it a richness worth having?

That, finally, seems to be a question which turns more on philosophical inclinations than formal requirements. For example, if we return to negation, there is a strong inclination to reduce the various occurrences of negation operators to one standard sentence operator. In formalizing our negative judgments, '*a* is non-*F*' yields as a stylistic variant to the regimented 'It is not the case that *a* is *F*', and '*a* nis *F*' (thank goodness, we may think) no longer occurs at all. The issue is, however, whether we can say all we wish to say, and preserve all the distinctions we wish to preserve with the single, external, form of negation. There is, after all, a familiar drive to distinguish internal from external negation. Chairs, it might be maintained, are neither astringent nor not, and one might distinguish saying that it is false that Pegasus has fingers from the motivating fact that, after all, the beast is a mythical horse (and horses lack fingers), from saying this from the motivating fact that Pegasus, after all, is mythical. The fact is, if one so distinguishes internal from external negation, they of course do not collapse into the single, external form. '*a* is non-*F*' implies, but is not implied by, 'It is not the case that *a* is *F*'. (Professor G. H. von Wright developed characteristic theses for distinctions concerning negation.[1]) Are there any reasonable or plausible grounds for supposing that it is at all worth our while to distinguish not only external and internal negation but also the two, putative, forms of internal negation?

---

[1] *On the Logic of Negation*, Societas Scientiarum Fennica, Commentationes Physico-Mathematicae 22, 4, Helsinki 1959.

Russell, in the *Lectures*, argued th   there are negative facts. Negative facts, presumably, are complexes which make true our true denials of atomic propositions. Given Russell's logical atomism, and in virtue of the fact that accordingly atomic propositions are logically independent, in the sense in which there are (positive) facts which make true our true atomic propositions, so too there must be negative facts which make true those denials of atomic propositions which are true.

Sellars, commenting on Russell, and picking up a reference to Wittgenstein's remarks on this theme in the *Tractatus*, says this:

The issue, however, as Wittgenstein saw, is not "are there negative facts?" but are there negative *basic* facts about objects. . . . Wittgenstein failed, in the *Tractatus*, to see that he is committed to the view that 'not-(aRb)' is true because some (positive) atomic proposition incompatible with 'aRb', thus 'aR'b', does correctly represent a and b. Thus, 'a does not precede b' is true because 'a succeeds b' is true.

A standard objection to this move is that the incompatibility of *preceding* and *succeeding* would itself be a negative fact, and an "objective" one at that. If one is going to allow objective negative facts about relations, why not allow basic negative facts? Why not say that what makes "not-(aRb) true is the fact that not-(aRb)?" The answer involves taking seriously the idea that 'basic proposition' is not only a *logical* idea, but an *epistemic* one. . . . we must not confuse the irreducibility of negative facts with the basicness of negative facts.[1]

Sellars goes on to urge a view of facts, as structures of objects, most congenial to the no-copula theory of predication. It is interesting, and mildly curious (only mildly, since Russell was not thinking in these terms at that time), that Russell who came to hold a no-copula theory (with "verbs occurring as verbs", not as objects) argues in contrast to Sellars for negative facts.

Let us here suppose those cases which tempt us to say that a thing is not a given way (not because it is some way incompatible with its being the given way but rather) because it merely lacks the property or feature in question. We assume for now, that is, with Sellars, that all properties fall into families the members of which are mutually incompatible. There is no special reason in this case necessarily to view the operator on predicates as a negation operator. We might think of it simply as a "flip-flop" operator, as though the predicate were written upside down (Ramsey) or backwards (Ayer). If a is even, it is flip-odd. And if a is odd, it is, rather than not-even, flip-even. There is, as Ayer once pointed out somewhere, no reason to suppose that either "a is odd" or "a is even" is the positive statement with the remaining one its negation. And there is no reason not to generalize flip-flop operations on predicates to predicates in families rather than in pairs. It expresses after all the idea of complementation, and not that of negation. But if so, and if there remains sufficient motivation

---

[1] Sellars, this volume, p. 86.

to distinguish internal and external negations to accommodate astringent chair cases and winged horses, then we had better have a negative copula. For although '*a* is flip-odd' implies that it is not the case that *a* is odd, the latter, we may hold, does not imply the former. The latter, we may suppose, is true of Pegasus or our given chair, but the former is not. Neither the chair nor Pegasus is either odd or flip-odd, since neither is the right sort of thing to be either. What we have, on such an account, is apparently this: '*a* is flip-even' implies '*a* nis even', which in turn implies 'it is not the case that *a* is even'. But the last does not in turn imply that *a* nis even, for any object, *a*. '*a* nis even' implies and is implied by '*a* is flip-even', and '*a* nis odd' (i.e. '*a* nis flip-even') implies and is implied by '*a* is even', as well as that *a* is flip-flip-even. If, then, predicates come in arrays of complements, and if internal negations are to be distinguished from external negations, we seem to require a negation operator on the copula. We shall wish to assert '$(x)(x$ nis F. if and only if. x is flip-F)' and we shall wish to deny '(x)(it is not the case that x is F. if and only if. x nis F)'. The ontological moral to the story of negative facts emerges in this way; internal negation is explicable in terms of complementation. Sellars is right in this respect in saying that there are irreducible negative propositions which nonetheless are not epistemically basic. But external negation remains to be explicated, and is not explicable in terms of complementation. It reflects the notion, not of being incompatible with something, but of being other than it. And the drive to find in negative facts the source of what makes such judgments true is not explained away by referring to complementation.

Russell's later, no-copula theory of facts owes us thus an account of otherness and complementation as well. And Russell still has a debt to pay in the new currency of his later, no-copula theory. He still owes us an account of the nature of the ascription of false beliefs to agents, the problem which lead to his earlier, unsatisfactory characterization of judgment in the *Problems.* That these problems still remain to interest and exercise us, is of course a tribute to Russell's memory and influence; a debt of gratitude is owed Sellars for isolating and renewing these themes from the complexity of Russell's work.

David Pears

Russell's Theories of Memory 1912–1921

Between 1912 and 1921 Russell produced two different theories of memory. The first appeared in *The Problems of Philosophy* (1912), and he adhered to it until 1919. It is true that he modified it towards the end of this period. But it remained essentially the same theory until 1919, when it was replaced by a new theory. The old theory had to go when he abandoned the ego and gave an account of judgment which, unlike the account that he had given in 1910,[1] dispensed with the ego.[2] I shall call the two theories of memory "Theory I" and "Theory II", and each of them must be understood against the background of the account of judgment with which it was associated.

Theory I

Theory I is sketched in *The Problems of Philosophy*. It relies mainly on acquaintance, which is a direct relation between subject and object. It is, therefore, not a representative theory.

But how much can acquaintance do across an interval of time? Did Russell really think that it can reach back into the past, and fasten on to a particular perceived more than thirty seconds ago? There is no doubt that he thought that acquaintance with a perceived particular lasts as long as this. For according to him this is the duration of the specious present. The controversial question is whether he allowed that it lasts beyond the limit of the specious present. The difference between these two kinds of memory may be marked in Russell's way: memory of the specious present is immediate, and memory that reaches back beyond the limit of the specious present is remote. Then the question is whether remote memory involves acquaintance with the previously perceived particular.

There is another question about his treatment of remote memory which needs to be answered first. He often says that he is concerned only with true remote memory. Here "true" means "genuine", and his point is that he is concerned only with genuine, or paradigmatic cases of remote memory. So we need to know which kind of remote memory he regards as the paradigm.

His treatment of immediate memory also raises two questions. First, he seems to attribute infallibility to it, and it is not clear why he thinks this true, or

[1] "On the Nature of Truth and Falsehood", in *Philosophical Essays*, London 1910. Page references are to *Philosophical Essays*.

[2] "On Propositions", in *Logic and Knowledge*, ed. R. C. Marsh, London 1956. Page references are to *Logic and Knowledge*.

necessary. It may have seemed to him to be necessary because immediate memory had to be infallible in order to perform the functions that he assigned to it in Theory I. But this raises the second question: What was the function that he assigned to it?

I shall begin with this last question. Russell assigned two distinct functions to immediate memory in this period. First, he regarded it as the source of our understanding of the concept "past". According to him we acquire this concept through our experience of the specious present. A sensation occurs, fades, and vanishes, and, when this happens, he thought that there is no change of identity between the moment when it comes into existence and the moment when it ceases to exist about thirty seconds later. So, according to him, we enjoy acquaintance with something which is literally past, and through this acquaintance we acquire the concept "past" in much the same way that we acquire the concept "red".

He describes this function of immediate memory in "On the Experience of Time" (1915):

No doubt, in cases of remembering something not very recent, we have often only acquaintance with an image, combined with the *judgment* that something like the image occurred in the past. But such memory is liable to error, and therefore does not involve *perception* of a fact of which "past" is a constituent. Since, however, the word 'past' has significance for us, there must be perception of facts in which it occurs, and in such cases memory must not be liable to error. . . .

It is essential that the object of immediate memory should be, at least in part, identical with the object previously given in sense, since otherwise immediate memory would not give acquaintance with what is past, and would not seem to account for our knowledge of the past. . . . The epistemological need of the immediate experience is to make us know what is meant by 'past', and to give us data on which our knowledge can be built.[1]

In the second of these two passages Russell alludes to the other function that he assigns to immediate memory. It "gives us data on which our knowledge can be built". This is a different function, because knowledge of truths is not the same thing as understanding of meanings. Immediate memory performs this function by giving us direct verification of the reliability of memory; we then extrapolate this result to remote memory. "When we use images as an aid to remembering, we judge that the images have a resemblance of a certain sort to certain past sense-data, enabling us to have knowledge by description concerning those sense-data, through acquaintance with the corresponding images together with a knowledge of the correspondence. The knowledge of the correspondence is obviously only possible through some knowledge concerning the past, which is not dependent on the images we now call up."[2]

[1] "On the Experience of Time", *Monist* (1915).
[2] "Sensation and Imagination", *Monist* (1915), p. 35.

"Sensation and Imagination" was also published in 1915. If it had been written at the same time as *The Problems of Philosophy*, we could have interpreted this as an allusion to acquaintance with particulars perceived in the remote past. For, as I shall show later, Russell really did believe in the possibility of such acquaintance in 1912. However, "Sensation and Imagination" must be read with "On the Experience of Time", which implies that the acquaintance which gives us direct knowledge of truths about our pasts does not reach back beyond the limit of the specious present. He was, therefore, changing his mind about the range of acquaintance with particulars perceived in the past. If he had still felt confident in 1915 that its range extended into the remote past, he would not have assigned this function specifically to immediate memory. The same is true of the other function that he assigns to immediate memory in 1915.

In the first of the two passages quoted from "On the Experience of Time", he says that immediate memory must be infallible. His reason is that, if it were not infallible, we could not acquire the concept "past" through it. In "On the Nature of Acquaintance" (p. 151) he gives what may be taken as a different reason, connected with the other function that he assigns to immediate memory: "If the past can never be experienced in memory, how, we must inquire, can it ever come to be known that the object now experienced in memory is at all similar to the past object? And if this cannot be known, the whole of our supposed knowledge of the past becomes illusory. . . ." If this passage had been written in 1912, it too could have been interpreted as an allusion to acquaintance with particulars perceived in the remote past. But "Sensation and Imagination" and "On the Experience of Time" are the immediate sequel to "On the Nature of Acquaintance", and so "experiencing the past in memory" must, at least, refer to immediate memory, and perhaps refers only to immediate memory.

But do either of these two reasons give sufficient support to the conclusion that immediate memory must be infallible? All that they really establish is that the two functions assigned to immediate memory require that it should be as reliable as perception. However, Russell's pre-1919 views about perception inclined him to treat it as infallible, and since immediate memory is a scarcely noticeable extension of perception, it would have a similar claim to infallibility. So, even if the two functions assigned to immediate memory did not require infallibility, he was moving along another road towards the conclusion that it was, in fact, infallible.

Before 1919 he treated sensation as if it amounted to perception. A sense-datum is presented to the ego, and this means that the ego is acquainted with the sense-datum. He said later that this account was mistaken, because it treated sensation as if it were a form of cognition,[1] whereas really it is only "that part

---

[1] *My Philosophical Development*, London 1957, p. 135.

of the total experience [sc. perception] which is due to the stimulus alone, independently of past history. This is a theoretical core in the total occurrence. The total occurrence is always an interpretation in which the sensational core has accretions embodying habits."[1]

In fact, his pre-1919 theory about the way in which acquaintance yields knowledge of perceptual truths was more elaborate than his later remarks suggest. In 1918 he said that a sense-datum is a simple particular and that it is the meaning of the logically proper name that I attach to it when I am acquainted with it.[2] But this was only an approximate statement of his view. For, at least at a slightly earlier date, he was inclined to think that some sense-data are too complex to be the bearers of logically proper names. For example, in 1914 he said:

There is some difficulty in deciding what is to be considered *one* sense-datum: often attention causes divisions to appear when, so far as can be discovered, there were no divisions before. An observed complex fact, such as that this patch of red is to the left of that patch of blue, is also to be regarded as a datum from our point of view: epistemologically it does not differ greatly from a simple sense-datum as regards its function in giving knowledge. Its *logical* structure is very different, however, from that of sense: *sense* gives acquaintance with particulars, and is thus a two-term relation in which the object can be *named* but not asserted, and is inherently incapable of truth or falsehood, whereas the observation of a complex fact, which may be suitably called "perception", is not a two-term relation, but involves the propositional form on the object side, and gives knowledge of a truth, not mere acquaintance with a particular.[3]

One reaction to this difference would have been to say that a datum of this complexity does not count as a sense-datum. But he did not take this line in 1912, because in *The Problems of Philosophy* he included data of this kind among sense-data.[4] If he still included them in 1918, he cannot have believed that all sense-data are fit to bear logically proper names.

He evidently did not feel the same doubts about what he calls "simple sense-data" in this passage—i.e. coloured patches and such-like.[5] A datum of this kind cannot be analysed into a group of simple particulars, and so he felt no hesitation in classifying it as a sense-datum. According to him, it is simple, in spite of possessing a property, and its simplicity enables it to bear a logically proper name. His next step was to allow acquaintance with simple sense-data to extend to their possession of their properties.

He also took a second step, which is, perhaps, equally understandable. He allowed acquaintance with the more complex kind of datum to extend to its

---

[1] ibid., p. 143.
[2] "The Philosophy of Logical Atomism", in *Philosophical Essays*, p. 200.
[3] "The Relation of Sense-Data to Physics", in *Mysticism and Logic*, London 1917, p. 147.
[4] *The Problems of Philosophy*, London 1912, p. 180.
[5] ibid., pp. 72, 178, and "Knowledge by Acquaintance and Knowledge by Description", in *Mysticism and Logic*, p. 213.

internal structure. For example, in Chapter II of *Principia Mathematica* he says:

Let us consider a complex object composed of two parts *a* and *b* standing to each other in the relation *R*. The complex object "*a*-in-the-relation-*R*-to-*b*" may be capable of being *perceived*; when perceived it is perceived as one object. Attention may show that it is complex, we then *judge* that *a* and *b* stand in the relation *R*. Such a judgment, being derived from perception by mere attention, may be called "a judgment of perception". This judgment of perception, considered as an actual occurrence, is a relation of four terms, namely *a* and *b* and *R* and the percipient. The perception, on the other hand, is a relation of two terms, namely "*a*-in-the-relation-*R*-to-*b*" and the percipient. Since an object of perception cannot be nothing, we cannot perceive "*a*-in-the-relation-*R*-to-*b*" unless *a* is in the relation *R* to *b*. Hence a judgment of perception, according to the above definition, must be true.[1]

In this passage he must mean that the percipient is acquainted with the complex object. This is made quite clear in the parallel treatment of this topic in *The Problems of Philosophy*.[2] So he certainly takes the second step, and allows acquaintance with a complex datum to extend to its internal structure.

This suggests the possibility of a third step. Could he not say that acquaintance with a datum, whether it be a simple sense-datum or a datum of the more complex kind, will yield infallible knowledge of a truth about it? In the passage quoted from *Principia Mathematica* he seems to be on the point of taking this third step. Admittedly, he distinguishes perception from judgment, just as in the parallel passage in *The Problems of Philosophy* he distinguishes acquaintance from judgment. But in each case the first thing seems to lead automatically to the second, and the second is said to be infallible.

However, he did not take the third step so precipitately. It is true that it is required by his doctrine "that error can only arise when we regard the immediate object, i.e. the sense-datum, as the mark of some physical object".[3] For this implies that we cannot go wrong so long as we confine ourselves to describing our sense-data without saying anything about their causes or configurations. But in fact he was more cautious, at least in the passage quoted from *Principia Mathematica*, which continues: "This does not mean that in a judgment which *appears* to us to be one of perception we are sure of not being in error, since we may err in thinking that our judgment has really been derived merely by analysis of what was perceived." So there is a proviso attached to the thesis that these judgments of perception are infallible: when I make the judgment I must confine myself to what can be extracted by analysis from the complex object—or, as he sometimes calls it, "the complex fact"[4]—with which I am acquainted. When I analyse the complex fact and "separate out its constituents", I may go

---

[1] *Principia Mathematica*, 1st ed., Cambridge 1910, vol. 1, p. 43.
[2] *The Problems of Philosophy*, pp. 178 ff.
[3] ibid., p. 172.
[4] ibid., p. 211.

wrong.[1] Presumably, this risk also attends judgments about so-called "simple sense-data".

So he never really took the third step. But his pre-1919 theory of judgment pushed him in that direction. For, according to that theory, when someone makes a judgment, the self is acquainted with the particulars and universals which are mentioned in it or in its analysis. To judge is to arrange these things in thought. If the author of the judgment is confronted with an array of the same things in a perceived fact, it might well seem that he could hardly go wrong. But really this would be an illusion, produced by neglect of the question, how the percipient identifies the things, and by concentration on the question, how they are arranged. It is no accident that so many of Russell's examples in this period involve spatial relations. Such examples focus attention on the internal structure of the perceived fact and suggest that the percipient can analyse it and report it without drawing on his memory of anything outside it.

He soon realized that this would be an impossible feat. But while he still held these theories of sensation and judgment, he was nearly led to ascribe infallibility to the percipient. Judgments of immediate memory had an almost equal right to the treatment. So he credited them with rather more reliability than reality or the two functions that he assigned to immediate memory required.

The next question for discussion is the question, what kind of remote memory Russell regarded as paradigmatic. This question is not too easy to answer, because he always specifies the phenomenon in a way that involves his theory about it. Thus in *The Problems of Philosophy*, at a time when, according to my interpretation, he maintained Theory I, he specifies paradigmatic remote memory in the following way:

There is some danger of confusion as to the nature of memory, owing to the fact that memory of an object is apt to be accompanied by an image of the object, and yet the image cannot be what constitutes memory. This is easily seen by merely noticing that the image is in the present, whereas what is remembered is known to be in the past. Moreover, we are certainly able to some extent to compare our image with the object remembered, so that we often know, within somewhat wide limits, how far our image is accurate; but this would be impossible, unless the object, as opposed to the image, were in some way before the mind. Thus the essence of memory is not constituted by the image, but by having immediately before the mind an object which is recognized as past.[2]

After he had adopted Theory II, he could no longer specify paradigmatic remote memory in this way. For Theory II is a representative theory of remote memory, and in it the function of acquaintance with particulars in the past had been entirely taken over by the occurrence of images. So in *The Analysis of Mind* (1921) he specifies paradigmatic remote memory by contrasting it with

[1] ibid., p. 214.
[2] ibid., p. 180.

habit-memory. "The recollection of a unique event cannot, so Bergson contends, be wholly constituted by habit, and is in fact something radically different from the memory which is habit. The recollection alone is true memory."[1]

Without going any further into the details imported by Theories I and II, I think that it is possible to discern the kind of case that he regarded as paradigmatic. We could describe it as the kind of case in which a person is in the most direct contact with his past that the current theory allows. But this is a metaphorical description. The test would be this: can the person check his memory impression or supplement it without using any resources except those provided by his own memory? If so, it is a paradigmatic memory. It is easy to understand Russell's picture of paradigmatic memory in the early stage of Theory I. Theory II introduces a complication, because it is not so easy to understand why he calls the contrasting cases habit-memories. Why should the checks and the supplementations not themselves be the effects of habit? More radically, how can we determine whether they are or not? It would be too simple to assume, as he does, that memories that come in words are always habit-memories.[2]

But perhaps it is sufficiently clear what phenomenon Russell regarded as the paradigmatic case of remote memory. About this phenomenon there remains one more question to be discussed. While he adhered to Theory I, did he allow that acquaintance with particulars reaches back beyond the limit of the specious present?

In my book *Bertrand Russell and the British Tradition in Philosophy*, I gave an affirmative answer to this question right down to 1919.[3] J. O. Urmson, in his review of my book, argues that this certainly does not fit "The Philosophy of Logical Atomism" (1917–18), and probably ought not to be read into *The Problems of Philosophy*.[4]

Perhaps the first point that should be made is that, if Russell ever did hold Theory I, the so-called "realist" theory of paradigmatic remote memory, he certainly never said that an event witnessed by a person in the past continues to exist, so that now, when he remembers it, the relation between the act and the object does not need to span a period of time. No doubt, others have said this, but if Russell treated paradigmatic remote memory like perception, at least he treated it like perception through a time-telescope. This is made very clear in two remarks about the "realist" theory which he made at a time when he certainly did not hold it.

Take . . . the remembering of a past event. The remembering occurs now, and is therefore necessarily not identical with the past event. So long as we retain the act, this need cause

---

[1] *The Analysis of Mind*, London 1921, p. 166.

[2] ibid., pp. 175–6.

[3] London 1967 (rev. ed. 1972), pp. 71, 151–2.

[4] J. O. Urmson, *Philosophical Review* 18, 4 (1969). See a note on this controversy by R. K. Perkins Jr. forthcoming in *Mind*.

no difficulty. The act of remembering occurs now, and has on this view a certain essential relation to the past event which it remembers.[1]

If we had retained the "subject" or "act" in knowledge, the whole problem of memory would have been comparatively simple. We could then have said that remembering is a direct relation between the present act or subject and the past occurrence remembered: the act of remembering is present, though its object is past.[2]

This is made even clearer in a passage that he wrote earlier, when he may still have been inclined to hold Theory I.

We are told [by Meinong] that it is impossible the presentation should exist now, if its content does not exist now. But if presentation consists wholly and solely, as we have contended, in a relation of subject and object, then a memory-presentation is a complex of which one constituent is present while the other is past. It is not clear that such a complex has any definite position in the time-series: the fact that the remembering subject is in the present is no sufficient reason for regarding the whole complex as present.[3]

But does this passage show that at the time of writing "On the Nature of Acquaintance" Russell actually held the "realist" theory of paradigmatic remote memory? It certainly seems to show this. For he is arguing against Meinong, and so might be expected not to put forward any thesis to which he did not subscribe at the time. However, "On the Nature of Acquaintance" has to be read in its context, because it is only the beginning of a complete book on the theory of knowledge which has not yet been published as a whole. "Sensation and Imagination" and "On the Experience of Time" are the next instalments of this book, and the two functions which he there ascribes to immediate memory clearly indicate that at the very least he is no longer confident about the "realist" theory of remote memory. In the unpublished part of the book (the *Theory of Knowledge* MS in the Bertrand Russell Archive, McMaster University) this is corroborated. He poses the question whether we have acquaintance with past particulars in remote memory, and his answer is that he is inclined to think that we do not, but that he is not quite sure.

So it is certain that he was doubtful about the point at the time of writing "On the Nature of Acquaintance". But in "The Philosophy of Logical Atomism" he says things which, as Urmson rightly insists,[4] show that he has now made up his mind, and no longer believes that acquaintance with particulars reaches beyond the limit of the specious present. However, if we go back to 1912, we find him clearly committing himself to the "realist" theory. The best evidence is the passage already quoted from *The Problems of Philosophy*, which continues:

[1] *The Analysis of Mind*, p. 21.
[2] ibid., p. 163.
[3] "On the Nature of Acquaintance", in *Logic and Knowledge*, p. 171.
[4] Urmson, loc. cit. "The Philosophy of Logical Atomism", pp. 201–3.

Thus the essence of memory is not constituted by the image, but by having immediately before the mind an object which is recognized as past. But for the fact of memory in this sense, we should not know that there ever was a past at all, nor would we be able to understand the word 'past' any more than a man born blind can understand the word 'light'. Thus there must be intuitive judgements of memory, and it is upon them, ultimately, that all our knowledge of the past depends.[1]

It is, of course, tempting to read this as the first statement of the thesis of "Sensation and Imagination" and "On the Experience of Time", that the two functions are performed by immediate memory. But this interpretation is ruled out by the examples which Russell proceeds to give. They are examples of recent and vivid memories, but the time-interval starts at half a minute and increases. This proves that when he refers to "the fact of memory in this sense", he does not mean immediate memory, but, rather, as I argued earlier, paradigmatic remote memory. It is true that he does not mention acquaintance in this passage, but there really is not any other relation which he could have believed to hold between the ego and the past particular.

So in 1912 Russell relied on acquaintance with past particulars not only in immediate memory, but also in paradigmatic remote memory. Consequently, when he investigated the certainty of memory-judgments, he found no sharp break at the point of transition from immediate to remote memory, and his scale of self-evident truths is continuously graded into the not so recent past.[2] The 1910 account of judgment applied to paradigmatic remote memory in the same way that it applied to immediate memory. In both cases alike a person is acquainted with a past fact and with the particulars and universals that are its constituents, and, since to make a judgment is to arrange these things in thought, it seems easy to secure correspondence between judgment and fact. So long as the memory remains paradigmatic, there is only a gradual decrease in certainty as the fact recedes into the past.

But Russell soon began to feel doubts about the range of acquaintance with past particulars, and by 1917 he had abandoned Theory I, the "realist" account of remote memory. However, some of the elements of Theory I still survived. For the ego still remained as one of the terms in the dual relation, acquaintance, even if there was now a severe restriction put on the range of the other terms.

Theory II

Before 1919, Theory I had already lost its most distinctive component, the thesis that we enjoy acquaintance with particulars perceived in the remote past. But it was still based on the assumption that in immediate memory, acquaintance with perceived particulars lasts as long as the specious present. When

---

[1] *The Problems of Philosophy*, p. 180.
[2] ibid., pp. 180–5.

Russell abandoned the ego in 1919, he ceased to regard acquaintance as a dual relation between ego and object. This development produced three consequences. First, it led him to formulate a new account of judgment, in which images play an essential role. This was a considerable change. For in his earlier account of judgment, the essential role was played by the direct relations acquaintance, and judging, which held between the ego and the objects outside the mind which were the constituents of the proposition judged to be true; images, if they occurred, were a luxury. The second consequence was that neither perception nor immediate memory could be reduced to mere acquaintance. For if acquaintance was not a dual relation between ego and object, it was no longer plausible to suppose that it amounted to knowledge. Interpretation was obviously needed, and interpretation required a point of support outside what was immediately given. The third consequence was that it became quite impossible to treat remote memory as a direct cognitive relation between the ego and past particulars. Russell had already reached this conclusion by another route, and it now became over-determined.

This complex series of changes is confusing, and I shall try to show that there is one point in it which confused Russell himself. In remote memory, images are now brought in for two distinct reasons. They are required as representative data, and they are also required as the elements out of which memory-propositions are formed. If we do not keep these two functions of images carefully separated, we shall confuse two opposed directions of fit. First, there is the case described by Wittgenstein: "But it is also possible for a face to come before my mind, and then for me to be able to draw it, without my remembering whose it is or when I have seen it."[1] Here the image would be a datum, and, if it struck me as familiar, it would pose the question, "Who is this?", and I would then try to fit a name to an image. But this direction of fit would be reversed if I started with the question, "What does Mr. A look like?". In this case my image would not lead to a question: rather, it would come as the answer to a question already asked. The direction of fit, therefore, would be reversed.

Now I am not going to argue that Russell simply confused these two cases with one another when he developed Theory II. What I shall try to show is that he did not distinguish between them sufficiently clearly, and that this produces flaws in the theory at several points.

But first something must be said about the new account of propositions, and the function of images in it. It is given in "On Propositions". His rejection of the subject made it necessary to find something else to put in its place. He puts what he calls "the content of the belief" in this position.[2] The content is what is believed, if it is a case of belief, and it is the same thing as the proposition. It is made up of words, images or both.[3] But images are the gold, and words are

[1] Wittgenstein, *Philosophical Investigations*, part 2, iii.
[2] "On Propositions", p. 307.
[3] ibid., p. 308.

only paper currency, because we understand the meanings of words only if we are able to get the right images. When words "operate without the medium of images, this seems to be a telescoped process. Thus the problem of the meaning of words is reduced to the problem of the meaning of images."[1] The meaning of an image depends partly on resemblance, but it is partly "within the control of our will. . . . The image of a triangle may mean one particular triangle or triangles in general."[2] Finally, in addition to words and images, sensations may occur as parts of propositions;[3] i.e. when someone makes a judgment about a sensation, the sensation itself may occur autonymously in the proposition. In such a case, the sensation functions in two different ways simultaneously, as a datum, and as a symbol of itself, i.e. autonymously.

This account of propositions is repeated in *The Analysis of Mind*, and the possibility of the autonymous occurrence of sensations is explained at greater length.[4] When it is applied to memory, the result is a theory with two layers: first, Russell analyses the general phenomenon of memory in animals as well as in human beings, and then, on this basis, he builds up a theory about what only human beings can achieve. One explanation of the superiority that he attributes to images is that, like Aristotle, he wants to show that there is a continuous development from animals to human beings. "It would seem that image-propositions are more primitive than word-propositions, and may well ante-date language. There is no reason why memory-images accompanied by that very simple belief-feeling which we decided to be the essence of memory, should not have occurred before language arose; indeed, it would be rash to assert positively that memory of this sort does not occur among the higher animals."[5] Another explanation of the supposed superiority of images is that, according to him, they express paradigmatic memories, whereas words express habit-memories. This view is connected with his failure to maintain a clear distinction between cases in which images function as data and cases in which they function as symbols. It is easy to see why he assigned both these functions to a single sensation occurring autonymously. For the sensation occurs now, and the proposition has to contain a reference to it and a description of it. But when an image occurs in a proposition of remote memory, what it refers to and describes is not itself, functioning as a datum, but something else which lies in the past.

When Russell applies his new account of propositions to remote memory, he modifies his 1915 thesis that pastness is one of their constituents. His view now is that a paradigmatic proposition of this kind consists of a tenseless core of images and that pastness is not signified by anything in its content. Pastness comes in

---

[1] ibid., pp. 302–3. cf. Berkeley, *Principles of Human Knowledge*, Introduction, para. xx.
[2] "On Propositions", p. 303.
[3] ibid., p. 311.
[4] *The Analysis of Mind*, pp. 201, 237–9.
[5] ibid., p. 242.

in an entirely different way, as a specific modification of the feeling of belief which he now takes over from Hume. This feeling, which attaches to propositions, has not only a generic form, bare non-temporal assent, but also two specific temporal forms, memory and expectation.[1] When he develops this theory of belief in *The Analysis of Mind*, he takes care to point out that, when a proposition about the past is believed on inductive grounds, pastness is signified by something in its content, and the attached feeling is non-temporal assent. Analogously, when a proposition about the future is believed on inductive grounds, futurity is usually signified by something in its content. The specific past-oriented feeling of belief is only needed for paradigmatic remote memories, and the specific future-oriented feeling of belief is only needed for what he calls "expectations". We might have supposed that he would have said "precognitions", but he says "expectations", and he is referring to a particular kind of inductively grounded belief: he means the kind of expectations that are unhesitatingly formed, and immediately and personally verified, like the expectation of thunder after lightning.[2]

The third consequence of his abandoning the ego was that his rejection of the "realist" theory of remote memory was now over-determined and irrevocable. This left him in a position in which he might have been expected to re-emphasize his 1915 thesis that remote memory depends on immediate memory not only for the acquisition of the concept "past" but also for the verification of the correspondence of image to original. But the curious thing is that he says very little about those two points in *The Analysis of Mind*. He said that "there may be a specific feeling of 'pastness', especially where immediate memory is concerned", and that "immediate memory is important because it bridges the gulf between sensations and the images which are their copies".[3] However, there is no development of these points, and it might appear that he believed that the concept "past" is acquired through remote memory.

If this was his view in *The Analysis of Mind*, the concept "past" would have to be derived from some property of the images that occur in remote memory. He mentions two properties of images which he might have regarded as the source of the concept. One is familiarity and the other is the property "which makes us regard them as referring to more or less remote portions of the past", and which he actually called "pastness".[4] But it is implausible to suppose that these properties of images, or any others, could play this role. No doubt, familiarity is a felt property of certain images. But it suggests the proposition "I have experienced something like this before" only to someone who already possesses the concept "past". Presumably, the same is true of whatever property Russell means by the "pastness" of an image. In general, such properties of images get

---

[1] "On Propositions", pp. 308, 311.
[2] *The Analysis of Mind*, pp. 176, 251–2.
[3] ibid., pp. 162, 175.
[4] ibid., pp. 161, 162.

their names from the propositions which they suggest, and they suggest propositions containing the concept "past" only to those who have already learned the meaning of that word at closer quarters. In some cases it would seem to be an illusion even to suggest that there is a property, or at least to suggest that it can be identified independently of the proposition which it suggests.

If all such theories about the source of the concept "past" are implausible, and if Russell has in reserve a more plausible theory, according to which we acquire it in a less remote way, it is natural to suppose that he is relying on such a theory in *The Analysis of Mind*. But there are two passages that seem to go against this interpretation. So if it is going to be adopted, the two passages must be reconciled with it.

One of the two passages occurs in *The Analysis of Mind*: "It might be contended that a memory-image acquires meaning only through the memory belief, which would seem, at least in the case of memory, to make belief more primitive than the meaning of images."[1] This is paradoxical because, if belief requires a proposition, and if the proposition is formed out of images, there would not be anything to believe until the images had acquired meanings. However, the paradox is put forward tentatively. But in the second passage, in "On Propositions", which was written earlier, he puts it forward without reservations:

It is clear that, when we remember by means of images, the images are accompanied by a belief, a belief which may be expressed (though with undue explicitness) by saying that they are felt to be copies of something that existed previously. And, without memory, images conld hardly acquire meaning. Thus the analysis of belief is essential even to a full account of the meaning of words and images—for the meaning of words, we found, depends on that of images, which in turn depends on memory, which is itself a form of belief.[2]

These obscure remarks amount to the suggestion that in the case of certain memory propositions belief comes before understanding. But how could that be so? It is just possible that what Russell meant was that among the propositions of remote memory there are some which function like ostensive definitions and produce understanding of the concept "past" in much the same way that "This is red" produces understanding of the concept "red". But he never says this, and in any case another interpretation fits his remarks better.

What they probably mean is that there is a certain property of images which leads us to give them a past reference and to believe that they correspond to past experiences of ours. This would only happen to us when we already possessed the concept "past". So in these passages, he would not be trying to explain our

[1] ibid., p. 235.
[2] "On Propositions", p. 306. The rest of the page references in this essay are to *The Analysis of Mind*.

acquisition of the concept, but only the fact that after we have acquired it we give certain images a past reference. The paradox is then less extreme. He is not saying that belief is more primitive than understanding in such cases, but only that it is more primitive than past reference. His idea is that an image occurs as a datum and strikes me as familiar, and so produces a belief in me, and then, in order to express this belief, I put the image into a proposition in which it has a reference to the past. This interpretation allows us to suppose that he still adhered to his 1915 theory about our acquisition of the concept "past".

Although this is almost certainly what he meant, it is still a paradoxical thesis. For when we scrutinize the details of this complex process, difficulties appear. First, consider the function assigned to familiarity. It must be remembered that Theory II has to explain the transition from the common achievements of higher animals and human beings to those that are peculiar to human beings. He begins with the common achievements, and builds up his theory from them. He points out that a person's belief that a particular image corresponds to a past experience of his, "must, in fundamental cases, be based on a characteristic of the image itself, since we cannot evoke the past bodily and compare it with the present image" (p. 161). The characteristic is familiarity, which, according to him, is a feeling which need not involve a proposition. "The judgment that what is familiar has been experienced before is a product of reflection, and is no part of the feeling of familiarity, such as a horse may be supposed to have when he returns to his stable" (p. 169). It is a feeling capable of degrees: "In an image of a well-known face, for example, some parts may feel more familiar than others; when this happens we have more belief in the accuracy of the familiar parts than in that of the unfamiliar parts. I think that it is by this means that we become critical of images not by some imageless memory with which we compare them" (pp. 161-2). In this passage he says nothing about the resources provided by immediate memory, and simply pits his new image theory of remote memory against his earlier "realist" theory.

But how much can be extracted from the feeling of familiarity? Does it really provide a general explanation of the fact that we refer certain images to the past and believe that they correspond to past experiences of ours? Or does it explain these two facts only in the special case described by Wittgenstein, where the image does not come in response to a question, and the direction of fit is the reverse? And even in this kind of case we might feel doubts about the function assigned to familiarity. Russell seems to import into this kind of case a definite reference to the past, which is only appropriate to the other kind of case, where the definite reference is supplied by the prior question. If an image strikes me as familiar, I only give it an indefinite reference to my past.

I am not arguing that he actually confuses the two opposed directions of fit. For he says that in human beings a familiar image suggests the claim "I have experienced something like this before", whereas recollection usually produces a claim such as "I had two eggs for breakfast", which expresses the attachment of the past-oriented feeling of belief to an image (p. 175). Now there are several differences between his descriptions of these two situations. In the first the claim is indefinite, the feeling is familiarity, and presumably no attempt at recollection has yet occurred: but in the second the claim is definite, the feeling is past-oriented belief, and there has probably been an attempt at recollection. However, he never explicitly draws the distinction between the two directions of fit, and he tries to show that the second type of case develops smoothly out of the first, without any sharp discontinuities. This is understandable, because his theory is an attempt to build up human memory out of elements that exist at the lower level of animal memory, and so it is natural for him to blur certain differences between the first case, which is quite like what happens when an animal remembers something, and the second case, which is not.

The fundamental reason for his lack of clarity about the differences between the two cases is his adoption of an image theory of propositions. The image which occurs in the situation described by Wittgenstein may be exactly like the image which would have occurred if the direction of fit had been reversed. Hence, it is only too easy to minimize the difference between the first situation, in which the image is a datum, and, perhaps, a sign, in the sense in which a colossal bang is a sign that something catastrophic has happened, and the second situation, which exhibits the reversed direction of fit, because the image is a symbol which is part of my propositional answer to the question about the appearance of my absent friend. This difference could not have been minimized by anyone who treated words rather than images as the primary components of propositions.

There are several other factors which join in the conspiracy to keep the difference between datum and symbol out of sight. The most important one is Russell's well-known assimilation of remote memory to sense-perception. "If [a sensation] is part of a perception [of a person], we may say that the person presented is an object of consciousness. For in this case, the sensation is a *sign* of the perceived object in much the same way in which a memory image is a sign of the remembered object" (p. 292). General assent to this description of memory-images is unlikely to be revoked even when they are evidently functioning as symbols.

His theory that sensations may occur autonymously in propositions may also play a part at this point. For when a sensation occurs autonymously in the judgment "___ is of Jones", where the blank is filled by the sensation itself, the difference between datum and symbol is very inconspicuous. It would be equally easy to miss if an image occurred autonymously in the judgment "___ has occurred before in my experience". Now he never actually says that a memory-image ought to be regarded as the past experience itself occurring autonymously in the present judgment. He could not have said that even when he held his "realist" theory of remote memory. For even then he did not think that the past experience recurred as a present object. And he was even further from being in a position to say it after he had given up the theory. However, in *The Analysis of Mind*, he does take a step in that direction. He says:

We might be tempted to put the memory-belief into the words: "Something like this image occurred". But such words would be very far from an accurate translation of the simplest kind of memory-belief. 'Something like this image' is a very complicated conception. In the simplest kind of memory we are not aware of the difference between an image and the sensation which it copies, which may be called its prototype. When the image is before us, we judge rather "This occurred". The image is not distinguished from the object which existed in the past: the word 'this' covers both, and enables us to have a memory-belief which does not introduce the complicated notion 'something like this'. (p. 179)

To say "this occurred" when confronted by a memory image, with no distinction made between the image and its prototype, is as close as he can get to saying "____ occurred" where the blank is filled by the prototype itself.

An auxiliary role is played by the fact that in certain cases the feeling of familiarity really does seem to develop quite smoothly into the past-oriented feeling of belief (though Russell never identifies the two feelings). In the situation described by Wittgenstein the image of the face strikes me as familiar, and, since I am a human being and not a horse, this is equivalent to saying that it strikes me that I have seen it somewhere before, even if only in a dream. But, according to Russell, if I accept this, I have a past-oriented feeling of belief directed on to the tenseless proposition, "I see this". So in this case it seems natural to say that the feeling of familiarity develops into the propositional attitude.

But when we look more deeply into the differences between the two so-called "feelings", it turns out to be much more plausible to say that they are two quite different things and that the second occurs after, and as a result of the first.

Consider familiarity. If we call it a felt property of certain things, we must take care to add that the proposition which it suggests is part of the criterion of identity of the feeling. Now what it suggests is a memory claim with an indefinite reference to the past. But Russell neglects this part of the criterion of identity of the felt property, because he concentrates on the feeling of familiarity rather than on the judgment that a thing is familiar, and, according to him, the indefinite memory-claim expresses a kind of recognition which "differs from the sense of familiarity by being cognitive: it is a belief or judgment, which the sense of familiarity is not" (p. 170) (cf. the remark already quoted about the horse and its stable). But though the judgment is not identical with the sense of familiarity, it is part of its criterion of identity. For even if a person does not formulate an indefinite memory-claim, we say that something struck him as familiar only because he would formulate it, or, at least, because he has a basis for formulating it: and though a horse could not formulate it, we say that something struck it as familiar only because it would have a basis for formulating it, if it could. So it is a mistake to speak of the feeling of familiarity as if its criterion of identity were independent of the justified tendency, perhaps counter-factual or even contrary to possibility, to formulate an indefinite memory-claim. Provided that this error is avoided, we may say that to feel the familiarity of a thing is to experience one of its properties. Of course, the property will be relational, because the thing may not be familiar to another person.

But those who hold that belief is a feeling can hardly classify it in the same way. For in this case the so-called "feeling" is the person's reaction to a proposition. When he considers it, he feels bound to assent to it. So in this case the proposition comes first and elicits the feeling, whereas in the other case the feeling comes first and generates the proposition.

Another connected difference is that the feeling of belief is directed on to the whole proposition and not on to any part of it. If it had been directed on to a part of it, we might have been able to regard it as the experience of a property of that part, like the feeling of familiarity. But this road is blocked, and the obstacle explains the development of Hume's account of the difference between "ideas of memory" and "ideas of imagination". Hume supposes that the former are distinguished by their vivacity. But if he meant vividness, his theory would be destroyed by the objection that it excludes the possibility of a memory-image of a foggy scene. This objection can be generalized: no pictorial property can serve to distinguish memory-images from the rest without excluding some possibility which ought not to be excluded. The object of the feeling of belief must be a whole proposition, and, if we say that it is an image, that will only be a brief way of referring to the proposition of which the image is a part, and so the feeling cannot be the experience of a pictorial property of the image.

When Hume appealed to vivacity, he really meant the force with which an image imposes itself on a person either immediately, as in memory, or mediately, as in causal belief. This suggestion obviously requires the image to be part of a proposition. In the case of memory the requirement would be met if, for example, I tried to recall the appearance of an absent friend. I might say that my image felt right, meaning that it felt right to me as the answer to a question, and, therefore, as part of a proposition. It would, of course, be a mistake to treat this as a cast-iron criterion of accuracy. For there is also the question of credentials: "How good is my memory?" But Hume's theory is correct to this extent: I am subjected to the force exerted by the mechanism of my memory, whatever that mechanism may be. This point is not substantially altered by Russell's suggestion that the indication of time is in the feeling rather than in the proposition.

It is clear that his theory about the way in which images function in memory will not fit the case in which an image occurs in response to a question. Why then did he not explicitly restrict the scope of his theory to the type of case described by Wittgenstein? The explanation seems to be that, when he develops his account of familiarity, he quietly imports into this kind of case a definite reference to the past which really belongs to the other kind of case with the opposite direction of fit.

This comes about in a rather complex way. The first point to notice is one that has already been mentioned: according to Russell, familiarity immediately suggests a memory-proposition to us, and leads us to believe it. Now this memory-proposition is, as he says, an indefinite one: e.g. "I have seen (something like) this window before". But without seeming to notice what he is doing, he substitutes a definite claim of the kind that I might, but need not be, able to make next: "In the bedroom in which I slept as a child, the window was like this" (and here an image occurs). This cannot be correct because the feeling of familiarity, by itself, can neither suggest nor lead me to believe a proposition referring to a definite past experience of mine. One way of getting such a proposition is to take a situation in which the direction of fit is reversed, because, for example, I am asked about the shape of the window in my childhood bedroom. But in that case I would not say that my image felt familiar, still less that it struck me as familiar. Rather, it would feel right. So Russell should not have imported the definite past reference into the case described by Wittgenstein, and in the other case, which exhibits the reverse direction of fit, he should not have appealed to the feeling of familiarity. If my answer to a question feels familiar, that may only be because it is my usual error.

Although Russell marks the difference between an indefinite memory-claim and a definite one, his discussion of the transition from the first to the second shows that he is not aware of its importance. He illustrates the transition with an example which is peculiar in two different ways (p. 176): the object which sets me going is not an image but a physical object, a wall with an array of pictures, and I feel that it is unfamiliar rather than familiar. The first of these two peculiarities tends to conceal the fact that there is any transition from the indefinite claim to the definite one, and the second introduces a complication which obscures the nature of the transition.

First, consider the second peculiarity, the fact that the arrangement of pictures strikes me as unfamiliar. If I made a memory-claim on the basis of this experience, it would be negative: "This array of pictures is unlike anything that I have seen before." No doubt, it is unlikely that I would make this indefinite claim in this particular case. But it is easy to think of examples in which an indefinite claim would be natural. But the important point is that such a claim is all that can be made on the basis of unfamiliarity, and that it is negative. Similarly, if I went beyond the basis of felt unfamiliarity, and said what, in particular, the arrangement of pictures was unlike, that too would be a negative claim. This is a tiresome complication, and Russell might equally well have given an example of familiarity and a positive claim.

The first peculiarity of his example is more important. Why is it that in this case I do not have to think very hard before coming up with a definite reference to my past, viz., to the wall when I last saw it? It is easier to answer this question for the positive case before considering the negative case. If the wall strikes me as familiar, no definite reference to the past can be based on that experience. It may be easy for me to provide a definite reference, but that is a further step. If, on the other hand, it strikes me as unfamiliar, it would be absurd to try to take this further step, because it strikes me as unlike anything that I have seen before, and there is no particular thing which it will turn out to be unlike. So why do I not have to think very hard before coming up with a definite reference to my past in Russell's negative example? The search for such a reference in this case ought to be more than difficult; it ought to be an absurdity.

The solution to this paradox is that in Russell's example the definite reference to my past does not just lie close at hand: rather, it is contained in the meaning of the original statement, that the wall strikes me as unfamiliar. Russell takes this to mean that it strikes me as unfamiliar-as-itself, or to put this in plain English, that it strikes me that it has changed in some way (cf. the horse returning to its stable). Of course, this experience would still leave me with a residual problem: In what way has it changed? But it would not leave me with the residual problem of finding a definite past reference. For the definite past reference to the thing itself at an earlier point of time is already included in the meaning of the word 'unfamiliar' in the original statement. In that statement it means self-unfamiliar. Similarly, if I had said that it struck me as familiar, I might have meant self-familiar.

At first sight, these complications might appear to facilitate a smooth transition from the feeling of familiarity or unfamiliarity to Russell's past-oriented feeling of belief in a proposition with a definite past reference. But that would be an illusion. It is absurd to try to find a definite past reference after an experience of general-unfamiliarity, and, though such a reference may be found after an experience of general-familiarity, the search for it is a further step. Moreover, when such a reference is already contained in the experience, that is only because it is a different experience. Self-familiarity is not the same thing as general-familiarity. Here we tend to talk about the feeling of familiarity as if it were always the same feeling, whatever claim might be involved in its description. But this is to ignore the fact that the appropriateness of these claims is part of the criterion of identity of the feelings. Nobody would make this mistake about the word 'strange'. A person may look strange by looking unlike anyone else, or, more easily, by looking unlike himself. In these two cases, the strangeness is obviously not the same property.

In any case, most of Russell's examples in *The Analysis of Mind* involve the familiarity of images, and there is no concept of self-familiarity for images. For how would I identify the earlier manifestation of this image which I am now having? Of course, we could improvise a method of identification. But that has not yet been done, nor is there any need to do it, whereas the method of identifying an earlier phase in the history of a material object has been settled, and it does answer to a need.

It may now be possible to explain Russell's insistence that the word 'this' refers both to the past experience and to the present image, with no distinction made between them (p. 179, already quoted). He may have been trying to construe the general-familiarity of an image in the typical situation described by Wittgenstein as a kind of self-familiarity. For when the specious present terminates, though the image detaches itself from the sensation and begins to lead a life of its own, they might both be regarded as phases in the history of a single entity, and this might suggest that a later phase—i.e. an image—might strike me as self-familiar, in much the same way that my childhood bedroom, if I returned to it, might strike me as self-familiar, or the horse's stable would strike it as self-familiar. However, this idea would be mistaken, because the horse and I have independent criteria for reidentifying the stable and the bedroom, but there are no such criteria for the entity which consists of a sensation followed by a long series of image-phases. The concept of 'the self-unfamiliarity of an image' breaks down in the same way.

It is worth noting that there is an analogy between Russell's theory of memory in *The Analysis of Mind*, and his theory of desire in the same book (Chapter III). In the latter discomfort plays a role like that of familiarity in the former. Discomfort is treated as an immediately recognizable causal property of a mental occurrence (pp. 66 and 75). It is the property of initiating a behaviour-cycle which terminates with the attainment of an object which removes the discomfort and so produces quiescence. According to Russell, a desire is simply a mental occurrence with this property. "A desire is called 'conscious' when it is accompanied by a true belief as to the state of affairs that will bring quiescence; otherwise it is called 'unconscious'." (p. 76).

Now Russell rightly insists that a true paradigmatic memory-claim must be caused by the experience to which it refers (p. 82). It follows that any paradigmatic memory-claim must implicitly involve a stipulation about its own causation. So suppose, as Russell does, that the claim is based on an image which strikes me as familiar (general-familiarity). Then the implied stipulation will be that this image was caused by some experience of mine that was like it (indefinite reference to my past).

Here we have a causal requirement about the past, which is analogous to Russell's causal requirement about the future in the case of desire. In order to exhibit the analogy I shall make the unrealistic assumption that any feeling of discomfort suggests and leads me to believe the proposition that it will cause a behaviour-cycle terminating in the attainment of some object that will remove it. Then the felt general-discomfort of a mental occurrence will be like Russell's felt general-familiarity of an image, which suggests, and leads me to believe the proposition that the image was caused by some similar prototype in my past. This proposition could be true, and yet I might not realize that it was true, and it might not even occur to me. In such a case it would be possible to say that the image was familiar, but did not strike me as familiar. Similarly, a person might want something and yet not be aware that he wanted anything. In such a case Russell would have to say that his awareness of his discomfort was totally suppressed. Conversely, an image might strike me as familiar when it was not familiar. Analogously, I might suffer from false-general-discomfort (like false-hunger). Moreover, an image might strike me as familiar when it was familiar, but not *because* it was familiar (normal causal requirement for memory not met). Analogously, my discomfort might not be the cause of the behaviour-cycle which led to its removal.

This theory of desire is unrealistic in many ways, but most obviously so when Russell tries to answer the question how I know what I want. For he can hardly suppose that every kind of object is associated with a recognizable type of discomfort. But, to pursue the analogy, it would be equally implausible to suppose that, when I make a definite memory-claim, I base it on a specific kind of familiarity in my image. It is very obvious that at this point in his theory of desire Russell ought to have brought in his other idea, that desire is an attitude to propositions, to be treated like belief.[1] This criticism of his theory of desire is closely analogous to my main criticism of Theory II about memory.

However, Theory II does not rely so heavily on immediately felt causal properties of mental occurrences. For, though he uses examples of self-familiarity, he does not go so far as to claim that the general feeling of familiarity is divisible into species which can be recognized immediately as pointing towards specific kinds of prototypes. However, he does make the transition from the feeling of general familiarity to the past-oriented feeling of belief in a way that blurs the distinction between data and symbols.

This development of Russell's ideas about memory illustrates a general feature of his philosophy. He sees the importance of propositions in the theory of knowledge, but he does not completely succeed in abandoning the point of view of his eighteenth-century predecessors, who were less aware of their importance. Consequently, he runs too closely together, even if he does not actually confuse, symbols and data, things that we do with things that happen to us, credentials with criteria, and other similarly related couples.

---

[1] "The Philosophy of Logical Atomism", pp. 218, 228.

Wesley C. Salmon

Memory and Perception in Human Knowledge[1]

"The general, though not universal, trustworthiness of memory is an independent postulate," wrote Russell in *Human Knowledge*. "It is necessary to much of our knowledge, and cannot be established by inference from anything that does not assume it" (p. 195).[2] In view of this statement, it is natural to wonder why, when he explicitly lists his postulates of scientific inference, no such postulate appears. We shall *not* attempt to explain this omission by supposing that he forgot to include it.

1. *Memory Premises*

According to the main thesis of *Human Knowledge*, scientific inference proceeds from two types of premises, general and particular. The particular premises are furnished by perception, memory, and testimony. The overall reliability of the testimony of other observers is secured by means of the postulate of analogy, which does appear in the official list (p. 493). This postulate enables us to infer that other human beings are observers; in so doing, it establishes the relevance of their behaviour, primarily their linguistic behaviour, to the scientific problems with which we are concerned. Our awareness of the testimony of others is, of course, based upon our perceptions and memories of what they write and say. Perception and memory thus remain as the fundamental sources of particular premises, while testimony assumes a derivative status.

One of Russell's major aims in *Human Knowledge* was to establish his claim

[1] This paper is a much expanded version of a paper, "Perception and Memory", which was presented at the meeting of the American Philosophical Association, Pacific Division, December, 1953, but was never published. It was motivated by Russell's discussion of memory in *Human Knowledge*, especially the statement quoted at the beginning of the paper. The present paper is not confined to the exposition of Russell's views; it is, rather, an attempt to deal with problems he raised, and in a spirit which is, I hope, in fundamental harmony with his approach to such problems. Perhaps the chief conviction I share with Russell is the view that the problems he discusses are of fundamental philosophical importance. I do not believe that philosophical developments subsequent to the writing of *Human Knowledge* have rendered them obsolete.

The author wishes to express his gratitude to the National Science Foundation for support of research on the foundations of inference in the empirical sciences. He is also indebted to Professor Merrilee Salmon for valuable critical comments on an earlier draft.

[2] *Human Knowledge: Its Scope and Limits*, New York 1948. Unidentified page references are to this book.

that among the premises of scientific inference are some synthetic general propositions. These premises are necessary if we are to be able to make inferences from the facts presented by perception and memory to other facts that we neither perceive nor remember. It is the function of Russell's postulates to furnish these general premises. Since the status of these postulates is a main concern of my paper "Russell on Scientific Inference",[1] I shall not discuss them further here. This essay will be confined to the sources of the particular premises of scientific inference.

According to Russell, both perception and memory arise from sensations. Sensations are unvarnished experiences that are free from interpretation with respect to anything outside of themselves. As such they cannot, in and of themselves, be mistaken. 'There are in fact no illusions of the senses, but only mistakes in interpreting sensational data as signs of things other than themselves' (p. 167). Although sensations have a kind of incorrigibility, Russell denies that they directly furnish the premises of scientific inference, for they do not constitute knowledge. "When we speak of 'knowledge', we generally imply a distinction between the knowing and what is known, but in sensation there is no such distinction" (p. 422).

Russell does characterize sensations as *sources* of knowledge (p. 422) and as *data* (p. 170), but it is important to distinguish data (or sources) from premises. The data are facts (p. 170); they are *causes* of the beliefs or judgments that we take as premises (p. 166). Perceptions and memories, rather than sensations, provide the actual premises.[2] And although Russell says that "in a critical scrutiny of our beliefs as to matters of fact we must wherever possible translate the causal transitions of primitive thinking into logical transitions", (p. 166), he continues to regard sensations as causes rather than premises.

Russell has a good deal to say about the way in which perceptions arise out of sensations. Perceptions, unlike sensations, do involve interpretations that go far beyond what is immediately given in sensory experience. When, to use one of Russell's favourite examples, we see a canoid patch, we interpret it as a dog, and we have implicit beliefs about its unseen parts and implicit expectations about its behaviour. The process by which this interpretation occurs can be understood in evolutionary terms. From frequent association of barking sounds with canoid patches, we develop an expectation that a dog, if he makes any sound at all, will make a barking sound. Such expectations will have practical value if the regularities by which they are generated persist in the future. This process involves elementary generalization which Russell calls "animal inference", not because it is about animals, but because it occurs at a pre-human

---

[1] This volume, pp. 183–208.

[2] In a later section of the book, Russell defines data as propositions (p. 392), but in that context he has already established the relationships between sensations and perceptions and between sensations and memories, and his immediate concern is the credibility of the premises furnished directly by perception and by memory.

level (p. 167). "The fact is that the generalization, in the form of a habit of expectation, occurs at a lower level than that of conscious thought, so that, when we begin to think consciously, we find ourselves believing the generalization, not, explicitly, on the basis of evidence, but as expressing what is implicit in our habit of expectation" (p. 168). This is the process Russell describes as "the filling out of the sensational core by means of animal inferences, until it becomes what is called 'perception'" (p. 169).

Although sensations are counted among the basic data of science, sensation alone does not provide the premises of scientific inference.[1] These premises are, rather, perceptual judgments. "Science starts, and must start, from rough and ready generalizations which are only approximately true, many of which exist as animal inferences before they are put into words" (p. 186). Thus, although perceptual judgments depend upon animal inferences, these are to be distinguished from scientific inferences. "The distinction between animal inference and scientific inference is this: in animal inference, the percept *A* causes the idea of *B*, but there is no awareness of the connection; in scientific inference (whether valid or invalid) there is a belief involving both *A* and *B*, which I have expressed by *A* is a sign of *B*. It is the occurrence of a single belief expressing a connection of *A* and *B* that distinguishes what is commonly called inference from what I call animal inference" (p. 186).[2]

Animal inference is obviously fallible; consequently, the perceptual judgments that arise from sensations via animal inferences are always infected with some degree of uncertainty. The relations between sensations and perceptual judgments involve "connections between the sensation and other facts outside of my momentary mental state, and these connections must be suitably related to the connection between the pure sensation and the rest of the mental state called a perceiving" (p. 422). "This expansion of the sensational core to produce what goes by the somewhat question-begging name of 'perception' is obviously only trustworthy in so far as our habits of association run parallel to processes in the external world. . . . Thus what we seem to know through the senses may be deceptive whenever the environment is different from what our past experience has led us to expect" (p. 170). Russell openly accepts the consequence that the premises of scientific inference fall short of certainty: "It must be understood that when I say that this or that is a premise, I do not mean that it is

---

[1] In Chapter 12 of *My Philosophical Development*, New York 1959, Russell reports that he abandoned the concept of sense data during the years 1919–21, and he gives the reasons. He never readopted the concept. From that point onward, Russell never accepted any form of phenomenalism.

[2] In this passage Russell speaks of the *percept* A rather than the *sensation* A, but that does not affect my point. In the context of this quotation he is dealing with common sense inference in which percepts of physical objects already exist, but the animal inference that occurs here has the same basic characteristic as that which occurs in the transition from sensations to perceptions.

certainly true; I mean only that it is something to be taken account of in arriving at the truth, but not itself inferred from something believed to be true . . . " (pp. 189–90). (I assume that the term 'inferred' in this last clause is intended in its usual sense, not in the sense that would include animal inference.) In Section 2 of "Russell on Scientific Inference" I discuss the problem of uncertainty of data; I believe this discussion supports Russell's contention that scientific inference may legitimately proceed from premises none of which are certain.

Russell does not include in his list of postulates one which asserts the general reliability of perception. He does not attempt to take as fundamental premises reports of sensations,[1] supplementing them with a general postulate that will validate the inference from sensations to external objects and events. Parallel remarks apply to memory.

Let us first make clear what is meant logically by saying that memory is a premise of knowledge. It would be a mistake to set up a general statement of the form: "What is remembered probably occurred." It is rather that each instance of memory is a premise. That is to say, we have beliefs about past occurrences which are not inferred from other beliefs. . . . (p. 188)

There is a distinction to be made here, which is not without importance. A recollection is a present fact: I remember now what I did yesterday. When I say that memory is a premise, I do not mean that from my present recollection I can infer the past event recollected. This may be in some sense true, but is not the important fact in this connection. The important fact is that the past occurrence is itself a premise for my knowledge.[2] (p. 189)

According to Russell, both perception and memory furnish premises purporting to contain information about particular things and events, and both of these types of premises fall short of certainty. Moreover, Russell argues, premises of both types are required, for without memory premises we could infer nothing either of our past or of the past history of the universe. The reliability of memory *cannot* be established on the basis of perceptual premises alone:

---

[1] It is, of course, important to distinguish sensations from reports of sensations. Although sensations contain no interpretive aspects which transcend their own content, reports of sensations, because they involve use of language, would not remain pure and free from the kind of interpretive elements that result from animal inference. In any case, Russell accepts neither sensations nor reports of sensations as premises of scientific inference.

[2] Disconcertingly, Russell continues this very passage: "It cannot be inferred from the present fact of my recollecting it except by assuming the general trustworthiness of memory, i.e., that an event remembered probably did take place. It is this that is the memory-premise of knowledge." Unless Russell is flatly contradicting the very explicit statement he has made on the preceding page, the word 'this' in his last sentence must refer to the past occurrence mentioned earlier in the paragraph, not to the general trustworthiness of memory to which it would seem naturally to refer.

What I wish to say about memory is that its general though not invariable trustworthiness is a premise of scientific knowledge, which is necessary if science is to be accepted as mainly true, but is not capable of being made even probable by arguments which do not assume memory. (p. 188)

The necessity of memory as a premise may be made evident by asking the question: What reason have we for rejecting the hypothesis that the world came into existence five minutes ago? If it had begun then just as, in fact, it then was, containing people with the habits and supposed memories that in fact people then had, there would be no possible way of finding out that they had only just begun to exist. Yet there is nothing logically impossible in the hypothesis. (p. 189)

This is, in fact, no more impossible than for God to have created Adam with a navel, or the earth with a plentiful supply of fossils.

Both memory and perception are related causally to sensations, and I should think, memory judgments as well as perceptual judgments arise from sensations by generally similar types of animal inference.[1] The main purpose of this paper is to discuss the relative evidential status of memory premises and perceptual premises, and in so doing, to compare the relation between sensation and perception with the relation between sensation and memory. I think it can plausibly be argued that the relationship is even closer than Russell seemed to be claiming. While David Pears has argued that the early Russell went too far in merging memory with perception,[2] I shall argue that the later Russell did not go far enough in that direction.

2. *Types of Memory*[3]

The term 'memory' refers to a wide variety of things. I remember the multiplication table and Kepler's second law. I do not remember how to extract a square root, although I do remember more than one occasion on which I learned how to do it. I remember my first view of the Great Salt Lake, though at the time I was convinced that it was a mirage. I remember Janos Starker's cello performance at the Russell Memorial held at Indiana University. I remember Mt. Rainier. I remember that the siege of the Alamo occurred in 1836, but I remember neither the battle (I am not *that* old) nor the building (I have never been in San Antonio); however, if I were a Texan I would certainly be exhorted to remember one or the other (I'm not sure which). I remember the murder of Lee Harvey Oswald. I have a childhood "memory" of my father frisking a

---

[1] In Section 4 I shall discuss the question of whether sensations can produce memories without generating intervening perceptions. I shall answer in the affirmative, but it will be seen that nothing much hinges upon this issue.

[2] In his paper, "Russell's Theories of Memory 1912–1921", this volume, pp. 117–137.

[3] My discussion in this section owes a great deal to Don Locke's interesting and informative little book, *Memory*, New York 1971.

garage proprietor he suspected of carrying a gun, but I have lots of independent evidence that no such event ever occurred.[1]

The foregoing list contains memories of at least three distinct types. (1) We remember abstract relations (the multiplication table), general facts (Kepler's laws), and particular facts which the subject has *not* experienced (the date of a battle). It has often been noted that this type of memory is usually dispositional in character. A person is said to remember the multiplication table whether he is doing arithmetic at the moment or not; to remember the multiplication table is to be able to give the correct value for the product of two small integers under appropriate stimulation. Similar remarks apply to the memory of general and particular facts. To remember Kepler's second law is to be able to state it or apply it in suitable circumstances; to remember the date of a battle is to be able to come up with the right number if asked. This type of remembering is very nearly tantamount simply to knowing (or retaining knowledge of) something that was learned at an earlier time. I shall call this type of memory 'propositional', for propositions are what we remember in cases of this sort.[2] When particular objects and events are involved, we remember propositions about them rather than remembering the objects or events themselves, since the objects or events were never experienced by the subject. When general facts are involved, it is more evident that propositions are remembered, for it is not even clear what would be meant by saying that one had experienced a general fact such as the equality of areas swept out by the radius vector of a planet in equal times. We might conceivably experience specific instances of that general fact, but it is hard to see how we could experience the general fact itself. The same point is even clearer in the memory of mathematical relations. Without something akin to Plato's doctrine of reminiscence it is hard to see how one could suppose there was any fact to be experienced. On some rare occasions propositional memory can, I believe, be occurrent rather than dispositional. If a young Texan has trouble giving the date of the siege of the Alamo, but after a great intellectual effort succeeds in bringing it to mind and says, "Now I remember! It was 1836!" it seems that he is engaged in an act of remembering in an occurrent sense.

(2) We also have memories of various skills, such as how to extract a square root, or how to ride a bicycle. Memory of this type has aptly been called "practical". Like propositional memory it is chiefly dispositional (once you have

---

[1] Late at night, after a long day of travel, my father stopped at a garage to have the battery charged, because the generator had ceased functioning. I had been asleep in the back seat and awoke as he was discussing arrangements. The most likely explanation of my "memory" is that the garage attendant answered a question to which he did not know the answer with the colloquial "Search me", and my overactive imagination supplied the rest.

[2] Don Locke calls this "factual" memory, but I am reluctant to use that term because (1) I doubt the propriety of calling mathematical relations "factual", and (2) what I shall call "retrospective" memory (Locke's "personal" memory) seems to have at least as much right to the title.

learned to ride a bike you never forget how—even though you never ride one again), but sometimes it may be occurrent (*now* it is coming back to me—how to extract the square root).

(3) Finally, there are memories of persons, objects, and events with which the subject has been directly acquainted; borrowing a term from Furlong, I shall call this type "retrospective memory".[1] Retrospective memory comes in both the dispositional and the occurrent forms. I can claim to remember Professor Starker in the dispositional sense, for I am confident of being able to recognize him upon meeting him again. I can remember him in the occurrent sense by forming a visual image, though imagery is not the only mechanism of occurrent memory. I can retrospectively remember an objective event such as a musical performance, or a subjective experience such as my first view of the Great Salt Lake. Moreover, I can remember the Great Salt Lake. Although remembering how to ride a bike does not qualify as retrospective memory, recollection of taking my sister's bike out into the back alley and learning to ride it does. Although remembering the date of the siege of the Alamo does not count as retrospective memory, recollection of looking it up in the encyclopaedia yesterday does. The murder of Lee Harvey Oswald is a borderline case, for I witnessed the murder, but with the aid of television, rather than spectacles or a telescope. Perhaps I can properly claim to have retrospective memory only of the "instant replay" rather than the murder itself.

Although I am not suggesting that either practical or propositional memory is unimportant—as a matter of fact, propositional memory is an indispensable component of scientific knowledge—I shall confine attention in this paper mainly to retrospective memory, and moreover, to the occurrent form. The reason for focusing attention so narrowly upon this one type is that our main concern—the problem with which Russell was trying to deal—is the problem of empirical knowledge of the past. The occurrent form of retrospective memory seems to constitute experience of the past; it seems to provide more or less direct acquaintance with past events and objects. Indeed, I shall argue that it constitutes experience of events as past that is strongly analogous to perceptual experience of events as present. Occurrent retrospective memory is the source of precisely the kind of premises about past events that Russell is discussing, and as such, it plays a central role in Russell's account of scientific inference.

Many philosophers have argued that terms like 'perceive' and 'see' are success words; consequently, they argue, we cannot correctly claim to see a lake in the middle of the desert if it is in fact a mirage, and I cannot claim to have seen a mirage when it was actually the Great Salt Lake. A similar thesis is sometimes applied to memory terms. I cannot properly say I remember my father frisking

---

[1] E. J. Furlong, "Memory", *Mind* 17 (1948). I differ from Furlong, however, in that I do not hold imaging to be an essential component of retrospective memory.

the garage owner if no such event actually occurred. This is, of course, just a matter of terminology. Whatever decision we make about it, we must still recognize that there are perceptual experiences which seem to provide acquaintance with external objects and events. We cannot, by inspection of the experience itself (and still less by linguistic legislation), tell whether such an experience is veridical or not. Nevertheless, these experiences give rise to perceptual beliefs and judgments about the objective world, and even though they are sometimes false, such judgments do constitute premises for scientific inference.

The same is true of memory. We have memory experiences which seem to provide acquaintance with things, persons, or events which are not part of that memory experience itself. The putative object of the alleged acquaintance may be a person or object that existed in the past, a physical event that occurred in the past, or a subjective experience that occurred in the past. Again, inspection of the memory experience itself does not enable us to tell reliably whether it is veridical or not; this fact notwithstanding, such memory experiences are the basis of memory judgments which are used as premises of scientific inference. Furlong's retrospective memory is memory of what *seem to be* particular objects or events with which the subject was acquainted at some previous time. Such memories are not necessarily—by definition—veridical. The "memory" of my father frisking the garage proprietor is retrospective memory, whether the event I seem to remember occurred or not.

It might be suggested that retrospective memory is always memory of a real or putative perceptual experience. Thus, it might be said, I can remember seeing the Great Salt Lake, but I cannot remember the Great Salt Lake itself as distinct from my seeing it. Similarly, the claim might run, I can remember seeing my father frisk the garage owner, but I cannot remember the frisking. In this case, either the recollection of the perceptions is veridical, but the perceptions themselves were not, or the memory itself is not veridical and the perceptual experiences I seem to remember did not actually occur. Either way, it is agreed that the frisking as an objective event did not occur as I retrospectively remember it.

I do not think this view is correct. Even if we were to agree (to what I specifically deny in Section 4) that a veridical retrospective memory of an object or event requires a previous veridical perception, I see no reason for supposing that the perceptual experience, rather than the perceived object or event itself, is the content of my retrospective memory experience. I think of my daughter, whom I have not seen for several weeks; I remember her even though I have completely forgotten the circumstances in which I last saw her. I am remembering her, but I am not remembering my seeing of her on any particular occasion. If I try to remember seeing her I can do so, but that is an entirely different memory. Similarly, I can remember Starker's cello performance; I remember him playing the cello, and I remember how profoundly moving was my experience at the time, but these are two different—though closely associated—memories.

There are several modes of retrospective memory. The mode that has been most widely discussed in the philosophical literature might be called "retrospective image-memory". In this mode, the memory experience has the phenomenological character of a direct presentation of an object or event, accompanied by a conviction that the object or event existed or occurred at some time in the past. This conviction may, of course, be mistaken, but it is nevertheless a feature of the memory experience. It is important to realize that the imagery need not be visual; the recollection of a musical performance would include auditory imagery, while the recollection of a fine dinner would include olfactory and gustatory images. When one perceives an object or event, part of what happens is that he has certain sensations. When one remembers an object or event in the retrospective image-memory mode, part of what happens is that certain sensations occur. Imaging, as I understand it, is the having of sensations similar to those one might have in the presence of the object of the image. When perception occurs, physical processes, such as light waves and sound waves, cause sensations. In retrospective image-memory, other processes cause similar sensations.

Another mode might be called "retrospective verbal-memory"; in this mode the memory experience consists of a verbal description of the event or object, along with the same kind of conviction about its past existence or occurrence. Retrospective verbal-memory must be clearly distinguished from propositional memory. In propositional memory, the experience that gives rise to the memory is an experience of a description or a statement, e.g. as uttered by a teacher or written in a book. In this kind of memory the subject is not directly acquainted with the event or object described. In retrospective verbal-memory, the experience that gives rise to the memory is an experience of an object or event (not a linguistic description of one); the subject forms his own description of what he has sensed, and that is the content of his memory.

There are other modes as well. When one meets a person who seems familiar and has a conviction that one has met that person before, or when one comes to a place and has the sense that one has been there before, we might say that retrospective memory in the "*déjà-vu* mode" is occurring. In this mode, the content of the memory seems to be the feeling of familiarity which is interpreted as the result of previous acquaintance.

Although this list of modes of retrospective memory is probably incomplete, I think it is comprehensive enough to show that imagery is not always a part of retrospective memory. How frequently memory does involve images I do not know. There is little doubt that image-memory sometimes occurs; its extent seems subject to considerable individual variation. Some people are quite adept at the use of images; indeed, eidetic imagery is an extreme form of the phenomenon. Others, like myself, seem to prefer symbol-mongering; they use images much less frequently. Russell reported that he hardly ever had images.[1]

Retrospective image-memory is, nevertheless, appealing for purposes of epistemological discussion, because it provides a vivid counterpart to perception. This is the type of memory Russell treats in *Human Knowledge*:

Memory is the purest example of mirror knowledge. When I remember a piece of music or a friend's face, my state of mind resembles, though with a difference, what it was when I heard the music or saw the face. (p. 422)

A memory is accurate . . . in proportion to its resemblance to a past fact. (p. 423)

I shall argue later (4) that imagery is quite inessential to retrospective memory, and that the various modes have equally good epistemological credentials. What is important about retrospective memory is not that it presents us with "pictures" of past objects or events, but rather that (when veridical) it provides us with information that results from acquaintance with those objects or events themselves. In the next section, however, I shall follow Russell in confining attention to retrospective image-memory, for such a procedure will facilitate the posing of a very fundamental issue.

3. *The Phenomenology of Perception and Memory*

In order to get started on an assessment of the relative epistemic merits of perception and memory, I shall begin by approaching them from a strictly phenomenological standpoint—that is, I shall attempt to examine both perception and retrospective image-memory in terms of their contents alone, without regard for what we know of their causal origins. From such a standpoint we can say that perception seems to present us with events that are simultaneous with our experience of them, while retrospective image-memory seems to present us with events that occurred earlier than our experience of them. We might say, rather crudely, that perception seems to provide pictures of things as they are, while retrospective memory (in the image mode) seems to supply pictures of things as they were. In using this approach we are temporarily adopting the stance of the pure epistemologist who, following a

---

[1] *An Outline of Philosophy*, Cleveland and New York 1960, p. 195. (This book was first published in London in 1927, and an American edition was published in 1927 under the title *Philosophy*.) In this work Russell discusses memory that does not involve images—what I have called "retrospective verbal-memory"—and accords it a great deal of importance, unlike his treatment in *Human Knowledge*. He says, "As regards the part played by images, I do not think this is essential. . . . Memory may depend on images. . . . But it may also be purely verbal. . . . I do not think there is anything in memory that absolutely demands images as opposed to words. . . . The most important point about memory is one which has nothing to do with images. . . . I mean the reference to the past" (pp. 195-6).

Cartesian method, endeavours to ascertain what we can learn about the world from experience alone, assuming that we have no factual knowledge whatever about anything outside of experience.

Although we know by educated common sense that the situation is considerably more complex than it seems on the surface, there may be some temptation to conclude, on the basis of phenomenological considerations alone, that perception has a stronger claim to reliability than memory has. In other words, it might be argued that the events presented in memory are presented as more remote from our present experience than the events presented in perception. On this basis it might further be argued that premises furnished by perceptual judgments are more reliable than premises furnished by memory judgments, so that memory premises are in need of some special sort of justification which is not required in the case of perceptual premises. Although I doubt that he ever argued for this view along the foregoing lines, Russell does seem to have accepted this conclusion, at least so it would appear from the passage quoted at the very beginning of this paper.

Since I wish to maintain the opposite position, namely, that memory stands in no need of any epistemological justification that differs from that required by perception, I shall refer to the foregoing argument and others closely related, as various forms of the *immediacy objection*. I hope to be able to counter it in each of its important forms.

There is little need to argue that the apparent immediacy of perception is no guarantee of its infallibility; we know that all too well from Cartesian arguments. In dreams we are presented with events that seem to be right there, but obviously this immediacy is not a reliable sign of veridicality. Similar things transpire with illusions and hallucinations. As Russell has frequently pointed out, suitable intervention in the nervous system of a subject could produce precisely the same experiential content as he has when he is perceiving veridically (p. 48). These considerations show that there is a kind of symmetry between perception and memory. Russell argues that memory requires justification because it is not incompatible with our experience to suppose that the world was created five minutes ago. In that case, most of our perceptions might be veridical while most of our memories would be illusory. Similarly, however, it is possible that during the night a malevolent psychophysiologist inserted a number of electrodes into my brain, producing all of my perceptual experiences by electrical stimulation of my central nervous system. In that case, most of my memories would be veridical while most of my perceptions would be illusory. Or, to abandon the science fiction, it is possible that I only dreamed I woke up this morning, and that my present perceptual experiences are actually dream experiences.[1] Perception and memory are separately and independently

---

[1] I once dreamed of waking up; I realized that it was a dream when, subsequently, I really awoke (I think). Russell reports having had a sequence of a hundred dreams of awaking (p. 172)!

subject to radical sceptical hypotheses, and neither of these hypotheses seems especially more devastating than the other.

It has sometimes been suggested that perceptual experiences are more vivid than memory experiences, and that this difference supplies both a criterion for distinguishing between the two kinds of experiences and a basis for claiming that perception is more reliable than memory. Even Russell seems to give some weight to this consideration when he says that vivid memories of apparently recent events are the most credible ones (p. 423). But Russell is also aware that memories are much more vivid and intense than some perceptions (p. 393). Anyone who has recently experienced the death of someone close is likely to find the memory of the funeral much more vivid than the perception of an aeroplane at the moment passing over at a very high altitude, especially if his current interest in the aeroplane is small. Thus, we must deny that the degree of vivacity or intensity of an experience bears any direct relationship even to the apparent temporal proximity of the event being experienced. There is no temptation, in the situation just described, to say that the funeral is happening now, but the aeroplane flew over some time ago. And certainly there is no hope that the sense of pastness of remembered events can be explained in terms of the lesser vividness of memory experiences, for a great many of our perceptual experiences strike us with minimal vividness (p. 393). We must, however, concede to Russell the point that vivid memory experiences are likely to feel compelling, so regardless of their epistemological credentials, they are apt to be taken as veridical. A similar point, I imagine, applies to vivid perceptions.

That vividness is not necessarily a reliable indicator of veridicality is apparent to anyone who has ever had a nightmare. Whether the Freudians are right or wrong about dreams being wish fulfilments, it seems reasonable to suppose that dreams do perform a psychic function. This function would be impaired if dreams came clearly marked as nonveridical experiences—just as bogus money would suffer a severe handicap if it came with the word 'counterfeit' conspicuously printed across its face. Descartes had a *theological* argument upon which he based his claim that clarity and distinctness (which may be related to vividness) of an experience is the criterion of veridicality, but there seems to be no *epistemological* argument for criteria of that type based either upon force and vivacity (Hume's terms) or upon clarity and distinctness. As Russell remarked, the pain Dr Johnson felt when he kicked the stone (which might have been exceedingly vivid if he was suffering from gout at the time) not only failed to prove the existence of the stone; it also failed to prove the existence of his toe (p. 173). We can conclude that, even if (contrary to fact) memory experiences were less vivid than perceptual experiences, this would not constitute a basis for judging that memory is less reliable than perception.

Another form in which the immediacy objection might be posed is in the claim that memory depends upon perception in a way in which perception does not depend upon memory. I have already argued against one version of this claim when I denied that every memory is given as a memory of a perceptual event—when I maintained, not only that it is possible, but that in fact we frequently do remember objects and events without explicitly remembering our perceptions of them. While we might admit, temporarily for the sake of argument, that such memories require previous perceptions of the events remembered, my present point is that the memory of the perception itself is not a necessary part of every memory experience. Thus, if we were inclined to argue that the memory presupposes the perception, the argument would take us beyond the confines of the phenomenological character of the memory experience. We shall consider this matter in the next section.

We may conclude at present that both perceptual experience and memory experience (of the retrospective image-memory variety at least) involve images that purport to present facts of one sort or another. There is no feature of the image or presentation itself that enables us to establish with certainty the veridicality of any such experience, whether it be perceptual or memorative.[1] Likewise, there is no phenomenological characteristic of the presentation that provides a sound basis for grading such experiences as more or less reliable— i.e. as more or less likely to be veridical. If we wish to establish that memory is less reliable than perception, extraneous considerations will have to be brought to bear.

4. *The Causal Theory of Perception and Memory*

The later Russell (post 1921 or so) espoused a causal theory of perception, and I might add, a causal theory of memory as well. He maintained that sensations are events in the history of an organism, but that they are not cognitive acts; sensations, by themselves, do not constitute knowledge. If, however, the organism lives in an environment that has been and will continue to be moderately hospitable to its survival, sensations will accumulate accretions that transform them into perceptions, which are cognitive acts. The reason that sensations have cognitive value—i.e. constitute a basis for knowledge of objective (often external) facts—is that they have certain specific kinds of causal relations to the external facts to which they bear witness. Such causal processes are extremely complex. Seeing a coloured object in daylight involves emission of photons from the sun, transmission of these photons across empty space and through the earth's atmosphere, their incidence upon the object in question, where some wave-lengths are absorbed and others are reflected, further transmission to the eye of the beholder, focusing in the lens of the eye prior to incidence upon the retina, stimulation of certain nerves which may trigger a complicated neural reaction, and the transmission of the nervous impulses to the brain of the subject.

---

[1] Here I am resurrecting the archaic adjective 'memorative', meaning pertaining to memory, because both of the current adjectives 'memorial' and 'mnemonic' have assumed more specialized senses.

This is the briefest sketch of what is involved in seeing, for example, a bird. And the most obvious consequence is that the process takes time. Light transmission is not instantaneous, and neither is the transmission of neural impulses. The light takes perhaps a few nanoseconds to travel from the bird to the eye, and the neural impulses take perhaps a few milliseconds to travel from the eye to the brain. We experience the bird as it was a few milliseconds earlier.

While this delay is insignificant for many purposes, it does imply that perceptual experiences are misleading insofar as they seem to present the object as it is just at the moment of the perception; more precisely, we make an incorrect inference if we conclude from the seeming immediacy of the presentation that it is strictly simultaneous with the event being perceived. Due to the much smaller speed of transmission of sound, common sense has pretty well absorbed the idea that when we hear a noise the event which caused it may no longer be occurring. And every schoolchild learns that light, in spite of its great speed, may take long periods of time to travel to us even from stars that can be seen with the naked eye. Thus, an astronomical event, such as the creation of a supernova, even though it is perceived as immediate, may be much farther in the past than a retrospectively remembered event such as yesterday's breakfast. It follows that perception is not always causally more immediate than is memory; the perceived event may be causally more remote from the perceptual experience than is the remembered event from the memorative experience.

These causal considerations suggest a physical basis for distinguishing perception from memory. In cases of memory and perception alike, certain events outside of the subject's body initiate causal processes that lead to other events inside of his body which we call "sensations". In the case of a perceptual experience, the sensations very promptly evoke the interpretative accretions that transform the sensations into a perception. In the case of memory, the sensations provide information that is somehow stored by the subject. Apparently, this can happen in at least two ways.

First, certain sensations of colour, shape, and sound may produce a perception of a dog, and information about the perceptual image is somehow stored in such a way that the image can be reproduced at a later time. I do not think that the percept itself, or a set of sensations, or an image is literally stored in memory. When the subject is no longer perceiving an object, the percept, the perceptual image, and the accompanying sensations cease to exist. But information about the sensations (and about the percept if there is one) can be stored in a way that enables the subject to produce a similar set of sensations at a later time. The process is somehow analogous to the way in which a computer can store information about an oscilloscope display, giving it the ability to reproduce the display later upon command. Or perhaps it is analogous to the way in which a TV programme can be stored on magnetic tape. Although I have no detailed knowledge of the neurological mechanism of such memory, it seems plausible to speculate that information, rather than an image, is stored, but in such a way that the subject has the capability of reproducing the image (or sensations) with more or less accuracy.

Second, the same sensations may lead to the verbal description, 'large black barking dog', and in this case information about the description is stored in a manner that makes it possible for the subject to reproduce the verbal description at a later time. This type of memory has an analogue in the ability of a computer equipped with a print-out device to provide, in printed form on a sheet of paper, the same data as were contained in the oscilloscope pattern. The oscilloscope pattern is an image; the printed information is a description, not a picture or image.

The transition from sensations to perception in the first case involves animal inference as we discussed above. The sensations in the second case give rise to the verbal formulation by another process of animal inference (or something very similar to it), and this is true, I believe, whether or not a perception mediates between the sensations and the description. The first process leads to retrospective image-memory; the second leads to retrospective verbal-memory. Perhaps some other process is involved in *déjà-vu* memory.

Although I do not know the physiological mechanisms of either image-memory or verbal-memory on the part of humans, there seems to be no doubt that human beings and computing machines are capable of both. In either case, the memory experience involves the retrieval of information, stored in one way or another; the subject seems to become aware of the retrospective character of the experience as a result of storing and retrieving the information. This suggests that we can roughly distinguish veridical memory from veridical perception by saying that, although the total duration of the physical process connecting the event experienced with the experience of it may be large in either kind of experience, the memory experience differs from the perceptual experience by having a significantly long portion of that causal process within the body of the subject. A better formulation would be that the delay involved in the generation of the perceptual experience from the sensations is not noticeable by the subject, while the delay in the production of the memory from the sensations is noticeable. In many cases of memory, the subject seems able to make a rough estimate of the amount of the delay, so that he can judge how long ago the recalled event occurred.

In discussing the generation of memories by sensations, we left open the question of whether those same sensations produced a perception in the process. Memory experiences can occur in both ways, I believe. I can vividly recall my first view of the rings of Saturn—that is, I can remember the celestial object and I can remember my experience of it at the time. Light from the sun, reflected by Saturn, had travelled from Saturn through my telescope to my eye. It took several minutes for the light to make the trip, and it took a few milliseconds for the retinal stimulation to cause a sensation in my brain. Almost immediately thereafter I perceived Saturn. At about the same time information derived from this experience was somehow stored in my brain, and I can bring it forth at will. In so doing, I can experience Saturn with its rings, as well as re-experiencing my psychological state when the focusing of the telescope suddenly brought the rings into clear ·view.

Another sort of thing can happen. Suppose that shortly after rain you are walking down the street engaged in intense discussion with a colleague, and that without the slightest interruption of the conversation you step aside to avoid a puddle. A few moments later someone asks you why you stepped aside back there, and you answer that it was because of the puddle. At the time the reaction was automatic; you did not notice the puddle and you did not consciously alter your path. You did, of course, have some sort of sensation that caused you to step aside, but you were not aware of either the sensation or your reaction to it. In such a case, it seems proper to say that there was a sensation without a perception. The subsequent question then focused attention upon the experience, producing a memory which is based upon sensations caused by the puddle, but not depending upon a perception of the puddle. Because such possibilities seem real enough, I now want to deny what I granted earlier for the sake of argument. It seems to me that memories can arise directly from sensations without requiring an intervening perception as a necessary part of the causal chain. I therefore reject that form of the immediacy objection that maintains the greater causal remoteness of memory experiences from their objects on the ground that every memory experience requires a perception as an intermediate part of the causal process.

Suppose, however, that I am wrong about the foregoing point, and that every veridical memory requires a perception as well as sensations. Or suppose even that I am right, but that, as a matter of fact, the vast majority of memories do arise from previous perceptions, so that the *general* reliability of memory is not materially affected by the possibility of a relatively few memories based only on sensation without perception. Even then, the immediacy objection still does not show that memories are less to be trusted than perceptions. There are two reasons, but the first is far less important than the second.

First, even if a memory that depends upon a previous perception is veridical, it does not follow as a logical necessity that the perception was veridical as well. For a memory experience to be veridical, it is only necessary that there be a certain relation of correspondence between the memory content and the fact remembered. This may be achieved by means of an illusory perception if the causal process of storage and retrieval imposes a distortion upon the perceptual content that compensates for the distortion involved in the perceptual experience. I think such corrective distortions may sometimes actually occur. For example, I see a somewhat unfamiliar bird in unusual light, and the colour impressions I get do not represent the correct colour of the bird, as seen in normal light. Thus, I am the victim of an illusory perception. Further observations of the same bird, or of other birds of the same species, subsequently familiarize me with the natural colour of the bird, so that later, when I remember the bird *as he appeared to me on that first occasion*, I remember him as appropriately coloured, not with the illusory colours that were produced by the unusual light. Whether such corrections of illusory perceptions occur frequently I do not know; I think they do occur, perhaps more often than we might suppose offhand, but my general response to the immediacy objection does not depend upon this phenomenon.

Second, and far more importantly, even if every memory depends upon a previous perception, and even if illusory perceptual experiences invariably lead to illusions of memory while veridical perceptions do not guarantee veridical memories, we still could not validly infer that perception is generally more reliable than memory in the context with which we are concerned. Our problem is whether the premises of scientific inference furnished by memory are generally less reliable than the premises supplied by perception. Let us look at the problem in this way. At a given time, a particular scientist is trying to draw a scientific conclusion of some sort. The information available to him consists of a large body of propositions or beliefs, some of which are derived from testimony (teachers, colleagues, journal articles, books), some from his own memory of events he has witnessed, and some from his current perceptions of what is going on around him at the time. We have already explained that testimony is derivative, so we should revise our description and say that all of the information attributable to testimony depends upon memories of things he has heard and read (assuming no one is talking to him at the moment and assuming that he is not at the moment engaged in reading a book or article). The crucial fact is that, for the most part, the information to which his memory testifies right now is distinct from that to which his current perception testifies. I say that this is true for the most part because the events he is now remembering are mainly distinct from the events he is now perceiving, though there may be no completely satisfactory way of distinguishing the memory of very recent events from the perception of current events when both appear in the same specious present. Aside from what goes on in the specious present with respect to what Russell calls "immediate memory" (p. 96), the content of the memory premises is entirely distinct from he content of the perceptual premises.

It must surely be admitted that some types of memory are more reliable than others. The scientist can be more certain about the adjustments he just made to his apparatus than he can about many events he recalls from his early childhood. Similarly, it must be admitted that some types of perception are more reliable than others. Perceptual judgments based upon careful and attentive observation under favourable conditions of lighting, etc., are more reliable than those based upon casual observation without particular attention and under unfavourable conditions. The scientist's perception of the meter reading that he is making carefully right now is certainly more reliable than his perception of words being spoken some distance away in a noisy laboratory in a conversation to which he is paying very little attention. Moreover, it also seems undeniable that some memories are more reliable than some perceptions. The scientist's memory of his recent adjustment of the apparatus is more reliable than his casual perception of the aforementioned conversation.

It is this last mentioned fact that is crucial to our argument. Even if every memory of a given event is less reliable than the corresponding perception of the very same event, it does not follow that the memory premises of a given scientific inference are less reliable than the perceptual premises of that same inference, for generally speaking the perceptual premises will refer to different events than the memory premises do. For example, a scientist might dream of performing an experiment, and he might bring to his dream a large store of veridical memory experiences, while at the same time having *only* illusory perceptual experiences.

With this last argument, it seems to me that the immediacy objection collapses entirely, even as it is applied to the causal account of both perception and memory. The conclusion is that memory premises and perceptual premises are on precisely the same footing; they demand the same sorts of justification, or they are equally free from the need of justification. And this is true of premises based on retrospective memory in any mode, not just in the image mode, for it is the information, not the image, that is important.

5. *P-m Posits*

Common sense seems to tell us that memory is, nevertheless, inferior to perception in reliability—not in every case, but by and large (p. 189). It does seem plausible to suppose that the relative frequency of veridicality among perceptual experiences is greater than for memory experiences. This judgment is based upon experience with perceptual and memory judgments, not upon a causal analysis of the processes involved. It is not that memory is or seems less immediate than perception, but rather that memory plays us false more often. To the question of how we know such facts (if indeed they are facts) the obvious answer is that we remember. I am not going to condemn this as a vicious circle or regress, for it seems to me that perception and memory together are used to criticize both perception and memory. In particular, it seems that memory plays an indispensable role in assessing the reliability of memory, and that there is nothing viciously circular about it. This account seems to me to be entirely within the spirit of Russell's approach (pp. 188-9, 391-6).

Russell has explained how sensations gather interpretive accretions, based in the first instance on animal inference, thereby becoming perceptions. When we see lightning nearby, we expect thunder. When we see a dog, we expect the sound he makes will be a barking sound. When we see a table, we expect it to feel solid and to stay put rather than vanishing spontaneously in a cloud of smoke. As sophistication increases, we accumulate further generalizations and theories. We come to believe in the quasi-permanence of written records. We even come to the point of expecting the part of the highway which looks wet ahead on a hot day to be dry when we get to it. These same accretions of animal inference, common sense inference, and scientific inference also fill out the sensations that give rise to memories. The results of such inferences can, of course, be used to check on the reliability of perceptions and memories. I perceive the pavement as wet, but my past experience enables me to correct the perception, because that kind of mirage is common under the circumstances. Moreover, when the thing that I perceived as a mirage stood still and neither receded into the distance nor vanished, I corrected the perception and regarded the thing perceived as the Great Salt Lake. If I seem to recall making an appointment for lunch today, but am not quite sure, I look in my date book for a record. General views about the constancy of such ink marks constitute an indispensable part of the check on this memory. Another crucial part is some recollection of the circumstances in which the notation was entered.

At any given time, our knowledge consists of various perceptions, memories, expectations based upon animal inference, and common sense generalizations. These all have to fit together in a coherent pattern (pp. 395–6). Sensations cannot be incompatible, but a series of them may upset a strong expectation. Perceptions and memories, by themselves, may be quite independent, but groups of them can be incompatible with common sense or scientific generalizations (p. 188). If, for instance, I dream that I see a friend whom I also know to have died, the perception of meeting him does not conflict with the memory of his death except in the presence of my faith in nonresurrection. Given such a conflict, I may summon many memories, and perhaps some additional perceptions, and decide that in this case the perceptual experience is illusory while the memory experience is veridical. This method of checking the veridicality of experience consists in taking a body of experiences and beliefs and attempting to ascertain whether any elements are in conflict with the bulk of it. A perceptual experience or a memory experience may be expurgated as illusory if it fails to fit in properly. This method obviously depends for its efficiency upon having a fairly large body of knowledge available for application at any given time.[1]

According to Russell (as noted above), sensations do not constitute knowledge; hence, their incorrigibility has little epistemological significance. Perceptions and memories do constitute knowledge, but they are uncertain.

---

[1] These remarks should not be taken as advocating a coherence theory of either truth or confirmation. Coherence is an important factor in the assessment of propositions, but it is coherence with a large body of judgments based upon experience—i.e., upon perceptions and memories—that is required. There is no suggestion here that all coherent bodies of propositions, regardless of their connections with experience, have any epistemic credentials.

Moreover, since perceptions and memories provide the basic premises concerning particular facts, there is no body of certain premises that fulfil this function (pp. 391-6). Perceptions and memories are caused by sensations, but sensations do not constitute an epistemological basis from which other things are inferred. Our evidential basis is the set of beliefs or judgments based upon our perceptual and memorative experiences. It is from these that we make scientific inferences. Sensations are then to be regarded as theoretical entities whose existence and nature can be inferred from the study of psychology and physiology. A comprehensive theory of the world and its inhabitants would have to include an explanation of how sensations are caused, an account of their part in the generation of perception and memory, and a treatment of the causes and circumstances in which illusions of perception and memory occur. All of this, I believe, is compatible with Russell's views on sensation, perception, and memory.

What is the status of the premises furnished by perception and memory? It can be aptly described in a word: they are *posits*. In the paper on scientific inference, I discussed Reichenbach's notion of the posit, how it functions in the theory of nondemonstrative inference, and Russell's attitude toward it. Let us call that type of posit an *inductive posit*. Basically, it is an assertion about the limit of a relative frequency—in Reichenbach's view, it is an assertion regarding the value of a probability. The inductive posit is a statement that is not known to be true, but it is nevertheless asserted tentatively and subject to future withdrawal or revision in the light of new evidence. As I explained in that paper, it is very similar in character to a Popperian conjecture. Inductive posits come in two varieties: blind and appraised. A blind posit is a statement that is made without any assessment of its reliability. A blind posit can be transformed into an appraised posit on the basis of further inference based upon further blind posits, but a blind posit can be appraised only at the cost of introducing a new blind posit.

Statements reporting perceptions and memories are also statements accepted tentatively as true, subject to revision or rejection in terms of additional evidence. Let us call these posits *p-m posits*. My argument about the illegitimacy of the immediacy objection is designed to show that there is no need to distinguish between "perceptual posits" and "memory posits"—that basically they have the same status and are adopted for the same reason—hence, the single concept of p-m posit. In the context of Reichenbach's theory, p-m posits would have a more fundamental place than inductive posits, for the empirical ascertainment of observed frequencies requires perceptions and memories of outcomes of trials—e.g. which side of the die landed uppermost when the die was tossed. When such posits are made simply on the basis of the corresponding perceptual or memorative experience they may be regarded as blind posits—their reliability is unassessed, perhaps because there is no reason to doubt them. But in the context of the dream, where p-m posits do not fit well with our other knowledge, they are subject to criticism; on the basis of such an examination we withdrew the perceptual judgment about meeting the deceased friend. A careful assessment elevates the memory-report of the funeral to the level of a very reliable p-m posit, and it lowers the perception-report of the subsequent meeting to the level of an almost surely illusory posit.

An interesting example of such an assessment of p-m posits occurred in the course of experiments on psycho-kinesis.[1] In an experiment in which a subject concentrated on six during many die tossings, an observer favourable to parapsychology counted significantly more sixes than would be expected by chance. Another observer, hostile to parapsychology, counted significantly fewer sixes than would be expected by chance—he, too, getting results that support the hypothesis that thoughts affect the outcome of the tosses, but negatively in his case. A camera revealed perceptual errors on both observers' parts. In this example, perceptual posits were criticized because they led to inductive posits that were incompatible with theories held by some of the investigators.

If, as a result of posits based on both perception and memory, and in the light of generalizations based upon animal inference, common sense inference, and scientific inference, we find that memory judgments are generally less reliable than perceptual judgments, then we will want to take that assessment into account in making our inferences. Indeed, in the paper on scientific inference, I reported that Richard Jeffrey has developed a theory of probability in which uncertain data can be handled. Unappraised p-m posits would, of course, be taken at face value as reliable, but appraised p-m posits could in principle be used with numerical indices of reliability attached. None of this suggests that there is any difficulty in principle in admitting blind p-m posits based upon perception and memory alike, subject to future appraisal should the need arise. In fact, the more blind posits the better, within reason, for the approach functions best on large amounts of accumulated evidence without being too fussy about reliability of what is initially admitted. It would be futile to try to screen all posits for reliability before allowing them to be used as premises at all.

6. *Precognitive Posits*

In our discussion of memory, we have been focusing attention upon ways of procuring knowledge of the past; in our discussion of perception we have been dealing with knowledge of events which at least purport to qualify as present. Turning attention now to the sources of knowledge of the future, we recognize immediately that there are common sense and scientific predictions which yield knowledge of the future, but these are obviously *conclusions* of inferences.

---

[1] See "Some Unorthodoxies of Modern Science" (A Symposium), *Proceedings of the American Philosophical Society* 96, 5 (1952).

Since our concern is primarily with the *premises* of scientific inference, we need say no more about such predictions. The question is whether we have more direct sources of knowledge of the future.

In addition to memories, which phenomenologically seem to reveal past events, and perceptions, which phenomenologically seem to reveal present events, we also have anticipative experiences which seem to reveal the future to us. Some of these future oriented experiences are simple expectations based upon habit and animal inference. We ready ourselves to hear a loud noise when we see lightning strike nearby; we brace ourselves for a jolt when we feel our automobile skid out of control. In many such cases the whole process is unconscious; the body seems to make predictions of which we become aware only if the expectation is not fulfilled. When this happens, the psychological response is one of surprise. A hunter who has "perceived" a deer in the brush should be surprised when it says "moo". Another type of future-oriented experience comes in the form of beliefs that are propositional in character, whether they are formulated in words or not. The jilted lover believes that his beloved will return, but this need not involve any images of her returning. This kind of anticipation may be thought to be analogous to retrospective verbal-memory, different only in that it is directed to the future rather than the past. Such a characterization is correct on the phenomenological level, but I shall argue in a moment that it breaks down when we look at the experiences causally. Finally, it seems undeniable that in some precognitive experiences we have an image of an object or event along with a conviction that it will exist or occur in the future. Such precognitive experiences are phenomenologically parallel to retrospective image-memory.

Since I have been suggesting that perceptions and memories give rise to p-m posits that legitimately serve as premises of scientific inference, it might be argued that we have no grounds for prohibiting the use of precognitive posits based upon the sort of experience that involves an image accompanied by a conviction that it corresponds to some future object or event.[1] This conclusion strikes me as entirely correct. We seem to experience some events retrospectively in memory; we seem to experience some events immediately in perception; we seem to experience some events prospectively in the type of precognitive experience I have just described. To each such experience there corresponds at least one posit that can be taken as a premise for scientific inference. But all such posits are subject to the critical analysis described for p-m posits in the last section; consequently, the fact that they have been admitted as premises at one stage of investigation does not mean that they will be permanently retained in that capacity. It may turn out that precognitive experiences

[1] Other types of anticipatory experience, such as I have just described, might serve as the basis for posits about the future, but those based upon precognitive images constitute the clearest case. The same analysis, in terms of the causal relation between event experienced and the posit, will apply to all kinds of future-oriented (prospective) posits.

are found to be so seldom veridical that we decide, in general, to prohibit the use of precognitive posits as scientific premises. But I do not think that this is the correct account of what happens, for I am not convinced that precognitive posits are *that* unreliable.

It seems to me rather that as our scientific accounts of perception and of the physical world develop with some degree of sophistication, causal theories arise according to which causes must temporally precede their effects. Into this framework we can fit a causal theory of perception (granting that the event perceived is earlier than, not strictly simultaneous with, the perception) and memory, but we cannot also maintain that precognitive experiences are actually caused by the precognized event. Hence, even if there are veridical precognitions, their relation to the precognized events is very different from the relations of veridical perceptions and memories to the events they reveal to us. Moreover, when the anticipation is of the propositional variety mentioned above, we must reject the analogy with retrospective verbal-memory, for the event or object described cannot be the cause of the anticipative belief about it. If there is a proper analogy, it is with propositional memory, which does not require that the subject already have personal acquaintance with the object or event to which the proposition refers.

We might wonder why so much emphasis should be placed on the causal theory of memory and perception. Is this difference between perception and memory on the one hand, and precognition on the other, so fundamental that it justifies us in excluding precognitive posits as premises of scientific inference, once science has become sophisticated enough to be able to recognize the difference? This is a very deep question, which I cannot treat here; much of the answer is furnished, I believe, by Reichenbach's penetrating discussion of the asymmetry of producing and recording, and by his analysis of the fact that in this physical world we can have records of the past but not of the future.[1] A veridical memory of an event is a more or less stable record of that event; a perception of an event is a fleeting and impermanent record of the event; but the nature of this physical world precludes precognitive records of the future. This distinction in status between p-m posits and precognitive posits is not an *a priori* prejudice; it is, instead, a result of the relatively sophisticated picture of the world furnished by contemporary science. It is just this kind of scientific knowledge that Russell insists he is taking for granted throughout *Human Knowledge*.

7. Conclusion

In my paper on Russell's treatment of scientific inference, I suggested *contra* Russell that nondemonstrative inference could be approached via inductive

---

[1] Hans Reichenbach, *The Direction of Time*, Berkeley and Los Angeles 1956, Chapter 4.

posits, thereby eliminating the need for special synthetic postulates to validate it. In this paper I am suggesting that Russell's approach to perception and memory would be hospitable to the admission of memory premises and perceptual premises on the same basis. If this is correct, the need for any *special* postulates to validate memory premises is avoided.

I should like to suggest, finally, that the concept of the p-m posit opens the way to pragmatic justification of their use as premises of scientific inference, without the need for justification by way of synthetic postulates. To argue this latter point—that the two concepts of posits, inductive and p-m, obviate the need for any synthetic postulates of scientific inference—is beyond the scope of this paper. But it is a possibility well worth considering, for it may hold the only key to the salvation of the empiricism Russell found himself forced reluctantly to abandon.

8. *Appendix: Past, Present, and Future*

Our contemporary view of the world, based upon educated common sense and science, regards time as a real feature both of physical reality and of our experience of it. Although modern physics informs us that time is a good deal more complex than common sense supposes, it does not impugn the reality of physical time. There are physical processes that have temporal duration, and some of the events that make up such processes occur earlier than others in the same process. The temporal relations of *earlier than* and *later than* have a secure place in physical theories. These relations are taken to be objective features of the physical world whether or not there are any sentient beings who are aware of them.

According to common sense, time has other attributes as well. What is real (or perhaps I should say "really real") is what is happening now. There seems to be a class of events that are located in the present; they are the ones that qualify for the special status of *happening now*. Others once had that exalted position but have lost it (never to regain it); they reside in the past. Other events have yet to achieve the station of presentness, but sooner or later they will; they reside in the future. Thus, time seems to be divided into three parts: past; present and future. This division has one conspicuous feature—its instability. The present is constantly moving, and as this goes on events move from the future, through the present, into the past. These events concomitantly come into being (they occur) and pass out of existence. Notice that the relations of *earlier than* and *later than* do not have this sort of instability. Aristotle's *Organon* was written earlier than Russell and Whitehead's *Principia Mathematica*; this always was true, is true right now, and always will be true.

Various philosophers have questioned the thoroughly objective status of the temporal concepts of past, present, and future. The most searching analysis is by Adolf Grünbaum, who argues that pastness, presentness, and futurity do not characterize objective events *simpliciter*, but rather, are *mind-dependent* properties analogous, somehow, to such mind-dependent secondary properties as colour and taste. He writes:

In the common-sense view of the world, it is of the very essence of time that events occur now, or are past or future. Furthermore, events are held to change with respect to belonging to the future or the present. Our commonplace use of tenses codifies our experience that any particular present is superseded by another whose event-content thereby 'comes into being'. It is this occurring *now* or coming into being of previously future events and their subsequent belonging to the past which is called "becoming".

. . . It is apparent that the becoming of physical events in our temporal awareness does not itself guarantee that becoming has a mind-independent physical status. Common-sense colour attributes, for example, surely *appear* to be properties of physical objects independently of our awareness of them and are held to be such by common-sense. And yet scientific theory tells us that they are mind-dependent qualities, like sweet and sour.

. . . The temporal relations of earlier (before) and later (after) can obtain between two physical events independently of the transient now, and of any minds. On the other hand, the classification of events into past, present, and future, which is inherent to becoming, requires reference to the transient now as well as to the relations of earlier and later. Hence the issue of the mind-dependence of becoming turns on the status of the transient now. . . . I can state my thesis as follows: Becoming is mind-dependent because it is not an attribute of physical events *per se* but requires the occurrence of states of *conceptualized awareness*. These states of awareness register the occurrence of physical and mental events as sustaining certain apparent time relations to the states of awareness.[1]

Grünbaum's provocative views on the mind-dependence of becoming, the now, and the present have led philosophers to wonder what kinds of properties or relations events could have which would render these temporal classifications mind-dependent.[2] It is *perhaps* not too difficult, if one accepts something like Russell's view of sensations, to see how a physical object that has a certain configuration of parts can (under appropriate conditions of observation) cause a sensation that has the property of being blue, even though the object itself does not literally have the quality of blueness independent of observation. Our philosophical tradition has prepared us for the distinction between primary *properties* and secondary *qualities*, explaining more or less satisfactorily the mind-dependent character of the latter. But, one might ask, when an event has the property of occurring now, what qualitative feature characterizes the sensation involved in the awareness of that event? The answer, it would seem, is that the sensation has the property of occurring in the psychological history of the observer, since every event that one is aware of as occurring is associated with

[1] Adolf Grünbaum, *Modern Science and Zeno's Paradoxes*, Middletown, Conn., 1967, pp. 7–8.

[2] The ensuing argument against Grünbaum's mind-dependence thesis is adapted from Ferrel Christensen's doctoral dissertation at Indiana University, "A Defense of Temporal Becoming", 1971.

some sensation or other. But every sensation the subject ever has belongs to his life history, and it is true *at all times* that the sensation is part of his life history. Thus, every event of which the observer is ever aware is associated with a sensation (or collection or sensations) that the observer has at some time or other. Clearly, then, the property of occurring to the observer at some time in his life history cannot count as the qualitative feature of sensations that distinguishes those associated with events that have the mind-dependent property of occurring now (even if we grant the very dubious supposition that it is a qualitative feature at all). It is unsuitable for this purpose precisely because it would *permanently* qualify every event of which the observer is ever aware as occurring now; it would, consequently, manifestly fail to distinguish those events that have the mind-dependent property of presentness from those that have the similarly mind-dependent properties of pastness or futurity. Events that we judge to involve something blue (e.g. a blue flash) are distinguished from those that we take to involve other colours by being permanently associated with sensations that are qualitatively blue. Events that are judged to be in the present cannot similarly be distinguished from events that are judged to be in the past or future by being permanently associated with sensations that have the quality of occurring within the experience of the subject. Grünbaum's analogy between the mind-dependence of now and the mind-dependence of secondary qualities, though of considerable heuristic value, does leave us with some unanswered questions.[1]

Our foregoing discussion of perception, memory, and precognition suggests some simple answers to some of the residual questions about the mind-dependence of past, present, and future. We have characterized memory as a way of experiencing events as past; we have characterized perception as a way of experiencing events as present; and we have characterized a type of precognition as a way of experiencing events as future. I think it is important to notice that each of the phrases, 'as past', 'as present', and 'as future', is an adverbial phrase qualifying the verb 'to experience'. The same point can be rephrased by saying that to remember an event is to experience it retrospectively, to perceive an event is to experience it presently, and that to have a precognition of an event is to experience it prospectively. The terms 'retrospectively', 'presently', and 'prospectively' are explicit adverbs, and they explicitly qualify the verb. These terms clearly refer to characteristics of the act of experiencing, not to any objective property of the events themselves or any objective temporal relations among the events themselves (without involving the awareness of these events). Nor, I think, do these features characterize the sensations upon which the awareness depends.

Grünbaum claims that "what confers nowness at a time *t* on either a physical

---

[1] It is noteworthy that the argument given in this paragraph resembles strikingly an argument Grünbaum has levelled against Reichenbach's claim that becoming has an objective physical status (Grünbaum, op. cit., pp. 29–30).

or a mental event is that the *experience* of the event satisfies the specified require-ments".[1] In order for an event to qualify as now, it is not sufficient that some sentient being is sensing it; it is not sufficient that some sensation is caused by it. Instead, the sensing organism *M* must be "*conceptually aware* of the following complex fact: that his having the experience of the event *coincides temporally* with an awareness of the fact that he has it at all".[2]

While I am not sure that Grünbaum would agree with the following re-formulation of his criterion, I should like to suggest that the characteristic which the experience must have in order to qualify the event experienced as present is that the experience be a perceptual experience—i.e. that the sensations occur and be transformed (by animal inference, etc.) into a perception without discernible delay. It seems to me that the "conceptual awareness" to which Grünbaum refers is distinguished from mere awareness in much the same way as sensations are distinguished from perceptions. The characteristic that qualifies an event as present, if this is the case, is that it is experienced perceptually. In a similar fashion, the characteristic that qualifies an event as being in the past is that it is experienced retrospectively—i.e. it is experienced in such a way that there is a noticeable time lapse between the sensations and the memory-aware-ness. The characteristic that qualifies an event as future is that it is experienced prospectively. On this basis, we see clearly that past, present, and future status of events is not determined by any simple characteristic of the sensations associated with it, but rather in terms of the process by which the sensations (which, for Russell, do not constitute knowledge) are transformed into a *cog-nitive* awareness. The adverbial nature of the terms 'retrospectively', 'presently', and 'prospectively' should serve to remind us that it is the process that is being characterized.

If a retrospective image-memory is to be veridical, its image must bear a suitable resemblance to a veridical perception the subject might have had (and in most cases actually did have) in the presence of the remembered object or event. The memory image is, of course, accompanied by a conviction of past-ness, and that is an essential part of the memorative experience. Similarly, if a retrospective verbal-memory is veridical, the verbal description of the remembered object or event was true of that object or event when it was experienced—at the time the subject had the sensations from which the memory arose. In such cases, the statement (or memory premise) based upon the memory is a statement in the past tense whose counterpart in the present tense was true when the remembered object or event was encountered by the subject. Thus, the memory premise "A large black barking dog *was* in the yard" corresponds (assuming the memory to be veridical) to the statement "A large black barking dog *is* in the yard", which would have represented a veridical perceptual

[1] ibid., p. 18.
[2] ibid., p. 17.

judgment at the time the dog was encountered. Our treatment of retrospective memory (especially in the verbal mode) serves to point up the adverbial character of the verb tenses, and to exhibit them as a primary way of expressing the retrospective character of the experience that is coordinated with the mind-dependent property of pastness.

I realize, of course, that I have been using phenomenological characterizations of the awareness; a scientific account of the processes involved in these various types of awareness demands many refinements. Precognition, for example, seems to be a way of perceiving future events—i.e. events that occur later than the awareness of them. Actually, as we concluded in a previous section, there is no way of perceiving future events if perception is regarded as a causal process. Perception, moreover, provides awareness that appears to be simultaneous with the event perceived. We know that precise simultaneity never obtains, though in many cases the awareness is simultaneous for all practical purposes.[1] The retrospective character of memory awareness is, in contrast, quite often a reliable guide to the time interval separating the awareness from the event of which the subject is aware. As I suggested above, this retrospective characteristic of memory experiences may be explained on the basis of an awareness of the interval separating the storage and the retrieval of the information supplied by memory. The pastness of the event remembered is then explained in terms of the storage of information being earlier than the retrieval of information. The retrospective character of a memory experience thus furnishes the pastness of the event by way of a present awareness (the memory experience) and the objective earlier than relation.[2]

The analysis of perception and memory that has been presented in this paper provides, if I am not mistaken, an especially clear account of the mind-dependence of past, present, and future. It seems to me to resolve some difficulties that may arise if we overwork the analogy between these temporal properties and typical secondary qualities. At the same time, I must add, it suggests a very

---

[1] I deliberately omit mention of the complexities the special theory of relativity confers upon the physical concept of simultaneity because the present discussion of past, present, and future is essentially restricted to the world line of the perceiving and remembering subject.

[2] Grünbaum (op. cit.) explicitly recognizes the import of the question "If our *experiences* of (extra and/or intradermal) physical events are causally dependent upon these events, how is it that the former *mental* event can properly qualify as being 'now', whereas the eliciting physical events *themselves* do not so qualify . . . ?" (p. 24). He realizes the legitimacy of the demand for a characterization of "features peculiar to the time of awareness" (p. 25), but he declines any attempt to provide it, remarking only that he is "*not* assuming that nowness is a *sensory quality* like red or sweet, but only that nowness and sensory qualities alike depend on awareness" (p. 25). Although I cannot claim to have offered a detailed explanation of the mechanisms of perceiving and remembering, I do suggest that the analysis of perception and memory offered in this paper offers plausible conjectures about the features of these processes that are most pertinent to awareness of pastness and presentness.

strong analogy between these temporal qualities and sensory qualities if one adopts an adverbial theory of sensing. These results constitute a pleasant bonus deriving from our treatment of the relation between perception and memory.

Grover Maxwell

The Later Bertrand Russell: Philosophical Revolutionary[1]

Whether one talks about the later Russell, the early Russell, or the middle Russell, most would agree that all these Bertrand Russells were unquestionably revolutionary on matters political, social, sexual, educational, etc. In fact it has been only within the past five to ten years that a significant segment of the population—consisting mostly of young people—has begun to catch up with Russell's advanced and profound positions on these subjects. As examples, two recent books which have received wide attention, Reich's *The Greening of America* and Jean-François Revel's *Without Marx or Jesus: The New American Revolution Has Begun*, have, in some places, almost caught up with the middle Russell, the Russell, say, at the time when he wrote *Marriage and Morals* (1929). And, as another example, educational groups very much like the so-called "free schools" or "open schools" that are popping up almost everywhere today, were not only advocated by Russell many years ago, but some were actually set up and run by him (at a financial loss, of course). It is redundant but I cannot resist adding that Russell saw, years ago, what most of us today admit (and even insist) is the truth about America's war guilt and war crimes in Vietnam. And, even if one does not admit the existence of such guilt, one must agree that the evidence provided by My Lai, the Pentagon Papers, etc., shows beyond doubt that the vilification, ridicule, and charges of senility levelled at Russell by almost all Americans, including its leading "liberals", were intemperate and unjustified.

It is interesting to speculate that much of what might be called "underground philosophy" and a great deal of the new life style of many of our young people really represent as much a fruition of such views of Russell as they do those of more commonly attributed sources such as Hesse, Sartre, Camus, etc.

However, as fascinating as I find all of this and as much as I admire and largely agree with these facets of Russell's thought, I have mentioned them mainly to emphasize that they are not the concern of this paper at all. It will be concerned, rather, with Russell's later technical philosophy—his metaphysics, epistemology, and philosophy of science, mainly the latter two. I define the "later Russell" as the Russell from *c.* 1925 onwards, about the time when he gave the Tarner Lectures, which were expanded and published as *The Analysis of*

[1] Some of the research that provided material for this essay was supported by the Minnesota Center for Philosophy of Science of the University of Minnesota, the Carnegie Corporation, and the National Science Foundation.

Matter in 1927. (*The Analysis of Mind*, by the way, published in 1921, should *by no means* be considered a companion piece of *The Analysis of Matter*. There are many reasons for this—e.g. in 1921 Russell still had not completely stopped his brief but notorious flirtation with phenomenalism. Ironically, as far as subject matter and theoretical content are concerned, *The Analysis of Matter* has a better claim to the title *The Analysis of Mind* than does the book so titled.)

In *The Analysis of Matter* there is contained, already in fairly detailed and complete form, the position on a number of central philosophical issues that he was to hold, with only minor changes, for the rest of his life. Among these subjects are perception and our knowledge of the external world (and of ourselves),[1] the development of his event ontology and, in considerable detail, his theory of space-time, as well as, as is indicated above, a different and more detailed and comprehensive account of his philosophy of mind, i.e. his later "solution" of the mind-body problem. Indeed, with the two important exceptions noted below, *Human Knowledge: Its Scope and Limits*,[2] which is his most complete and definitive book on these issues, may justly be considered mainly a rewrite of *The Analysis of Matter*. The exceptions are his work on probability, induction, and confirmation (he calls it "non-demonstrative inference"), which appear for the first time in any detail in *Human Knowledge* and the development of his construction of space-time out of causal relations among events, which is given in considerably more detail in *The Analysis of Matter* than in *Human Knowledge*.

Before continuing this theme, I should like to re-emphasize how drastic is the transition from the Russell of the period *c.* 1914 to *c.* 1922, to the post-1924 Russell. And before commenting on the substantive philosophical transition, I feel constrained to make a few socio-academic remarks. As Russell himself has noted,[3] the philosophy of the later Russell has either been neglected or grossly misunderstood and misrepresented by other philosophers. It is not my purpose to speculate about causes of this remarkable treatment (or, rather, mistreatment) of "the philosopher of the century" here. However, one reason popularly proposed for neglecting his later views must be vigorously controverted, i.e. that they were the views of a doddering old man already well advanced into senility. For, as is explained above, most of the main views of the later Russell, with one important exception (his work on "non-demonstrative inference") are already given in *The Analysis of Matter*. Now when the lectures on which this book is based were given, Russell was fifty-three years old. Any suggestion that, at such

---

[1] Unfortunately his book, *Our Knowledge of the External World*, is usually the last book of his on the subject that most philosophers seem to have read (judging from the nature and frequency of references one encounters in the literature). This is extremely unfortunate for it too belongs, in large part, to his brief phenomenalistic period. The view he advocates in *The Analysis of Matter* is entirely different in many vital respects.

[2] New York 1948.

[3] e.g., *My Philosophical Development*, New York 1959, p. 27. I have also discussed this matter in some detail in "Theories, Perception, and Structural Realism", *Pittsburgh Studies in the Philosophy of Science* 4 (1970).

an age, senility or dotage was already beginning to set in, especially such a suggestion concerning Bertrand Russell, may certainly be dismissed without comment.

Whatever the causes may be, the neglect and lack of understanding (often, it seems, the deliberate misunderstanding) of this later work of Russell have the same dimensions of scandal and disastrous loss for the realms of philosophy and science as the rejection, vilification, and ridicule of his political, social, and ethical views have for the concerns for the future of humanity. For, in the philosophical areas mentioned above and discussed below, I do not think it an exaggeration to say that the solutions (tentative ones, of course) and considerations offered by Russell are more advanced, more complete, and closer to the truth than the others (virtually all of them oblivious of Russell's later work) that fill the journals and books of the past few decades.

One such case is Russell's treatment of the currently much-discussed problems about the meaning of *theoretical terms*, or better, the problems about the nature of theoretical (unobservable) entities and the status and extent of our knowledge about them. Already in *The Analysis of Matter* and in more detail in *Human Knowledge*, Russell offers an attractive and, to me, a thoroughly convincing solution to the major ontological and epistemological difficulties in this area.[1] In accomplishing this, he relies on two well-known devices from his earlier philosophy, his *theory of descriptions*—both *definite* and *indefinite* descriptions, and his distinction between knowledge by description and knowledge by acquaintance as well as his *principle of acquaintance*. Only a gross misunderstanding of the later Russell and of the principle of acquaintance itself can be responsible for the opinion of many philosophers that Russell's continued adherence to it indicated that he continued to support phenomenalism where common sense knowledge is concerned and some kind of instrumentalism for the interpretation of scientific theories. Nothing could be further from the truth; the later Russell was a strong realist both regarding the external (mind independent) world *and* the unobservables of scientific theories.

Admittedly, there appears at first glance to be an insuperable difficulty for one who wants to maintain both realism and the principle of acquaintance, especially if he holds, as did Russell, that we are acquainted only with items in our direct (private) experience. For the principle of acquaintance is the contention that *every proposition that we can understand must contain only constituents with which we are acquainted*. But the difficulty *is* only apparent and was, indeed, already completely circumvented by the *early* Russell's doctrines on descriptions and on knowledge by acquaintance and knowledge by description. For example,

---

[1] I have discussed this at some length in my "Russell on Perception: A Study in Philosophical Method", in David Pears (ed.), *Bertrand Russell: A Collection of Critical Essays*, New York 1972, and in even more detail in my "Structural Realism and the Meaning of Theoretical Terms", in M. Radner and S. Winokur (eds.), *Analyses of Theories and Methods of Physics and Psychology*, *Minnesota Studies in the Philosophy of Science* 4 (1970).

we can understand the proposition that the author of *Waverley* wrote *Marmion* even if we do not know *who* wrote *Waverley* (or *Marmion*), i.e. even if we are not *acquainted* with the author of *Waverley*. In Russell's terminology the author of *Waverley* (whoever he was) is not a constituent of the proposition that the author of *Waverley* wrote *Marmion*. Nevertheless, if I truly assert that the author of *Waverley* wrote *Marmion*, I have managed to *denote* the individual that wrote *Waverley* (and *Marmion*) even though he is not a *constituent* of the proposition asserted. The proposition can, therefore, for Russell, denote and thus, in one sense, refer to or, in one sense, be *about* something that is not one of its *constituents*.

At this point, one might be tempted to accuse Russell of playing fast and loose with the word 'constituent'—of stipulating a "persuasive" definition of it in order to have his epistemological cake, the principle of acquaintance, and eat the ontological cake of realism as well. But putting the objection in this manner takes all of the sting out of it; the objection, put thus, answers itself. It is just the beauty of the combination of the distinction between knowledge by acquaintance and knowledge by description with the principle of acquaintance that it yields a *concept empiricist*[1] theory of meaning (an epistemological matter) and, at the same time, provides for a robust realism with respect to the external world and its unobservables (an ontological matter). Our knowledge of unobservables, that is, our knowledge of items with which we are not acquainted, is *knowledge by description*, and we denote or, in *one* legitimate sense of 'refer', refer to such items by descriptive phrases, both *definite* and *indefinite*.

Using a linguistic approach, we may put the principle of acquaintance: in any declarative sentence that we can understand, every descriptive (non-logical) term must have as its direct referent an item with which we are acquainted. We can understand 'The author of *Waverley* wrote *Marmion*', for we are, let us common-sensically assume, acquainted with the property of *being an author*, with *Waverley*, with the property (the relation of) *writing* and with *Marmion* all of which comprise *and* exhaust the direct referents of the descriptive terms of the sentence in quotes. However, provided a certain *contingent* assumption is true, the sentence has another referent, an *indirect* one; it refers to (or *denotes*) *indirectly* whoever it was that wrote *Waverley*, provided that some one individual *did* write it (the contingent assumption just mentioned above). Such indirect reference to items with which we are not acquainted and of which our knowledge is knowledge by description is accomplished by purely logical

[1] Russell's later writings clearly reject *judgment empiricism*, the doctrine that all of our knowledge must be confirmed wholly by experience (or observation). This is most explicit, of course, in his development of his theory of non-demonstrative inference in *Human Knowledge*. Thus, he rejects the empiricism that is prevalent today, the kind advocated, for example, by logical positivism, logical empiricism, and related views. However, he makes it abundantly clear that rejection of *judgment* empiricism is entirely consistent with, indeed quite congenial with, his staunch adherence to the *concept* empiricism expressed by the principle of acquaintance.

terms in combination with terms whose *direct* referents are items with which we are acquainted.

If we write the sentence in question as:

$$(\exists x)[Wxw \cdot (y)(Wyw \supset x = y) \cdot Wxm]$$

where '*Wuv*' stands for '*u* wrote *v*', '*w*' stands for *Waverley* and '*m*' stands for *Marmion*, we may say that the indirect reference is accomplished, in this case, by an existentially quantified variable and other logical terms in combination with descriptive terms such as '*W*' and '*w*' whose *direct* referents are items of acquaintance. In this case, we refer, *indirectly*, to an individual, to whoever wrote *Waverley*, even though we do not name him (her, it, . . .) and, indeed, even though we do not know who (or what) he (or she, or it) *is*.[1] Similarly, we can refer to unobservable properties, even if we do not know *what* the properties are to which we refer. In such a case, the reference to the property is indirect and is accomplished by means of existentially quantified *predicate* variables and other logical terms in combination, again, with terms whose *direct* referents are items of acquaintance. Proceeding in this manner, all theoretical terms, *that is* all terms purporting to refer directly to unobservables (to items with which we are not acquainted), whether they be individuals, properties, or classes, can be eliminated and replaced by existentially quantified variables of the corresponding logical type. The result, of course, is the Ramsey sentence.[2]

The Ramsey sentence of a theory is a weaker assertion than the original theory *only* in that it does not "name" the unobservable properties, classes, and individuals involved but refers to them *indirectly* (in the sense of "indirect reference" under discussion). It makes explicit the fact that our knowledge of unobservables is knowledge by description and that *we do not know what* the unobservable entities of our theories *are*, even though we do know something about them: we know what our theories, duly "Ramseyfied", assert about them. This is just another way of stating Russell's claim that our knowledge in these realms is knowledge of *structural* properties *only* and that we are ignorant of what the "intrinsic" properties in these realms *are*.[3] But, although "Ramsey-fication" eliminates theoretical terms, it in no way eliminates reference to (and

---

[1] The question as to *how* we know that the author of *Waverley* wrote *Marmion* is a question for *confirmation theory* and one that it is not necessary to answer when we are discussing the *meaning* of such a knowledge claim. Obviously we *can* have excellent and overwhelming evidence (similar stylistic idiosyncrasies in the two texts, etc.) that the same person wrote both *Waverley* and *Marmion* even if we have no idea of who the author is.

[2] For a more detailed (although different) discussion of the Ramsey sentence approach, as well as the equivalent model-theoretic approach, see my "Structural Realism and the Meaning of Theoretical Terms", where references to earlier work by Ramsey, Carnap and others are also given.

[3] Since for Russell nothing is observable except items in our direct experience, all properties (and individuals) of the external world are unobservable; all of our knowledge of them is, thus, knowledge by description and knowledge of structure only: we do not know what any of the intrinsic properties of the external world *are*.

(structural) knowledge about) theoretical (unobservable) entities. Indeed, we have just covered the details of how the reference to unobservables remains as *indirect reference* and the knowledge remains as (structural) knowledge by description. The limitations that the Ramsey sentence makes explicit, and which Russell[1] made equally explicit in an equivalent though terminologically somewhat different way, are therefore *purely epistemic* limitations: *they impose no ontological restrictions whatever*. It has been a serious mistake, therefore, to suppose, as have many philosophers, that adoption of the Ramsey-sentence approach entails any rejection of realism. The ontological status of unobservables is in no way impugned by the fact that our knowledge of them is by description only or that it is of purely structural matters, any more than our ignorance of who wrote *Waverley*, were we so ignorant, would condemn Sir Walter Scott to non-existence or to a shadowy ontological nether world. Neither Russell's principle of acquaintance nor its explication by means of the Ramsey device have any ontological implications, and, moreover, they greatly facilitate the implementation of a vigorously realist view. Such a view was strongly advocated by Russell.[2]

In summary, on this point, Russell solved in a simple, straightforward, and entirely satisfactory manner a problem about which volumes and journalfuls are still being written today. He showed us how to dispose of the problem about the meaning of theoretical terms by showing how to *eliminate* theoretical terms without in any way eliminating reference to theoretical entities. When the observable is limited to items in our direct experience, as Russell persuasively argues it should be limited, this same approach becomes a solution to the traditional problems about perception and our knowledge of the external world. Russell's principle of acquaintance, his doctrine of knowledge by acquaintance and knowledge by description, and his theory of description, especially when implemented by the Ramsey sentence or by an equivalent, simple model-theoretic approach, clarify his claims that our knowledge of

[1] Apparently Russell was not acquainted with Ramsey's approach to these matters (see Frank Ramsey, *The Foundations of Mathematics (and Other Essays)*, New York 1956). However, it is easily shown that his approach and Ramsey's are equivalent, Ramsey's being somewhat more elegant and transparent. For details, see again my "Structural Realism and the Meaning of Theoretical Terms".

[2] The theory of *indirect reference* that I have just outlined provides a foundation for a more comprehensive theory of meaning. More specifically, it contains the means for clarifying the syntactical dimensions of meaning of descriptive terms in a natural—or in any applied—language as opposed to the directly referential or "purely semantical" component. It thereby answers any charge that it is merely a naive "Fido-Fido" view and, at the same time, takes into account the legitimate portion of the "meaning is use" doctrine. For, just as many putatively proper names are more properly regarded as abbreviations of definite descriptions, so are many predicates best thought of as abbreviations for descriptive phrases (definite in some cases but, more often, indefinite) which refer *indirectly* to properties with which the language community is not acquainted.

what is in the external world is limited to its structural properties (although we know *that* its intrinsic, or first-order properties are "out there" too).

Russell's views on the matters just discussed are, of course, similar to *representative realism*, and the two main objections usually made against it have been made against Russell's position. These objections are answered by showing that their force derives in large measure from a faulty view of non-demonstrative inference (I shall return to this later) and by showing how (via Ramsey sentences, etc. above), we can refer to properties (indirectly and abstractly) that have never been (or ever will be) exemplified in our experience. Other philosophers have held similar views about perception, of course, beginning perhaps with Democritus and the early Greek Sceptics and passing down through Galileo, Locke, Eddington, W. Sellars (along with his father Roy Wood Sellars and the other "Critical Realists"). But Russell's views on these matters seem to have developed independently and in quite a novel manner. More importantly, I shall try to show later that, when combined with his event ontology and his associated theory of space-time, they provide the only satisfactory mind-body "identity theory"—the only satisfactory mind-body *monism* with which I am acquainted. If Russell's later philosophy can make good on this matter, surely its radically revolutionary character cannot be seriously questioned.[1]

Russell rejects *substance* metaphysics altogether and replace *things*—clumps of matter (physical objects), etc. with classes or families of *events*. Examples of one kind of events are: a twinge of pain, the occurrence of a patch of red in the visual field, etc. These examples are events such that we know *what* they are. This is *not* true of the events that comprise the vast bulk of the physical (external) world. We do not know *what* these events are; we do not know their intrinsic nature; we do not know *what* the first-order properties are that are exemplified in them. What we do know, if our theories from physics, etc. and refined common sense are true or close to the truth, are some of the structural properties (mostly relational) of these events. The most prominent of such properties are the causal relations that hold among the events. Russell's theory of space-time amounts to "constructing" space-time out of events and their causal relationships to each other—a truly *relational* theory of space-time. Thus, as he puts it: "When the causal relations of an event are known, its position in space-time follows tautologically."[2] Since we have already located mental events (the occurrence of perceptive experiences, etc.) in the causal network, they thereby acquire a spatio-temporal location, and a kind of mind-body "identity theory" automatically follows as a consequence of the theory. I believe that the matter can be made more clear if we adopt definitions of "mental" and "physical" slightly different from Russell's. Let us call anything "a physical event" that is in the causal (and, thus, in the spatio-temporal) network, and something will be called "a

---

[1] The summary in the next few paragraphs of Russell's view on this matter is taken mainly from my "Russell on Perception: A Study in Philosophical Method".

[2] P. A. Schilpp (ed.), *The Philosophy of Bertrand Russell*, Evanston, Ill., 1944, p. 705.

mental event" if and only if it is an event in our direct experience (as Russell puts it, if it (or its ingredients) can be known otherwise than by inference—in Russell's special sense of 'inference' discussed, e.g. in *Human Knowledge*).[1] Now, since mental events are in space-time—i.e. they play a causal role—it follows that all mental events are physical events. Since there *are* such things as mental events, it also follows that some physical events are mental events; of what other physical events are like, or what their intrinsic nature is we are ignorant, so ignorant, Russell says, that we do not know whether they are similar to (in their first order or intrinsic properties) or totally different from the events in our experience (whose first order or intrinsic properties we do know by acquaintance). What we do know about physical events (including those that are mental, although about these we know more besides) are (some of) their structural or higher order properties, the more important of which give their spatio-temporal (or causal) structure.

At the risk of repetition, I must stress a point of crucial importance. The mental events that comprise our experience, that we live through and know in all of their qualitative richness *really are physical events* (they *really are* mental events too, of course). As with other physical events, each has its own position in the spatio-temporal—causal—network and is *not* an epiphenomenal or parallelistic correlate of some other "truly physical" event that is supposed to play the "real" spatio-temporal or causal role. There *is* no such *other* physical event at the spatio-temporal locus in question. Every "truly mental" event is also "truly physical" (though not conversely so far as we know). We regard mental events differently from other physical events because they comprise our experience and, thus, we know their intrinsic properties as well as their structural ones.

Since the brain, like all portions of matter, consists of a family—or families—of events, causally related in appropriate ways, and since neurophysiology and psychophysiology gives us the causal locus that it does for the events that comprise our experience (our thoughts, feelings, etc.), it follows that our thoughts and feelings are, quite literally, among the constituents of our brains. (Perhaps, e.g., *some* of the members of a certain family of events that comprise a certain electron in the brain *really are* mental events. This is indeed crude. But we shall, perhaps, have to wait for further developments (better theories) in physics, neurophysiology, etc. before anything less crude can be posed.)

As Russell says, this theory may seem fantastic, but he clearly believes it is true or close to the truth and, at any rate, that it is the theory best supported by the evidence from science and enlightened common sense. Not the least component of its support comes from the fact that contemporary physics seems much better formulable using an event ontology than it is using a *substance* one. In

---

[1] Russell first defines "mental event" in this manner and then defines a "physical event" as one not known (or not known to be known) except by inference.

physics today, the "dematerialization of matter" is virtually complete. Be that as it may, I do not believe that there are any insurmountable obstacles to *understanding* the theory, especially if we remember the commonplace from the history of science that, when novel theories are proposed, old words take on meanings that, while they are quite similar to the old meanings in many respects, are sometimes bewilderingly different from them in others. And Russell's famous statement, which, he says, profoundly shocked Ernest Nagel—and others as well[1]—is seen to be an unexceptionable consequence of the theory. The statement is to the effect that when a physiologist examines another man's brain what he really sees is a portion of his own brain. Of course, the word 'see' here has a somewhat different meaning from its ordinary one. For its ordinary use is, in the main, a naïve realist one; to say that we *see* something ordinarily implies that we perceive something external. But according to Russell we never see *anything* in this ordinary sense of 'see'. All that we ever perceive visually are ingredients of the events that comprise our experience and are, thus, literally in (or are constituents of) our own brains. Russell provides for avoidance of misunderstanding here by his distinction between physical space and perceptual space, e.g. visual space. Physical space, we recall, is constructed out of events and their causal inter-relationships, but my visual space, in which I am aware of qualitative extension, shapes, locations of colour patches and other visual "percepts", is an ingredient of events in my experience. Thus all of my visual space, no matter over how many miles common sense may indicate that it spreads, is located at a point or within a small volume in physical space, in, as a matter of fact, my (physical) brain. Consider the physiologist's percept that common sense mistakenly identifies with the other man's brain. This percept is really located in the physiologist's (private) visual space although, of course, the other man's brain does play a crucial causal role in producing it. Let us refer to this percept as the physiologist's percept of the other man's brain. Then it is quite clear that the physiologist's percept of the other man's brain is external to the physiologist's percept of his own body (in the physiologist's visual space), while both percepts are in the physiologist's brain in physical space.

The difference between this kind of mind-body monism and traditional materialistic mind-body theories is extreme. Traditional materialism took our conception and knowledge of matter, of the physical, to be straightforward and unproblematic. The mental, on the other hand, was held to be not only problematic but metaphysically and epistemologically undesirable, what with its alleged privacy or subjectivity, ineffability, etc., and therefore it was thought to be something best got rid of, or at any rate swept under the rug of epiphenomenalism or put into the closet of psychophysical parallelism. Traditional materialism's conception of matter was one that resulted from naïve realism or from a not too pervasive modification thereof. Matter was something

---

[1] Schilpp (ed.), *The Philosophy of Bertrand Russell*, p. 705.

good and solid. One could *see* and *feel* that it was good and solid; as Russell says, it was bumpable into. Modern science, however, according to Russell, makes necessary the drastic revision of our conception of matter that has been discussed in this paper. It turns out that we cannot see or feel matter at all, except for those events in our visual and tactile experience that comprise a small portion of our brains. Our traditional notions of matter, rather than those of mind, turn out to be the problematic ones. Traditional materialism, by accepting common sense naïve realism, fell into the error of identifying visual and tactile percepts with the physical objects that are merely (one crucial part of) their causes. Thus, contrary to what traditional materialism wanted, the mental remains every bit as mental as anyone could hope for, in spite of the fact that it is also physical. However, the portion of physical events that are mental, as far as we know today, is subject to the same principles and laws of nature as the rest of the physical world. Russell's mind-body monism retains this much in common with materialism. Whether or not further investigation will reveal that additional natural laws are required for the mental realm remains an open question.

In view of all of the hooting and scoffing to which Russell's later philosophy of mind has been subjected, it is especially gratifying to see that approaches quite similar to his are beginning to find favour with a number of leading *scientists* who are interested in very general problems in areas such as perception, neurophysiology, neuropsychology, psychophysiology, etc. Scientists in such fields have, of course, long been interested in the philosophical issues involved. Eccles, for example, has long ago settled for a dualistic interactionist answer to the mind-body "world-knot". However, the current work of Gibson (a psychologist) on perception—I am told by a former student of his, whose opinion I respect (Robert Shaw at the Center for Human Learning of the University of Minnesota), and by others—is quite congenial with Russell's kind of thinking, in spite of the fact that Gibson claims to defend a kind of "direct realism"; his use of the term seems to be different from that of most philosophers. Several papers by Gordon Globus, a psychiatrist at the University of California at Irvine, on the mind-body problem—papers not yet published, but which are excellent in my opinion and in that of some of my colleagues—are all very much along Russellian lines. The same is true of much of the work of the noted Karl Pribram, a neurophysiologist at Stanford University (see, for instance, his book, *Languages of the Brain*, Englewood Cliffs, N.J., 1971).

I have saved until last what I consider to be the most revolutionary of all of Russell's later ideas, especially when one considers the views that prevail in most philosophical circles in the English speaking world today. It is a view, in fact, of which Russell himself seemed only dimly aware, although he did make fairly explicit remarks about it from time to time. I am talking about what Russell took to be the nature and function of the entire business of philosophical inquiry. We can begin by mentioning his most general views on the matter, views that he *did* state explicitly and emphatically again and again in *Human Knowledge* and in *My Philosophical Development*. First of all, he emphatically rejects the claim that philosophical problems are, in general, pseudo-problems, as he does the claim that they are to be settled exclusively or even mainly by the analysis of language—or by the application of logic alone (in *Human Knowledge*, for instance, he says that "logic is no part of philosophy"). Surely his views on this are too well known to require further comment here, especially his views on "ordinary language" philosophy. However, it should be noted that he ends up being almost as strongly opposed to the linguistic, "logical reconstruction" approach of, e.g. Carnap and similar philosophers as he is to the "Oxbridge Analysts". He maintained the contrary view, again explicitly, emphatically, and repeatedly, that it is the business of philosophy to discover *truth* (or as close as we can get to truth) *about the real world*. And, although my statement of the views that he makes absolutely explicit has just ended, it does not require very careful study of the texts to see that by truth here he means *significant, important*, and indeed (this is the crucial point) *contingent* truth.

It is here that we must speculate about Russell's implicit views, and thus, things become more difficult. However, it seems to me that it was surely Russell's gradually evolving new views on induction—or confirmation theory— or the relation between evidence and what is evidenced—on what he called "non-demonstrative inference"—that drastically altered his former views and brought about his later views on the nature of philosophical activity. Here I can only give a bare summary of his later thinking on these matters.[1]

First of all, he became more and more convinced of the conclusiveness of Hume's critique of inductive reasoning. He believed that the attempts of Reichenbach and others to give even a "pragmatic" justification or "vindication" of induction or "the straight rule" (of statistical inference) were forever doomed to failure.

As far as I know, Russell never studied the work of Karl Popper or his disciples. However, in *My Philosophical Development*, p. 27, he had already come to see that the important and interesting theories in science, even in physics, are not viably falsifiable (*pace* Popper). It is doubtful whether Russell saw the other equally conclusive reason why the falsification approach fails to eliminate Hume's problem (i.e. given any number of data whatever there will be an infinite number of mutually incompatible theories that will explain the data equally well)[2] but I shall not discuss that matter here.

To make a long story short, Russell recognized what seems to me inescapable: all of our general knowledge and practically all of our singular knowledge of any interest or importance rests upon assumptions that are not tested or testable by experience or observation. As noted above, although Russell remained a

[1] I have argued this matter in some detail in my "Theories, Perception, and Structural Realism" and "Russell on Perception: A Study in Philosophical Method".

[2] See my two papers mentioned above.

concept empiricist until his death, he completely abandoned judgment empiricism. This is exactly the opposite of the position that most English-speaking philosophers defend today.

At this point there emerge two (incompatible) prongs of Russell's thought. One of them he makes explicit in considerable detail in Parts V and VI of *Human Knowledge* and in the chapter titled "Non-Demonstrative Inference" in *My Philosophical Development*. Here he takes the untested, untestable, and, in this sense, non-empirical (though nevertheless contingent) assumptions upon which our significant knowledge of the world and ourselves rest to be his notorious six "Postulates of Scientific Inference". But, in spite of my boundless admiration for Russell's later work, I do not think that he ever used these postulates significantly or ever showed how they could do much for anyone, be he scientist, philosopher, or man-in-the-street.[1]

The other prong of Russell's thought is one that is incompatible with his "Postulates-of-Scientific-Inference" approach. Again, to make a long story short, it is something like the following. The philosopher *and* the scientist after first seeing and trying to understand whatever particular problem it is that they are interested in must then propose theories that, if true, would solve their problem. That is, he holds that both proceed hypothetico-deductively. They must propose theories that, if true, would *explain* their data or their per-plexities or whatever it is that wants explaining. For example, as explained above, Russell held that what physics tells us plus his own *theory* of space-time (based on his event ontology) plus certain other assumptions already discussed *explain* satisfactorily all of the perplexities about the relationship between mental events and physical events that have puzzled thinkers throughout the centuries. This and other traditional philosophical problems mentioned above, were, I have argued (see references above), for Russell contingent problems, differing, if at all, only in degree and not in kind from (other) genuine scientific problems.[2]

---

[1] There is one exception; they produced the beautiful last paragraph of *Human Knowledge*:

But although our postulates can, in this way, be fitted into a framework which has what we may call an empiricist "flavour" [here "empiricist" must obviously refer to *concept empiricism*], it remains undeniable that our knowledge of them, in so far as we do know them, cannot be based upon experience, though all their verifiable consequences are such as experience will confirm. In this sense, it must be admitted, empiricism as a theory of knowledge has proved inadequate, though less so than any other previous theory of knowledge. Indeed, such inadequacies as we have seemed to find in empiricism have been discovered by strict adherence to a doctrine by which empiricist philosophy has been in-spired: that all human knowledge is uncertain, inexact, and partial. To this doctrine we have not found any limitation whatever.

[2] Russell's recognition that observations and logic alone, no matter how liberal one's (reasonable) interpretation of 'logic' is, are insufficient for scientific knowledge and equally so for mundane common sense knowledge puts him squarely in the camp of those who

The fact that even the later Russell claims that he attacks such problems by the "method of analysis" should not deceive one. For there is detailed textual evidence that by "analysis" *here* he means neither *breaking a whole down into its parts* (although he has used such a meaning at times) nor does he mean anything resembling currently popular "philosophical (or logical) analysis". The textual evidence is overwhelming that by "analysis" here he must mean something like *proposing a theory that explains what we take to be the facts relevant to the problem at hand.* For example, as early as 1913 he said: "Every truly philosophical problem is a problem of *analysis*; and in problems of *analysis* the best method is that which sets out from *results* and arrives at the *premises*" (my italics).[1] And as early as 1927 (*The Analysis of Matter*, p. 194) he expressly endorses hypothetico-deductive reasoning as being the mode of reasoning used in science. In other words, "analysis" here can only mean what I take most enlightened philosophers today to believe the method of science to be, i.e. *hypothetico-deductive* (or better, *hypothetico-inferential*) reasoning.[2]

Russell, as far as I know, never really worried about the crucial problem that still faces us today in confirmation theory: i.e. given that whatever our relevant data may be there is an infinitude of mutually incompatible theories that would explain them. But being the wishful mortal that I am, my guess is that he would have given an answer similar to mine: we must dream up as many plausible theories as we can that will do the job[3] and then sit back and, first of all, hope that we have been so almost unbelievably lucky as to get anywhere close to the truth and, then, make a *subjective guess* as to which *proposed* theory has the highest *objective* prior (not *a priori*) probability.[4]

It is in such a manner, i.e. by means of hypothetico-inferential reasoning, I believe, that the later Russell justifies his preference for realism over either solipsism, idealism, instrumentalism, or behaviourism, for monism over dualism, and for Relativity Theory over Newtonian Mechanics, etc. And he says explicitly: "I do not pretend that the above theory [the theories of his I have discussed about perception and the external world, the relation of mind and

---

reject all fashionable strictures on "scientific method". As already noted, he has no sympathy with instrumentalism, phenomenalism, and other restrictive methodologies. At times, it is true, he has used a behaviouristic approach to certain epistemological problems. But close examination shows that such an approach was always a supplementary, nonexclusive alternative—one that told only part of the story. He explicitly rejects behaviourism and operationism as epistemological or ontological views as well as exclusive methodological premises for science.

[1] *Monist* (1913), quoted by Alan Wood in the addendum to *My Philosophical Development*.

[2] For more detail on Russell's meaning of "the method of analysis" see my "Russell on Perception: A Study in Philosophical Method".

[3] Unfortunately (maybe fortunately?) we usually are bright enough to come up with only one or two such theories.

[4] See my "Corroboration without Demarcation", in P. A. Schilpp (ed.), *The Philosophy of Karl Popper*, La Salle, Ill., 1973.

matter, etc.] can be proved. What I contend is that *like the theories of physics, it cannot be disproved*, and gives an answer to problems which older theorists have found puzzling. *I do not think that any prudent person will claim more than this for any theory.*"[1]

Russell, then, wants to return philosophy to what I believe is her rightful position, which some have called "the Queen of the Sciences". And, as I have claimed elsewhere ("Russell on Perception: A Study in Philosophical Method") his later philosophy has provided solutions in the sense that science provides solutions—tentative ones—for which many contemporary philosophers (and scientists, e.g. psychologists, neurophysiologists, and especially psychophysiologists) are still groping. But whether I am right about this or not, I have absolutely no doubt that his later philosophy deserves immeasurably more study than it has received and that our knowledge will be extensively enriched when this is forthcoming.

---

[1] Russell, *My Philosophical Development*, p. 27; my italics.

Wesley C. Salmon

Russell on Scientific Inference or *Will the Real Deductivist Please Stand Up?*

By the time he had reached the age of forty (*c.* 1912), Bertrand Russell had confronted some of the most profound problems concerning the nature of mathematical knowledge and deductive logic, and he had produced results which have had a lasting effect upon our understanding of these issues. The shoulders of this benevolent giant have supported many successors who have tried to see further, and in some cases succeeded. For these achievements he has received much well-deserved recognition and honour.

Russell never supposed, however, that deductive logic could be the whole story concerning scientific inference. He made this point explicitly in the famous chapter on "Induction" in *The Problems of Philosophy* (1912) while considering ways to "extend our knowledge beyond the sphere of our private experience". For many years Russell continued to be concerned with the nature of scientific knowledge in such works as *Our Knowledge of the External World* (1914), *The Analysis of Mind* (1921), *The Analysis of Matter* (1927), and *An Inquiry into Meaning and Truth* (1940), to mention only the most important works in the period between *Principia Mathematica* (1910–13) and the volume on Russell in *The Library of Living Philosophers* (1946).[1]

Russell seemed to feel, nevertheless, that there was a problem of induction with which he had not yet dealt adequately. In the lead article in the Schilpp volume, "Bertrand Russell's Logic", Hans Reichenbach requested further clarification of Russell's views on induction. In response Russell wrote: "It is clear that induction is needed to establish almost all of our empirical beliefs, and that it is not deducible from any or all of the principles of deductive logic. . . . I do not see any way out of a dogmatic assertion that we know the inductive principle, or some equivalent; the only alternative is to throw over almost everything that is regarded as knowledge by science and common sense".[2] After some remarks about insincere doubting, as practiced by professional philosophers, he continues:

But if we are unwilling to profess disbeliefs that we are incapable of entertaining, the result of logical analysis is to increase the number of independent premises that we accept in our analysis of knowledge. Among such premises I should put some principle by means

[1] P. A. Schilpp (ed.), *The Philosophy of Bertrand Russell*, Evanston, Ill., 1944.
[2] ibid., p. 683.

of which induction can be justified. What exactly this principle should be is a difficult question, which I hope to deal with at some not distant date, if circumstances permit.[1]

Human Knowledge, Its Scope and Limits (1948) is Russell's attempt to carry out the promised investigation. He concludes that the principle of induction (by enumeration) is false, and that inferences conducted in conformity to that principle, even when they have true premises, will usually have false conclusions. This does not lead Russell to abandon induction entirely; rather, it leads him to seek restrictions that can be imposed upon induction so as to secure the probability of inductive conclusions. The net result is the postulation of several principles, but the principle of induction is not among them. A restricted form of the inductive principle is, however, derivable from them.[2]

Russell never wavered from the view that science involves *some* sort of non-demonstrative inference. He chooses not to call it "induction", reserving that term for induction by enumeration. *Human Knowledge* thus embodies Russell's mature attempt to provide an analysis of non-demonstrative inference in science. The author of that work had been publishing serious philosophical works for more than half a century; his first book in the philosophy of science, *An Essay on the Foundations of Geometry*, was published fifty-one years earlier in 1897. Moreover, it was preceded by enough articles to get anyone a promotion to Associate Professor in almost any American university, to say nothing of his book on *German Social Democracy* (1896). Like Socrates, Russell was widely regarded as a corruptor of the youth, but unlike Socrates, he could hardly be accused of failure to publish. Although *Human Knowledge* represents the culmination of Russell's epistemological thought, surprisingly little attention was paid to the theory of non-demonstrative inference developed in it. Small wonder that Russell, in *My Philosophical Development* (1959), written about a decade after *Human Knowledge*, should express frank disappointment at this general neglect. In view of his epoch-making contributions to the theory of demonstrative inference, the least we can do is to make some serious efforts to understand just what Russell was driving at.[3] Even though we may end up rejecting Russell's solution, we can learn some extremely important lessons regarding non-demonstrative inference.

1. *The Dilemma of Solipsism and Empiricism*

There are two distinct ways of attacking the theory of knowledge. One is the Cartesian approach, which consists in finding a secure epistemological basis

---

[1] ibid., p. 684.

[2] *My Philosophical Development*, New York 1959, p. 200.

[3] I realize that my arguments in this paragraph are largely *ad hominem*, but this type of argument, though deductively fallacious, may upon occasion be a valid form of non-demonstrative inference.

upon which one can reconstruct, from scratch, the edifice of knowledge. The other is a more nearly Kantian approach, in which one somehow accepts, at least in broad outlines, the body of currently accepted scientific knowledge, attempting to account for it by means of a logical analysis of the relation between the results of science and the evidence upon which they rest. Both approaches involve what is called "rational reconstruction", but the first proceeds from the evidential ground up, while the second proceeds from the theoretic superstructure down. As Russell says, the two approaches should be compatible and complementary, like digging a tunnel through a mountain from both ends.[1] In practice, however, they seem to diverge widely, failing miserably to meet in the middle.

Russell examines these alternative approaches, and, in effect draws out a dilemma: we must either accept solipsism of the present moment, or admit that there are non-empirical postulates which must be accepted as probably true. Solipsism comes in two varieties, ontological and methodological. The ontological solipsist is committed to the view that nothing *exists* apart from the contents of his own consciousness. The methodological solipsist holds merely that the contents of his own consciousness constitute the sum total of all *evidence* from which everything else must be constructed or inferred. Whichever type of solipsism you adopt, however, Russell argues that you are logically committed to a solipsism of the present moment. Without some independent assurance about the reliability of memory the very existence of the past is uncertain, and without the principle of induction the future can likewise be doubted. The Cartesian *cogito*, if properly interpreted, yields no permanent self with a past or future, but only a momentary disembodied conscious experience.

Although methodological solipsism may seem relatively benign, compared with ontological solipsism, Russell argues that the former leads to the latter, at least if one is an empiricist. If you accept the principle of empiricism—that the sole basis for any factual claim lies in experience—then methodological solipsism leads to ontological solipsism. In the absence of synthetic non-empirical premises, nothing can be inferred beyond the confines of one's own momentary conscious experience. This follows from the fundamental principle, emphasized by both Hume and Russell, that distinct events are logically independent of one another.[2] From premises that refer only to events within experience, it is impossible to deduce anything about things and events that lie outside of experience. It is only by postulating such principles as the general reliability of memory and induction (or principles sufficient to validate induction), that one can, so to speak, break out of solitary confinement.

Russell's resolution of the dilemma—call it *the dilemma of solipsism and empiricism*—is unequivocal: solipsism of the present moment is a doctrine that

---

[1] *My Philosophical Development*, p. 205.
[2] *Human Knowledge*, New York 1948, pp. 174-5.

cannot be refuted, but it cannot be held sincerely. To underline the absurdity of solipsism, Russell mentions a letter he received from the logician Christine Ladd Franklin, espousing solipsism herself and expressing dismay that there are so few other philosophers who do likewise![1]

Russell's dilemma of solipsism and empiricism seems strongly reminiscent of the Hume-Kant confrontation. On the one hand, Hume's analysis of knowledge was based upon a thoroughgoing empiricism, and it led to an intolerable scepticism. Russell mentioned Hume explicitly when he spoke of the *professional* doubts of philosophers. Kant's transcendental deduction, on the other hand, accepts scientific knowledge as real, and it results in synthetic *a priori* propositions. Russell emphatically denies that his postulates of knowledge achieve the status of synthetic *a priori* truths,[2] but it does seem fair to say that they result from a kind of transcendental deduction. Russell's unwillingness to embrace empiricism, if the price is solipsism of the present moment, reminds one of Thomas Reid's celebrated condemnation of Hume's empiricism:

A traveller of good judgment may mistake his way, and be unawares led into a wrong track; and while the road is fair before him, he may go on without suspicion and be followed by others; but when it ends in a coal-pit, it requires no great judgment to know that he hath gone wrong.[3]

It is worth remarking, I think, that the method of Cartesian doubt made a good deal more sense in the first half of the seventeenth century than it does in the last half of the twentieth. Descartes could sincerely maintain that what was paraded before him as scientific knowledge was sufficiently doubtful and insecure to require thoroughgoing scrutiny or revision. A twentieth-century philosopher who feigned sincere scepticism about modern physics—after all the wonders of the nuclear age—would be a preposterous figure. This is *not* to say that scrutiny of the epistemological foundations of science is misplaced. But the aim of such investigations is not to question seriously the acceptability of the bulk of contemporary science; rather, it is to understand the logical structure of science more or less as is. As Russell remarked, no philosophical argument to prove the wholesale falsity of modern science could conceivably be as convincing as the results of physics themselves.[4]

2. Probability and Certainty

The Cartesian method of doubt was designed by its author to yield certainty of scientific knowledge. Russell is thoroughly aware that such a goal is unattain-

---

[1] ibid., p. 180.

[2] *My Philosophical Development*, pp. 201–2.

[3] Thomas Reid, *An Inquiry into the Human Mind*, Chapter 1, Section 8; quoted by Roderick M. Chisholm, *Perceiving*, Ithaca, N.Y., 1957, p. 75.

[4] *My Philosophical Development*, p. 207.

able, and that the best for which we can ever hope are scientific results that are probable. Such probable conclusions require, of course, premises given by experience, but even then, according to Russell, it is impossible to infer validly the probability of the desired conclusions without the aid of supplementary general premises. As we have noted above, Russell explicitly, repeatedly, and emphatically denies that these additional general premises—his postulates of scientific inference—can be known with certainty. Thus, among the *premises* of knowledge are statements that are merely probable.

Furthermore, accepting (as he does) the overall correctness of modern science, Russell regards perception as a causal process, originating generally in external events and terminating with certain events in the brain. These latter events in the brain are usually correlated with external events, and hence, they can be taken as evidence for the external events. There are, of course, illusions, hallucinations, and dreams; consequently, the mental events that constitute the content of experience are not absolutely reliable guides to external reality, but they do provide a probabilistic basis for inference. If we regard the content of *perceptual* experiences (which Russell distinguishes sharply from "sense-data") as premises for scientific inference, we shall have to admit that these premises, like the aforementioned general premises, are uncertain. Thus, Russell maintains, all of the (non-trivial) premises—both particular and general—of scientific knowledge are uncertain.

Russell clearly realizes that this view has an awkward aspect, for the theory of probability seems to demand that some statements be accorded the status of certainty as a basis for assigning degrees of probability to others. In the logical theory of probability advanced by John Maynard Keynes (1921)—a system with which Russell was long acquainted—probability is a relation between two propositions, evidence and hypothesis. The hypothesis is said to have a degree of probability relative to the evidence; the evidence, however, is given, and no uncertainty or degree of probability attaches to it. In Reichenbach's frequency theory as well, Russell maintained, probability is defined in terms of given relative frequencies of occurrences, and no probability or uncertainty attaches to these. Hence, as Russell carefully pointed out, it is difficult to see how any probabilities at all can be generated on the basis of uncertain premises.

One of the standard responses to this problem has been to retreat into some form of phenomenalism based upon incorrigible phenomenal reports or sense-data statements. This position had been adopted by some of the early logical positivists, by A. J. Ayer in *The Foundations of Empirical Knowledge* (1953), and especially by C. I. Lewis in *Analysis of Knowledge and Valuation* (1946). Among these influential authors, Lewis at least had explicitly formulated the principle "If anything is to be probable, then something must be certain",[1] and had recognized it as a motivation for his distinction between "terminating

---

[1] C. I. Lewis, *Analysis of Knowledge and Valuation*, La Salle, Ill., 1946, p. 186.

judgments" and "non-terminating judgments". Russell himself, much earlier, had briefly espoused phenomenalism, but that went the way of some of his other early marriages.[1] At the time of writing *Human Knowledge* Russell does not see phenomenalism as a viable answer to the problem. He concludes, instead, that "the mathematical aspects of probability have less to do than might be thought with the problems of scientific inference".[2]

Russell maintains, in consequence, that there are two kinds of probability: one, a finite-frequency concept, that is governed by the mathematical calculus of probability; the other a concept of degree of credibility that need not satisfy the mathematical calculus, but can be applied more broadly.[3] This thesis is quite similar to Carnap's theory of the two types of probability,[4] with the crucial difference that both of Carnap's concepts fulfil the axioms of the mathematical calculus. Carnap's theory, however, still faces the problem to which Russell calls attention; like its predecessor, Keynes's logical theory, it cannot handle uncertain evidence. Although various authors, including Popper and Reichenbach, explicitly rejected phenomenalism (or any other theory incorporating incorrigible basic statements),[5] I do not think any of them had shown formally how to come to terms with this problem. It was only with the recent work of Richard Jeffrey[6] that, as far as I know, a formal theory of probability capable of accommodating uncertain evidence was developed. The problem of uncertain evidence was clearly recognized and acknowledged by Russell, but not solved by him; it is a problem whose resolution required a simple—but extremely important—technical development.

3. *The Grue Problem*

In the course of his argument that the principle of induction—i.e. induction by enumeration—will generally lead to false conclusions, Russell shows how to construct classes in which induction will, with overwhelming frequency, go wrong.[7] Although he does not invent cute predicates like Nelson Goodman's 'grue' and 'bleen',[8] the classes he defines have the same fundamental import for induction as Goodman's pathological predicates. As Goodman defines these

---

[1] See paper by Grover Maxwell in this volume, pp. 169–182.

[2] *My Philosophical Development*, p. 193.

[3] *Human Knowledge*, p. 381.

[4] Rudolf Carnap, *Logical Foundations of Probability*, Chicago 1950.

[5] Karl R. Popper, *The Logic of Scientific Discovery*, New York 1959, Chapter 5; Hans Reichenbach, *Experience and Prediction*, Chicago 1938, Chapters 3–4.

[6] Richard Jeffrey, *The Logic of Decision*, New York 1965, Chapter 11; and "Probable Knowledge" in Imre Lakatos (ed.), *The Problem of Inductive Logic*, Amsterdam 1968, pp. 166–80.

[7] *Human Knowledge*, pp. 404, 414.

[8] Nelson Goodman, *Fact, Fiction, and Forecast*, Cambridge, Mass., 1955; 2nd ed., Indianapolis, Ind., 1965.

terms, it will be recalled, an object x is grue at time t if x is green and t is earlier than t_0 (midnight December 31, AD 2000) or x is blue and t is later than t_0. It follows that an object which exists in both the twentieth and twenty-first centuries can be and remain grue only if it is green before the end of the twentieth century and blue thereafter. Goodman then points out that whatever inductive evidence we have for the generalization "All emeralds are green", seems likewise to be inductive evidence for the statement "All emeralds are grue". If there are any emeralds after the turn of the century, at least one of these generalizations must be false. Since we obviously can define such peculiar predicates ad lib, there is no problem in showing that most of our inductions from true premises will have false conclusions. Goodman concludes that we must find a basis for determining which predicates are projectable, and which are not.

Russell puts the problem this way, If we have examined the first n members $a_1, \ldots, a_n$, of a class A and found all of them to be members of B, we may wish to predict that the next member, a_{n+1}, will also be a member of B. If, however, we allow complete latitude in the choice of the class B, our class B may turn out to include only $a_1, \ldots, a_n$, and nothing else, or it may include everything in the universe except a_{n+1}, or anything in between these two extremes, all of which result in a false inductive conclusion. Russell, too, seeks restrictions for his classes that will rule out the unwanted types of induction. He maintains that the difficulty arises out of the use of classes that are defined extensionally, or partly extensionally. He concludes that the inductive principle must be restricted so as to apply only to classes defined intensionally; at least, no explicit reference to *unobserved* members of the class is permitted in the definition. The inductive principle involves a relation among intensions; it cannot legitimately be used to deal with relations among just any arbitrary classes that can be specified extensionally. He proposes to rule out the use of such "manufactured" classes—i.e. classes defined by reference to (unobserved) particular individuals—where inductive reasoning is concerned.[1]

Russell's move is precisely the one made by Carnap in reply to Goodman.[2] Carnap characterized Goodman's peculiar predicates as "positional", because of the explicit reference in their definitions to the particular time t_0, the moment of transition from the twentieth to the twenty-first century; ordinary predicates like 'green' and 'blue' were termed "purely qualitative".

Carnap's answer to Goodman was widely regarded as inadequate, because Carnap never really said what constitutes a purely qualitative predicate. We

[1] *Human Knowledge*, pp. 414–15.

[2] Goodman, "A Query on Confirmation", *Journal of Philosophy* 43 (1946); and "On Infirmities of Confirmation Theory", *Philosophy and Phenomenological Research* 8 (1947–8); Carnap, "On the Application of Inductive Logic", *Philosophy and Phenomenological Research* 8 (1947–8); and "Reply to Nelson Goodman", *Philosophy and Phenomenological Research* 8 (1947–8).

all feel intuitively that 'grue' and 'bleen' are not purely qualitative, but are, rather, "positional" predicates, while our familiar 'green' and 'blue' are purely qualitative. Goodman points out, however, that whereas 'grue' and 'bleen' are positional relative to 'green' and 'blue' taken as primitive, 'green' and 'blue' become positional, and hence not purely qualitative, if the Goodmanesque predicates 'grue' and 'bleen' are taken as primitive. It is basically a matter of familiarity of usage, Goodman claims, that makes 'green' and 'blue' seem qualitative while 'grue' and 'bleen' seem positional, peculiar, and pathological.[1] To speakers of a grue-bleen language, presumably, the opposite would seem to be the case. It appears that the positional status of 'grue' and 'bleen' is a result of mere historical accident.

Russell does not take up this latter twist to the Goodman argument, and for a very good reason. It would not have occurred to Russell that, as Goodman seems sometimes to be suggesting, the choice of primitive predicates for the language of science is an arbitrary matter—that is, that you are equally free to choose the green–blue or the grue–bleen language. Russell argues repeatedly, and soundly I think, that not all of our descriptive terms can be defined verbally. Rather, some of them have to be defined by some sort of ostensive process. It is relatively easy to see how, even acknowledging the familiar difficulties associated with ostensive definition, terms like 'green' and 'blue' can be defined ostensively. Green things all bear a certain degree of observational resemblance to one another, and the same goes for blue things. Grue things, on the other hand, do not all resemble one another in a similar way: grue things observed just before the critical time t_0 will be qualitatively dissimilar to grue things observed just after that date.[2] Since our ostensive definitions must be given before the date of the qualitative switch, it is difficult to see how it would be possible to offer a set of positive instances which all grue things resemble, and a set of negative things from which all grue things differ, with any hope of establishing the applicability of the predicate 'grue' to green things before the year 2000 and to blue things after the year 2000. The demand for a primitive descriptive scientific vocabulary that can be provided by ostensive definition will block the admission of the Goodman-type predicates that we feel are positional in character.[3] The impossibility of providing ostensive definitions for such predicates forms a sound basis for characterizing them as positional or not purely qualitative. It is not that such predicates are to be forever blocked from admission to the language of science, but only that they cannot enter as ostensively defined primitive predicates.

[1] Goodman, *Fact, Fiction, and Forecast*, Chapter 3, Section 4.

[2] Goodman, "Positionality and Pictures", *Philosophical Review* 69, 4 (1960).

[3] See Wesley C. Salmon, "On Vindicating Induction", in Henry E. Kyburg and Ernest Nagel (eds.), *Induction: Some Current Issues*, Middletown, Conn., 1963, for further discussion of the argument that ostensive definability is the basis for distinguishing normal from pathological predicates.

It is worth noting, parenthetically, that ostensive definitions themselves involve explicit reference to particular individuals. In order to define a predicate such as 'green', a number of positive instances are identified which a new object must resemble if it is to qualify as green, and quite possibly a set of negative instances are also given to exemplify non-green. This fact does not, however, disqualify ostensively defined predicates (or classes) from being considered intensional under Russell's definition. In defining intensionally specified classes—those that are to qualify as not being "manufactured"— Russell requires that no explicit mention be made of unobserved members of the class.[1] The positive and negative instances of an ostensive definition are presumably already observed, so ostensively defined predicates (or classes) are not thereby disqualified. Intuitively, this approach seems sound, for the positive instances are used in conjunction with a "similarity clause"—a statement to the effect that these instances and all that resemble them have the property in question (e.g. green). The similarity clause establishes the fundamentally intensional nature of the definition, for it makes a certain qualitative similarity the essential defining characteristic.

Certain types of positional predicates can be defined ostensively. Suppose we have a table top with a line down the middle dividing the left from the right side, and suppose a large number of coloured objects rest upon the table. There is no reason why we cannot ostensively define a predicate 'gruespat' (standing for spatially grue) which will apply to objects that are green and to the left of the dividing line, and to objects that are blue and to the right side of the dividing line. The feasibility of this procedure obviously depends upon the possibility of displaying positive and negative instances on both sides of the table—that is, on both sides of the positional dividing line. If, however, the table were arranged with a cover over the right-hand side, so that positive and negative instances from only one side of the positional divider could be displayed, it appears impossible to provide an adequate ostensive definition of 'gruespat'. In the former case, the object which constitutes the positional marker is an observed object (though, to be sure, it is not a member of the class of objects to which we want to apply our new predicate), while in the latter case the dividing line is effectively unobserved—more importantly, all objects on one side of that line are unobserved. The latter case is, of course, analogous to Goodman's predicate 'grue', as long as our observations all occur before the onset of the twenty-first century. Thus, although Russell's formulations may need a little tidying up, his basic idea that an intensional class is one whose definition involves no reference to particular *unobserved* objects appears to provide an adequate method for handling "manufactured" or Goodmanesque predicates.

No one could accuse Russell of lacking an interest in language; his

[1] *Human Knowledge*, pp. 404, 414.

contributions to the philosophy of language are of supreme importance in the entire development of twentieth-century analytic philosophy. Unlike other philosophers who have had an overwhelming interest in philosophy of language —e.g. some logical positivists in early phases of their thought, and quite probably Goodman in some contexts—Russell never lost sight of the fact that the languages of science and common sense are designed to fulfil descriptive functions, and that the fulfilment of these functions demands a mechanism whereby words can be made to refer to objective physical things. While other philosophers were enchanted with the charms of syntax, Russell never lost sight of the semantical aspects of the language of science. As a consequence, he remained fully conscious of the basic ostensive nature of the scientific language. He could never be victimized by the Goodman grue-bleen paradox, a puzzle that takes a serious toll among philosophers who concentrate too exclusively upon the syntactical aspects of language.

4. The Hypothetico-Deductive Method

The treatment of "manufactured" predicates exemplifies the sort of thing Russell set out to do in connection with induction, namely, to show what restrictions must be imposed to make it a satisfactory principle of scientific inference. Russell remarks that the inductions he wants to block are precisely the kinds that would be ruled out by common sense.[1] However, a logical principle whose applicability has to be determined by common sense hardly qualifies as a logical principle. It is incumbent upon us to formulate the conditions explicitly. The restriction to classes that are not manufactured is one example.

The basic problem can be seen from the mathematical calculus of probability (especially by examining Bayes's theorem); generalizations cannot, in general, be made probable by induction. In other words, instances of a generalization do not necessarily confirm it, unless it happens to be a generalization of the right sort in the first place. Generalizations involving manufactured classes are certainly generalizations of the wrong sort, but it hardly seems likely that merely ruling out such classes is sufficient to do the job.

At this point it might be tempting to say that induction by enumeration is not the right way to approach a scientific hypothesis in the first place. Scientific inference, it might be maintained, is basically hypothetico-deductive; the method of science does not involve establishing general laws by finding instances of them, but rather confirming theories by deducing consequences and testing them experimentally. Scientific inference, according to this view, is not typified by finding observational instances of "All crows are black", but rather by predicting the outcome of the torsion balance experiment as a deduction

---

[1] *Human Knowledge*, pp. 417–18; *My Philosophical Development*, p. 190.

from Newton's theory, and then verifying the predicted result by performing the experiment.

Russell's argument against this naïve hypothetico-deductive account of scientific method is devastating. The hypothetico-deductive schema is nothing other than the fallacy of affirming the consequent. From the hypothesis 'Pigs have wings' in conjunction with the acknowledged fact that pigs are good to eat, it follows that some winged creatures are good to eat. Upon ascertaining that some winged creatures are good to eat, we have a hypothetico-deductive confirmation of the hypothesis "Pigs have wings".[1] To the possible rejoinder that the hypothetico-deductive method does not establish hypotheses conclusively, but only with a probability, Reichenbach tersely remarks that he does not think it even probable that pigs have wings.[2]

One reason, of course, that we find the argument silly is because we already know that the hypothesis is false, but that does not mean that the *inference* would have been any less silly otherwise. For, suppose we did not already know the truth of the hypothesis. Should we then regard the edibility of chickens, ducks, and turkeys as any kind of evidence for the wingedness of pigs? Or suppose that, not knowing what a platypus is, I travel to Australia, am served platypus, and find it edible. (To put an additional kink in the argument, suppose they tell me that it is also known as "duckbill"!) Would it then be reasonable for me to conclude that it (probably) has wings? Hardly, for wingedness and edibility are not closely associated properties, and we can be fully aware of that fact without knowing whether the platypus (or the hog) has wings. We know that some, but not all, winged creatures are good to eat; we also know that such wingless creatures as cows, sheep, rabbits, goats, deer, trout, catfish, etc., are edible as well.

This example illustrates, incidentally, Russell's repeated insistence that one fact can be evidence for another only if certain factual relations obtain in the world. In this world, edibility is not evidence of wingedness; in some other possible world they might be closely associated properties, and one would then be evidence for the other. In rejecting the "pigs have wings" inference we are, of course, relying upon background knowledge. Russell maintains that non-demonstrative inference always depends upon background knowledge. According to Reichenbach, in contrast, there is such a thing as legitimate primitive induction by enumeration in the absence of background knowledge. He would therefore allow that there are possible circumstances *in this world* in which an observed association between edibility and wingedness could support an inductive inference to the conclusion that what is edible is (probably) winged, but in the face of accumulating evidence of the lack of association,

[1] "Dewey's 'New Logic'", in Schilpp (ed.), *The Philosophy of John Dewey*, New York 1939, p. 149.
[2] Hans Reichenbach, "Bertrand Russell's Logic", in Schilpp (ed.), *The Philosophy of Bertrand Russell*, p. 48.

such an inductive conclusion would have to be revoked. Neither Russell nor Reichenbach ever suggests the legitimacy of ignoring available relevant background information.

If we ask further whether the hypothetico-deductive method might have any inductive merit, in spite of being an obvious deductive fallacy, Russell points out that it is basically no different from induction by enumeration. To accept a scientific hypothesis as true involves at least accepting all of its observational consequences; it may involve more than that, but it cannot involve any less. A hypothetico-deductive test is just a check on the truth of one of the logical consequences of the hypothesis. Repeated testing of this sort constitutes an induction by enumeration on the instances of the following generalization: "All observational consequences of this hypothesis are true." Thus, the hypothetico-deductive method by itself has no better credentials than induction by enumeration.[1] We have already seen that Russell regards induction by enumeration as unacceptable unless it is qualified by restrictions on the types of generalizations it can be used to support. In strictly parallel fashion, he argues, the hypothetico-deductive method is correct only with respect to certain types of hypotheses. It remains to determine under what conditions the hypothetico-deductive method—which is really not distinct from induction by enumeration—is a sound method.

In attempting to answer this question, Russell examines Keynes's theory of probability with some care and a good deal of sympathy. By invoking Bayes's theorem, Keynes shows that a hypothesis can be confirmed, i.e. rendered probable, if it has a non-vanishing prior probability. Keynes used the principle of limited independent variety in order to achieve suitable prior probabilities for scientific hypotheses. Russell does not find this particular principle adequate, so he introduces a set of postulates of his own. But they are invoked for precisely the same purpose, and they fulfil the same function.[2] Russell's theory of scientific inference is, consequently, explicitly and straightforwardly a Bayesian one, and like any Bayesian approach, it faces difficult questions about the nature and status of prior probabilities.

5. *Statements v. Rules*

Russell's search, as he often reminds us, is for some suitable *premises* for scientific inference. He devotes considerable attention to what he calls "the *principle* of induction", and he frequently remarks on its *falsity*. It therefore appears that he regards the principle as a statement—either a universal or a statistical generalization—to the effect that if all observed *A* are *B*, then all *A* are *B*. This statement is not true for all classes *A* and *B*, nor even for most. The crucial point at this

[1] *Human Knowledge*, p. 417.
[2] *My Philosophical Development*, pp. 200–1.

juncture is that Russell is looking for a *statement* that will serve as a premise of arguments, not for a *rule* of inference to which arguments may conform. Russell apparently regards the deductive forms of arguments as the only acceptable ones. If scientific arguments are to be acceptable they must be cast into deductive form. This can only be done by finding suitable premises which can be used to render scientific inference deductively valid.[1]

If deduction is the only acceptable form of argument, we may easily wonder why Russell talks so much about non-demonstrative inference. It would seem that demonstrative inference is the only admissible kind. The answer, I believe, is that Russell regards most of the inferences of common sense and science as enthymemes—as incomplete deductions that need additional premises to become valid inferences. In considering the fundamental problem of inference from the observed to the unobserved, Russell quite explicitly points out that, from a set of premises about observed objects alone, it is impossible validly to deduce any conclusion about unobserved objects; in particular, it is impossible to deduce any scientific generalization that pertains to both observed and unobserved objects.[2] Since such an inference cannot be deductive, but nevertheless must be admitted if we are to have knowledge extending beyond the immediate contents of experience, Russell concludes that non-demonstrative inference is indispensable. But in attempting to account for this type of inference, Russell does not seem to consider seriously the possibility of looking for non-demonstrative *rules* of inference which would characterize some non-deductive logic. To be sure, Russell does occasionally speak of non-deductive "forms of inference",[3] but he *never* to my knowledge proposes a *rule* of inference, though he frequently and repeatedly discussed the need for additional premises. The only logic is, for Russell, deductive; non-demonstrative inferences are merely valid deductions with suppressed premises. Russell makes this point particularly obvious when he maintains that the data of sense are not adequate by themselves to establish the conclusions required by science and common sense; they must be supplemented by general statements which Russell also calls "data". When, in certain contexts, he speaks of the uncertainty of the data, he is speaking, in part at least, about the uncertainty of the general premises required to make our inferences valid.[4]

Russell consistently maintained that scientific results are never completely certain; this thesis is compatible with the view that all inference is deductive. Probabilistic conclusions can obviously be deduced from probabilistic

---

[1] This statement may seem to involve a highly controversial interpretation of Russell, but I believe that *My Philosophical Development*, Chapter 16, "Non-Demonstrative Inference", provides ample evidence for this view of Russell's approach. Furthermore, Part 6 of *Human Knowledge* seems to admit no other reading.

[2] *Human Knowledge*, pp. 504–7.

[3] *My Philosophical Development*, p. 207.

[4] *Human Knowledge*, p. 384.

premises. The use of Bayes's theorem is compatible with this general approach, for it is, after all, a mathematical theorem, and its use does not render any inferences non-deductive. From probability values fed into the theorem one gets other values out just by turning the crank.

Any argument, no matter how flagrantly invalid, can be considered an enthymeme and rendered valid by the addition of a suitable premise. The whole issue then revolves around the status of the new premise, for the acceptability of the original argument then hinges upon the plausibility of the additional premise. Russell is fully aware of this point, and he searches for postulates that will be plausible premises for scientific inference. Such premises must be probablistic statements, for non-demonstrative scientific inferences sometimes have true premises and a false conclusion. Even after a premise which makes the inference a valid deduction is added, the original premises are still true and the original conclusion false. If a strong principle of uniformity of nature were the additional premise, the first such instance of a non-demonstrative inference with true premises and a false conclusion would constitute a conclusive falsification of this new premise.[1] The only way to avoid such a consequence, as far as I can see, is to make the additional premise a probability statement, and also to weaken the original conclusion by making it a probability statement as well.

Russell's approach, as he is clearly aware, raises the extremely difficult and fundamental problem of the status of the additional premises—i.e. Russell's postulates of scientific inference. He is under no illusions about the possibility of proving such postulates. Whether they are universal statements or statistical statements, Hume's arguments show that they cannot be proved or even rendered probable. Thus, we must ask, what reason have we for accepting them? Russell answers, essentially, that they are not known to be false and they do the job. We accept them because we need them to account for the very possibility of scientific knowledge. We need them to keep us out of the coal pit of solipsism. Without them, says Russell, "science is moonshine".[2]

6. Validation v. Vindication

There is, it seems to me, a different way to approach the problem Russell is grappling with, namely, to seek one or more *rules*, not premises, to account for the logic of scientific inference. This alternative implies that there is a kind of logic other than deductive logic—a genuinely non-demonstrative logic with its own non-deductive rules—what is usually called "inductive logic". Indeed, if we loosen up the meaning of "induction", so that it refers to any kind of non-demonstrative inference, not just induction by enumeration, the usual terminology is extremely natural.

[1] This point was made by A. J. Ayer in a talk at Indiana University several years ago.
[2] *Human Knowledge*, p. 505.

I am not suggesting that the problem is automatically solved by the demand for a rule instead of a statement. Rules are as much in need of justification as are statements. And in a wide variety of circumstances, the appropriate justification of a rule consists in proving the truth of a corresponding statement. I do not see any advantage in replacing the statement "Copper conducts electricity" by the rule "Given the statement 'This is copper', you may infer the statement 'This conducts electricity'." The supposition that any significant philosophical problem is avoided by replacing the law with the rule seems to me quite mistaken. Similarly, if justification of a rule of induction by enumeration required proof of the statement "If all observed *A* are *B*, then, usually, all *A* are *B*", nothing substantial would be gained by concentrating upon the rule rather than the statement.

The problem of justifying a rule, however, need not be the same as proving a strictly corresponding statement. This point was made most convincingly by Herbert Feigl in his classic article, "De Principiis non Disputandum . . . ?" (1950),[1] in which he makes the distinction between two types of justification, *validation* and *vindication*. In this terminology, to validate a statement is to prove its truth (either with certainty or to a high degree of probability), while to validate a rule consists in deriving it from some other rule or principle. Thus, for example, in many systems of formal logic the rule of conditional proof can be validated by proving the deduction theorem, which says that whatever can be deduced by means of the rule of conditional proof can likewise be proved without its aid.

Vindication is a different sort of justification. To vindicate a rule is to show that it serves some particular purpose whose desirability has been agreed upon. For example, the deductive rule of modus ponens is justified by means of a theorem in the metalanguage which says that the rule is truth-preserving—that is, that its adoption will never enable us to deduce false conclusions from true premises. Since inference which fulfils just such a condition is the aim of deduction, the argument constitutes an appropriate justification—in the sense of vindication—for the use of modus ponens.[2]

It is agreed on all sides that induction cannot be proved truth-preserving, for that is only to say that it is not deduction. All parties agree that it would be nice if we could prove induction to be frequently truth-preserving, but Hume's arguments seem to demonstrate conclusively that no such pleasant result can be established. Proof of either of these conditions would certainly constitute a vindication of induction, but the distinction between vindicating a rule and validating a universal or statistical general statement would not be very interesting. In the face of the impossibility of any such vindication, based upon

[1] Herbert Feigl, "De Principiis non Disputandum . . . ?" in Max Black (ed.), *Philosophical Analysis*, Ithaca, N.Y., 1950, pp. 113–31.
[2] Only pragmatists of an especially crass variety, e.g. Blaise Pascal, William James, or Josef Goebbels, are concerned with *vindication* of *statements*.

a proof of the universal or frequent success of induction, what can be done? —In the words of the TV commercial, "What's a mother to do?"

One alternative is to *postulate* its frequent success; this is the path Russell took. Another alternative is to deny that there is any such thing as non-demonstrative or inductive inference; that is the path Popper took.[1] Another alternative is to claim that we have an intuitive sense of inductive validity to which we can appeal for justification; that is the path Carnap took.[2] Another alternative is to say that it was a silly question in the first place; that is the path that Strawson took.[3] Another alternative is to swallow circular reasoning without boggling; that is the path of Black and Braithwaite.[4] Hume took up backgammon.

At this point, Feigl's distinction between validation and vindication may be of real help. In making this distinction, at least insofar as it applies to the problem of induction, Feigl is essentially endorsing Reichenbach's attempt to provide a pragmatic justification of induction,[5] even in the face of the afore-mentioned impossibility of proving either that induction will be successful or will probably be successful. Reichenbach attempted to show that induction will work if any systematic method of predicting the future will. Reichenbach emphatically denies that this claim implies that induction will be successful; it implies only that induction will be successful *if* any method is.[6]

7. *Postulates, Conjectures, and Posits*

Reichenbach attempted to make this point in his article in the Schilpp volume, when he said,

But as soon as this assumption is discarded ["Hume's tacit presupposition that what is claimed as knowledge must be proven as true"], the difficulties for a justification of induction are eliminated. I do not wish to say that we can at least demonstrate the in-ductive conclusion to be probable. The analysis of the theory of probability shows that not even this proof can be given. But a way out of Hume's scepticism can be shown when knowledge is conceived, not as a system of propositions having a determinable truth value or probability value, but as a system of posits used as tools for predicting the future. The question of whether the inductive inference represents a good tool can then be answered in the affirmative.[7]

---

[1] Popper, *The Logic of Scientific Discovery.*

[2] Carnap, "Replies and Systematic Expositions", in Schilpp (ed.), *The Philosophy of Rudolf Carnap*, La Salle, Ill., 1964, pp. 977–9.

[3] P. F. Strawson, *Introduction to Logical Theory*, London 1952, Chapter 9.

[4] Max Black, *Problems of Analysis*, Ithaca, N.Y. 1954, Chapter 11; R. B. Braithwaite, *Scientific Explanation*, New York 1953, Chapter 8.

[5] Feigl, op. cit., pp. 136–7.

[6] Reichenbach, *The Theory of Probability*, Berkeley and Los Angeles 1949, pp. 473–5.

[7] Schilpp (ed.), *The Philosophy of Bertrand Russell*, p. 49.

Russell replies curtly,

But I do not see what difference is made by regarding knowledge as a "tool"; if it is to be a good "tool for predicting the future", the future must be such as it predicts. If not, it is no better than astrology.[1]

This exchange is unfortunate; because of Reichenbach's terminology, Russell clearly did not see the force of his argument. But whatever the reasons for misunderstanding, Reichenbach does have an argument which is designed to show that induction *is* a better tool than astrology for predicting the future,[2] even though neither method can be proved in advance to yield successful predictions. For, Reichenbach had argued, if the future is predictable—if any method, including astrology, can achieve predictive success—then induction will predict the future successfully. This argument of Reichenbach has been criticized by many authors on many scores; indeed, I have presented what I consider conclusive refutations.[3] The point is *not* that Reichenbach produced the thoroughly adequate justification he thought he had achieved; rather, he showed a direction in which the search for a justification could proceed without prior condemnation to futility because of Hume's arguments.

When Russell returns to the subject of induction in *Human Knowledge*, he does ask whether there is any reason to believe a principle of induction true, or if not, "is there nevertheless any reason to *act* as if it were true?"[4] At this point he reconsiders the possibility of a pragmatic justification, and he re-examines Reichenbach's concept of the posit. Russell offers several arguments against Reichenbach's notion. For one thing, he advances the argument which I characterized above as essentially Goodman's "grue-bleen" objection. He formulates the argument and offers what I take to be a sound solution. The result is that Reichenbach's method of positing needs precisely the restriction Russell advocates, namely, that it should be applied only to "non-manufactured" predicates. This condition can be appended to Reichenbach's rules without undue strain.[5]

For another thing, Russell and Reichenbach become embroiled in needless controversy centring around the concept of truth. The entire discussion would have benefited enormously, I believe, if both disputants (but especially Reichenbach) had taken Tarski's analysis of truth to heart.

Moreover, I think Russell is in error when he characterizes Reichenbach's *blind* posit as a "decision to treat some proposition as true although we have no good ground for doing so".[6] For Reichenbach, the blind posit is contrasted with

[1] ibid., p. 683.
[2] Reichenbach, *Experience and Prediction*, pp. 353–4.
[3] Wesley C. Salmon, "The Predictive Inference", *Philosophy of Science* 24 (1957).
[4] *Human Knowledge*, p. 400; Russell's italics.
[5] Salmon, "On Vindicating Induction".
[6] *Human Knowledge*, p. 413.

the appraised posit; the appraised posit has a "weight" or numerical value attached, while the blind posit has no such numerical evaluation. But this does not mean that there is no good reason for making the posit. Reichenbach's justification of induction provides just the good reason needed; to posit is to adopt the method of prediction which must yield successful prediction if any method will. That *is* a good reason. The posit is called "blind" because we don't know *how good* a posit it is.[1] That does *not* mean it is no good!

Russell's most significant remark on the concept of the posit may lie in the comment: "I am not concerned to deny that some posit is necessary if there is to be any probability in favour of predictions, but I am concerned to deny that the posit required is Reichenbach's."[2] What, then, is the chief difference between Reichenbach's posit and the kind of posit Russell will countenance? Reichenbach is willing to admit a genuine rule of non-demonstrative, or inductive, inference which yields predictive posits. Russell prefers to posit his synthetic postulates of scientific inference, which then serve as auxiliary premises sufficient to render scientific inference deductive. The issue seems to revolve around the fundamental question of *whether there is such a thing as non-demonstrative inference* in any sense other than the trivial enthymematic sense.

Russell is not the only important twentieth-century philosopher to react to Hume's critique of induction by denying the admissibility of any kind of non-demonstrative inference. Karl Popper has done the same thing in maintaining that it is no business of science to try to confirm scientific hypotheses—that the proper aim of science is to offer bold explanatory conjectures and to subject them to severe testing.[3] Russell was perfectly clear in his recognition that observational evidence supplemented only by deductive inference could never enable us to make inferences to the future. When confronted with this fact, some of Popper's followers have answered that prediction is not a genuine scientific aim—i.e. that science is concerned with explanation, not prediction.[4] Popper himself claims that the corroboration of a theory, which is a measure of its goodness, is purely retrospective and has no predictive content, but he also maintains that "there is not even anything irrational in relying for practical purposes upon well-tested theories, for no more rational course of action is open to us."[5] The real question, I suppose, is whether any other course of action

[1] Reichenbach, *Theory of Probability*, p. 446.

[2] *Human Knowledge*, p. 413.

[3] Popper, "Science: Conjectures and Refutations", in *Conjectures and Refutations*, New York 1962. For a more recent summary of his views on this question, see Popper, "Conjectural Knowledge: My Solution of the Problem of Induction', *Revue Internationale de Philosophie* 95–6 (1971).

[4] J. W. N. Watkins, "Non-Inductive Corroboration", in Imre Lakatos (ed.), *The Problem of Inductive Logic*, Amsterdam 1968, pp. 61–6.

[5] Popper, *Conjectures and Refutations*, p. 51. See also "Conjectural Knowledge", pp. 184–5, 187–8.

could be *less* rational, given Popper's view that scientific theories can only be refuted, never established.

I find it nearly impossible to take such a view seriously. While the theory of nuclear fission was undoubtedly a very significant explanatory hypothesis, its predictive significance should not be overlooked. Scientists building the first man-made nuclear reactor in the West Stands at Chicago deduced various consequences from their theories, not only to carry out an important test, but also to predict whether the stadium and perhaps the whole city of Chicago would go up if a critical mass of U^{235} were assembled. And their colleagues in New Mexico had to predict whether the detonation of an atomic bomb over the sand of the desert would initiate a chain reaction in which the sand, and perhaps the whole surface of the earth, would participate. Such predictions had to be made, and it is hard to believe that anyone would have been just as happy to have them made by a seer with a crystal ball. To the notion that science has no predictive function, the proper response seems to be that of Russell to solipsism: though logically irrefutable (perhaps), it certainly cannot be maintained sincerely.

If scientific theories do have predictive import—if they can, indeed, serve as a basis for *rational* practical behaviour—then Popper's *pure* deductivism cannot be maintained. Unless Popper is willing to admit synthetic postulates after the fashion of Russell, it seems that he must be committed to the use of some form of non-demonstrative inference. The method of conjecture and refutation, advanced by Popper, may be just such a method, though Popper would vehemently deny this characterization. According to Popper, in employing the method of science we advance bold explanatory theories as conjectures. These conjectures are never finally accepted; they are tentatively accepted only as long as they withstand serious efforts at falsification, only until they are refuted in the course of a severe test. It is no part of the method of science, Popper maintains, to attempt to confirm hypotheses by finding positive evidence for them; rather, the method of science consists in subjecting hypotheses to severe tests—the more severe the better—in the attempt to *falsify* them. Conjectures that have withstood severe tests without being refuted are accepted tentatively for purposes of further testing and scientific explanation—and for purposes of prediction as well, I should add, for that function seems undeniable. As Popper has said:

Hume was right in stressing that our theories cannot be validly inferred from what we can know to be true—neither from observations nor from anything else. He concluded from this that our belief in them was irrational. . . . If, however, the term 'belief' is taken to cover our critical acceptance of scientific theories—a *tentative* acceptance combined with an eagerness to revise the theory if we succeed in designing a test which it cannot pass—then Hume was wrong. In such an acceptance of theories there is nothing irrational. There is not even anything irrational in relying for practical purposes upon well-tested theories, for no more rational course of action is open to us.

Assume that we have deliberately made it our task to live in this unknown world of ours; to adjust ourselves to it as well as we can; to take advantage of the opportunities we can find in it; and to explain it, *if* possible (we need not asume that it is), and as far as possible, with the help of laws and explanatory theories. *If we have made this our task, then there is no more rational procedure than the method of trial and error—of conjecture and refutation*: of boldly proposing theories; of trying our best to show that these are erroneous; and of accepting them tentatively if our critical efforts are unsuccessful.[1]

This passage, though taken from a section in which Popper is discussing Hume's *psychological* theories, seems to offer a clear and straightforward account of Popper's views on the logic and methodology of science. In later sections of the same paper, in which the *logic* of science is the explicit topic of discussion, he says, "The actual procedure of science is to operate with conjectures: to jump to conclusions—often after one single observation . . . "[2] He continues, moreover:

So long as a theory stands up to the severest tests we can design, it is accepted; if it does not it is rejected. But it is never inferred, in any sense, from the empirical evidence. There is neither a psychological nor a logical induction. *Only the falsity of the theory can be inferred from empirical evidence, and this inference is a purely deductive one.*[3]

Scientific theories, according to Popper, are conjectures that are put forward without proof or verification; they are neither inferred from empirical data nor rendered probable by such data. They are nevertheless accepted, but only tentatively, with the understanding that new evidence may lead to their revision or rejection.

According to Reichenbach, "*A posit is a statement with which we deal as true, although its truth value is unknown*".[4] He distinguishes two kinds of posits, appraised posits and blind (or anticipative) posits. It is the status of the blind posit that is crucial in the present context. In discussing the justification of induction he says: "Again the concept of *posit* will be used for the interpretation of the statements to be considered. The statement that the observed frequency will persist can be maintained only in the sense of a posit, since it is obvious that we cannot prove it to be true."[5] After pointing out, in effect, that we can no more assign a probability value than we can a truth value, he continues: "The inductive posit is not meant to be a final posit. We have the possibility of correcting a first posit, of replacing it by a new one when new observations have led to different results."[6] In a brief hint at the justification of the method of positing,

[1] ibid., Popper's italics.

[2] ibid., p. 53.

[3] ibid., pp. 54–5, Popper's italics.

[4] Reichenbach, *Theory of Probability*, p. 373, Reichenbach's italics.

[5] ibid., p. 445, Reichenbach's italics.

[6] ibid. Blind posits can also be transformed into appraised posits by means of suitable inductive inferences, but this process always involves the introduction of new blind posits.

Reichenbach adds, "The inductive procedure, therefore, has the character of a method of *trial and error* so devised that, for sequences having a limiting frequency, it will automatically lead to success in a finite number of steps. It may be called a *self-corrective method*, or an *asymptotic method*."[1]

The similarities between Popper's conjectures and Reichenbach's posits are striking—I do not believe that the above quotations misrepresent the views of either author, e.g. by being taken out of context, or by virtue of some matter of emphasis. On the contrary, it seems to me that extended consideration of their discussions of these concepts simply reinforces the feeling of similarity. Both authors maintain that certain scientific statements are "accepted" or "treated as true" even though they cannot be proved to be true or probable. Both emphasize the tentative status of the statement, making it subject to rejection or revision in the light of further evidence; both use the characterization as a method of trial and error. Both authors claim that these statements are useful for prediction or practical action. In addition, both authors provide a methodology for conjecturing or positing, as the case may be. Popper offers such criteria as simplicity, content, and falsifiability as a guide to the selection of theories (or hypotheses) to be advanced as conjectures; Reichenbach offers the rule of induction as a method for selecting inductive posits. Moreover, both authors seem to offer vindications for their methodological prescriptions: Reichenbach brings forth his famous "pragmatic justification"; Popper argues that his method enables us to learn of our mistakes as early as possible. Each of these arguments is explicitly related to the fulfilment of a desired aim—the ascertainment of limiting frequency values for Reichenbach; the promulgation of powerful explanatory theories for Popper. Finally, both authors explicitly insist that their methodologies are justified even though it is impossible to prove that they will realize their respective aims.

In stressing the similarities between Popper and Reichenbach, I am not suggesting that their views are identical. I believe that their approaches are similar, in that they both seek to vindicate rules (or methods) of non-demonstrative inference, though they differ in their willingness to describe the situation in this way.[2] The statements they posit are different, the rules they advance are different, and the vindications they offer are different. It is, however, an interesting

---

[1] ibid., p. 446, Reichenbach's italics.

[2] This is not meant as a psychological statement about Popper's motives or intentions; I am simply trying to compare the two logical theories. Though, as I remarked above, Popper would reject this way of characterizing his theory, his view seems to contain the elements of a theory of non-demonstrative inference according to rules that may well be capable of vindication in terms of the considerations Popper himself supplies. On such an interpretation we might even make sense of the inescapable predictive import of scientific theories.

The feature of Popper's doctrine that strikes me as totally unacceptable is his unconditional denial of the possibility of non-demonstrative inference, particularly inferences with predictive conclusions. But this denial seems to me to be an unnecessary appendage to his

question whether the two systems are compatible or complementary. Reichenbach's system seems best suited to establish low level (universal or statistical) laws; Popper's system seems best adapted to dealing with high level theories. If there is only one fundamental mode of non-demonstrative inference in science, then at most one of them can be acceptable. But by what argument could we expect to establish any such condition of mutual exclusion?

Three extremely tough-minded philosophers—Russell, Reichenbach, and Popper—have all confronted the problem of non-demonstrative inference in science. Reichenbach responds by advocating, and attempting to justify, an inductive rule for positing limiting frequencies. Popper responds by advocating a method of conjecturing (positing) explanatory theories, and he offers methodological considerations for adopting such a method. Both Reichenbach and Popper offer methods of positing, and both of them offer pragmatic justifications (i.e. vindications) for these methods. Russell, on the other hand, posits postulates of scientific inference, and claims that we have to *know* these postulates if we are to account for scientific inference. He is clearly aware that this view leads to an abandonment of empiricism, but tough-mindedly he accepts this consequence. If, however, he had seen the possibility of pragmatic vindication of posits themselves, or of a method of positing, then he would have had the path between the horns of his dilemma of solipsism and empiricism. In that case he would have been able to avoid the postulational approach which he himself criticized with superlative succinct cogency: It has all the advantages of theft over honest toil.[1]

8. *Historical Postscript: Russell and Carnap*

I remarked above on the similarity between Carnap's and Russell's views of the theory of probability: both authors adopt a dual conception, combining a frequency concept with a rational credibility concept. Russell reports that he did his main work on this problem shortly after his return to England from America in 1944.[2] In 1945, Carnap published his well-known article, "On Inductive Logic",[3] which provided an illuminating summary of what was later was to be contained in his systematic treatise, *Logical Foundations of Probability* (1950). I know of no evidence that prior to writing *Human Knowledge* Russell was aware of Carnap's work on probability; at least, Carnap's work seems not

---

important methodological insights, and one that is hard to reconcile with his claim that it is *rational* to use well-tested theories for purposes of practical action.

The most fundamental difference between Popper and Reichenbach seems to lie in the denial *v.* the affirmation of the need for pragmatic vindication of a mode of non-demonstrative inference.

[1] *Introduction to Mathematical Philosophy*, London 1919, p. 71.
[2] *My Philosophical Development*, p. 190.
[3] Carnap, "On Inductive Logic", *Philosophy of Science* 12 (1945).

to have had any significant bearing on Russell's thought regarding probability. The only important relation between Russell and Carnap on probability and induction seems to be the profound influence Keynes had on both of them.

Even a cursory comparison of *Human Knowledge* and *Logical Foundations of Probability* serves to reveal the marked contrast between the care and rigour of Carnap's work and the somewhat "slap-dash" appearance of Russell's treatment. The term "slap-dash" is Russell's; in *My Philosophical Development* he indicates that the style of presentation may have hidden the considerable effort that went into the development of the ideas expounded in *Human Knowledge*.[1] Nevertheless, it is undeniable that Carnap's exemplary precision goes far beyond anything that was even implicit in Russell's presentation. Carnap tried to do for inductive logic what Russell and Whitehead had done for deductive logic in *Principia Mathematica*. Carnap's work exhibits the same sort of rigour to which the authors of the *Principia* had aspired, while Russell's treatment of non-demonstrative inference certainly does not. Carnap's work consequently attracted the major attention of those interested in inductive logic, especially those who hoped to use the tools of mathematical logic in this domain. This may explain why Russell's work suffered almost total neglect.[2] His postulates seemed very imprecise in formulation, and he made no rigorous deductions from them. Before we proclaim oblivion a suitable fate for Russell's treatment of scientific inference, however, let us reconsider the nature of the task he was attempting to accomplish. A good case can be made, I believe, for denying that Russell's work on non-demonstrative inference was rendered obsolete by Carnap.

As Russell emphatically and repeatedly asserted, his aim was an epistemological analysis of the body of scientific knowledge then regarded as reasonably well-founded. Russell was attempting to provide a basis for assigning appropriate

---

[1] *My Philosophical Development*, p. 190.

[2] Another reason for the widespread neglect of Russell's treatment of non-demonstrative inference may be the general disrepute into which serious consideration of Hume's problem of the justification of induction fell, primarily as a result of the linguistic approach to philosophy. In his well-known article, "Russell's Doubts about Induction", *Mind* 18 (1949), Paul Edwards argues that the problem of induction as posed by Russell in *Problems of Philosophy* can be dissolved on the basis of ordinary usage. The consequence, if Edwards were correct, would be that one of the central issues to which Russell addresses himself in *Human Knowledge* is a pseudo-problem. William Hay, in his famous review-article on *Human Knowledge*, "Bertrand Russell on the Justification of Induction", *Philosophy of Science* 17 (1950), argues in a similar vein. In consequence, Hay suggests that the main contribution of Russell lay in his part in developing the tools provided by *Principia Mathematica*, with which others, but not Russell, might make significant progress in dealing with the problems of scientific inference. Russell—rightly in my opinion—regards linguistic dissolution of fundamental epistemological problems as unworthy, easy evasions of important issues. Russell never allowed himself to take such evasive action, and he reacted with understandable bitterness—see Chapter 18, "Some Replies to Criticism", in *My Philosophical Development*—to those who were unwilling to grapple with the hard philosophical problems on which he had expended so much intellectual effort over more than half a century.

antecedent (prior) probabilities to the kinds of laws and theories that made up the body of real science as it was seen around 1944–5. It hardly needs remarking that science—at the dawn of the "nuclear age"—contained theories in the fullest sense of the word, involving reference to highly theoretical entities. Carnap, by contrast, constructed a rigorous inductive logic that was, at the time of *Logical Foundations*, restricted to first order languages with logically independent one-place primitive predicates—and even this had to be swallowed along with the bitter requirement of descriptive completeness![1] In 1950, two years after publication of Russell's *Human Knowledge*, Carnap had an inductive logic that could be applied only within languages that did not even contain relational predicates, to say nothing of theoretical terms; at the same time such languages had to be regarded as completely adequate to express all of the truths of empirical science. This same inductive logic assigned zero prior probability to every universal generalization expressible in the language,[2] with the consequence that every statement that could conceivably be a candidate for a scientific law was incapable in principle of ever obtaining a non-zero *posterior* probability on any finite amount of observational evidence. Genuine theoretical statements could never even get smuggled into the language.[3] By no stretch of the imagination could Carnap be said to have achieved the aim for which Russell was striving, namely, a satisfactory basis for assigning prior probabilities to scientific theories. Only with the work of Hintikka (1966)[4] was it shown how Carnap's system could be consistently modified so as to allow universal generalizations to achieve non-zero prior, and consequently posterior, probabilities. Theoretical statements still remain problematic. Carnap was, in a limited sense, engaged in the same enterprise as Russell—namely an *a priori* assignment of prior probabilities as a basis for a workable logic of non-demonstrative inference. Russell offered his synthetic postulates of scientific inference as statements known on some *extra-empirical basis* which would be capable of lending non-zero prior probabilities to scientific statements; Carnap supplied *a priori* measure functions that assign prior probabilities to state descriptions.

Viewed in this light, it seems fair to say that Carnap had developed a *precise logical system* that could not possibly do the job of providing a rational reconstruction of actual scientific knowledge, while Russell had provided *very imprecise suggestions* that might hold some promise of eventual success. Carnap

---

[1] Carnap, *Logical Foundations of Probability*, p. 74.

[2] This statement applies to the language L∞ which contains infinitely many individual constants, though only a finite number of predicate terms.

[3] I am fully aware that much important work in the subsequent twenty years by Carnap and several co-workers—e.g. Kemeny, Hintikka, and Jeffrey—has resulted in significant extensions of scope and power of Carnap's inductive logic, but I am trying to clarify the situation that existed in induction and probability at about the time of Russell's *Human Knowledge*.

[4] Jaakko Hintikka, "A Two-Dimensional Continuum of Inductive Methods", in Jaakko Hintikka and P. Suppes (eds.), *Aspects of Inductive Logic*, Amsterdam 1966.

was, of course, utterly frank in admitting and explaining the shortcomings of his system, and he devoted considerable effort during the last twenty years of his life to enriching and extending it. Russell, too, was aware of the limitations of his work; he placed no great confidence in his actual formulations of the postulates, and felt sure that they could be improved.[1] I am inclined to feel that the relationship between the work of Russell and Carnap at this point nicely exemplifies Russell's metaphor of digging a tunnel through a mountain from both sides.

To clarify this situation further, it might be helpful to look back at Russell's work on the foundations of mathematics. By the time Russell took up the topic in 1900, nineteenth-century mathematicians and logicians had arithmetized analysis and Peano had provided an axiomatic formulation of arithmetic. Much progress had been made in working from the theoretical superstructure down toward the foundations—the superstructure (arithmetic and the infinitesimal calculus) was in quite good order but the fundamental logical basis had yet to be clarified. Those digging from one side had largely done their job, and that may have made it easier for those digging from the other side. But whether or not the job was easier, success, if achieved, could more readily be recognized. When Russell turned away from the work in the foundations of mathematics, a logical reconstruction of the whole of mathematical analysis was reasonably near completion. Although much remained to be done, and many important surprises were in store, one could look with considerable intellectual satisfaction at the entire reconstruction from fundamental logical foundation to the upper reaches of the discipline. The science of mathematics as a whole seemed to be in pretty good logical shape.

No such situation existed in inductive logic and foundations of empirical science in 1950, nor does it at present. The gap between the real science and the logical foundations (even if one has few qualms about the legitimacy of Carnap's inductive logic as far as it goes) is something like the abyss between Euclid's axiomatized geometry and Aristotle's theory of the syllogism. Hence, it is understandable that Russell, as one intensely interested in the logical structure of real scientific knowledge, should attempt to sketch, even with imprecision and lack of rigour, a way in which the logical gap can be bridged. While Carnap was busy making vast and important improvements in Keynes's theory of probability, Russell was trying to show how that theory could be made relevant to the epistemology of real science. These remarks are not intended to disparage Carnap's work on inductive logic in the least; rather, they are designed to suggest the extent to which Carnap and Russell were devoted to the same task, but in complementary ways. They are intended to show, moreover, that Carnap's work did not render Russell's superfluous. Russell's postulates of scientific knowledge may yet hold important clues for those who, like

---

[1] *Human Knowledge*, p. 474; *My Philosophical Development*, p. 205.

Carnap and Russell, believes that the *a priori* assignment of antecedent probabilities constitutes an indispensable part of the logical reconstruction of scientific inference.[1]

Acknowledgment

The author wishes to express his gratitude to the National Science Foundation for support of research on scientific inference, and to Adolf Grünbaum for many valuable criticisms of a draft of this essay.

---

[1] For Carnap, of course, posterior degree of confirmation statements are also *a priori*, but the evaluation of scientific hypotheses depends upon synthetic evidence statements as well as analytic degree of confirmation statements.

Richard Wollheim

Bertrand Russell and The Liberal Tradition

Bertrand Russell was born on 18 May 1872, in time, by twelve months, to have John Stuart Mill for his godfather—"so far as is possible in a non-religious sense".[1] At this period, Mill's ideas on political and social matters were in the ascendancy in advanced and even liberal circles. Russell died on 2 February 1970, and in the intervening ninety-seven years much had happened, both in the world of ideas and in the world of politics, to challenge Mill's social philosophy. His ideas had come to seem thin and irrelevant: intellectually thin, and politically irrelevant. It would, I think, be a matter only of simplification, and not of grave distortion, to look on the whole of Russell's social philosophy as an attempt, a sustained attempt, to repair that of John Stuart Mill: to supplement its deficiencies, to relate it to new ideas, and to demonstrate its applicability to the ever-changing realities of the twentieth century.

But if this is a correct characterization of Russell's work as a political thinker, this does not mean that he was actuated merely by piety, ancestral or intellectual. Russell's concern with social issues was direct. It is an interesting, and perhaps a surprising, fact that if you look at a list of Russell's works currently in print, you will find that half are devoted to political and social matters, taken in a broad sense. But these are not evenly distributed over his career. Their production falls into certain distinct periods, and these correspond to what were for Russell happenings of considerable political or personal moment: the horrors of the First World War, the Russian revolution and the attendant hopes and fears, the upbringing of his own children, and the superpower politics that followed the uneasy peace of 1945. Where Russell exaggerates, and where indeed I fail to follow what he had in mind, is in the assertion, which he was fond of making, that his political thinking had intellectually nothing to do with his general philosophy. Nor do I find Russell's argument for this assertion— namely, that, though he agreed with Hume on most points of general philosophy, he was in total disagreement with him on politics—as convincing as Russell would like it to be. But there is at least this to the assertion: that it corrects the error of thinking of Russell's political ideas as a mere application of his general philosophy, designed to round off the picture as it were. It restores to them the immediacy of their inspiration.

The central tenets of John Stuart Mill's social philosophy are to be found in his essay *On Liberty* and in what he says there about the relation between society and

---

[1] P. A. Schilpp (ed.), *The Philosophy of Bertrand Russell*, Evanston, Ill., 1944, p. 3.

the individual or, in his words, "the proper limits of state intervention". For the purpose of defining these limits Mill divided the desires (and hence the actions that derive from these desires) into two broad groups, which are intended to be exclusive and exhaustive: the self-regarding and (though the phrase is not Mill's) the other-regarding. The limits of state action may then be laid down as follows: as far as self-regarding desires are concerned, the state has no right to interfere with their satisfaction; in this area the individual enjoys complete freedom. As far as other-regarding desires are concerned, the state has an *a priori* right to interfere with their satisfaction, but whether this *a priori* right may be justifiably exercised depends upon a further calculation. And this is whether interference with the satisfaction of such a desire would increase the overall happiness of the community: or whether the frustration that the individual would experience if his desire is forbidden him is outweighed by the unpleasure that other individuals would suffer if his desire is permitted him. Mill's social philosophy is given, we can now see, in two stages: a Principle, which fixes the possible rights of the state and where these must end, and a Practical Maxim, which fixes within these limits the actual rights of the state.

Mill's Principle has given rise to much discussion, and it is generally felt that, before it can be found acceptable as the ground of a social policy, two sets of questions about it must be adequately answered. The first set includes such questions as the following: Is the distinction between the two sorts of desire tenable? If so, how are they related? Are the two sorts of desire of equal value to the individual, or has he a stronger interest in the satisfaction of one sort than in that of the other? Is the state right to confine its activity to the satisfaction or frustration of existing desires, or should it not also concern itself with the formation or modification of desires? This last question serves as a bridge to the second set of questions that Mill's Principle provokes. This set includes such questions as: Under what conditions is Mill's Principle likely to be adopted? What are the general conditions under which its operation is certain to be beneficial? How is it related to the forms of economic and social organization? In other words, Mill's social philosophy, as expressed in his thesis of the proper spheres of the individual and the state, needs to be supplemented in two ways: first, by a theory of human nature and, secondly, by a theory of society.

Of course, I do not want to suggest that Mill himself was unaware of all this. There is much both in his work on the mind and in his economic writings that is highly relevant to the thesis of *On Liberty*, and what Mill wrote in that essay is often made to seem considerably more naïve than it really is, just because this necessary background is ignored. Nevertheless, whatever the explanation, and some of it may lie in historical accident, Russell showed himself, in certain respects, more alive than Mill to the needs of liberal theory, or to what it required in the way of reinforcement or expanison. In this paper I intend to consider, first, what Russell had to say about man, secondly, what he had to say about society, in his attempt to enrich or to justify the political theory he inherited.

First, then, man. In his *Principles of Social Reconstruction*, which was written in 1915, delivered as lectures in 1916, and remained probably the finest expression of Russell's political attitude, we find, in the Preface, the following statement of intent: "My aim" he writes, "is to suggest a philosophy of politics based upon the belief that impulse has more effect than conscious purpose in moulding men's lives."[1] The important word here is "impulse", and for the importance of impulse itself conclusive evidence had, Russell felt, been provided in recent years from two sources: on the one hand, by psychology, by which he meant (roughly) psychoanalysis, towards which he retained a respectful if distant attitude[2]; and, on the other hand, by the outbreak of the First World War, which was, of course, going on as Russell wrote. But to see the import of this admission for liberalism as Russell saw it, we must understand how he conceived impulse. Though in the passage I have quoted impulse is contrasted with conscious purpose, essentially it is contrasted with desire. "All human activity," Russell writes a few pages later, "springs from two sources: impulse and desire."[3] And this contrast, of which we hear little in Russell's "official" philosophy of mind, remains a theme throughout his social philosophy.[4] Desire takes for its object something which is distant, possibly both in space and in time: and integral or essential to a desire is the belief that the object desired will somehow or other satisfy one if one gets it. Impulse, by contrast, is immediate: it is directed towards something which one wants to do or have, here and now, and it is unmediated by the belief that that towards which one has an impulse will have desirable results or satisfying consequences. Impulse lies in the moment, desire is shaped by foresight, and Russell's first point would be that any political philosophy that held that only desire had to be taken account of and that consequently overlooked impulse, like Mill's theory at any rate as I have presented it, is to that degree inadequate.

But suppose we admit impulse as something which any adequate political theory must take account of, does that require a serious amendment to Mill's principle of state action? And if it doesn't, if the principle can still stand, does

[1] *Principles of Social Reconstruction*, London 1916, p. 5.
[2] Russell would seem to have drawn his knowledge of pyscho-analysis largely from Bernard Hart, *The Psychology of Insanity*, Cambridge 1912: a work which Russell quotes with admiration in the *Principles of Social Reconstruction* and, again, in *The Analysis of Mind*, London 1921. Hart writes in the Preface to his book that a very large number of its leading ideas are "due to the genius of Prof. Freud of Vienna, probably the most original and fertile thinker who has yet entered the field of abnormal pyschology".
[3] ibid., pp. 12 ff.
[4] e.g. *Political Ideals* (original edition New York 1917), London 1963, p. 68; *Authority and the Individual*, London 1949, p. 63; *Human Society in Ethics and Politics*, London 1954, p. 176.

the admission add to, or detract from, the acceptability of the principle?

By and large Russell would not seem to have thought that the admission of impulse as such required any change in Mill's Principle. That is, he seems to have thought that whatever method was adopted for dividing desires into those which fell, at least potentially, into the jurisdiction of the state and those which fell outside it, could, broadly speaking, equally well, equally justifiably, apply to impulses. (I say "broadly speaking", "by and large", because there is a suggestion recurrent in Russell's thinking that impulse should be given some kind of priority over desire, and this Russell justifies on grounds of preserving spontaneity, a vital value in human life: but, quite apart from the dubiousness of the justification—that is, whether the spontaneous can rightly be equated with the impulsive in Russell's sense—there is the further question how far the resultant policy admits of application in the public, as opposed merely to the private, domain.)

If, then, the admission of impulse does not as such make Mill's Principle inapplicable, does it do anything to affect its plausibility? What I have in mind is this: it might be said that Mill's Principle by making some desires actionable by the state though others remain free of it, safeguards society certainly, but at the expense of the individual. The appearance of liberalism is preserved, but the reality is collectivist. For, to the individual, are not all his desires equally of significance, and how is he to accept the fact that, though he may indulge some, others are or can be forbidden him? Well, obviously one line of defence here would be to try to show that the desires in the matter of which the individual's rights are less than absolute mean less to him: they are in some way disposable, whereas those in whose exercise he is safeguarded are crucial to him. But how is this to be shown? Well, once again, one way (though only *one* way) of doing this would be to show that other-regarding desires (or at any rate the anti-social subset of them) could, in principle, be argued away, though to do this one would first have to establish that desires are amenable to reason. Now in point of fact it is common ground to both Mill and Russell that in some limited sense desires are amenable to reason. For, though every desire has a core that is not amenable to reason, argument can secure a hold on desire in so far as every desire contains (which we have seen it does) a belief about means to ends: a belief, that is, that what is desired will bring satisfaction. For that belief can be disproved. Indeed, Mill went on to think that, when the state recorded its opposition to a certain desire by associating a punishment to its satisfaction, it thereby constructed a practical argument calculated to dissolve that desire. For though the object that was desired might bring satisfaction by or in itself, it certainly would not if it always came attended by punishment.

However, Russell was insistent, as we have also seen, that impulses are not amenable to reason even in the limited sense in which desires are. And this follows from the fact that impulses do not contain a belief about means and ends: they have no constituent upon which argument can gain a grip. Now, if this is so, then the recognition that there are impulses as well as desires, and that Mill's Principle must apply to both, can only have the effect of making the Principle more anti-individualist, more collectivist than liberals took it to be. Over a considerable range of his inner drives, the individual will have to tolerate a degree of frustration that he seemingly has no reason to accept.

But to this Russell had an answer. And his answer was based on another feature of impulses that set them in contrast to desires. Desires can be regulated by reason whereas impulses can't be. But impulses, just because of their immediacy, can find substitute satisfactions in a way not open to desire. Russell developed the point in his Reith Lectures given in 1948 and published under the title *Authority and the Individual*,[1] but in substance the point had been there since the writings of the First World War. Indeed, in *The Principles of Social Reconstruction* Russell laid it down that one of the marks by which a political institution is to be judged is the degree to which it succeeds in moulding impulse in a favourable direction: that is, moulding it in such a way that it ceases to run counter to the legitimate exercise of state action.[2] And to the charge that this is more oppressive than anything that could be envisaged under the heading of the frustration of desire, Russell had his reply. For him the only kind of state action that we can without reservation call oppressive is that which involves the bending of the individual's will or getting him to do what he doesn't want to do.[3] Whether the moulding of impulse is oppressive or not cannot be decided in the abstract. To think that it can—and here I to a small degree run ahead of my own exegesis of Russell's argument—means ignoring the fact that impulse and desire are, of necessity, shaped by external forces, or that the socialized individual is the product of education. Accordingly, if the issue is to be resolved, all depends on *how* impulse is moulded or on the principles of state interference to which it, impulse, is being made to conform.

And this brings us to the second of the two things that Russell has to say about man that bear upon liberal theory. Having divided the sources of human action into desire and impulse, Russell then went on to divide both desires and impulses into two groups: desires and impulses which are creative, and desires and impulses which are possessive.[4] This distinction, repeated throughout Russell's social writings, turns out to be a distinction of great political significance. For the creative desires and impulses of man are inherently harmonious, whereas the possessive desires are inherently conflictive: and in both cases along two dimensions. The different creative desires and impulses of a single individual cohere, and so do the creative desires and impulses of different individuals: similarly for the possessive desires and impulses of individuals and the disharmonies to which they give rise. Indeed, in *Human Society in Ethics and Politics*, which is

---

[1] *Authority and the Individual*, pp. 17–18, 35–6, 93.

[2] *The Principles of Social Reconstruction*, p. 36.

[3] ibid., p. 230.

[4] ibid., p. 162; *Political Ideals*, pp. 11 ff., 71 ff.

where Russell comes closest to conventional utilitarianism, he begins by invoking the notion of "compossibility of desire". "Right desires will be those that are capable of being compossible with as many other desires as possible; wrong desires will be those that can only be satisfied by thwarting other desires."[1] But by the end of the book, the distinction with which Russell is operating is that between creative and possessive desires and impulses. And the result, he clearly thinks, is extensionally equivalent. Now, this being so, it seemed only natural to Russell that this distinction should replace Mill's distinction between self-regarding and other-regarding desires and that the principle of state interference should be reformulated in terms of it. The principle thus reformulated Russell called the Principle of Growth, and it became his central political belief.

In point of fact what I have just said about the relation of Russell's Principle to Mill's is not quite accurate. For whereas, as we have seen, Mill's social philosophy contains both a Principle and a Practical Maxim for the determination of state action, Russell would seem to have made do with his Principle of Growth, which therefore takes over the function of both. It is the unique determinant of legitimate state action: though it is worth pointing out that Russell's concern with the demarcation between the legitimate and the illegitimate in state action was more approximate or generalized than Mill's. Or, to put it another way, in formulating the Principle of Growth, Russell, unlike Mill, would seem to have been interested not so much in separating those actions where the state had no right to intervene, no matter what conditions held, from those actions where the state might or could have a right, given certain further conditions, as in separating those actions where the state had no right to intervene, however this came about, *a priori* or *a posteriori*, from those actions where it had such a right. In consequence, the creative impulses and desires are the heirs not solely to the self-regarding desires but to the self-regarding desires plus those desires which would on an overall calculation be reckoned beneficial.

If this is right, a natural question to raise is whether Russell and Mill would be likely to find themselves in agreement on the actual desires or the actual actions with which the state is entitled to interfere. The presumption is that they would. But I think that it is impossible to be altogether certain on this point, because of a very obvious lacuna in Russell's thinking. For Russell has nothing to say about how we are to classify desires seemingly of one kind which are instrumental to the satisfaction of desires of another kind: for instance, and most relevantly, desires which are, at their face value, possessive desires but which are motivated by creative desires. (So I desire a table on which to write the book that I desire to write.) Without an answer to this question it is impossible to be certain about the overlap or otherwise between what in practice would follow from the

---

[1] *Human Society in Ethics and Politics*, p. 59.

recommendations in principle of the two authors. However this we do know: that, even if there were a total concurrence between them about what actions they think the state could legitimately interfere with and what actions they think it should not, the grounds on which they would think this would differ. So we must ask, which of the two accounts provides the more attractive rationale for state action? And here I think the advantage lies with Russell. For, given what Russell assumes about the creative impulses and desires, his account is more firmly rooted in the nature of man. Instead of the state being set over and against the individual, now allowing him, now forbidding him, to do what he wants, the state, even when it does frustrate the individual, is also in a sense taking his side against himself.

But of course we cannot delay the question, Why should we accept Russell's assumptions about the creative energies of man? What entitled him to take so optimistic a view of their role in the life of the individual and the life of society? The answer comes in two parts.

For the view that the creative energies of one and the same individual are harmonious, Russell relied heavily on his theory of education. I think that any acceptable political philosophy must contain a theory of education—just as any acceptable moral philosophy must contain a theory of self-development—for it is only against the background of the making of the citizen, or the making of the agent, that a distinction between legitimate and illegitimate obligation, whether civil or moral, can be formulated. Russell saw this. The details of his theory of education do not concern us, but the way in which he saw the relation between the creative and the possessive desires and impulses in the child's development does. For Russell did not think that these were two independent sets of desires and impulses, each potential in the human being, and that a good, i.e. a free, form of education would allow one set to flourish and would cause the other to die of inanition. Rather it was Russell's view that one set of desires and impulses is a transform of the other, and that a good, i.e. a predominantly free, form of education will ensure that the transformation goes the right way round. Now, given that the two sets of impulses and desires are transforms of one another, and do not have independent sources, it is not surprising that one set should be internally harmonious. For this fact about it should explain why there is such a transform, since the possession of internal harmony would account for its social or biological value. Of course, what we need to explain is not only why there should be a set of desires and impulses that is internally harmonious, but how this harmony comes about or what is its "secret". Russell's answer, again not surprising, is that the secret of the harmony is that all the harmonious impulses and desires derive from the man's conception of himself, or the "intimate centre in each human being".[1] Since this intimate centre has most to fear from external pressures, it falls into place that creative impulses and desires

[1] *Principles of Social Reconstruction*, p. 24.

are the form that the energies of the individual will take, if he is allowed to develop freely, i.e. has a good education.

For the view that the creative energies of different individuals are harmonious one with another, Russell relied very largely on the contrast within impulses and desires in terms of which "creative" is defined: that is, he relied on the necessary truth that the creative desires do not involve possession. In *Political Ideals*, he writes of "the creative or constructive impulses, which aim at bringing into the world or making available for use the kind of goods in which there is no privacy and no possession".[1] Now, if this is true of creative impulses and desires, moreover if it is necessarily true of them, then it follows that there is no space within which they can, indeed within which they could, bring individuals into conflict with one another.

Having surveyed what Russell brought to traditional liberal theory from the theory of man, we might now seem to be ready to turn to what he thought the theory of society could contribute to it. But I want to postpone that for a moment while we look, in slightly greater substance, at those energies of man which Russell thought it legitimate for the state to curb, or which were thought by him to be, at any rate in excess of a certain degree, not merely other-regarding but anti-social. Russell's phrase (as we have seen) is "the possessive impulses or desires", but in all his writings he makes it clear that he has not exclusively in mind that which draws men to possess property. There is also the drive to power and this, in Russell's view, is the supreme menace in society. It is the supreme menace for two reasons, which need to be kept apart. In the first place, the love of power is the strongest of all the possessive impulses and desires: stronger, for instance, than the love of property. Indeed in *Power*, possibly his best-known though by no means his best book on politics, Russell argues that the love of property in its objectionable form—that is, where it is boundless and so in principle unsatisfiable—is just a manifestation of the love of power.[2] Secondly, the love of power is the supreme menace because it attacks that area of others which is most precious to them. For, given that the best life is that which involves the creative energies, the indispensable value for the individual who wishes to be creative must be his freedom. Freedom is, of course, only an instrumental value, but instrumental for all those more significant than itself. "Freedom", is how Russell puts it, "is the greatest of political goods"[3]—adding, in a footnote, "I do not say the greatest of *all* goods. The best things come from the exercise of man's creative energies, but to exercise them he must be free." Of course Russell recognized that the individual needs also material security, but this, he thought, need amount to no more than "a moderate competence".[4] "It is true," he writes, with that simplicity of expression he always adopted when

[1] *Political Ideals*, pp. 11–12.
[2] *Power: A New Social Analysis*, New York 1938, p. 10.
[3] *Roads to Freedom*, London 1918, p. 82 and n.
[4] *Power*, p. 10.

passions were likely to run high, "that poverty is a great evil, but it is not true that material prosperity is in itself a great good."[1] In holding that the love of power is the great evil in society, and, more particularly in holding this for the reasons for which he did, Russell felt that he put himself in opposition to Marxism. For all his life, from the writing of *German Social Democracy* in 1896 onwards, Russell wrote as though Marxism was committed to a belief in the supremacy of the economic motive: as far as he was concerned, the economic motive had been given by Marx pride of place both in analysing existing society and in working out the society of the future.[2] Whether this was a simple misunderstanding on Russell's part, or whether it was a subtle interpretation, it is genuinely hard to say. I shall in a moment come to a point on which divergence between Russell and Marxism is beyond dispute.

It is now time to look at what Russell contributed to liberal theory from the side of society. If we continue to take Mill's essay *On Liberty* as Russell's starting-point, it is clearly a defect of that essay that it gives little or no indication of the kind of society in which the policies it supports are likely to be realized. At the time of composition Mill had abandoned belief in *laisser-faire* as a principle of practical politics, and was sympathetic to socialism, but in the essay he gives no real indication of the state of his thinking. What did Russell do to make good this deficiency?

If I may seem to have spent an excessive amount of time on what Russell brought to liberal social philosophy from the theory of man, this will, I hope, pay off. For when we look to see what kind of society Russell thought was desirable for the realization of the Principle of Growth, we find that every proposal that he made follows directly from psychological considerations. Every change in institutions that he recommended was designed either to curb the lust for power or to provide the freedom necessary for the cultivation of creativity or directly to stimulate creativity. It was with these objectives in mind that Russell advocated a wide range of reforms: equality of wealth and property; economic security, in the form of a basic wage, democratic institutions, with insistence that the constituencies should be small and the issues of genuine moment; workers' control in industry; the freedom of women; the revitalization of work, its techniques and conditions; the spread of leisure; the rejection of superfluous technology; and the establishment of world government.

On these recommendations note two points. First, Russell, unlike many advocates of democracy, was never content with the mere existence of a certain kind of institution—say, a representative institution: he also thought it necessary that the institution should achieve the end for which it was introduced and by

---

[1] *Roads to Freedom*, p. 113.

[2] e.g. *German Social Democracy*, London 1896, pp. 7–8; *The Practice and Theory of Bolshevism*, London 1920, p. 65; *Power*, p. 10.

reference to which it was justified. So, in *The Practice and Theory of Bolshevism*, written in 1920 after a visit to the USSR, Russell goes so far as to say that there are "two different things that may be meant" by democracy. We may mean Parliamentary democracy or we may mean "the participation of the people in affairs".[1] Now, if it is confusing to think of these as different meanings of democracy, Russell was surely right to suggest that it is the mark of degeneracy in liberal tradition to make a crude identification of this or that social ideal with those institutions which might, or could, realize them. Secondly, Russell certainly moved beyond the range of conventional liberal thinking when he proposed state action whose aim was not merely to provide the conditions in which individuals could work out their own fulfilment if they wanted to, but also to encourage or reinforce them in this project. I am thinking specifically of Russell's concern with the quality of work, and the lead he looked to from the political authority in the matter of making work more creative. In this respect as in many others, Russell belonged to the more full-blooded tradition of British Socialism, as represented by William Morris and the Guild Socialists, rather than to the more attenuated version associated with the Labour Party.

But the most significant single feature of Russell's theory of society is that it reveals no belief whatsoever in what might be called fundamental social forms. Each institution is accepted or rejected by Russell on its own merits, depending on how far it satisfies or frustrates the aspirations of man. Questions whether one institution might necessitate or be necessitated by another are never allowed to enter into the calculation: because, presumably, Russell did not believe in such necessitation. And it is this that I had in mind when I talked just now of one indisputable divergence between Russell and Marxism.

For Russell the indispensable elements of any serious political position were a conception of the end and a conception of the means necessary to attain it. If either is missing, there are grave dangers. If there is a conception of the end to be realized but no assessment of the means to be employed or of proximate aims, a sense of drama will take over and, though there may be much personal heroism, even martyrdom, the chances are that the world will not be made a happier place.[2] If there is a conception of the means to be employed but no vision of what human life might be, the steps that are most likely to be taken are those which, while possibly upsetting many people at the time, do nothing for the furtherance of liberty or equality: and as an example of this, Russell quoted— with considerable foresight we might think, for he was writing in 1917—the nationalization of the railways after due compensation had been paid to their owners and their subsequent control by state boards.[3] But a graver danger stems from the fact that, if there is no end, there is equally no way to assess, not just

[1] *The Practice and Theory of Bolshevism*, p. 94.
[2] e.g. *Political Ideals*, pp. 38–40; *The Practice and Theory of Bolshevism*, p. 95.
[3] *Political Ideals*, pp. 43–6.

the efficacy, but the moral validity, of the means. In his last years Russell liked to recall a radio programme in which he had taken part with Lord Samuel, an official sage of the time, and Lord Samuel had made the familiar objection that it is wrong ever to make the end justify the means. "What else", Russell had asked, "could justify the means?"[1] In other words, for Russell most of the types of action that fell into the domain of political judgment were not unqualifiedly good or bad, but the context in which they occurred—notably, the end for which they were done, whether this was a good thing, and whether they were likely to achieve it—would be decisive. Take, for instance, Russell's own attitude to war. By and large Russell thought war totally wrong, but he thought that extreme circumstances might justify it: for instance, in the case of the Second World War against Nazi aggression, and again, in South-east Asia against American aggression. Over the years Russell had many grave charges to bring against Soviet Communism. But Soviet Communism had at least this constructive feature: that, by specifying both its end and the means to which it was committed, it offered itself up to critical appraisal—from which, in Russell's opinion, it came out pretty badly.

But the gravest danger of all attendant upon having no clear political aim, no vision of social life as it should be, is in effect the subject-matter of perhaps the most brilliant of Russell's political writings: *The Scientific Outlook*, written in 1931. "To say that we live in an age of science," the book opens, "is a commonplace, but like most commonplaces it is only partially true."[2] For if our ancestors would consider present society very scientific, it is likely that to our descendants it will seem the reverse. And Russell then proceeds to describe many different ways in which society might effectively be permeated by science. Industry, government, education, the propagation of the species, could all become scientific. The picture of "the scientific society", as it defines itself in Russell's ironical prose, gradually takes on the character of a nightmare. How can this be? The truth is that for Russell science could mean a body of knowledge, or it could mean a technique,[3] and in portraying the scientific society what Russell did in effect was to articulate a society in which science as technique, not science as knowledge, is realized to the maximum. But a society in which there is an idolatrous attachment to a means and no consciousness of end is fairly soon likely to find an end imposed on it: imposed on it by the means to which it lies in bondage. By the time we come to the leaders of this scientific society we are not surprised to learn that "the fact that they can do something that no one previously thought it possible to do is to them a sufficient reason for doing it."[4]

Russell twice lost his position on account of his social views. He was twice

[1] Rupert Crawshay Williams, *Russell Remembered*, London 1970, p. 27.
[2] *The Scientific Outlook*, London 1931, p. 9.
[3] ibid., pp. 10–11; cf. *Authority and the Individual*, p. 55.
[4] *The Scientific Outlook*, p. 274.

imprisoned for them. His last sustained political action, the Tribunal on American War Crimes in Vietnam, was met by a conspiracy of silence round the world. The fact that he was an intellectual genius made it easier for those who purveyed a more comfortable view of life to present him as a simpleton. He endured this too. He continued in the belief that, the desire for power aside, the most socially dangerous conditions of mind were boredom and the love of excitement.

George Nakhnikian

Some Questions about Bertrand Russell's Liberalism

Professor Wollheim believes that Russell's social theory is an improvement over Mill's. I wonder. Wollheim is right that Russell's distinction between the creative and the possessive impulses is integral to his social theory. Wollheim further believes that according to Russell this distinction is extensionally equivalent to the distinction between right desires and wrong desires, respectively defined to mean desires that are capable of being compossible with as many other desires as possible and desires that can only be satisfied by thwarting other desires. Russell reiterates the principle of compossibility of desire as late as 1943:

> What I hold practically is something like Leibniz's maximum of compossibles. I regard satisfaction of desire as *per se* good, no matter what or whose the desire; sometimes desires are compatible, sometimes not. If A and B desire to marry each other, both can be satisfied; if each desires to murder the other without being murdered at least one must be disappointed. Therefore marriage is better than murder, and love is better than hate.[1]

The principle is dubious. If A and B desire to kill each other, not caring what else happens, both can be satisfied; if each desires to kill the other without being killed, at least one must be disappointed. If we argue as Russell does we must conclude that killing each other is better than killing and not being killed, and this is by no means obvious.

Moreover, even if Russell's theory were in some ways an improvement over Mill's, Russell's liberalism is misleading for another and more serious reason. I agree with Russell that mankind can rid itself of many evils through economic and political reforms. But Russell thinks that these reforms are sufficient for doing away with all evils, those that are visited upon people by others and by physical nature as well as those that come from "defects in the character or aptitudes of the sufferer: among these are ignorance, lack of will, and violent passions".[2] I, on the other hand, believe that there are evils that exist because of the human condition itself. They are not due to avoidable ignorance, or lack of will, or violent passions or anything else of that sort. Nothing can be done to rid men of them. I want to explain this single point.

In *Proposed Roads to Freedom* Russell says: "The only human relations that have value are those that are rooted in mutual freedom, where there is no

---

[1] P. A. Schilpp (ed.), *The Philosophy of Bertrand Russell*, Evanston, Ill., 1944, p. 740.
[2] *Proposed Roads to Freedom*, New York 1919, p. 188.

domination and no slavery, no tie except affection, no economic or conventional necessity to preserve the external show when the inner life is dead."[1] With a slight emendation this statement is a correct value judgment. The *most rewarding* or *best* human relations are the ones that Russell is describing. But they are not the only ones that have value at all. Neurotic relationships are not "rooted in mutual freedom" but the satisfaction of neurotic needs is a good. Where Russell goes seriously wrong is in thinking that "when the evil heritage of economic slavery has ceased to mould our instincts" the most rewarding human relations will become a commonplace instead of being, as they now are, rare. Russell's mistake consists in thinking that "the whole basis of these evils is economic".[2] However, later Russell modified this view. In his *The Practice and Theory of Bolshevism*, Russell clearly says that abolishing capitalism is not enough to eliminate oppression and cruelty. There is also need for political reform. If we combine Russell's earlier and later views, we find him holding that economic and political reform is a sufficient condition for improving human relationships. I shall refer to this as "Russell's thesis".

Russell's thesis is an integral part of his liberalism. Russell's liberalism is a theory about means and ends. The end is to realize "some new system of society by which life may become richer, more full of joy and less full of preventable evils than it is at present".[3] Russell examines various theories as to the best means for achieving this end: anarchism, various forms of socialism and syndicalism. Wollheim correctly observes that "Russell certainly moved beyond the range of conventional liberal thinking when he proposed state action whose aim was not merely to provide the conditions in which individuals could work out their own fulfilment if they wanted to, but also to encourage or reinforce them in this project".[4] The means in Russell liberalism is a social organization that performs these functions well. Such a society, on Russell's view, must be socialist in its economy because Russell divides an individual's impulses and desires into the creative (good) and possessive (bad) and, so the argument goes, only under socialism is it possible to curb the possessive impulses and desires and free the creative ones for full expression. Russell's thesis thus is an integral part of his liberalism. It is part of Russell's theory about the right means for achieving the reforms that he and many other social theorists deem to be desirable.

Russell's thesis is not true. Underlying the error is an incomplete catalogue of "the evils in the lives we know of". This is how Russell views them:

When we consider the evils in the lives we know of, we find that they may be roughly

---

[1] *Proposed Roads to Freedom*, p. 204.

[2] ibid., p. 206. The word "these" refers to bad relationships between spouses, but Russell implies that the analysis extends to all human relationships gone wrong. The evils of power, too, are due to bad economic arrangements.

[3] *Proposed Roads to Freedom*, p. viii. This is a representative statement.

[4] Wollheim, this volume, p. 218.

divided into three classes. There are, first, those due to physical nature: among these are death, pain and the difficulty of making the soil yield a subsistence. These we will call "physical evils". Second, we may put those that spring from defects in the character or aptitudes of the sufferer: among these are ignorance, lack of will, and violent passions. These we will call "evils of character". Third come those that depend upon the power of one individual or group over another: these comprise not only obvious tyranny, but all interference with free development, whether by force or by excessive mental influence such as may occur in education. These we will call "evils of power". A social system may be judged by its bearing upon these three kinds of evils.[1]

Russell sees that suffering is caused by choices a person makes because of some defect of character. We may add that in an imperfect world nobility of character also may bring suffering. A man who resists tyranny because of heroic integrity can be transformed into a cowering wretch by the powers that he resists. This sort of thing can be avoided if the world is reformed so as to make tyranny impossible. It might even be, although I doubt it, that proper upbringing in a good society may eliminate the recurrence of defects in people's character.

However, Russell fails to note that individuals suffer for still another reason. The suffering that he overlooks differs from the woes that a man incurs because his character is defective. A human being is susceptible of change. Some people do and others do not change, but everyone is subject to change at any time in the course of his life. The time and nature of this kind of change is unpredictable. A choice made at a certain time in a man's life may be the only attractive alternative open to him given his makeup at the time. He may be a tightly controlled person at the time he makes the choice. Then, for some unaccountable reason, his defences collapse, he feels needs that he did not allow himself to feel heretofore, and the consequences of his choice frustrate his present needs causing him anguish. Such a person may also suffer from the sheer shock of the change. He may not understand what is happening to him. He may mistake the change for an onset of insanity. He may feel suicidally depressed because nothing that gave meaning and direction to his life has a hold on him any longer, and he has not yet found new meaning and purpose. If a man comes out whole from this kind of suffering, he will have gained a new and better life, but there is no guarantee that he will make it. Most of all, there is, as far as I can see, no economic reform that will prevent this kind of suffering. The possibility of it is inherent in the very condition of being human.

Russell's thesis is prominent in *Proposed Roads to Freedom*. To be sure in his later works he sometimes expresses the belief that one must take into account psychological factors that are not definable in terms of economic factors. In *Freedom and Organization*, for instance, Russell lists as "the main causes of political [including social and cultural] change from 1814 to 1914" economic

---

[1] *Proposed Roads to Freedom*, p. 188.

technique, political ideas and ideals, outstanding men, and chance.[1] In *The Practice and Theory of Bolshevism* Russell thinks that food, shelter, clothing, and sex are the basic needs of man, and four passions "acquisitiveness, vanity, rivalry and love of power [are] prime movers of almost all that happens in politics".[2] But Russell's conviction that psychological factors are irreducible to economic ones is quite consistent with the view he holds in *Proposed Roads to Freedom* that economic and political reform is a sufficient condition for improving human relationships. Russell believes that within a decent economic and political system "The process of leading men's thoughts and imagination away from the use of force will be greatly accelerated. . . . In a world where all men and women enjoy economic freedom, there will not be the same habit of command, nor, consequently, the same love of despotism. . . . In such a world, most of the nightmares that lurk in the background of men's minds will no longer exist; on the other hand, ambition and desire to excel will have to take nobler forms than those that are encouraged by a commercial society."[3] Human relations will be conceived in mutual freedom

when the evil heritage of economic slavery has ceased to mould our instincts. Husbands and wives, parents and children, will be only held together by affection: where that has died, it will be recognized that nothing worth preserving is left. Because affection will be free, men and women will not find in private life an outlet and stimulus to the love of domineering, but all that is creative in their love will have the freer scope. Reverence for whatever makes the soul in those who are loved will be less rare than it is now: nowadays, many men love their wives in the way in which they love mutton, as something to devour and destroy. But in the love that goes with reverence there is a joy of quite another order than any to be found by mastery, a joy which satisfies the spirit and not only the instincts; and satisfaction of instinct and spirit at once is necessary to a happy life, or indeed to any existence that is to bring out the best impulses of which a man or woman is capable.[4]

A life lived in this spirit—the spirit that aims at creating rather than possessing—has a certain fundamental happiness, of which it cannot be wholly robbed by adverse circumstances. This is the way of life recommended in the Gospels, and by all the great teachers of the world. Those who have found it are freed from the tyranny of fear, since what they value most in their lives is not at the mercy of outside power. If all men could summon up the courage and the vision to live in this way in spite of obstacles and discouragement, there would be no need for the regeneration of the world to begin by political and economic reform: all that is needed in the way of reform would come automatically, without resistance, owing to the moral regeneration of individuals. But the teaching of Christ has been nominally accepted by the world for many centuries, and yet those who follow it are still persecuted as they were before the time of Constantine. Experience has proved that few are able to see through the apparent evils of an outcast's

[1] *Freedom and Organization, 1814–1914*, London 1934.
[2] *The Practice and Theory of Bolshevism*, London 1920, p. 133.
[3] *Proposed Roads to Freedom*, pp. 202–3.
[4] ibid., p. 206.

life to the inner joy that comes of faith and creative hope. If the domination of fear is to be overcome, it is not enough, as regards the mass of men, to preach courage and indifference to misfortune: it is necessary to remove the causes of fear, to make a good life no longer an unsuccessful one in a worldly sense, and to diminish the harm that can be inflicted upon those who are not wary in self-defence.[1]

What Russell is saying is that people are too cowardly to live a life of creative love. They are afraid of not achieving worldly success, and the only way that these fears can be removed is through economic and political reform. He is right that the life of creative love has an inner joy that is of priceless value. He is also right that not many live that way. But he is altogether mistaken in thinking that to live that life men need only summon up the necessary courage and vision, or failing that, have their fears and anxieties removed by economic and political reform. The fact that men very rarely experience the joys of creative love has been recognized by observers as diverse in their interpretation and explanation of this fact as Jesus, Freud, the Buddha, and the existentialists. They all agree on one point: that the cure is not in economic and political reform. This is not to say that such reforms are not desirable. It is only to recognize that the sickness of man's spirit cuts across economic and political systems. A man cannot give or receive love and acceptance unless he loves and accepts himself. Economic and social degradation do seem to ruin a man's capacity for loving and accepting himself, but these factors do not explain all cases of self-rejection. The number is legion of socially and professionally prominent and economically secure men who experience suicidal depression. Many deeply disturbed adolescents are sometimes so depressed. These sorts of troubles spoil human relationships and they seem to afflict people of both sexes, of all ages, under different social and economic systems. The cure for them is not economic. It requires remaking oneself. That requires help from others, but success or failure depends ultimately on the inner resources of the individual.

The pain that a man estranged from himself feels is not an unmitigated disaster. Indeed, for those who succeed in remaking themselves into love-giving and love-receiving people, this pain is an instrumental good. Without it rebirth is impossible. But not all who need to be reborn make it. Some never feel the pain. Others feel it, but they lack the inner resources necessary for rebirth. In either case there is loss of vitality and joy. There is either psychological or physical suicide. These are great misfortunes, and there is no reason to think that economic and political reforms can do away with them.

Russell's thesis is, therefore, false. Economic and political reforms can at best eliminate suffering that comes from physical nature, defects of character, and abuse of power. Even on this there is wide-ranging disagreement. Still it is reasonable to believe that economic and political reforms can go a long way

[1] ibid., pp. 187–8.

towards reducing the suffering that comes from these sources. The recalcitrant examples are in cases of suffering that come from self-hatred.

Because there is ample evidence in Russell's public life as well as in his writings that he was thoroughly familiar with the phenomenon of spiritual malaise, I am puzzled by the fact that when he writes on social theory he seems to lose sight of spiritual malaise as a source of evil that is beyond economic or political remedy.

Even admitting all this, a more-up-to-date version of Russell's liberalism, one that recognizes the limitations of economic and political reform, seems to me to be a sensible political philosophy.

Ralph Schoenman

Bertrand Russell and The Peace Movement

Bertrand Russell's preoccupation with questions of war and peace was lifelong. Over a period of seventy-five years the attitude of political movements and of nation states to this issue had predominant weight in deciding Russell's relationship to them. Long before global war had become a matter of annihilation of the species, Russell felt it to be the clearest expression of moral cowardice and irrationality. If his attitude to peace and the politics of social conflict is to be made comprehensible, it is necessary to discern the essentially empirical approach he favoured. He never felt comfortable with political and sociological theory which rooted war in a specific economic and social system.

This was true despite the fact that during his last years his views reflect a radical estimate of the relationship between capitalism and armed conflict. Close examination makes clear, however, that, for Russell, the category of American imperialism—an order requiring world empire—did not arise from a law of social development. To him it was simply power which had compelled the rulers of American capitalism to use an army for the protection of its investments. He came to recognize that crushing social revolution and the arms economy were designed to prevent mass unemployment and to secure hegemony over rivals for markets, the better to obtain investment zones which could not be challenged. Russell did not arrive at this consonance with Marxist, indeed Leninist, critiques of the social dynamics of capitalism in an imperial phase because he shared their philosophical or theoretical assumptions. He was, in fact, a caustic critic of Marxist theory and Leninist practice over many years. His first book on *German Social Democracy* was an orthodox liberal attack upon the Marxism of the German movement. His books on anarchism, syndicalism and guild socialism, such as *Principles of Social Reconstruction, Roads to Freedom, The Practice and Theory of Bolshevism, Power* and *Authority and the Individual* continue his essential approach.

Nonetheless, his attitude toward capitalism and American imperialism during his last years bears a decidedly Marxist character. It is precisely in this apparent anomaly that the deceptive paradox of Russell's lifelong political posture can be found. He rarely hesitated to accept the correctness of a specific set of data, even when he had rejected the critique derived from it in the form of a universal law or a hypothesis propounding a general theory of society.

By the end of 1964 Russell had concluded reluctantly that American capitalism controlled the State in America and used its armed might to effect and perpetuate global imperial rule. All his political actions and pronouncements during this last period reflect that premise, for which a vast and eloquent array of evidence was assembled in polemical form. The aim was to awaken people to the view that American imperialism was pursuing counter-revolutionary politics on a world scale, yet Russell believed this to be neither necessary nor inherent in the development of capitalism. It gave his views an urgency, but it left him at times despairing over the means which seemed required to defeat so brutal a system of society. As this assessment of American capitalism was one to which he came only reluctantly and upon confronting evidence and arguments which appeared irrefutable, he upheld these views in some sorrow. He continued to hope that popular pressure might dissuade rulers from their destructive course.

Liberals and social democrats were confounded by Russell's adherence to a Bolshevik view of war and peace during the 1960s, and a few revolutionaries mistakenly thought Russell had come round to Marxism in his last, most combative years. He had become, through the force of events in which he was involved, perturbed over the world activity of the American ruling class. He acknowledged the documentation of its corporate power and its international workings, but he by no means thought through the ways in which the oppressed could overcome this colossus.

All his life he looked pragmatically at social questions. This gave him a peculiar strength in that he did not require a holistic view to act with radical daring and commitment. It contained a weakness because he appeared impulsive, frequently inconsistent and prone to invoke the most inflamed rhetoric for incompatible positions within the space of a few years—and sometimes months.

It would be a mistake to think that Russell lacked an underlying political philosophy. His very eclecticism, pragmatic daring, penchant for a practical response to each new situation and scepticism about historical laws of social development comprised an essentially liberal sensibility. But Russell's underlying liberalism was that of the bourgeois revolutionary period. The radical assault on arbitrary authority, privilege, suppression of personal liberty and the grosser forms of exploitation—this was the liberalism which suffused his mind. It led him to the Labour Party and even to Fabianism, Guild Socialism and Syndicalism. Yet these pragmatic credos, radical as they sometimes appear in his thinking, were rooted in the social categories of Locke, Bentham and Mill.

It was his radical but bourgeois sensibility which sought always to reconcile change with reform and political democracy with class conciliation. The political ideals which guided Russell and informed his politics throughout his life were reason, common sense, enlightened self-interest and avoidance, where possible, of social clash or crisis.

Neither misery nor folly seems to me any part of the inevitable lot of man. And I am convinced that intelligence, patience and eloquence can, sooner or later, lead the human race out of its self-imposed tortures, provided it does not exterminate itself meanwhile.

228

On the basis of this belief, I have had always a certain degree of optimism, although as I have grown older, the optimism has grown more sober and the happy issue more distant. The causes of unhappiness in the past and in the present are not difficult to ascertain. There have been poverty, pestilence and famine, which were due to man's inadequate mastery of nature. There have been wars, oppressions and tortures which have been due to men's hostility to their fellow men. And there have been morbid miseries fostered by gloomy creeds, which have led men into profound inner discords that made all outward prosperity of no avail.[1]

When authority and the dominant social order violated common sense, elementary political liberties or economic needs, Russell would become aroused to radical politics in pursuit of liberal goals. But, significantly, his liberalism derived from the radical movement in early bourgeois society—its revolutions and its boldest reforms. Later liberalism often offended Russell as jaded and a veiled apology for the established order. Russell was to be in conflict periodically with liberals and social democrats who embraced an ageing capitalism which inherited the ruling role of privilege and authority it had earlier dethroned. In the First World War, these sentiments crystallized in Russell's thinking and experience.

An understanding of the confidence and anachronistic recklessness with which an aristocratic Russell embraced radical positions requires an appreciation of a bizarre feature of British history, the absence of a genuine bourgeois revolution in England. The Glorious Revolution deferred it and the defeat of the French Revolution aborted it. British landed aristocracy instead effected bourgeois reforms, presiding over that improbable miscegenation wherein rising industrialists were made aristocrats by decree.

One architect of this unwieldly class amalgam was Russell's grandfather. Lord John visited Napoleon at Elba and introduced that paradigm of bourgeois legislation, the Reform Bill of 1832. He removed legal disabilities from the Jews and effected free trade. The formal Empire was forestalled in favour of a liberal version of neo-colonial penetration of world markets. The Whigs shaped Bertrand Russell. Mill was his godfather and Lord John his guardian who raised him. "History stops in 1815," Russell was fond of saying, "after that it's gossip, family gossip."

The death of his parents, who were advocates of contraception, free thinking and women's suffrage, led to the setting aside of their will, which had provided for Russell to be raised by bohemian and radical pre-Raphaelites. Instead, he suffered the disciplinarian and austere household of his eminent grandparents. He was afflicted by loneliness, terrible isolation and pain. The passion engendered by his loss imparted to his politics their peculiar driving force. He acted out in his public life the isolation and sense of personal injury which he had felt so early. The unfairness and irrationality of this sudden onslaught upon his infant life, brought about by the death of both his parents within

---

[1] *Portraits from Memory*, New York 1969, p. 55.

months of each other, compelled him to seek out and to rail against apparent injustice. He would switch from one political posture to another while bringing to bear the same conviction, because he felt that whatever wrong he perceived at a given moment deserved it.

When the First World War broke out, I thought it was a folly and a crime on the part of every one of the Powers involved on both sides. I hoped that England might remain neutral and when this did not happen, I continued to protest. I found myself isolated from my former friends and, what I minded even more, estranged from the current of the national life.

This theme of isolation is repeated throughout his life.

The end of the First War was . . . the prelude to an even more complete isolation.[1]

It was an isolation attendant upon publication of *The Practice and Theory of Bolshevism* (1920). In this book Russell warned of authoritarian tendencies in Leninism and reacted strongly to the cultural primitivism he saw in Russia, particularly as it reflected itself within the Bolshevik party. The magnitude of the bureaucratic tyranny which emerged under Stalin was not imagined by Russell. The police state, later to be installed and cemented with mass murder, required the physical liquidation of the Bolshevik leadership and a total dismantling of their political institutions. Russell, having been prescient about the incipient degeneration of revolutionary power, was later misled by his own initial insight, because he saw continuity rather than demolition in the development from Lenin's soviets to Stalin's labour camps. But in this book he professed himself at one with the aims of Bolshevism while warning of elitism and intolerance in the leadership. Thus, his sympathies with the revolution isolated him from established opinion and his harsh criticisms of the Bolsheviks alienated him from friends who preferred applause to analysis.

The leitmotif emerges strongly in a mock obituary written by him in 1937:

By the death of the third Earl Russell . . . a link with the very distant past is severed. . . . [His] outlook, which is reminiscent of Bentham, has become rare in this age. . . . His life for all its waywardness had a certain anachronistic consistency, reminiscent of that of the aristocratic rebels of the early 19th century. His principles were curious, but such as they were, they governed his actions . . . politically, during his last years, he was as isolated as Milton after the Restoration. He was the last survivor of a dead epoch.[2]

An aspect of his own sense of being out of step was the stridency with which he would uphold any view even if it invalidated an earlier judgment. He was also prone to praise opinions or acts which seemed to him just, even if he were

[1] ibid., pp. 6, 7.
[2] *Unpopular Essays*, New York 1950, p. 173.

approving those with whom he was in general disagreement. After a scathing assessment of the German Marxists in his first book, he writes:

[Their opposition to the Franco-Prussian war was] one of the most honourable facts in their whole history.[1]

He would, moreover, determine his attitude to others on the basis of how they measured up to his sense of rectitude, for he suspected that people had an infinite capacity to rationalize the offences of their side. Hence, he seemed to them unpredictable, wayward and flighty.

Russell attributed all subsequent disasters—from Italian and German fascism to the Second World War—to the First World War. His support of the pacifist movement in its opposition to the First World War did not, as widely alleged, mean that he was a pacifist.[2]

Neither then nor later did I think all war wrong. It was *that* war, not all war that I condemned.[3]

In 1937, when the prospect of a second inter-imperial world conflict seemed imminent, Russell opposed all sides equally. In his mock obituary written in that year he predicted:

In the Second World War, he (Russell) took no public part, having escaped to a neutral country before its outbreak. In private conversation, he was wont to say that homicidal lunatics were well employed in killing each other but that sensible men would keep out of their way while they were doing it.[4]

This was the thesis of *Which Way to Peace?* in which he recommended that invading German troops should be treated as tourists. He was to become ashamed of that book and of the pacifist stance he took towards Hitler's Germany. But he had grasped that Britain and France were in conflict with Germany for reasons of imperial rivalry, markets and colonial domain. Sane men would not be forced to choose between them. Here is a further instance of Russell's radical impulse transcending his Whig frame of reference. The Marxist view of the Second World War was little different from its assessment of the First World War, and this too was Russell's response. Both sides were seeking markets and exploited their people through a ruling class. The business of socialists was to

[1] *German Social Democracy*, New York 1965, p. 81.

[2] Later, during his opposition to the war in Indo-China, the press universally described him as a pacifist. This was because if he were against any war on principle, his specific charges of aggression, imperialism and atrocity could be discounted.

[3] *Portraits from Memory*, p. 6.

[4] *Unpopular Essays*, pp. 174-5.

oppose all these regimes rather than support one against the other. Nonetheless, when Hitlerism became transparent, Russell abandoned his view.

Very largely as a result of our follies, Nazi Germany had to be fought if human life was to remain tolerable.[1]

Thus, he found himself supporting conservative regimes because of the circumstance of their opposition to Hitler. This orthodoxy with respect to the Second World War was to colour his politics for fifteen years.

Russell was now caught in a familiar dilemma. He wanted to oppose Nazism and he distrusted the governments of the Western powers. These were the same States which had launched the First World War. He perceived no alternative to supporting these regimes in Britain and the United States. That *they* were concerned solely with establishing an imperial order of their own was an idea he himself had voiced. But his political inclinations involved appeals to reasonable men, hoping to dissuade them from folly. He did not often act as if he were confronting a structure of power whose thrust transcended the vagaries of particular leaders and whose institutions disallowed the changes he sought from those who manned them. When methods of gentle argument in the form of articles or addresses proved inadequate he would agitate among the populace, but still out of the hope that officialdom could be induced to act differently by resulting pressure.

In sum, his radical periods were in pursuit of liberal ends; when he abandoned his radical politics of method, he was swiftly assimilated by established power. In failing to persist in his critique of British and American capitalism because they were now in conflict with fascist states, he prepared to sanction the cold war which followed the Second World Imperial Conflict. This development was rooted as well in the fact that Russell did not, at heart, believe the wars and social evils he perceived to be irretrievably part of the fabric of capitalist society. He harboured the wish that public pronouncements in the name of common sense could turn the tables.

In crisis he would go beyond the appeals to governments and seek in popular movements the lever with which to pressure change in state policies. At these moments he would assume the mantle of a radical agitator, if not organizer. But he was, even at these times, inhibited by his fears that revolutionary struggle would not necessarily end the wars and injustices he opposed. Most important of all, Russell did not acknowledge any social agency of the revolutionary transformation to which he implicitly aspired. The working class was not evident to him as this agency because its subjective consciousness appeared to him a barrier to the implementation of what had to be done. And lacking a route to such an agency of drastic change, Russell condemned himself to the role of gadfly—an individual who could rail and rally but ultimately on his

---

[1] *Portraits from Memory*, p. 7.

own and in self-effected isolation. In truth, he found this posture at once more suited to his political abilities and his personal need.

There were, however, serious intellectual doubts which inhibited him from engaging wholeheartedly in mass movements with revolutionary aims. He felt that cultural excellence and unique achievement were the product of favoured circumstance. The tutoring, elite schooling and other accoutrements of class privilege seemed to him responsible for outstanding achievement and, although he disliked the undemocratic, he distrusted the assumption that its removal would have no detrimental consequences. Russell had many aristocratic attributes which infused his entire sensibility. It provided him with strength when standing out against orthodoxy but it sapped his confidence in the outcome of dramatic change. He was influenced by bourgeois trepidations which dissolved revolutionary transformation into categories like "mass society". He felt that excellence came from the special nurturing of individual talent and that mediocrity or cultural decline would follow the overthrow of privilege. He desired its overthrow but he mourned in advance some of the consequences as he saw them. Russell knew that oppressed peoples harboured talented women and men denied the opportunity to grow. But he did not believe in the creative energy and untapped possibilities in great masses of ordinary men and women, except perhaps as an abstract hope for a distant future.

Great evils, such as nuclear war or the genocidal conflict inflicted on the Vietnamese, moved him to place these reservations far behind the moral imperative of action against barbarity. If social upheaval set back cultural advance for a time, it was a lesser price to pay than acquiescence in butchery. But this very formulation expressed his scepticism regarding the liberation assumed by revolutionaries for society at large.

Russell, despite his criticisms of elitism, did not believe that impoverished or uneducated people would quickly overcome deprivation. The consequences of denial might last generations. It followed that venality and irrationality would not disappear the moment radical change had occurred. Powerful figures employing revolutionary rhetoric and pretension would cloak their own ambitions as they exploited people anew. But the new injustice would be harder to oppose because it presented itself in the garb of revolutionary emancipation. And in colonial countries, change would entail dislocation of a magnitude creating chaos and an ensuing coercion required to install a stable regime. Cultural backwardness would prevent popular control from taking hold for long. Russell did not believe that peasants or workers were capable of controlling the functionaries who would administer. In his heart, he was not certain it was desirable they should. He harboured ideas of more than cultural inferiority and could not entirely accept that cultural and technological deprivation were caused by exploitation alone. Implicit here was a racial judgment, which often led him to feel that revolution in the colonial world would produce regimes worse than those displaced.

There was a perpetual conflict in him between his loathing for unjust or privileged rule and his distrust of the inherent capacity of the deprived. He tended, therefore, to temper his opposition to governmental injustice by avoiding allegiance to mass movements for the establishment of popular power. All of these fears had been made a central part of his political thought by Stalin's consolidation of power, which brought to pass, on a scale which his most nightmarish imaginings had not anticipated, those very evils which inhibited him from going beyond vocal dissent.

The radical component of his Whig sensibility had been checked by Stalin's crimes. The regime in Russia gave play in Russell to the other element of bourgeois thought, a distrust of the ultimate capacities of masses of men and a sense that a cultivated stratum of responsible people should somehow prevail. It was always clear to him that states and rulers would commit follies requiring opposition, but Stalin reconciled him more readily to his own society. Russell did not perceive the break in continuity between the Bolshevik revolution and Stalin and he became an active anti-Communist. He did so because he fully believed Stalin's self-serving and false contention that Stalinism continued the politics of Marx and Lenin in Russia and in the world at large.

With the end of the Second World War, Russell became pre-occupied by two questions: nuclear weaponry and Stalin's police tyranny. In Stalin's state of privileged autocrats professing to represent a political movement of liberation and equality, Russell saw more than Bonapartist degeneration. The fate of the Russian revolution deepened, indeed fixed, his apprehension that this was a probable fate both of revolutionary politics and revolutionary parties. This cut him off from avenues without which he lacked any vision of how his own aspirations for society might be implemented or how he might sustain the social struggles he periodically felt compelled to espouse.

In 1945 Russell warned in the House of Lords of the feasibility of a fusion weapon. Unless, he argued, disarmament occurred before that moment, the arms race would produce a war of global destruction. He could find no method or political stratagem for avoiding this calamity. He favoured a world government and for years associated himself with world federalist societies. Once again he reverted to the classic nineteenth-century liberalism which had shaped him. Such a world government was to be effected through agreement by member states who would surrender their sovereignty to the world body even as local regions had come to do in the formation of the nation state. But the problem with this perspective lay in the fact that the rulers of states with clashing economic and political interests were to be the authors of a world order which pre-supposed transcending those interests.

Since only powerful states could enforce this agreement, Russell's quest for world order reduced itself to an appeal for a great power *modus vivendi*, carving up the planet and ratifying the division of spoils in a formal agreement backed by the armed forces of the participating states. Nonetheless, implicit in Russell's pursuit of some form of emergency agreement between the great powers was an end to his advocacy of the cold war. To urge such collaboration precluded being a partisan of either side. Russell hoped that, in time, the world body itself would become the dominant authority, its power transcending the particular national units composing it. There was no room for social revolution in this schema. Russell, in his preoccupation with the devastating consequences of a new war, was inclined to let other problems take care of themselves. His Whiggism perceived the states involved as power units and the social composition or class character of these states was of marginal interest when compared to the dangers of war.

There was, however, a considerable lag in Russell's thinking. Although advocating world government, until the H-bomb test of 1954 he remained fixed in his stance of cold warrior. Stalin's Russia presented a picture of secret police, brutal suppression of all political and cultural freedom, concentration camps, and the cynical use of Aesopian language to describe official policy. 'Peace loving', 'democratic', 'progressive', and other words of good coin were invoked to describe their opposite. Russell reacted to Stalin's Russia with revulsion and fear. Unlike many liberals and social democrats, he had not been an apologist for Stalin between 1927 and 1945. But like them he accepted Stalin's claim that his regime and the politics of the Stalinist movement were Marxism and Bolshevism in practice and theory.

This is crucial in understanding Russell's political advocacy. As long as he accepted that Stalinism was Marxist practice, he was rendered an unwitting supporter of a series of official lies in the West, in their way as Aesopian and concealing of cruelty as those which shocked him in Russia. The main difference is that the victims of capitalism were most visible in the colonies during this period, while those of Stalin inhabited his national territory or border states absorbed within it. Russell's strength derived from the fact that he had never apologized for Stalin's crimes because they were labelled socialist, a claim few liberals or social democrats, from Shaw to the Webbs, could make. But Russell now swallowed the fiction that Stalin's Russia was bent upon world conquest through revolutionary war, espionage and intrigue. He saw a direct relationship between the absence of internal democracy in Russia and an adventurist policy of military conquest. He did not understand that the privileged and autocratic caste which had usurped the revolution in Russia feared revolution in other countries because the spread of revolution undermined their control over the anti-capitalist movement. It would cause their criminal acts to be criticized, exposed and resisted in the name of revolution itself.

Here was a Russia which, under Stalin, had opposed a revolution in China in 1927, making Chiang Kai-shek a member of the Communist International. It had prevented through the Comintern a single strike or street demonstration in opposition to Hitler by a German Communist party able to poll ten million votes. It had opposed socialist revolution in Spain from 1936 to 1939, prevented it in France and Italy in 1945, supported the French occupation of Indo-China and North Africa and signed an agreement at Yalta and Potsdam opposing any revolutionary development in Indo-China for twenty-five years. As late as 1949, months before the defeat of Chiang, Stalin was urging upon the Chinese a coalition under Chiang's rule.

Apart from the counter-revolutionary dynamic of the foreign policy of Stalin's regime, in the aftermath of the Second World War Russia was so decimated that it hardly possessed a standing factory. It had nearly thirty million more women than men. Millions of those able-bodied men alive in Russia were in forced labour camps under the guard of tens of thousands more. The United States had dropped atomic bombs on Japan six months *after* Japan had sued for surrender, signalling a willingness to use this weapon against the Soviet Union. The United States possessed a nuclear monopoly and a vast preponderance of productive power.

Western capitalism presented this Russia as a revolutionary power bent upon world military conquest! This fiction was trumpeted precisely to disguise the displacement by the United States of the colonial powers as American capitalism sought world conquest for its investments and control. Ironically enough, because liberals and social democrats had for almost twenty years accepted Stalin's description of his brutal regime as socialist and humane, because they had applauded his reactionary foreign policy which sought sphere of influence accommodations in exchange for the active undermining of the revolutionary movement in other countries, these liberals and social democrats were now morally impotent to expose the cynical decrying by the Western powers of the nature of Stalin's rule. They now repeated for Western capital what they had performed for Stalin: they concealed the nature of the regime. It was American capitalism which deployed the reaction to Stalinism to mask its own plans for world control conducted in the name of protecting a free world. The Stalinist movement itself, calling itself Communist and revolutionary, lent verisimilitude to the propaganda of Western capital because each purge trial and suppression of liberty in Eastern Europe was hailed as democratic and progressive. But Stalin, through the wholesale killing of Bolshevik leaders and cadre, had long achieved the transformation of the Communist movement from an international league of revolutionists committed to lead popular revolutionary movements, into unquestioning agents of a clique's view of Russian state interests. These interests invariably sacrificed revolutionary possibility to cynical diplomatic deals or criminal adventures with the same end. The sordidness of this configuration served to depoliticize many and, in Russell's case, to reconcile him to the legitimacy of capitalist rule.

It was to be the war in Vietnam which enabled Russell to see in retrospect for the first time the dynamics of American foreign policy. But in 1945, pillaging the planet, usurping world resources, using military and financial "aid" to resurrect corporate capital, installing puppet regimes and pursuing counter-revolutionary war—none of these stratagems was remotely apparent to Russell as the real pattern and practice of American power. On the contrary, he perceived only the façade of that power, its formal democracy and its tolerance of civil liberty. The war in Vietnam crystallized for Russell as for others the possession of the State by a ruling class of concentrated capital, and he then understood that civil liberty was allowed because, through empire, American capital was able to forestall economic hardship and the ensuing mass disaffection which would challenge capitalism in the heartland.

At the end of the Second World War, such a view would have seemed to him out of keeping with evident reality, a mechanical and vulgar Marxism believed only by satraps of Stalin. He believed then that America and Britain were not only democratic in political life, but defensive in relation to Russia. The Russian menace and threat of war, manufactured so cynically, was believed by him.

When the United States made perfunctory proposals to disarm contingent upon a permanent inspection within Russia tantamount to espionage, Russell advocated this policy. Thus when Bernard Baruch called in 1947 for a pooling of nuclear energy under the aegis of the United Nations, Russell supported this plan as a concrete step towards a monopoly of nuclear arms by a world authority. The Baruch plan had two objectives. It would have frozen nuclear weapons before Russia could develop its own weaponry, rendering American nuclear hegemony permanent. It made the United Nations the regulatory and inspecting body. But the Russians were as aware as anyone else that the United States financed the United Nations and controlled it politically, and that United Nations functionaries from participating states were universally wealthy, conservative members of their own ruling class. It was a disarmament plan designed to legitimize rapid US rearmament and the arming of Western Europe.

Russell believed that political democracy was threatened by Russia, and panicked. He feared that unless Stalin were prevented immediately from extending his rule, an inevitable nuclear arms race would ensue, leaving people the invidious choice of acquiescence in such conquest or one hundred million dead in a nuclear war. Thus, to Russell, the Baruch plan was a last hope for internationalizing atomic energy. Stalin's rejection of it persuaded Russell that to avoid a nuclear war in the future, preventative war should be threatened unless Stalin gave way. He no more perceived that American power and its military bases installed or preserved client regimes than he grasped that the formal democracy retained in North America and Western Europe was tenuously linked to the continued despoliation of three continents.

All these relationships, derived from a Marxist critique of capitalism as an international phenomenon, were obscured by observing capitalism as it worked at the centre of privilege. It was rather like gauging the industrial revolution by examining the art collection of the mine owners while ignoring the men in the pits. Russell, however, was in this period mainly concerned to expose the dangers of Stalinism and to act against its threat to liberty as the Western capitalists defined it. He acted openly for the British government and undertook on their behalf an official mission to urge West German resistance to the Berlin blockade. In 1950 he went to Norway urging immediate membership in NATO. He did not yet perceive the thrust of post-war American policy to displace European colonialism with its own capital penetration. The end of the British empire was evident to him and welcome. But the advent of the American empire was hidden from him by the fact that Stalin's tyranny permitted this American power to present its rapacity in defensive terms.

Nor did he see the end of colonialism as a formal development, important as Indian independence had been to him. He had been President of the India League with Krishna Menon as his secretary, but he did not yet understand the role of the Indian national bourgeoisie as guardians of foreign capital in the sub-continent. It took the Sino-Indian conflict and his perception of Nehru's regime as a foil for US Asian strategy, to which he came after involvement with the events, for such relationships to become part of his own political understanding.

Unlike many who were appalled by Stalin, Russell did not abandon a passionate role in political life. Some former radicals, who had been taken in, compensated by manning the cultural barricades of the CIA, even as they had, with Stalin's blessing, administered the predecessor of the CIA, the OSS. They were now jaded, disillusioned and impotent. Russell did not defend Western capitalism and its foreign interests out of apostasy. He was convinced that Western bourgeois democracy both possessed greater liberty and less inclination to visit war on mankind than did Stalin's Russia. But he soon discovered that his anti-Communist colleagues were not truly distressed by Stalin's hostility to civil liberty, for they eagerly supported the elimination of the civil liberties of Communists, critics of American policy and opponents of capitalism.

Sidney Hook and various intellectuals in the Congress of Cultural Freedom were shocked to discover that Russell's anti-Stalinism was principled. He hated the lack of freedom in Russia and thus would not tolerate a witch-hunt in the United States. He was forced to resign. Thus, two interlocking developments began to cause a shift in his thinking. First, the acquisition of nuclear weapons by the Soviet Union, and secondly the rampant assault on civil liberty, academic freedom and critical intelligence in the United States. The FBI and the investigating committees, which aimed at preventing any opposition to foreign wars or the consolidation of capitalist power, began to shake Russell in his estimate of the political democracy practised in the West.

A third factor should be mentioned. Russell became worried by the fact that he was taken up by the establishment. He had been totally and ruthlessly attacked for his opposition to the First World War. It wasn't merely his dismissal from Cambridge, his imprisonment or being banned from the coasts on the ground that he would signal to U-boats. It was also the silence and collusion of his closest colleagues. When these very types began to acclaim him, when the BBC wanted him for Third Programme talks, when Cambridge invited him and King George awarded him an Order of Merit, he became worried. And when he received the Nobel Prize, now nearly eighty, not for his technical work but for literature, Russell smelled a rat. "I used to look at myself in the mirror," he would tell me, "and ask myself what despicable thing have I done to gain favour with these scoundrels?" It worked at him. He knew intuitively that he was serving ends not his own and he knew it before he arrived at an intellectual formulation of it.

Russell believed that good men were in jeopardy when mediocre men did them honour. It was not to be long before these admirers were writing attacks on his rashness, impetuousness, gullibility and senility, returning to their form of the First World War. No awards came then. "You'll see," he often told me, "they won't wait five minutes after my eyes close before they claim the corpse." As it was they moved quicker than that.

The Bikini tests of 1954 were a watershed in Russell's political life. H-bombs in production posed the question of annihilation of the planet. He pulled sharply away from the political direction of the previous ten years. He felt that the human race would die out, and soon, unless an international authority could achieve disarmament, especially nuclear disarmament.

Russell undertook to organize a movement of scientists from East and West to propose solutions to the arms race. He wrote to Einstein, who signed jointly with him an appeal he drafted. He read it over the BBC at Christmas. It was entitled "Man's Peril".

There lies before us, if we choose, continued progress in happiness, knowledge and wisdom. Shall we instead choose death because we can not forget our quarrels? I appeal as a human being to human beings. Remember your humanity and forget the rest. If you can do so the way lies open to a new Paradise; if you cannot, nothing lies before you but universal death.[1]

The mood was much accentuated by Stalin's death. The prospect of change in Russia influenced Russell, for a nuclear arms race made even less sense. Russell now engaged Khrushchev, Eisenhower and Dulles in an exchange. He was very much affected by the invasion of Suez as it showed the dominating colonialism of Western capitalism to be intensely alive. And if the crushing of the Hungarian revolution appalled him, it carried with it the possibility of continued resistance to the Stalinist regimes which Russell had feared were immutable and impossible to overcome. Khrushchev's conciliatory tone in the

---

[1] ibid., p. 238.

debate influenced him further. Russell viewed willingness to reach disarmament agreements as the transcendent issue. It was against the grain for him to acknowledge that the Russians had persistently offered disarmament pacts and security agreements to the Western powers which were rejected.

Gradually, through his own direct involvement, Russell saw that the United States was pressing the arms race both because the military expenditure stabilized capitalism and because the world was to be policed for counter-revolution. But in the early stages, he interpreted this as old habit, or maintaining an arms race for its own sake. That the Russians were seeking to curtail it and reach agreement was puzzling to him. In seeking to explain this, he moved in surprising directions. First, he began to accept that militarism was economically linked to American capitalism. Secondly, he began to see that American militarism was part of an imperial thrust designed to defend markets, install puppet regimes and crush any social revolution which dared challenge this global control.

This emerging view of American power and of capitalism was not easily arrived at and was slow to come. He resisted the evidence and accepted it painfully, and then from one whom he had come to trust. It shattered almost all his political preconceptions about the cold war and the nature of Stalinism. If American capitalism were a malignant world force imposing an arms race, how was he to assess the Soviet pursuit of accommodation with such an imperial system?

Only now did Russell begin to reassess his view of Stalin and his regime. Whereas before Russell had considered the threat of military expansion to emanate from Russia, now, in retrospect, he began to see Stalin as the constant maker of global deals—with Hitler, with Churchill and with Roosevelt and Truman—deals aimed not at advancing revolution but at aborting it in exchange for capitalist support for his own regime. Moreover, if the thrust towards world domination and world intervention were American, then acquiescence in this by the Soviet Union was to be regarded in a very different light. Seen from this perspective, Russian reasonableness and accommodation were not a virtue, but a different kind of crime. For it entailed a willingness to police the world jointly with the capitalist states and to use Communist parties globally to prevent revolution, not make it.

Over this ten-year period beginning in 1955 Russell moved from a view of Stalin and of Soviet policy which saw them as aggressive to one which viewed them as conciliatory. As Russell undertook campaigns specifically directed against US imperialism and sought the counsel of close associates concerned with the conduct of these campaigns, he moved to a view of Stalin and his successors which saw them make deals, like those made by gangster trade union leaders with large corporations at the expense of the rank and file. Stalin's tyranny now was associated not with foreign adventure but with avoidance of international revolution, for fear of revolutionary consequences within Russia itself.

The path upon which Russell set his foot in 1955 led him slowly to a political posture one hundred and eighty degrees from his starting point. He was propelled by feverish involvement in the events of the period but also by a particular association. At the time of his early involvement in the Campaign for Nuclear Disarmament he served as its honorary President. As such he did not play a direct role; he spoke periodically to mass rallies but left the operation of the Campaign to such as its chairman, Canon Collins of St. Paul's.

As a mood developed for more radical action than the Campaign's leadership desired, I approached Russell with plans for a movement of mass civil disobedience capable of obstructing the nuclear facilities and leading to large strikes on the part of rank and file trade unionists. Russell had felt himself very much a figurehead in the CND, and yearned to make a significant difference in the world, despite his great age. He wished to influence the times drastically in a direction away from mass destruction but he did not see how to go about it. He was drawn to my plans and to the radical enthusiasm with which they were advanced. It stimulated him to be joined to the prospect of a developing movement and he appealed to me to undertake it. In so doing, Bertrand Russell now entered an arena of strategy, tactics, organization and police repression. His own energy and determination were considerable, but he looked to me to make these aspirations actual. He often felt unsure and sought a trusted intimate whose enthusiasm might sustain his own. Because my own views were anti-capitalist and moving in a revolutionary direction, it was inevitable that our endless discussions and plans would bear the imprint of this association.

The radical character of his transformation was considerable. The hostility now directed towards him because of it was not feigned. Those in power or fawning upon it were appalled by the spectre of Russell's great international prestige mobilized in support of social revolution at home and abroad. As the authorities felt that the vigour of a younger man, who would enlarge Russell's impact by granting it organizational form, was particularly dangerous, steps were taken. After three imprisonments, deportation proceedings were begun against me, even as my extradition had earlier been sought. The ancient cry of "outside agitator", invoked by authority to discount the possibility of indigenous disaffection, was now modified to suit the circumstance. Russell, it was widely suggested, had fallen under an evil and manipulative influence, one who exploited the failing powers of a once grand old man.

The press and other media sincerely disbelieved that a man of such remarkable independence of mind would, in his late eighties, change so drastically his approach to the world. But despite the constant appearances of Russell on television, the public speeches and the endless interviews—activity scarcely possible in one of tired mind—the press continued to chorus that he was senile and used. It was more palatable to maintain that Russell had been taken over by a sinister young revolutionary, and many of the perpetrators of the fable believed it. Its power derived partly from the great disparity in our ages but also from the fact that it touched a partial truth. Russell needed someone who could represent him, shield him in part from the onslaughts of the media, engage organizationally in the events of the day and whose strong convictions would correspond to his own. It went without saying that such a relationship required trust even as it reflected influence. Both the government and the press concentrated on this relationship as a way of avoiding having to engage the issues on their merits and as a means of insulating the public from the impact of Russell's advocacy. But the more feverishly his enemies sought to separate us, the more intense and important became the friendship and political partnership. There was a growing dialectic between Russell's association with bitter social struggles against the established order, his alienation from servers of power and fence-sitters, and a deepening dependence upon the young revolutionary with whom he worked to these ends. He sometimes pulled back when unnerved by the direction his involvement was leading him. These hesitations covered such later occurrences as the aid provided to armed revolutionary struggles by the Russell Foundation or the financial and other support received by us from governments and revolutionary movements. In weighing these decisions, which were so removed from the political choices facing him in tamer times, he counted upon and trusted my judgment.

His wife and his more conventional friends, whose views were not his own, could neither grasp nor sympathize with such politics and wished him out of it. The feverish activity, the unbridled animus of the public media, the steady stream of exotic and unfamiliar visitors, the secret plottings and ambitious plans—all these alarmed and unsteadied the staid companions of quieter days. "Bertie," Edith Russell would call out, "there's a black man coming to see you!" "Oh," Russell would reply, "Where's he from?" "Greece, Turkey, one of those places," would be the disgusted answer.

They feared personally the deadly hostility of the State. They blamed, resented and connived against the political associate and friend whom Russell had sought out and to whom he had become so close. They brought inordinate pressure on Russell to desist. This domestic situation was an open secret, one others tried to exploit for similar ends. As long as his strength lasted, Russell would not accede to the pressures or demands.

I will now turn to Russell's writings of this period to impart something of the flavour of the transformation that took place in him. In 1959, when he had moved to a posture of seeking to mediate between the two blocs and to effect agreements, Russell wrote as follows in *Common Sense and Nuclear Warfare*:

The peril involved in nuclear war is one which affects all mankind and one, therefore, in which the interests of all mankind are at one . . . The arguments that should be employed in a campaign against nuclear weapons are such as should appeal with equal force to Eastern and Western blocs and also to uncommitted nations since they are concerned solely with the welfare of the human species as a whole.[1]

Two years later, in 1961, Russell's involvement in open anti-State activity impelled him to re-examine the relationship between war and exploitation in *Has Man A Future?*:

More than half the population of the world is undernourished, not because it need be, but because the richer nations prefer killing each other to keeping the poorer nations alive and helping them to achieve a higher standard of living. Nothing . . . induces the richer nations to help the others except the hope of buying their support in the cold war. Why should we not, instead, use our wealth to buy their support for a secure peace? . . . There is a fear fostered by those who are interested in the armament industry that disarmament might cause a disastrous economic dislocation.[2]

By 1963 Russell had been involved in the Cuban crisis and the Sino-Indian conflict and was clarifying the perceptions he had gained about the aggressiveness of American capital. He stated in *Unarmed Victory*:

I dislike Communism because it is undemocratic and capitalism because it favours exploitation. But whenever the question of peace and war is relevant, the merits of either side become insignificant in comparison with the importance of peace . . . It has happened that in the disputes with which this book is concerned the Communist side has been the less bellicose. . .[3]

A year later in 1964 the war in Vietnam galvanized Russell into imparting a decided character to his public views, reflected in *War and Atrocity in Vietnam*:

Should America engage in a naked war of conquest which will be clearly seen as such? . . . Atrocity has characterized the conduct of the war throughout its history . . . [and shows] the extent to which it is possible to hide or disguise terrible crimes . . .[4]

Two months later, in an article significantly entitled "Free World Barbarism", Russell allowed oblique correction of his recent past:

A distressing aspect of world politics is the extent to which liberals and even socialists have accepted the basic assumptions of the large and powerful forces behind the Cold War. The role of the United States as a perpetual intruder in the international affairs of other nations is taken as sacred. The right of the United States to interfere in counties, if the social and political policies of those countries are incompatible with private economic power, is happily accepted. Instead of questioning how private corporate

[1] *Common Sense and Nuclear Warfare*, London 1959, p. 11.
[2] *Has Man a Future?*, London 1961, p. 122.
[3] *Unarmed Victory*, New York 1963, pp. 14–15.
[4] *War Crimes in Vietnam*, New York 1967, p. 56.

capitalism and its overseas commitments have become identified with American interests, liberals and many socialists accept this sinister sleight of hand.[1]

By 1966, in "Peace through Resistance to US Imperialism", the words have an open revolutionary tone:

Throughout the world today increasing numbers of people concerned with peace and with social justice are describing US imperialism as the common destroyer of peace and justice. To some, the expression 'US imperialism' appears a cliché, because it is not part of their own experience. We in the West are the beneficiaries of imperialism. The spoils of exploitation are the means of our corruption. Because imperialism is not part of our experience, we do not recognize the aptness of the description for the economic and political policies of what Eisenhower termed the "military industrial complex".[2]

In the same period, Russell appears no longer in doubt about the action necessary nor, for that matter, in doubt about how to assess conciliation on the part of the Soviet Union towards this imperial power:

If the Soviet Union in its desire for peace seeks to gain favour with the United States by minimizing or even opposing the struggle for national liberation and socialism, neither peace nor justice will be achieved. US imperialism has provided us with all the evidence to which we are entitled as to its nature and practice . . . When the people of Peru, Guatemala, Venezuela, Colombia, Vietnam, Thailand, Congo, the Cameroons, the United States, Britain—all the people demonstrate, struggle and resist, nuclear power is of no avail. Let us join together to resist US imperialism.[3]

In 1967 a call was issued for a War Crimes Tribunal in the following terms:

It is not enough to identify the criminal. The United States must be isolated and rendered incapable of further crimes. I hope that America's remaining allies will be forced to desert the alliances which bind them together. I hope the American people will repudiate resolutely the abject course on which their rulers have embarked . . . I hope that the peoples of the Third World will take heart from the example of the Vietnamese and join further in dismantling the American empire. It is the attempt to create empires that produces war crimes . . . There is only one way to remove starvation and disease in the poor countries—to overthrow the puppet regimes and create a revolution capable of withstanding American power. This is what has happened in Vietnam. This is why the United States has used every form of torture and experimental murder in its efforts to crush the Vietnamese revolution.[4]

Later in the year Russell's article condemns that peaceful coexistence which had governed his thinking in the period of his anti-nuclear agitation:

[1] ibid., p. 56.
[2] ibid., p. 94.
[3] ibid., p. 100.
[4] *Against the Crime of Silence*, New York 1970, pp. 4, 38.

I have supported peaceful coexistence out of the conviction that conflict in a nuclear age can only be disastrous. This conviction was based upon the hope that the US could be persuaded to come to an agreement with socialist and communist countries. It is now painfully clear that US imperialism cannot be persuaded to end its aggression, its exploitation or its cruelty. In every part of the world, the source of war and of suffering lies at the door of US imperialism. Wherever there is hunger, wherever there is exploitative tyranny, wherever people are tortured and the masses left to rot under the weight of disease and starvation, the force which holds down the people stems from Washington.[1]

It is a marked progression from 1945, and we would do well to return to the political point of departure a decade later. When Russell and Einstein issued the appeal to scientists of East and West, they hoped that Nehru would finance and host the first meeting of this movement. At first he agreed, but quickly acceded to US pressure. Onassis offered to foot the bill if the meetings were held in Monte Carlo! This was considered an inappropriate setting and was not accepted. Finally, Cyrus Eaton, the Canadian magnate, agreed to host and finance the first meeting on condition that the Nobel laureates agreed to take the name of the small Nova Scotian village in which Eaton was born. This was the origin of the Pugwash movement which also held its first conference in the village of that name. It was Russell's first organized effort to advance disarmament. The gathering of eminent men of science, particularly from the countries of NATO and the Warsaw Pact, was to seek together the basis for disarmament and then agitate for these agreements among their respective governments. The date was 1955 and the premise guiding both Russell and this movement was that scientists who had expert knowledge on the subject of disarmament need only arrive at agreement on the technical facets of disarmament and the governments would be obliged to pay heed to their findings.

The scientists, however, found themselves divided along political lines. Eaton, who had financed the gathering, knew well that the Russians sought to stabilize the world so they could defend without duress their own social privilege and political control. He was among those North American capitalists who saw in the regime of the Soviet rulers the best agency for preventing social upheaval, because they could expect the Soviet leadership to direct the Communist movement to support stable bourgeois regimes safe for investment.

But American scientists such as Glass, Wiesner, Rabinowitch and Brown aspired to influence policy *à la* Kissinger. They opposed proposals which went beyond limited arms controls. Linus Pauling, on the other hand, led a large agitation against nuclear testing, gathering signatures throughout the world to place before the United Nations. His findings impressed Russell. He showed how nuclear tests killed thousands of unborn in future generations. He calculated the total devastation consequent upon nuclear war. He documented the persistent

---

[1] *War Crimes in Vietnam*, p. 99.

record of American frustration of proposals to regulate Russo-American relations, proposals initiated by the Russians. In doing this, Pauling exposed the extent to which American Pugwash scientists were covert defenders of official American intransigence, often in the pathetic illusion that their influence would be enhanced by appointment to some advisory position. The American scientists engaged in a series of behind the scenes manoeuvres to impugn the scientific integrity and veracity of Pauling, casting doubt both upon his data and his motives. Glass and others wrote along these lines in the *Bulletin of Atomic Scientists* while Rabinowitch, its editor, gave prominence to their attacks and restricted Pauling's replies. Rotblat, the chairman of Pugwash, sympathized with the attacks upon Pauling and manoeuvred to dissuade Russell from supporting Pauling in any way. The campaign against Pauling was as unprincipled as it was venomous, for it was directed not merely against his opinions but against his honour, with consequences affecting his life's work.

As a friend of Pauling's I brought before Russell's notice the full extent of the campaign. Russell was angered and intervened for Pauling which prompted Rotblat to impugn me in turn. It was all rather sordid and neatly indicative of the limitations affecting such conferences where the political colouring of comprising elements went unacknowledged. Russell, in any event, was moving too quickly to be contained within Pugwash politics.

He acted to oppose nuclear testing through a British Committee set up for the purpose. This quickly evolved into a full Campaign for Nuclear Disarmament advocating unilateral British abandonment of the Bomb. With mass rallies and marches the movement acquired substantial support. Its radical wing was led by pacifists who practised small scale civil disobedience. Russell encouraged them.

Many of those in the CND were Labour Party politicians who viewed the Campaign as a vehicle for shifting the Labour Party to a policy of neutralism. Their brief success at one Labour Party convention in 1960 was reversed by Gaitskell in 1961 and now the mood for more radical action expanded dramatically. The mass march in Easter 1959 had drawn one hundred thousand, but we were saying to the movement:

We are living from moment to moment with the imminent prospect of annihilation. The weapons are on a hair trigger. The radar can't tell a goose from a cabinet minister. Join our annual march.[1]

The disparity between the danger described and the remedy offered was too great. Some of us active in the campaign now began to organize mass civil disobedience with a minimum pledged number of participants of two thousand for an action. In this way, we could assure any potential participant that we would go ahead with at least two thousand or delay the action until we had

[1] Leaflet of the Youth Campaign for Nuclear Disarmament, 1959.

such numbers. Thus, we could guarantee the mass character of the demonstration, encouraging many more to come out than might have been the case if a potential participant could not have known in advance whether there would be fifteen or three hundred. I wrote to Russell who asked me to discuss the proposition in detail. It was the beginning of our close association. The Canon of St. Paul's, Chairman of the CND, turned me in to Scotland Yard, but he only incensed Russell, who decided to declare openly for mass civil disobedience.

We invited one hundred prominent people to conspire openly for mass illegal action, daring the government to arrest Henry Moore, Benjamin Britten, Lord Boyd-Orr, Vanessa Redgrave, Augustus John, Robert Bolt, Doris Lessing, etc., etc. The huge growth of the Committee of One Hundred was checked when the government brought out five thousand troops and the police of six counties. The charges were now under the Official Secrets Act and the penalties risked were fourteen years. But we had a Committee of One Hundred in the docks, among the railway workers, steel apprentices and South Welsh Miners. Committees had spread as far as Norway, Germany, Greece and India. The arrests, police raids, press hysteria and physical assaults brought Bertrand Russell at the age of eighty-eight into active leadership of a tumultuous social struggle and completed the process of his alienation from Western capitalism.

Speaking constantly to mass audiences, he declared at the time of the Berlin crisis of 1961 that "Kennedy and Macmillan were worse than Hitler".[1] By 1962, the Committee had been smashed by the repression, but Russell was the acknowledged voice of a world-wide struggle against nuclear war. We were besieged by hundreds of letters weekly. The correspondence with heads of state, rebel leaders in prison such as Ben Bella and with every peace movement was well advanced.

We were approached by a group of huge industrialists led by the Swedish magnate and colleague of Krupp, Axel Wenner-Gren. They, Onassis and Eaton feared their profits would be blown up and favoured a neutral Europe which could trade with the East free of the burdens of NATO and of the domination of American capital. This was a harbinger of the Gaullist current, that disaffection of European capital now strong enough to be wary of their American overlords and with ambitions of their own.

The clandestine murder of Wenner-Gren introduced us to a series of political assassinations, encompassing figures as disparate as the Kennedy brothers and brave comrades ranging from Malcolm X, Pia Gama da Pinto in Kenya, Lumumba in Congo, Ben Barka in Morocco, Felix Moumié in Cameroons and my dear friend Khalid Zaki in Iraq. Khalid had been a close associate in the Foundation.

---

[1] Speech to the first Annual Conference of the Midlands Region Youth Campaign for Nuclear Disarmament, Birmingham, April 5, 1961.

The execution of John Kennedy caused us to establish the *Who Killed Kennedy Committee?*, on the basis of information we obtained from Mark Lane and from the District Attorney's office in Dallas from which a file was photocopied and sent. The investigation documented not only the fraudulence of the Warren Commission Report, but also the role of the US government in the killing, primarily through the Defence Intelligence Agency. Russell's association with the campaign we now launched to make the evidence known inspired a powerful and co-ordinated counter-campaign of vilification orchestrated throughout the established press. It was even more virulent among liberal apologists, including such gadflies as I. F. Stone. Russell's association with this effort, and the article "Sixteen Questions on the Assassination", caused the publication everywhere of attacks asserting his senility and representing me as a manipulator with psychopathic hostility towards the United States.

When all the findings were published in Mark Lane's book *Rush to Judgement*, and later in Jim Garrison's *A Heritage of Stone*,[1] the slanderers of Russell, now proved to be liars, never retracted a word. They merely enlarged the slander for their campaign of abuse over his support of the National Liberation Front in Vietnam. In any event, the international mafia of the CIA was most evident. The knowledge burned away any illusions Russell may have retained about the workings of the military-industrial world order, to which he began to respond as to a gangster league.

The Cubans informed us in mid-1962 of impending invasion and Russell and I tried to alert public opinion. During the missile crisis we were in close touch and negotiations with Khrushchev, Gromyko and other principals. The missiles were ground-to-air, without nuclear warheads, and amply lied about by Kennedy to include in their supposed range cities from which he required majorities. The British foreign minister confirmed the former and Goldwater declared the latter. Step by step the press of events and our continuous dialogue moved Russell beyond neutrality. I carried out a series of meetings with heads of state, taking proposals which we had weighed carefully. The discussions with President Kassim in Baghdad, and with his foreign minister, Hashim Jawad, about oil nationalization were followed in ten weeks by his assassination. I carried proposals from the Egyptian leadership to Ben Gurion, but the negotiations were abortive because the Israelis had no interest in abandoning their role as a vehicle for American power. The Egyptians were ready to persuade the Accra Assembly to assign one million dollars to a Russell Foundation, but our request to Nasser to release one thousand political prisoners, most of them on the left, killed the plan.

This feverish activity in country after country grew apace with the prominence Russell now assumed in the world movement. By creating a

---

[1] Mark Lane, *Rush to Judgment*, New York 1966; Jim Garrison, *A Heritage of Stone*, New York 1970.

Russell Foundation, I was able to deploy this influence to campaign in forty countries for the release of political prisoners, for intervention by Russell commanded response and brought international attention to the plight of the victim concerned. The process entailed intricate negotiations, which took me out of Britain increasingly, and made Russell more vulnerable to the pressures upon him to cut back his activity and moderate his radical direction. But he was still able to reject the suggestion, and the activity intensified. Elaborate negotiations unfolded to secure the release of political prisoners in Eastern Europe and of Jews in the Soviet Union.

Fresh upon the execution of Kennedy, the Johnson regime and its successor proceeded to overthrow Nkrumah, Soekarno, Obote, Ben Bella, Modibo Keita, and Goulart and to murder more revolutionaries. We were again caught up in efforts to warn and to forestall. This growing contact at intimate levels with the so-called neutral states brought us to the conclusion that such regimes, although in conflict with the United States and in quest of greater autonomy, could not spare their people the hunger which arises from exploitation, because of the very bourgeois character of the regimes themselves. Ultimately, they either capitulated to American pressure or fell in CIA coups because they feared to alienate their own privileged class by creating a social transformation for their populace. They thereby forfeited the popular support which was a pre-requisite for resistance to the US coups and plots. After each trip in which we sought to warn regimes of plots against them, I found Russell increasingly responsive to argument about the limitations of such governments and social formations in power.

But the incredible difficulty of challenging American power and economic dominion was dramatized for Russell by the fate of the Vietnamese. It is true that the Sino-Indian war much affected Russell's understanding of the obstacles facing the impoverished. When I saw Nehru, he was virtually under military house arrest as his government carried out military plans to encircle the Chinese revolution. The data provided for us by Chou En-lai during four trips influenced Russell considerably in his approach to world politics. But China's very eagerness for accommodation, which first appealed to Russell in relation to the Indian conflict, came to be understood by him as dangerous to the revolutionary interests of other peoples. Upon returning from Indonesia, I gave him a horrendous account of the bloodbath caused by the CIA coup, costing in a period of three months some one million lives. There the Chinese had supported a policy of collaboration by the Indonesian Communist movement with Soekarno, the spokesman for the Indonesian bourgeoisie. The failure of the Indonesian Communists to allow, let alone lead, a resistance to the fascist coup led to the slaughter. The Chinese party, like its counterpart in the Soviet Union, discouraged revolutionary struggle abroad if it could obtain favourable trade or other dispensations from the Indonesian bourgeois regime of Soekarno. They were to repeat this opportunism in Ceylon, Pakistan, Sudan and Iraq with comparable consequences to the revolutionary struggles in those countries. This paradigm of Stalinist politics was cited to Russell wherever it occurred, and he came to view the Chinese as he had the Russians—not as revolutionists but as functionaries of a privileged caste in power, whose conflicts with imperialism they would resolve where possible at the expense of revolution in other lands.

This was the mood which accompanied our preoccupation with helping movements struggling for revolutionary change in many places. The deep involvement with the Vietnamese revolution was not merely a matter of defending Vietnam from the genocide inflicted upon her by American power. It was as well part of a concern for the global struggle of peoples similarly afflicted and equally determined to withstand the American reprisal. We prepared an appeal to Kosygin to provide Soviet air force as a screen over Vietnam to protect her from the saturation bombings launched day in and out. This public request was made without illusion, for I had amply informed Russell about Kosygin's message of support to the right-wing army coup and its use of Soviet arms in liquidating the Maoist Communist Party of Indonesia. The statements we issued criticized Kosygin's marginal help to Vietnam and called for international support for the Vietnamese through the launching of struggles elsewhere, to spread thin the power of American imperialism. This was the substance of Che Guevara's call, and we became involved in his strategy and his fate.

There were several specific events which deepened the consciousness I sought to impart to Russell concerning the exigencies facing opponents of social oppression. The conspiracy to kill Kennedy, which we had spent much time in documenting and exposing through the *Who Killed Kennedy Committee?*, helped to disabuse Russell of any residual illusion about the character of the power of the Pentagon and intelligence agencies. The murder of Lambrakis, hero of *Z*, who led the march organized by the Bertrand Russell Committee of One Hundred in Greece, made an enormous impression, all the more because our funeral demonstration of 1,000,000 brought down the government.

These were the stages on the road to the Vietnam Solidarity Campaign and the War Crimes Tribunal. This tribunal was designed to provide a Commission of Inquiry to set out in the form of indictment a vast body of *prima facie* evidence concerning genocide in Vietnam. We saw the task to be one of creating a forum for the exposure of data widely known, not acknowledged as such and terrible in their cumulative impact. The attempts to dismiss the Tribunal because it was not a court with subpoena powers were beside the point. It *was* a partial body of committed men with massive evidence which we wished to dramatize. The data and their verifiability were the test, not a fake impartiality which no judge in any trial has ever possessed.

These years brought great internal strife. The Soviets and the French Communists opposed the Tribunal as too radical, seeking as they do for an accommodation with the United States at the expense of the revolution in South

Vietnam. The very dependence of the Vietnamese on the trickle of Sino-Soviet aid rendered them vulnerable to the placement by Russia and China of their state interests before the Vietnamese revolution. These disputes were amply reflected within the tribunal

Faced with these problems, we sought to obtain coordinated international support for Vietnam from revolutionary movements in the field, in Latin America and Africa. I went to Bolivia for six months with a Foundation team. During this period the press attacks were unmerciful. Hacks such as Flora Lewis wrote the most blatant abuse, such as her absurd statement in *Look* magazine that Russell had had an affair with his wife's sister. It was not merely that Russell was then in his nineties, but that his wife did not have a sister! Lewis's British equivalent was Bernard Levin, who also specialized in the most scurrilous abuse, focused upon Russell's mental acuity.

The murder of Che and the machinations of the pro-Soviet Communist Party of Bolivia undercut Foundation plans. As the Czechoslovak struggle against Stalinism unfolded in 1968, we warned against Soviet intervention and sought to build support for the Czechs. The invasion of Czechoslovakia by a half million Soviet troops moving to the borders of West Germany occurred without so much as a NATO alert, let alone an alarmed response from the United States.

We had warned of a *quid pro quo* whereby a free hand for Stalinism faced with socialist revolt in Czechoslovakia was exchanged by the United States for a free hand to bomb in Indo-China. This was alluded to by Brezhnev to Svoboda in Moscow and expanded upon by Czech participants in our Stockholm conference. I had spent five months preparing this conference in support of the Czechs. But 1968 proved a decisive year.

Over the years, the funding of the plethora of activities of the Russell Foundation had been a critical problem, resolved at first through support from sympathizers or from governments sympathetic to facets of our work. We now made a decision to create an archive of Russell's letters and documents, going back over a lifetime and including the most explosive contemporary materials. These brought the prospect of very large sums, and with them a sordid attempt to seize their control, as Russell began to fail. Russell's decline prevented him from playing a part in the troubles afflicting the Foundation, and the Foundation's decline was in step with Russell's.

The British authorities had for years sought to separate me from Russell. Upon my release from prison in Bolivia they finally banned me from returning to Britain. The convergence of Russell's incapacity, my inability to return to the country and the sudden advent of substantial funds made things easier for hangers-on who preferred that the organization concentrate on British questions, foregoing the risks attendant upon involvement with revolutions abroad. Russell's wife was well disposed to this point of view. Suddenly, The Vietnam Solidarity Campaign, of which I was the Chairman and Russell the President, was cut off both from Foundation funds and offices. Five directors and administrators resigned. The dubiousness of these proceedings brought on attempts to associate Russell with this coup, the better to grant it *post hoc* legitimacy. I was summarily removed from the Foundation directorate. The offices of the organization were moved to Nottingham and a rather remarkable period of activity was ended. These events, and the elements involved, will be discussed elsewhere.

Russell had travelled an incredible distance in his political evolution since 1945.

(1) He feared that Stalin's tyranny meant expansion and the danger of a new war.

(2) He regarded such a danger as intolerable if both sides had weapons of mass destruction.

(3) He advocated preventative war against Russia unless Stalin accepted the freezing of nuclear weapons.

(4) Stalin's death and the witch-hunt in the United States caused him to become more neutral between the two giant powers.

(5) H-bomb tests led him to plunge into a Campaign for Nuclear Disarmament and for prevention of the spread of nuclear weapons of mass destruction.

(6) American belligerence and military posture opened his eyes to Soviet conciliation.

(7) Through Pugwash, he inclined to Soviet disarmament proposals.

(8) The CND and Committee of One Hundred threw him actively into a struggle against US militarism and NATO.

(9) The Russell Foundation involved him with neutrals in resisting US pressure and belligerence.

(10) Vietnam brought Russell into the politics of revolutionary war.

(11) He began to view Soviet conciliation towards the United States not as a good, but as an expression of self-serving cynicism.

(12) Russell identified United States imperialism as the primary obstacle to peace and social change.

This evolution grew out of the exigencies of his own activism. It was not an inevitable progress. It would most likely not have occurred without the close association he formed with a young, wilful, radicalizing activist, at the close of the 1950s. He was not always comfortable with the direction he took and the consequent isolation from his family and friends pained him. His role crystallized in 1960 with the formation of the Committee of One Hundred. It was a remarkable renewal at the age of eighty-eight.

The lessons he learned in that decade have been understood by a handful of revolutionaries before him and since. But it is with them that reside the hopes of a liberated world which inspired Bertrand Russell.

Edward F. Sherman

Bertrand Russell and the Peace Movement: Liberal Consistency or Radical Change?

Mr. Schoenman's paper (p. 227) provides an interesting and persuasive account of the evolution of Bertrand Russell's political thought in the post-Second World War period. As Russell's secretary and close companion during most of the 1960s, Mr. Schoenman is in a unique position to discuss the last active phase of Russell's career. This period of Russell's life, when he had forsaken philosophy for political activism, has generally been ignored by scholars, and most of our information about Russell comes from the popular press, which was singularly unsympathetic to his causes. Russell was frequently pictured as a senile old man, no longer capable of creative and discriminating thought, who was being used by radicals for their own political purposes.[1] Mr. Schoenman's account helps to dispel, or at least to modify, that image. He indicates that Russell's intellectual vigour during this period was undiminished and that Russell was responding actively and creatively to the fast-moving political developments in the world around him. Scholarly consideration of Russell's last political period is overdue, and Mr. Schoenman's paper is an important contribution to that enterprise.

A significant theme running through Mr. Schoenman's paper is that Russell's radicalization during the 1950s and 1960s constituted a substantial break from the liberalism which had characterized his political and social philosophy. Mr. Schoenman, of course, played a significant role in this radicalization process as the driving force behind many of the radical political activities of the Russell Foundation in the 1960s. He describes the process as "a growing dialectic between Russell's association with bitter social struggles against the established order, his alienation from servers of power and fence-sitters and a deepening dependence upon the young revolutionary with whom he worked to these ends" and indicates that Russell "sometimes pulled back when unnerved by the direction his involvement was leading him". It is not surprising that Mr. Schoenman, recognizing the importance of his own role in Russell's development, would see Russell's evolution as a break with, indeed a repudiation of, his liberal past. But the intensity of Mr. Schoenman's own Marxist views seems to have affected his perception of the significance of Russell's lifelong liberalism in his political development in the 1960s. Portions of the paper, such as Mr. Schoenman's revisionist theory of post-Second World War history, seem to be

[1] See Levin, "Bertrand Russell: Prosecutor, Judge and Jury", *N.Y. Times Magazine* (19 Feb., 1967), p. 24.

prompted more by his own desire to elaborate an internally-consistent Marxist interpretation than to explain Russell's political thought. It is hard to believe that Russell, who generally eschewed ideological jargon, would have been entirely comfortable with terms like those which crop up throughout Mr. Schoenman's account—like "early bourgeois society", "second inter-imperial world conflict", and "international mafia of the CIA"—or with some of the more involved theories of world-wide capitalist conspiracy suggested by Mr. Schoenman.

There can be no doubt that Russell came to reassess the nature of American capitalism in the 1960s and to consider its Cold War foreign policies as anti-democratic and imperialistic in their world-wide effect. This position, as Mr. Schoenman notes, was a considerable change from Russell's attitudes in the 1950s when fear of Communism and a nuclear holocaust gave him a much more benign view of American policies. But Russell is not unique in making this change in the 1960s, and even the intensity of his anti-Americanism is not unusual. Many liberals of the 1960s had a similar change of heart. It is true that Russell's attack upon American foreign policy in the late 1960s went much farther than the criticisms of most liberals. Russell, in his last political book, *War Crimes in Vietnam* (1967), and in his public pronouncements in the middle and late 1960s, was no longer willing to view Vietnam and other American foreign policy actions simply as mistakes, but saw them as the product of a concerted imperialistic policy controlled by military and corporate interests. He wrote in February, 1965 that America "has developed a new policy, the aim of which is to transfer to America as much as possible of what used to belong to Western European Powers"[1] and thus to preserve colonialism in another form. In his "Appeal to the American Conscience" on 18 June, 1966, Russell said:

From Vietnam to the Dominican Republic, from the Middle East to the Congo, the economic interests of a few big corporations linked to the arms industry and the military itself determine what happens to American lives. It is on their orders that the United States invades and oppresses starving and helpless people.[2]

This is strong stuff, but it is not necessarily uncharacteristic of a liberal sensibility. It does not require a Marxist orientation to recognize in the American military-industrial establishment a capacity for misuse of power and, indeed, for imperialism on a grand scale. Many American liberals had begun in the 1950s to see dangerous interventionist tendencies in American foreign policy and to discern an undue concentration of power in the military-industrial establishment.

Mr. Schoenman shows some ambivalence in his assessment of the degree to which Russell finally embraced Marxism. He states that Russell arrived at a

[1] *War Crimes in Vietnam*, New York 1967, p. 76.
[2] ibid., p. 120.

"consonance with Marxist, indeed, Leninist critiques of the social dynamics of capitalism in an imperial phase" but not because he "shared their philosophical or theoretical assumptions". However, he remarks later in the paper that Russell's attitude "toward capitalism and American imperialism during his last years bears a decidedly Marxist character" which he explains by the fact that Russell "rarely hesitated to accept the correctness of a specific set of data, even when he had rejected the critique derived from it in the form of a universal law or a hypothesis propounding a general theory of society". This assessment is troubling, first, because it assumes that Russell's views were Marxist and second, because the claim that Russell accepted the data as proving the Marxist position even if he couldn't bring himself to accept the general theory is especially patronizing to Russell and self-serving to Mr. Schoenman. This patronizing attitude is also apparent in other places where Mr. Schoenman observes that Russell "did not understand" underlying complexities—such as that Stalinism was not true to Marxism or that the working class possesses sufficient consciousness to be the agency for revolutionary change—always with the implication that Russell finally saw the light, factually if not theoretically, and accepted the Marxist position *à la* Schoenman.

Mr. Schoenman's thesis that Russell's ultimate political development in the 1960s required a rejection of his liberal ideals misjudges, I believe, the nature of contemporary liberalism. Mr. Schoenman states that "Russell's liberalism was that of the bourgeois revolutionary period. The radical assault on arbitrary authority, privilege, suppression of personal liberty and the grosser forms of exploitation—this was the liberalism which suffused his mind." These ideals were certainly at the root of Russell's political liberalism which he fashioned early in his life. However, liberalism is not an immutable creed, nor even an entirely consistent set of political, economic, and social ideals. Liberalism has grown and changed as the twentieth century progressed, as exemplified by the fact that orthodox economic liberals are the conservatives of the twentieth century. Liberalism has, in fact, assimilated a variety of ideas associated with Marx—such as recognition of the potential for class exploitation in a capitalist society—while still rejecting the Marxist emphasis upon historical consistency and inexorability and holding to the Lockean emphasis upon limitation and separation of powers and protection of individual rights.

It is true that liberalism has been less sensitive to the potential for exploitation by nationalistic imperialism at an international level, as demonstrated by the patriotically nationalistic position taken by liberals in both Europe and the United States from the First World War onward (a position rejected by Russell in the First World War and again in the late Cold War and Vietnam War periods). Mr. Schoenman is perceptive in observing that Russell had been obscured from appreciating the imperialistic characteristics of American capitalism in the early Cold War period "by observing capitalism solely as it worked at the centre of privilege". However, the traditional liberal distrust of concentration of power led inevitably to a re-examination of the American employment of its vast military and economic power around the globe, resulting in the conclusion of many liberals by at least the 1960s that the United States, in its "arrogance of power", had become an imperialistic force. Whatever the impact of Mr. Schoenman's Marxism upon Russell, Russell's critique of American foreign policy is consistent with the spirit, though not necessarily the vocabulary, of contemporary liberalism.

Russell's political liberalism was very much related to his philosophical views. Throughout his life he held to similar values in politics and philosophy—he was individualistic rather than state-centred, democratic rather than authoritarian, pragmatic rather than ideological, empirical rather than theoretical, rational rather than emotional, international rather than parochial. These ideals are expressed in his distaste for Plato and Hegel, whom he considered to embody the spirit of totalitarianism. He found them to be refuted not by sceptics, such as Protagoras and Hume, but by empiricists, such as Democritus and Locke:

The only philosophy that affords a theoretical justification of democracy, and that accords with democracy in its temper of mind, is empiricism. Locke, who may be regarded, so far as the modern world is concerned, as the founder of empiricism, makes it clear how closely this is connected with his views on liberty and toleration, and with his opposition to absolute monarchy. He is never tired of emphasizing the uncertainty of most of our knowledge, not with a sceptical intention such as Hume's, but with the intention of making men aware that they *may* be mistaken, and that they should take account of this possibility in all their dealings with men of opinions different from their own.[1]

Russell believed that liberalism was a "recurrent product of commerce",[2] and thus was more likely to provide a political and economic system with a high degree of freedom and individuality. He recognized, however, that the liberal ideal had not actually been accomplished, that capitalism had permitted maldistribution of wealth, and that there could be "an imperialistic commerce" which prevented the free commerce which liberalism sought.[3] Still he clung to the ideals of democracy, anti-authoritarianism, and individualism, always maintaining that somehow those values had to be preserved in any political system. He was a lifelong opponent of Marxism. He heavily criticized Marxist ideology in his 1896 study, *German Social Democracy*, and nothing, even in his last book, *War Crimes in Vietnam*, seems to have changed that assessment. Despite the suggestions by Mr. Schoenman that Russell's disagreement was simply with Stalinism, his opposition to Marxism goes to its basic philosophical tenets. He saw Marx as an outgrowth of Hegel, accusing Marx of taking over

[1] *Unpopular Essays*, New York 1950, p. 14.
[2] ibid., p. 15.
[3] ibid.

"some of his most fanciful tenets, more particularly the belief that history develops according to a logical plan, and is concerned, like the purely abstract dialectic, to find ways of avoiding self-contradiction".[1] Russell's reluctance to view the class struggle as the only way to social change and, as criticized by Mr. Schoenman, his difficulty in accepting the working class as the agency of change is consistent with his opposition to theoretical Marxism. Russell's dislike for the centralization of power in the Party, which he saw as inevitable in a Marxist state, reflected deeply-felt liberal ideals.

Russell recognized that democracy, at least in western Europe and the United States, had failed to accomplish a proper distribution of wealth and that Marxist economics went to the heart of this failure. However, he rejected the political authoritarianism which seemed to accompany Marxism in practice. He wrote, in 1938:

Political democracy, while it solves a part of our problems, does not by any means solve the whole. Marx pointed out that there could be no real equalization of power through politics alone, while economic power remained monarchical or oligarchic. It followed that economic power must be in the hands of the State, and that the State must be democratic. Those who profess, at the present day, to be Marx's followers, have kept only the half of his doctrine, and have thrown over the demand that the State should be democratic. They have thus concentrated both economic and political power in the hands of an oligarchy, which has become, in consequence, more powerful and more able to exercise tyranny than any oligarchy of former times.[2]

Russell's solution was a fairly traditional British liberal philosophy of democratic socialism which put ownership or control of basic industrial enterprises in the government, but attempted to preserve a democratic state. It was a compromise which did not entirely satisfy either his traditional liberal concern with the individual or his social activist desire for greater social and economic justice. However, he accepted the compromise as essential to provide sufficient checks upon the government to prevent totalitarianism. Thus, it is not surprising that Russell should have had such antipathy for Communism under Stalin and yet have been so enthusiastic about it under Ho Chi Minh. In North Vietnam, he saw a government engaged in a nationalistic struggle which enjoyed the overwhelming support of the people. The nation was small enough and the style of Ho Chi Minh plebeian enough to prevent the gulf between the people and the rulers which disturbed Russell in other Communist nations. It had certain elements of a participatory democracy, and even its unfortunate totalitarian aspects, which Russell must have recognized, might be explained by wartime exigencies. This does not mean that Russell had foresaken his carefully-limited liberal-socialistic state model, but that, given the problems of emerging nations

[1] ibid., p. 13.
[2] *Power: A New Social Analysis*, New York 1938, reprinted in R. Egner and L. Denonn (eds.), *The Basic Writings of Bertrand Russell*, New York 1961, p. 669.

struggling against colonialism and underdevelopment, he saw no other effective model.

Russell was an odd mixture of the sensitive social activist and the rational social observer. He was raised in the tradition of enlightened aristocratic liberalism. He says of the British leaders of the 1880s when he was a boy that they were "all 'good' men: they were patient, painstaking, in favour of change only when a detailed and careful investigation had persuaded them that it was necessary in some particular respect. They advocated reforms, and in general their advocacy was successful, so that the world improved very fast; but their temper was not that of rebels."[1] He recognized the failings in this philosophy, but he was also disturbed by their opposites such as the rebels who first attracted notice in the 1890s in the sphere of literature—Ibsen, Strindberg, and Nietzsche —who, he said, were "more sweeping and passionate" but had an "impulse towards destruction and violence".[2] Russell tried to avoid that impulse while still not becoming complacent towards social injustice. He embraced pacifism and proved the strength of his convictions by going to jail for expressing pacifist views in the First World War. He was never a total pacifist, always insisting that it was only certain wars which he could not support. However, pacifism, or perhaps more correctly selective conscientious objection and non-violence, was always an important force in Russell's life, deriving its impact from its moral stance and its basic rationality.

Russell's approach to politics after the Second World War was basically consistent with his positions over the previous fifty years. Despite Mr. Schoenman's characterization of Russell's attempts to achieve some sort of nuclear limitation and detente as simply Cold War western orthodoxy, these attempts reflected Russell's intense concern over the division of the world into two camps and the likelihood of nuclear war. Russell's suggestion that the United States impose a nuclear *pax Americana* was unfortunate and one which he lived to regret, but it was much more the product of a fear that Russian expansionism and American willingness to resort to nuclear weapons would destroy the world. Even in this period Russell's proposals were basically internationalist, an attempt to impose a more rational world order through the United Nations or, as a temporary substitute, even through NATO.

By the middle 1950s, Russell had become a leader in the efforts of organized scientists to devise solutions to the arms race, and, as Mr. Schoenman points out, he began to lose favour with the Western governments as his solutions no longer coincided with their Cold War objectives. This involvement brought him into more contact with anti-establishment and radical persons, and his "Ban-the-Bomb" attitudes began to develop into more sharply defined criticisms of western Cold War policies. In many ways Russell's disenchantment

[1] *The Rationalist Annual*, London 1938, reprinted in Egner and Denonn, op. cit., p. 35.
[2] ibid., p. 36.

with western policies in the 1950s paralleled the growing recognition of the United States that it possessed the power to contain the threat of expansionist Communism abroad and its disposition to use that power around the globe to protect and solidify American political and economic power. Mr. Schoenman, of course, would reject that interpretation, seeing instead a well-conceived American imperialistic plan to rule the world from the very start of the Cold War. But the reason for Russell's failure to see through western Cold War policies after the war may have been simply that those policies had not yet taken the dangerous drift which Russell found, by the late 1950s, he could not support.

Mr. Schoenman's observation that by Russell's civil disobedience in 1961 with the Committee of One Hundred, he "threw in completely with the radicals", helps to explain many of Russell's subsequent actions. He was now leader of a movement and had a well-staffed organization, including Mr. Schoenman, behind him. From this time on, Russell no longer spoke simply as an individual, but as the head of a movement, and his thoughts and writing, although in many cases still his own, were the inevitable product of a collegial enterprise. 1962 was an important year for Russell, perhaps the zenith of his lifelong attempts to influence public affairs. In October, he was in constant telegraphic communication with President Kennedy, Mr. Krushchev, and other world leaders over the Cuban missile crisis. His pleas for restraint were responded to favourably by Krushchev in a public letter and may indeed have influenced the outcome of the crisis. In November, he played a similar role in the short Sino-Indian War. It was the philosopher's finest hour, buttering up, wheedling, lecturing world leaders by telegram and press releases ("What is to happen," he telegraphed Mr. Nehru, "to the chances for peace if India too defines honour and integrity in terms of national pride, victory in war, and military defeat of aggressors?").[1]

The Russell organization, generally acting through the Russell Foundation, broadened and radicalized its objectives after the telegram-sending days of 1962. By the middle 1960s Mr. Schoenman was flying around the world, conferring with leaders and more often with radical dissidents and revolutionaries, and Russell money was aiding many a radical cause. "Russell and the Foundation," as Mr. Schoenman describes it, "became preoccupied with helping movements which would bring social transformation to their countries and which would resist the American reprisal." The Foundation was involved with Che Guevara's abortive attempt to create a revolutionary movement in Bolivia (Mr. Schoenman says elliptically, "we became involved in his strategy and his fate") and in other revolutions.

Mr. Schoenman's account of Russell's involvement in revolutionary activities is especially unsatisfying because of its lack of insight into Russell's own political

---

[1] *Unarmed Victory*, New York 1963, p. 110.

and philosophical principles. Mr. Schoenman describes this period of Russell's career simply as a series of revolutionary activities with little theoretical inspiration other than the desire to bring about revolutionary change everywhere. His account has a sort of adventure story tempo, with Mr. Schoenman leading Russell into ever more revolutionary exploits. "The feverish activity in country after country," Mr. Schoenman writes, "grew apace with the prominence Russell now assumed in the world movement. By creating a Russell Foundation, I was able to deploy this influence to campaign in forty countries for the release of political prisoners, for intervention by Russell commanded response and brought international attention to the plight of the victim concerned."

It is probably true, as Mr. Schoenman indicates and as his critics have charged, that the activities of the Russell Foundation very much reflected Mr. Schoenman's own dispositions. But, as Mr. Schoenman also maintains, it does not appear that Russell was unaware of the direction the Foundation was taking or that he opposed it. Given at least Russell's tacit acceptance of that direction, it seems unlikely that he viewed the Foundation's programme as simply inciting revolution against the established order around the world. Russell believed too strongly in rationality to don the mantle of an indiscriminate inciter of revolutions. He had long professed a distaste for revolutions. He wrote in 1957:

I do not wish to suggest that revolutions are never necessary, but I do wish to suggest that they are not short cuts to the millennium. There is no short cut to the good life, whether individual or social. To build up the good life, we must build up intelligence, self-control and sympathy. This is a quantitative matter, a matter of gradual improvement, of early training, of educational experiment. Only impatience prompts the belief in the possibility of sudden improvement.[1]

However, Russell had come, by this time, to view American imperialism as an intractable force which could not be dealt with except by countervailing power. In a piece entitled "Peace Through Resistance to US Imperialism", in January 1966, he wrote:

Peaceful coexistence, therefore, cannot be achieved by requesting US imperialism to behave better. Peace cannot be realized by placing hopes on the goodwill of those whose power depends on the continuation of such exploitation and on the ever-increasing scale of military production. The system which oppresses the people of the world is international, co-ordinated and powerful; but it is hateful and oppressive and in various ways resisted by the people of the world.

A united and co-ordinate resistance to this exploitation and domination must be forged. The popular struggle of oppressed people will remove the resources from the control of US imperialism and, in so doing, strengthen the people of the United States itself, who

---

[1] *Why I Am Not a Christian*, New York 1957, reprinted in Egner and Denonn, op. cit., pp. 383-4.

are striving first to understand and second to overcome the cruel rulers who have usurped their revolution and their government. This, in my view, is the way to create a secure peace, rather than a tenuous and immoral acquiescence in US domination, which can neither work nor be tolerated by humane men.[1]

Despite these revolutionary sentiments, it is unlikely that Russell himself was much involved in spreading the seed of revolution around the world. These words were written in particular reference to Vietnam, where the case for the revolution which had been going on for thirty years against colonial powers was strong. In fact, it was Vietnam almost entirely which took Russell's attention and energy in the last years of his life, and much of what he said and wrote has to be understood in that context.

Russell's opposition to the Vietnam War and his War Crimes Tribunal were the last activities of his career. He challenged American involvement in Vietnam from the introduction of "advisers" by President Kennedy in the early 1960s and raised questions concerning American involvement there long before they began to concern most Americans. American policies directly offended his liberal sensibilities, both by the fact of American intervention and the manner in which the United States and South Vietnam conducted the war. Many of his early attacks were based upon the way in which the war was being conducted, the use of chemicals, napalm, and defoliation, the uprooting of civilian populations, and the establishment of political prisoner camps by the South Vietnamese. In April 1963, a letter which he wrote to the *New York Times* charging the United States with a "war of annihilation" in Vietnam and with the use of napalm and harmful defoliation chemicals was answered by an editorial attacking him for "an unthinking receptivity to the most transparent Communist propaganda".[2] Russell issued a vast number of statements on the war which took on an escalating intensity as the American involvement in Vietnam grew. Some of these are contained in his last book, *War Crimes in Vietnam* (the assistance of Mr. Schoenman is acknowledged in the introduction). It is a patchy book, containing an excellent introduction by Russell with a relatively reasoned and factual history of the Vietnam conflict, and a moving "Report from Vietnam" in 1966 by Mr. Schoenman which sensitively and graphically describes the effects of government repression in South Vietnam and American bombing and chemical warfare in North Vietnam. However, there is much political rhetoric in the book, and here, for the first time in Russell's published writing, we find highly dogmatic and Marxist terminology. The pieces are generally short, often taken from press releases and public letters issued by Russell, and one can only wonder at the degree of collegial input.

The War Crimes Tribunal, held in Stockholm and Copenhagen in 1967, was

---

[1] *War Crimes in Vietnam*, pp. 99–100.
[2] ibid., pp. 31–3.

a fitting conclusion for Russell's career. Its conception, as an attempt by prominent scholars, men of letters, and political and social leaders the world over to assess responsibility for violations of the international laws of war when the nations have failed to provide a legal mechanism for the task, was a creative and noble one. By invoking the international laws of war and the Nuremberg precedent, the Tribunal was a reaffirmation of Russell's faith in the rule of law and internationalism. However, the Tribunal lacked adequate precedent for its authority and, without the ability or, it appears, much desire to present both sides, it lacked all semblance of impartiality. Its function thus degenerated into one of publicity, serving at its best as a source of information and a jogger of consciences and at its worst simply as a purveyor of propaganda. Its informational value was hampered from the beginning by a bad press which labelled it as a propaganda stunt and then generally ignored its hearings and testimony.

Russell's hope that through the War Crimes Tribunal "the peoples of the world shall be aroused as never before, the better to prevent the repetition of this tragedy elsewhere"[1] was not accomplished, but the Tribunal, over the long run, served some purpose. It did provide the first documented evidence of American violations of the laws of war in Vietnam. The Tribunal had six international investigation teams, containing surgeons, biochemists, lawyers, directors of clinics and hospitals, trade union executives, and journalists, who gathered evidence in Vietnam.[2] The evidence was generally not subjected to adequate cross-examination and rebuttal, but some, particularly the physical evidence and the testimony of eye-witnesses, provided powerful proof of the disastrous effects of American weaponry upon the population and land of Vietnam and of unlawful conduct by some American ground troops. The image of the Tribunal has been considerably improved since the revelations of My Lai and other American atrocities in Vietnam and the disclosures of the impact of American tactics and bombing schemes in Vietnam.

The Tribunal also served as an experiment in, perhaps even a precedent for, attempts by private citizens to find ways to enforce international law in the tradition of Nuremberg. The fact that men and women of importance from all over the world were willing to serve on the Tribunal (the twenty-two scholars, writers, jurists, and political figures on the Tribunal generally had leftist sympathies but included many highly respected figures such as Jean-Paul Sartre, Simone de Beauvoir, James Baldwin, and Peter Weiss) indicated that such tribunals might have an impact upon the actions of powerful nations. Russell expressed this philosophy in his introduction to the published proceedings of the Tribunal, entitled *Against the Crime of Silence*:

War crimes are the actions of powers whose arrogance leads them to believe that they are

[1] ibid., p. 124.
[2] Letter to the Editor from Ralph Schoenman, *N.Y. Times*, 16 April, 1967, VI, p. 144.

above the law. Might, they argue, is right. The world needs to establish and apply certain criteria in considering inhuman actions by great powers. These should not be the criteria convenient to the victor, as at Nuremberg, but those which enable private citizens to make compelling judgments on the injustices committed by any great power.[1]

The force of such a tribunal lies not in its power to impose sanctions, for it has none, but in its ability to invoke the moral outrage of the peoples of the international community. It recognizes that although the nations have failed to implement the international law standards established at Nuremberg and in the international conventions regulating the laws of war, moral opprobrium is still a potent force. It also helps to maintain international common law standards which might otherwise be lost by failure of nations to recognize them as customary international law. Professor Richard A. Falk of Princeton University has noted the role of morality in international law:

It is important, then, that the sense of moral outrage widely shared by peoples and government is itself relevant to the identification of rules of international law. Such shared attitudes identify the limits of acceptable behaviour and possess or come to possess the quality of law. Therefore, the legal quality of war acts in Vietnam cannot be separated from the moral reaction to their commission. Attributing this moral agency to international law is especially necessary in view of the absence of legislative procedures available to bring a new law into being and administrative procedures to interpret existing law in light of changed circumstances.[2]

It is doubtful that anyone other than Russell, with his prestige as a philosopher, his reputation as a man of good faith, his organization, and his world-wide contacts, could have convened a forum with the resources, both investigatory and communicatory, and the impact of the War Crimes Tribunal. Despite its obvious limitations and defects, the Tribunal served as a reminder of the power of moral suasion and the determination of the peoples of the world not to permit the standards of Nuremberg to be subordinated to national interests or to be lost because of ineffective means of enforcement. It was a fitting re-assertion of Russell's faith in the capacity of man finally to impose rationality and humanism upon his actions within the world community.

[1] J. Duffett (ed.), *Against the Crime of Silence: Proceedings of the Russell International War Crimes Tribunal*, Flanders, N.J., and London, 1968.
[2] Clergy and Laymen Concerned About Vietnam, *In the Name of America: The Conduct of the War in Vietnam by the Armed Forces of the United States as shown by Published Reports*, 1968, p. 25.

Bibliography I: Works by Russell

Articles that first appeared in early periodicals are referred to, where possible, in more easily accessible reprinted versions. American editions are listed when they have been used in this book.

Against the Crime of Silence, New York 1970.
The Analysis of Matter, London 1927.
The Analysis of Mind, London 1921.
"Appeal to the American Conscience", in *War Crimes in Vietnam*, London and New York 1967.
Authority and the Individual, London 1949.

Common Sense and Nuclear Warfare, London 1949.

"Dewey's 'New Logic' ", in P. A. Schilpp (ed.), *The Philosophy of John Dewey*, New York 1939.

Essay on the Foundations of Geometry, London 1897.

"Free World Barbarism", in *War Crimes in Vietnam*, London and New York 1967.
Freedom and Organization, 1914–1949, London 1934.

German Social Democracy, London 1896, New York 1965.

Has Man a Future? London 1961.
Human Knowledge: Its Scope and Limits, London and New York 1948.
Human Society in Ethics and Politics, London 1954.

An Inquiry into Meaning and Truth, London and New York 1940.

"Knowledge by Acquaintance and Knowledge by Description", in *Mysticism and Logic*, London 1917, New York 1929.

Lectures on the Philosophy of Logic and Atomism, in R. C. Marsh (ed.), *Logic and Knowledge*, London 1956.

"Letter to Frege", in J. van Heijenoort (ed.), *From Frege to Gödel*, Harvard 1967.
"Logical Atomism", in *Logic and Knowledge*, ed. R. C. Marsh, London 1956.

Marriage and Morals, London 1961.
My Philosophical Development, London 1957, New York 1959.
Mysticism and Logic, London 1917, New York 1929.

"The Nature of Sense-Data: A Reply to Dr. Dawes Hicks", *Mind*, n.s. 22 (1913).
"The Nature of Truth", *Mind* (1906). The first two sections of this paper are reprinted as "The Monistic Theory of Truth" in *Philosophical Essays*, London 1910.

"On the Experience of Time", *Monist* (1915).
"On the Nature of Acquaintance", in *Logic and Knowledge*, London 1956.
"On the Nature of Truth and Falsehood", in *Philosophical Essays*, London 1910. This is the rewritten third section of "The Nature of Truth".
"On Propositions", in *Logic and Knowledge*, London 1956.
Our Knowledge of the External World, London 1914.
An Outline of Philosophy, London 1927, Cleveland and New York 1960. An American edition was originally published in 1927 entitled *Philosophy*.

"Peace through Resistance to US Imperialism", in *War Crimes in Vietnam*, London and New York 1967.
Philosophy, New York 1927. Published in England under the title *Outline of Philosophy*.
"The Philosophy of Logical Atomism", in *Logic and Knowledge*, London 1956. Also in *Philosophical Essays*, London 1910.
Philosophical Essays, London 1910.
Political Ideals, New York 1917.
Portraits from Memory and other Essays, New York 1969.
Power: A New Social Analysis, New York 1938. Also in R. Egner and L. Denonn (eds.), *The Basic Writings of Bertrand Russell*, New York 1961.
The Practice and Theory of Bolshevism, London 1920.
Principia Mathematica (with A. N. Whitehead), Cambridge 1910–13; 2nd edn. Cambridge 1925.
Principles of Social Reconstruction, London 1916.
The Problems of Philosophy, London 1912.

The Rationalist Annual, London 1938. Also in R. Egner and L. Denonn (eds.), *The Basic Writings of Bertrand Russell*, New York 1961.
"The Relation of Sense-Data to Physics", in *Mysticism and Logic*, London 1917.

Roads to Freedom: Socialism, Anarchism, and Syndicalism, London 1918. Published in New York in 1919 as *Proposed Roads to Freedom*.

The Scientific Outlook, London 1931.
"Sensation and Imagination", *Monist* (1915).

Unarmed Victory, New York 1963.
Unpopular Essays, London and New York 1950.

"War and Atrocity in Vietnam", in *War Crimes in Vietnam*, London and New York 1967.
War Crimes in Vietnam, London and New York 1967.
Which Way to Peace? London 1936.
Why I am Not a Christian, in R. Egner and L. Denonn (eds.), *The Basic Writings of Bertrand Russell*, New York 1961.

Bibliography II: Other Works

Ayer, A. J. *The Foundations of Empirical Knowledge*, London 1953.

Adams, E. M. (ed.). *Categorical Analysis*, Chapel Hill, N.C., 1964. (Collection of the papers of Everett W. Hall.)

Anderson, A. and N. Belnap. "A Simple Proof of Gödel's Completeness Theorem" (abstract), *Journal of Symbolic Logic*, 24, 4 (1959).

Bergmann, G. "Ontological Alternatives", in E. D. Klemke (ed.), *Essays on Frege*, Urbana, Ill., 1968.

Black, Max (ed.). *Philosophical Analysis*, Ithaca, N.Y., 1950.

—— *Problems of Analysis*, Ithaca, N.Y., 1954.

Braithwaite, R. B. *Scientific Explanation*, New York 1953.

Carnap, Rudolf. "On Inductive Logic", *Philosophy of Science*, (1945). 12

—— "On the Application of Deductive Logic", *Philosophy and Phenomenological Research*, 8 (1947–8).

—— "Reply to Nelson Goodman", *Philosophy and Phenomenological Research*, 8 (1947–8).

—— *Logical Foundations of Probability*, Chicago 1950.

—— "Replies and Systematic Expositions", in P. A. Schilpp (ed.), *The Philosophy of Rudolf Carnap*, La Salle, Ill., 1964.

Chisholm, Roderick M. *Perceiving: A Philosophical Study*, Ithaca, N.Y., 1957.

—— "On the Observability of the Self", *Philosophy and Phenomenological Research*, 30 (1969). Also in P. Kurtz (ed.), *Language and Human Nature: A French-American Philosophers' Dialogue*, St. Louis 1971.

Christensen, Ferrel. "A Defense of Temporal Becoming", doctoral dissertation at Indiana University, 1971.

Church, A. *Introduction to Mathematical Logic*, Princeton 1956.

Clark, Romane. "Concerning the Logic of Predicate Modifiers", *Nous*, 4 (1970).

Clergy and Laymen Concerned about Vietnam. *In the Name of America: The Conduct of the War in Vietnam by the Armed Forces of the United States as shown by the Published Reports, 1968.*

Cocchiarella, Nino B. "Properties as Individuals in Formal Ontology", *Nous*, 6 (1972).

—— "Fregean Semantics for a Realist Ontology", forthcoming in *Notre Dame Journal of Formal Logic*.

Cocchiarella, Nino B. "Whither Russell's Paradox of Predication?" forthcoming in M. K. Muntz (ed.), *Logic and Ontology*, New York.

Duffett, J. (ed.). *Against the Crime of Silence: Proceedings of the Russell International War Crimes Tribunal*, Flanders, N.J., and London, 1968.

Edwards, Paul. "Russell's Doubts about Induction", *Mind*, 18 (1949).
Egner, R. and L. Dennon (eds.). *The Basic Writings of Bertrand Russell*, New York 1961.

Feigl, Herbert. "De Principiis non Disputandum . . . ?" in Max Black (ed.), *Philosophical Analysis*, Ithaca, N.Y., 1950.
Fraassen, Bas C. van. "Facts and Tautological Entailments", *Journal of Philosophy*, 66 (1969).
Furlong, E. J. "Memory", *Mind*, 17 (1948).

Gandy, R. O. "On the Axiom of Extensionality: Part I", *Journal of Symbolic Logic*, 21 (1956).
Garrison, Jim. *A Heritage of Stone*, New York 1971.
Gödel, K. "Russell's Mathematical Logic", in P. A. Schilpp (ed.), *The Philosophy of Bertrand Russell*, Evanston, Ill., 1944.
—— "Über formal unentscheidbare Sätze der *Principia Mathematica* und verwandter Systeme I", *Monatshefte für Mathematik und Physik*, 38 (1931).
Goodman, Nelson. "A Query on Confirmation", *Journal of Philosophy*, 18 (1946).
—— "On Infirmities of Confirmation Theory", *Philosophy and Phenomenological Research*, 8 (1947–8).
—— *Fact, Fiction and Forecast*, Cambridge, Mass., 1955.
—— "Positionality and Pictures", *Philosophical Review*, 69, 4 (1960).
Grossman, R. "Frege's Ontology", in E. D. Klemke (ed.), *Essays on Frege*, Urbana, Ill., 1968.
Grünbaum, Adolf. *Modern Science and Zeno's Paradoxes*, Middletown, Conn., 1967.

Hall, Everett W. "The Forms of Sentences and the Dimensions of Reality", in E. M. Adams (ed.), *Categorical Analysis*, North Carolina 1964.
Hay, William. "Bertrand Russell on the Justification of Induction", *Philosophy of Science*, 17 (1950).
Heijenoort, J. van. "Logic as Calculus and Logic as Language", *Synthese*, 17, 3 (1967).
Hintikka, Jaakko. "A Two-Dimensional Continuum of Inductive Methods", in Jaakko Hintikka and Patrick Suppes (eds.), *Aspects of Inductive Logic*, Amsterdam 1966.

Jeffrey, Richard. *The Logic of Decision*, New York 1965.
—— "Probable Knowledge", in Imre Lakatos (ed.), *The Problem of Inductive Logic*, Amsterdam 1968.
Jensen, R. "On the Consistency of a Slight(?) Modification of Quine's 'New Foundations' ", *Synthese*, 19 (1968).

Kyburg, Henry E. and Ernest Nagel (eds.). *Induction: Some Current Issues*, Middletown, Conn., 1963.

Lakatos, Imre (ed.). *The Problem of Inductive Logic*, Amsterdam 1968.
Lane, Mark. *Rush to Judgement*, New York 1966.
Lewis, C. I. *Analysis of Knowledge and Valuation*, La Salle, Ill., 1946.
Locke, Don. *Memory*, New York 1971.

Maxwell, Grover. "Structural Realism and the Meaning of Theoretical Terms", in M. Radner and S. Winokur (eds.), *Analyses of Theories and Methods of Physics and Psychology*, Minnesota Studies in the Philosophy of Science, 6 (1970).
—— *Theories, Perception, and Structural Realism*, Pittsburgh Studies in the Philosophy of Science, 4 (1970).
—— "Russell on Perception: A Study in Philosophical Method", in David Pears (ed.), *Bertrand Russell: A Collection of Critical Essays*, New York 1972.
—— "Corroboration without Demarcation", in P. A. Schilpp (ed.), *The Philosophy of Karl Popper*, La Salle, Ill., 1967.
Montague, R. "Semantic Closure and Non-Finite Axiomatizability", in Montague, *Infinitistic Methods*, New York 1959.

Pears, David. *Bertrand Russell and the British Tradition in Philosophy*, London 1967. Rev. edn. 1972.
—— (ed.). *Bertrand Russell: A Collection of Critical Essays*, New York 1972.
Popper, Karl R. *The Logic of Scientific Discovery*, New York 1959.
—— "Science: Conjectures and Refutations", in *Conjectures and Refutations*, New York 1962.
—— "Conjectural Knowledge: My Solution to the Problem of Induction", *Revue Internationale de Philosophie*, 95,5 (1971).
Pribram, Carl. *Languages of the Brain*, Englewood Cliffs, N.J., 1971.

Quine, W. van O. "New Foundations", in *American Mathematical Monthly*, 44 (1937).
—— *Philosophy of Logic*, Englewood Cliffs, N.J., 1970.
Quine, W. van O. and N. Goodman. "Steps towards a Constructive Nominalism", *Journal of Symbolic Logic*, 12, 4 (1947).

Radner, M. and S. Winokur (eds.). *Analyses of Theoretical Methods of Physics and Psychology*, Minnesota Studies in the Philosophy of Science, 4 (1970).

Ramsey, Frank. *The Foundations of Mathematics (and Other Essays)*, New York 1956.

Reich, Charles. *The Greening of America*, New York 1970.

Reichenbach, Hans. *Experience and Prediction*, Chicago 1938.

—— *The Theory of Probability*, Berkeley and Los Angeles 1949.

—— *The Direction of Time*, Berkeley and Los Angeles 1956.

Revel, Jean-François. *Without Marx or Jesus: the New American Revolution has Begun*, translated by J. F. Bernard, London 1972.

Rosser, Barkley. "Extensions of Some Theorems of Gödel and Church", *Journal of Symbolic Logic*, 1 (1936).

—— "Gödel Theorems for Non-Constructive Logics", *Journal of Symbolic Logic*, 2 (1937).

Salmon, Wesley C. "Some Unorthodoxies of Modern Science" (A Symposium), *Proceedings of the American Philosophical Society*, 96, 5 (1952).

—— "The Predictive Inference", *Philosophy of Science*, 24 (1957).

—— "On Vindicating Induction", in Henry E. Kyburg and Ernest Nagel (eds.), *Induction: Some Current Issues*, Middletown, Conn., 1963.

Schilpp, P. A. (ed.). *The Philosophy of Bertrand Russell*, Evanston, Ill., 1944.

—— *The Philosophy of John Dewey*, New York 1939, 1951.

—— *The Philosophy of Rudolf Carnap*, New York 1964.

Schütte, K. *Beweistheorie*, Berlin 1960.

Strawson, P. F. *Introduction to Logical Theory*, London 1952.

Takahashi, H. "A Proof of Cut-Elimination Theorem in Simple Type-Theory," *Journal of the Mathematical Society of Japan*, 19, 4 (1967).

Urmson, J. O. "Review of *Bertrand Russell and the British Tradition in Philosophy*, by David Pears", *Philosophical Review*, 18, 4 (1969).

Watkins, J. W. N. "Non-Inductive Corroboration", in Imre Lakatos (ed.), *The Problem of Inductive Logic*, Amsterdam 1968.

Williams, Rupert Crawshay. *Russell Remembered*, London 1970.

Wittgenstein, L. *Tractatus Logico-Philosophicus*, with an Introduction by Bertrand Russell, London 1922.

—— *Philosophical Investigations*, translated by G. E. M. Anscombe, Oxford 1953.

—— "Logical Form", *Proceedings of the Aristotelian Society*, Supplementary Vol. 9 (1929).

Wright, G. H. von. *On the Logic of Negation*, Societas Scientiarum Fennica, Commentationes Physico-Mathematicae, 22, 4, Helsinki 1959.

Index

A Heritage of Stone, 248
abstract: entity, 95, 110, 112; object, 108; singular, 110, 112
abstraction: class, 3, 6; relational, 3, 8
acquaintance, 58, 59, 60, 61, 62, 63, 64, 65, 66, 67, 68, 69, 70, 102, 103, 104, 105, 106, 107, 108, 109, 117, 119, 120, 121, 123, 124, 125, 126, 145, 146, 148, 161, 173; cognitive character of, 59; epistemic character of, 59, 100, 103; knowledge by, 63, 64, 100, 103, 104, 105, 107, 171; nature of, 47–56; principle of, 57, 58, 91, 96, 97, 98, 99, 100, 171, 172
act, 57, 71, 72, 76, 102, 103, 104, 105, 106, 107, 123, 124; cognitive, 151; of remembering, 124
Adams, E. M., 113 n.
adjective(s), 93, 104
adverbial theory, 97, 98
Against the Crime of Silence, 244, 262
aggression: American, 219; Nazi, 219, 227, 232, 236, 237, 238, 243, 246, 249, 250
America, Latin, 251
American Philosophical Association, 139 n.
analysis, method of, 181
Analysis of Knowledge and Valuation, 187
Analysis of Matter, The, 81, 170, 171, 181, 183
Analysis of Mind, The, 68, 71, 82, 122, 123, 124, 127, 128, 129, 132, 135, 136, 170, 183, 211
anarchism, 222, 227
ancestral, 8, 9, 21, 27, 36, 37
Anderson, A., 12, 16
appearance, 47, 49, 50
Aristotle, 29, 127, 162, 207
arithmetic, axiomatic formulation of, 207
ascription, act of, 106
Aspects of Inductive Logic, 206
assent, non-temporal, 128
asymptotic method (of inductive procedure), 203
atomic bomb, 236
atomism, logical, 34
attribute(s), 59, 73, 76, 108
attribute, word, 73
Authority and the Individual, 211, 213, 219, 227
aware(ness), 53, 54, 55, 62, 106, 107, 166
awareness: cognitive, 165; temporal, 163
Ayer, A. J., 115, 187, 196

Baldwin, J., 262
Baruch, B., 237
Basic Writings of Bertrand Russell, The, 257 n.
Bayes' theorem, 192, 194, 196
becoming, mind-dependence of, 163
Begriffsschrift, 30

behaviour-cycle, 136, 137
behaviourism, 75, 181
being, 30, 31, 33, 34, 42, 43, 46, 107, 109
belief, 55, 68, 69, 70, 71, 72, 74, 75, 76, 77, 83, 85, 90, 91, 96, 97, 98, 100, 126, 128, 129, 130, 132, 133, 135, 136, 140, 142, 155, 157, 158, 161, 201 n.; dispositional, 96; empirical, 183; episodic, 96; fact, 70; false, 75, 110; feeling, 86 n.; past-oriented feeling of, 131, 132, 137; perceptual, 146; proposition, 85, 160; relation, 76; sentence, 75; statement, 76, 96
Belnap, N., 12, 16
Ben Bella, 247
Ben Gurion, 248
Bentham, J., 228
Bergmann, G., 30 n., 31 n.
Berkeley, G., 127
Berlin blockade, 238
Bertrand Russell: A Collection of Critical Essays, 171
Bertrand Russell and the British Tradition in Philosophy, 123
Bertrand Russell Archive, McMaster University, 124
Bertrand Russell Committee of One Hundred in Greece, 250
Beweistheorie, 21
Black, M., 198
Bolivia, 251
Bolshevik(s), 228, 230, 234, 235, 236
Boole, 30
Bradley, 78, 81, 82, 83, 84, 88, 95
Braithwaite, R. B., 198
Brezhnev, 251
Britain, 231, 232, 238, 244, 246, 249, 258
Buddha, 225

calculus, infinitesimal, 207
Campaign for Nuclear Disarmament, 241, 246, 247, 252
Camus, A., 169
capitalism, 222, 227, 228, 229, 232, 235, 236, 237, 238, 239, 240, 247
cardinal, 27, 29, 37, 52
Carnap, R., 173, 179, 188, 189, 198, 204–8
Carnegie Corporation, 169
Cartesian (arguments), 149, 184, 185
Categorical Analysis, 113 n.
category, 34, 95
causal chain, 154
causal theory (of perception and memory), 151–6, 161

Index

instrumentalism, 181
internal (negation), 116
internality, 33
Introduction to Logical Theory, 198
Introduction to Mathematical Philosophy, 31 n., 204
invariant, 26
isolation, 230
Italy, 236
iteration, 36, 37

James, William, 197
Japanese Journal of Mathematics, 1
Jeffrey, R., 159, 188, 206 n.
Johnson, Dr., 150
Johnson, President L. B., 249
John, Lord, 229
Journal of the Mathematical Society of Japan, 1
Journal of Philosophy, 111 n., 189 n.
Journal of Symbolic Logic, 1, 2, 34 n.
judgment, 58, 60, 68, 69, 102, 103, 105, 106, 107, 108, 109, 110, 111, 112, 113, 114, 116, 117, 118, 121, 122, 125, 126, 127, 131, 132, 140, 141, 146, 149, 157, 158, 186; empiricism, 172, 180; false, 101, 102; memory, 159; perceptual, 141, 153, 156, 159, 165; terminating and non-terminating, 188
justification, 197; epistemic, 47
juxtaposition, spatial, 98

Kant, I., 186
Kantian, 185; cognitive holism, 104
Kassim, President, 248
Kennedy, President J. F., 247, 248, 249, 250, 259, 261
key, Russellian, 64
Keynes, John Maynard, 187, 188, 194, 205, 207
Klemke, E. D., 30, 31 n.
knowledge, 58, 61, 62, 66, 69, 124, 126, 140, 142, 151, 157, 159, 183, 187, 198; by acquaintance; 63, 64, 100, 103, 104, 105, 107, 171, 172, common sense, 180; by description, 64, 118, 171, 172, 173; of the external world, 170; of the future, 1, 159, 160; intuitive, 62, 68, 70; mathematical, 183; of matter, 177; of the past, 125, 145, 159; perceptual, 100, 107; of the present, 159; scientific, 143, 145, 180, 186, 187, 196, 207; sources of, 140; theory of, 47–56, 124, 137, 184; of things, 55, 58, 67, 103, 107; of truths, 55, 56, 58, 59, 60, 67, 103, 105, 107, 119, 120, 121; of unobservables, 172
"Knowledge by Acquaintance and Knowledge by Description", 48, 51, 53 n., 55 n., 120
Krishna Menon, 238
Krushchev, N., 239, 248, 259
Kurtz, P., 50
Kyburg, Henry E., 190 n.

Labour Party, 218, 228, 246
Lakatos, Imre, 188 n., 200 n.
Lane, Mark, 248
language, analysis of, 179
Language and Human Nature: A French–American Philosopher's Dialogue, 50
Languages of the Brain, 178

Lectures on the Philosophy of Logical Atomism, 70, 74, 75, 101, 108, 109, 110
Leibniz, G. W., 19, 26, 27, 30, 221
Lenin, V. I., 227, 230, 234, 255
Leninist practice, 227
Leonard, 34
Lesniewski, 34
level(s), 19, 20, 22, 111
Lewis, C. I., 187
liberal(s), 169, 228, 235, 254
liberal theory, 213, 216, 217
"liberal" tradition, 209
liberalism: Bertrand Russell's, 221–6, 227, 229, 232, 253, 255, 256, 257; nineteenth-century, 234
Library of Living Philosophers, The, 183
linkage, 44
location, 15
Locke, 143, 144, 175, 228, 255, 256
logic, 1, 16, 33, 180; deductive, 183, 205; inductive, 205, 206, 207; mathematical, 29–32, 205; principles of, 47; second-order, 37–42
Logic and Knowledge, 51, 54 n., 67 n., 70, 71 n., 72 n., 101, 108, 117 n., 124
Logic and Ontology, 110 n.
Logic of Decision, The, 188 n.
Logic of Scientific Discovery, The, 188, 198 n.
logical (idea), 86, 115
Logical Atomism, 72
logical equivalence, 82
"Logical Form", 87
Logical Foundations of Probability, 188, 204, 205, 206

M, system, 2, 9, 10, 11, 12, 13, 15, 16, 17; theorem, 9, 10, 16
Macmillan, H., 247
man, theory of, 216, 217
Marriage and Morals, 169
Marsh, R. C., 51, 61 n., 101 n., 108 n., 117
Marx, K., 234
Marxism, 217, 218, 227, 228, 231, 235, 254, 255, 256, 257, 261
"mass society", 233
mass term, 66, 111
materialism, traditional, 177, 178
material things, 47
mathematics, 1, 207; foundations of, 29–46; philosophy of, 32, 35, 36
matter, 178, 182; dematerialization of, 177
maximum of compossibles, 221
Maxwell, G., 188
meaning, 59; postulate, 39, 45; theory of, 84, 95
Meinong, 71, 72, 76, 124
membership, 38, 39, 40, 41, 42, 44; relation, theory of, 35, 37, 41, 46; symbol, 110, 111
memory, 117–37, 139–67, 185; theory I, 117–25; theory II, 125–37; awareness, 165, 166; belief, 84, 129, 132; claim, 132, 133, 134, 136, 137; dispositional, 144; experience, 146, 147, 150, 151, 153, 154, 156, 157, 166; -image, 127, 129, 131, 132, 133; immediate, 117, 118, 119, 122, 124, 125, 126, 128, 130, 155; -judgment, 125, 149, 156; paradigmatic, 123, 125, 127, 128;